THE CENTRAL SCHOOL OF SPEECH AND DRAMA
UNIVERSITY OF LONDON

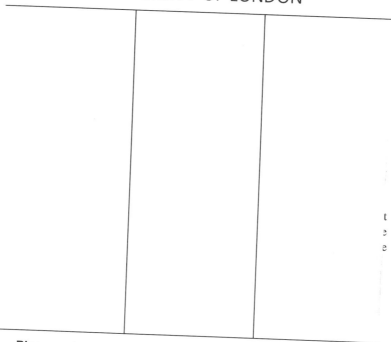

t
ɔ
ə

CAMBRIDGE TEXTBOOKS IN LINGUISTICS

General editors: S. R. ANDERSON, P. AUSTIN, J. BRESNAN,
B. COMRIE, W. DRESSLER, C. J. EWEN, R. HUDDLESTON,
R. LASS, D. LIGHTFOOT, I. ROBERTS, S. ROMAINE,
N. V. SMITH, N. VINCENT

Tone

MOIRA YIP

University College London

CAMBRIDGE
UNIVERSITY PRESS

PUBLISHED BY THE PRESS SYNDICATE OF THE UNIVERSITY OF CAMBRIDGE
The Pitt Building, Trumpington Street, Cambridge, United Kingdom

CAMBRIDGE UNIVERSITY PRESS
The Edinburgh Building, Cambridge CB2 2RU, UK
40 West 20th Street, New York, NY 10011-4211, USA
477 Williamston Road, Port Melbourne, VIC 3207, Australia
Ruiz de Alarcón 13, 28014 Madrid, Spain
Dock House, The Waterfront, Cape Town 8001, South Africa

http://www.cambridge.org

First published 2002

Printed in the United Kingdom at the University Press, Cambridge

Typeface Times 10/13pt   *System* QuarkXpress® [TB]

A catalogue record for this book is available from the British Library

ISBN 0 521 77314 8 hardback
ISBN 0 521 77445 4 paperback

This book is dedicated to the memory of my father
Bill Winsland, 1920–2001, who taught me my first
word of a tone language, Kikuyu, many, many years ago.
Little did he know where it would lead.

Contents

Figures

Maps

Preface

This book is designed for students of linguistics who want to learn more about tone. It assumes a basic knowledge of phonological theory such as might be acquired in a year-long phonology course, but it does not assume any particular prior exposure to work on tone. The theoretical chapters of the book are framed in Optimality Theory (OT), but should be intelligible to students with no previous background in OT.

The book is suitable for a semester-long course on tonal phonology at the advanced undergraduate or graduate level. The theoretical chapters include some simple exercises, and the answers are given at the end of each chapter. It is also hoped that the book will be a useful reference work on the fundamentals of tone, and to this end it includes extensive references to both primary fieldwork sources and to theoretical works. An effort has been made to give broad coverage of tone languages, both typologically and geographically.

Acknowledgements

This book could not have been written without the help of a number of people. My thanks go first and foremost to Neil Smith. He first suggested I should write this book, he found me office space at a time when I had no professional home, and he read every chapter in first draft, within days, and gave me back detailed and probing comments. It has been a privilege to work with him.

Particular thanks also to Akin Akinlabi, Larry Hyman and Scott Myers, who took the time to give me detailed comments on the manuscript, thereby saving me from numerous embarrassing mistakes.

This book has also benefited from help and comments from many other people over the last two years, including Mary Bradshaw, Nick Clements, Bruce Connell, Jerry Edmondson, Dan Everett, Colleen Fitzgerald, Seldron Geziben, Sharon Hargus, Joyce McDonough, David Odden, Stuart Rosen, Bernard Tranel, Justin Watkins, Yi Xu, and the participants in talks and seminars at University College London and the School of Oriental and African Studies. Some of you have read parts of the manuscript and given me honest feedback, some of you have pointed me in the right directions for references or data, some of you have asked pointed questions to which I then had to find out the answers. To all of you, my thanks.

All errors, misjudgements and misrepresentations are of course my own responsibility.

Notation systems, symbols and abbreviations

Segmental transcriptions will be those of the original source, unless otherwise noted.

Accent marks

Acute accent: á   high tone
Grave accent: à   low tone
Macron: ā   mid tone
In combination: ǎ   rising tone
                    â   falling tone
[Note: occasionally accents are used to show stress instead; this will be explicitly noted where relevant.]

Numerical systems

Asianist: 5 = high tone, 1 = low tone
Meso-americanist: 1 = high tone, 5 = low tone
Both: 2 digits in sequence show starting and ending pitches, so 35 is a contour tone.

Other symbols

φ   foot
σ   syllable
μ   mora
word-boundary; occasionally used for phrase-boundaries
H%   phonological phrase boundary tone
H// intonational phrase boundary tone

!H   downstepped H

Ⓗ   floating H

H*   accentual H, which associates to the stressed syllable

F_0 fundamental frequency, in Hertz

OT conventions

☞   winning candidate in OT tableau

*   constraint violation

*!   fatal constraint violation

shading   cell whose violations, if any, are now irrelevant, since a higher
           ranked constraint has decided things

C1 >> C2   C1 ranked higher than C2, shown by left-to-right placement in
           tableau

Glossary of terms and abbreviations

ballistic	Ballistically stressed syllables have post-vocalic aspiration, and are articulated more forcefully than controlled stressed syllables. They often rise slightly in pitch at the end, whereas controlled stressed syllables show a gradual decrease. The last part of a ballistically stressed syllable shows aperiodic noise, characteristic of aspiration.
Bernoulli's Law	A high-velocity airstream passing through a narrow opening exerts a sucking effect on the walls of the opening, drawing them together.
contour tone	A tone that changes pitch during its duration, either rising or falling.
debuccalization	Loss of all oral articulations, leaving only a laryngeal such as [h] or [ʔ].
declination	An overall fall in pitch as an utterance proceeds, possibly due to a drop in sub-glottal pressure.
default tones	A tone inserted on a toneless syllable at the end of the phonology. Usually a low tone.
docking	The association of a floating tone to a tone-bearing unit (TBU).
downdrift	The lowering of a H tone after an overt L tone. Sometimes called automatic downstep.
downstep	The lowering of H in the absence of an overt L tone, but usually caused by a floating L. Sometimes called non-automatic downstep. Used in this book on occasions as a cover term for both downdrift and downstep.
extrametricality	The exclusion of a peripheral element (syllable, mora, TBU) from some process, such as tone association or stress calculations.
gradient assessment	Calculation of the *extent* to which a constraint is violated, instead of a pass/no pass approach. Used especially in assessing alignment, so that the greater the misalignment, the more violations are counted.

iambic	Right-prominent binary feet, usually weight-sensitive.
LF	Term used by syntacticians, short for Logical Form.
modal voice	Normal phonation, no breathiness or creakiness.
mora	A weight unit: a light syllable has one, a heavy syllable has two. Long vowels always have two. Coda consonants may or may not count for weight i.e. may or may not have a mora.
non-automatic	See 'downstep' above.
OCP	Obligatory Contour Principle: Adjacent identical elements are prohibited.
PF	Term used by syntacticians, short for Phonetic Form. Always used in its abbreviated form. Could more appropriately be called Phonological Form.
polarity	Choice of the opposite tone to the adjacent tone, so that H roots take L suffixes, and vice-versa.
prosodic	Relating to the phonological constituent structure in which syllables are grouped into feet, feet into prosodic words, prosodic words into phonological phrases, and phrases into intonational phrases. Domains in which prominence is assigned. Often syntactically conditioned.
register	Three different senses: (1) Tonal range of the voice is divided into two *registers*, [+Upper] and [−Upper]. Refers only to pitch. Most common usage in this book. (2) Voice quality distinctions, such as modal *register* vs. creaky *register*. (3) Frequency at which a tone is realized at that point in an utterance. In this usage, downstep lowers the *register* on which H tones are realized.
rhyme	The part of the syllable starting with the nuclear vowel, and including all post-nuclear material.
Richness of the Base	An OT term, arising from the impossibility of restricting inputs in an output-based theory. All possible inputs must thus be considered.
sandhi	Phonological process which happen between words. In this book, usually tonal changes.
secret language	Language disguise games used by children (or sometimes teenagers or criminals!), in which the language is distorted in a regular way unintelligible to the outsider.
SPE	Sound Pattern of English (Chomsky and Halle 1968)

TBU	Tone-Bearing Unit. Syllable or mora, and perhaps vowel. The entity to which tones associate.
trochaic	A left-headed binary foot, usually evenly weighted. May be two moras, or two syllables.
UG	Universal Grammar.
ultima	The final syllable/mora.
UR	Underlying Representation.
VOT	Voice onset time.

Alphabetical list of OT constraints

Faithfulness constraints

*ASSOCIATE (=*ASSOC)
*DELETE
DEP-IO
DEP-MORA
DEP-T
*DISASSOCIATE (=*DISASSOC)
FAITH-BR
HEAD-MAX-T (includes FAITHNUCLEARTONE)
IDENT-IO
IDENT-T
INTEGRITY
LINEARITY
MAX-BR (TONE)
MAX-IO
MAX (LAR)
MAX-T (=MAX-IO (TONE))
NOCROSSING
NOFUSION
OUTPUTOUTPUTMATCH (=OO-MATCH)
PARSE-σ
PRESWEIGHT
REALIZE-MORPH
TONALPROMINENCEFAITH

Markedness constraints

ALIGN-L
ALIGN-R

S<small>PACE</small>-100%
S<small>PECIFY</small>-T
S<small>PREAD</small>
S<small>TRESS</small>=H
S<small>TRESS</small>T<small>O</small>W<small>EIGHT</small>P<small>RINCIPLE</small> (SWP)
*T<small>ONE</small> (=*T)
*T<small>ROUGH</small>
*V<small>OICE</small>
W<small>EIGHT</small>T<small>O</small>S<small>TRESS</small>P<small>RINCIPLE</small> (WSP)
W<small>RAP</small>-XP

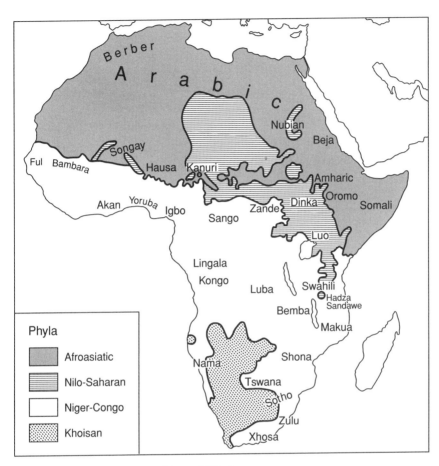

Map 1. *Africa, from Heine and Nurse 2000: 2*

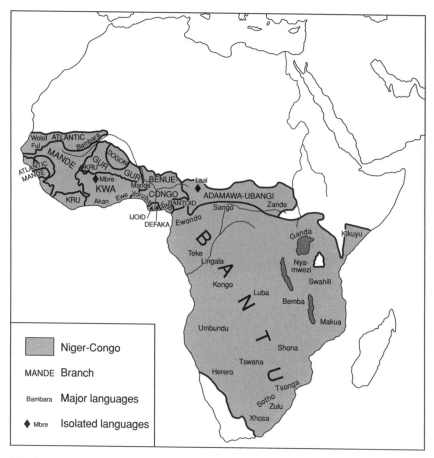

Map 2.   *Niger-Congo, from Heine and Nurse 2000: 12*

Map 3.   *Sinitic languages, from Lyovin 1997, Map VIII*

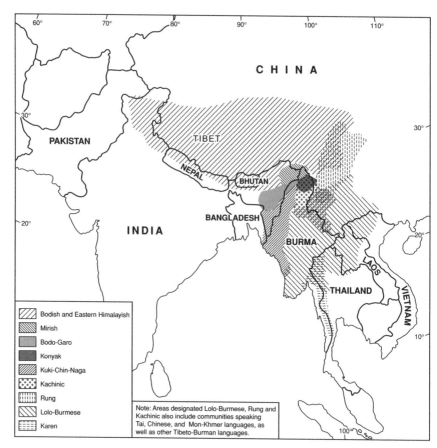

Map 4.   *Sino-Tibetan languages, excluding Sinitic, from Lyovin 1997, Map VII*

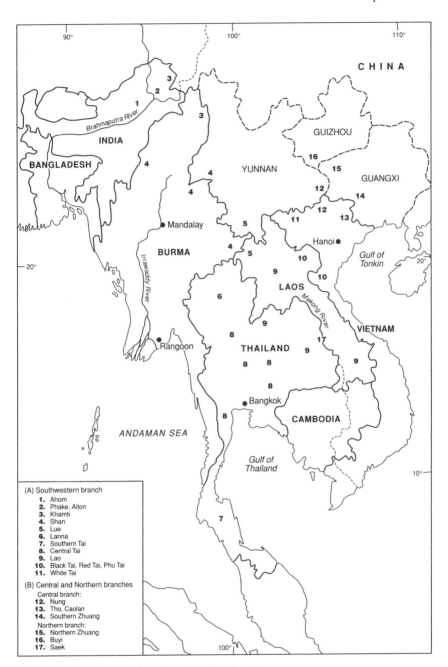

Map 5.   *Thai languages, from Lyovin 1997, Map IX*

Map 6.   *Austronesian languages, from Lyovin 1997, Map VI*

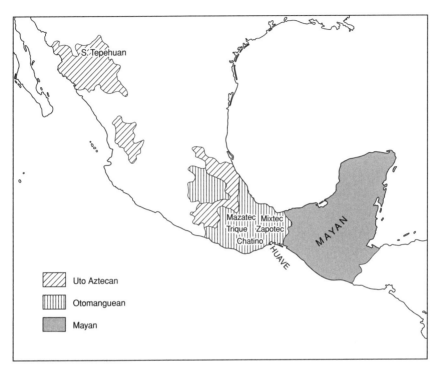

Map 7. *Meso-America, from Suarez 1983, Map 1*

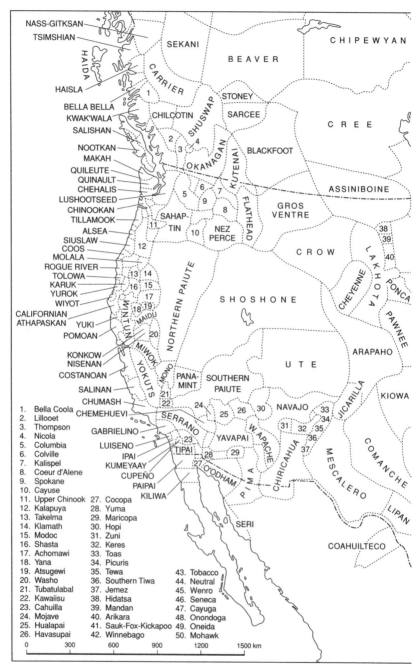

1. Bella Coola
2. Lillooet
3. Thompson
4. Nicola
5. Columbia
6. Colville
7. Kalispel
8. Coeur d'Alene
9. Spokane
10. Cayuse
11. Upper Chinook
12. Kalapuya
13. Takelma
14. Klamath
15. Modoc
16. Shasta
17. Achomawi
18. Yana
19. Atsugewi
20. Washo
21. Tubatulabal
22. Kawaiisu
23. Cahuilla
24. Mojave
25. Hualapai
26. Havasupai
27. Cocopa
28. Yuma
29. Maricopa
30. Hopi
31. Zuni
32. Keres
33. Toas
34. Picuris
35. Tewa
36. Southern Tiwa
37. Jemez
38. Hidatsa
39. Mandan
40. Arikara
41. Sauk-Fox-Kickapoo
42. Winnebago
43. Tobacco
44. Neutral
45. Wenro
46. Seneca
47. Cayuga
48. Onondoga
49. Oneida
50. Mohawk

0   300   600   900   1200   1500 km

Map 8.   *North America, from Mithun 1999, Map 1b*

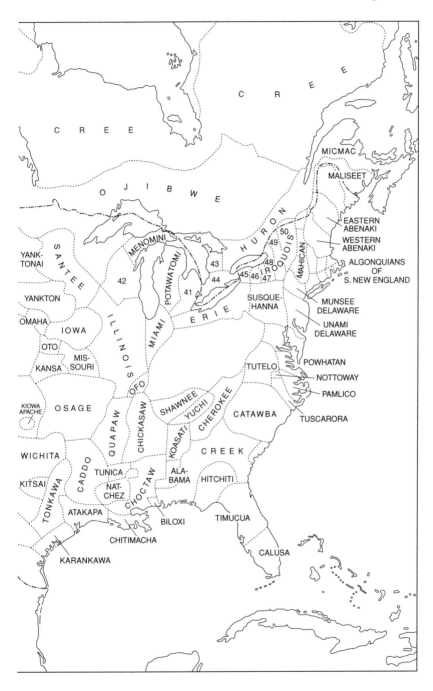

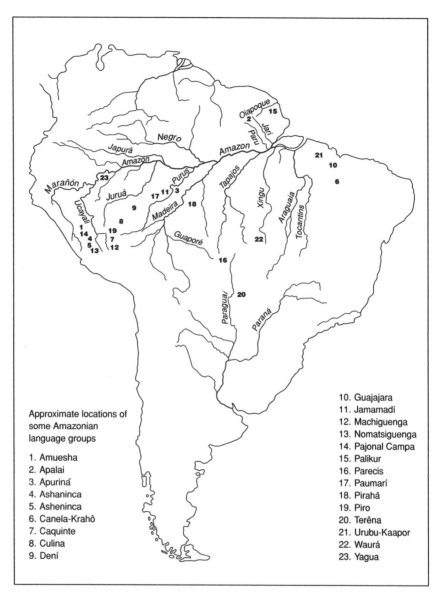

Approximate locations of
some Amazonian
language groups

1. Amuesha
2. Apalai
3. Apurinã
4. Ashaninca
5. Asheninca
6. Canela-Krahô
7. Caquinte
8. Culina
9. Dení

10. Guajajara
11. Jamamadí
12. Machiguenga
13. Nomatsiguenga
14. Pajonal Campa
15. Palikur
16. Parecis
17. Paumarí
18. Pirahã
19. Piro
20. Terêna
21. Urubu-Kaapor
22. Waurá
23. Yagua

Map 9.   *South America, from Derbyshire and Pullum 1986, vol. 1*

1
Introduction

Among the sounds of languages, consonants and vowels need no explanation to the lay person, but tones are another matter entirely. Tell someone you are writing a book about 'Tone', and they look blank, and yet by some estimates as much as 60–70 per cent of the world's languages are tonal. Begin to explain that you are interested in languages that use the pitch of the voice to convey meaning, and more often than not you will be interrupted with a remark such as 'Oh, that must be really interesting: those emotions and nuances and subtleties are so important when we're speaking!' Politely explain that actually you are interested in languages that use pitch to distinguish one word from another, not just to convey subtleties, and most people will assume that such languages are rare, and probably spoken only by isolated communities in less developed countries – until you point out that Mandarin Chinese (885,000,000 speakers), Yoruba (20,000,000) and Swedish (9,000,000) are all tonal.

Perhaps because of these misapprehensions (particularly prevalent in Western cultures), even among linguists tone is sometimes seen as a specialized topic that the general linguist can largely ignore. Undergraduate courses often pay it only cursory attention, and even graduate courses may devote no more than a class or two to the topic. The goal of this book is to fill that gap. It assumes a basic knowledge of phonological theory, but no prior acquaintance with the phonology of tone.

1.1   What is a tone language?

In all languages vowel height and consonantal place of articulation are central to conveying the meanings of words, and so we do not usually categorize languages as being 'vowel-height languages' or 'place-of-articulation languages'. Tone is different in that only a subset of languages (albeit a rather large subset!) make use of it in this way. For a linguist, then, tone has a very specific meaning. A language is a 'tone language' if the pitch of the word can change the meaning of the word. Not just its nuances, but its core meaning. In Cantonese, for example, the syllable [yau] (which we might spell 'yow' to rhyme with 'how' in English), can be said with one of six different pitches, and has six different meanings:

(1)   *[yau] in Cantonese*
        high level   'worry'
        high rising   'paint (noun)'
        mid level   'thin'
        low level   'again'
        very low level   'oil'
        low rising   'have'

In longer words, it matters *where* the tones go. For example, in Dagaare, a Gur language spoken in Ghana, a bisyllabic word can be first low then high, or the reverse, and the meaning changes completely; the acute accents show high tone, and the grave accents show low tone.

(2)   LH   yṳ̀òrí̧   'penis'
        HL   yú̧ó̧rì   'name'

In other languages, the only thing that matters is that the lexical tone of a word appear somewhere in that word, but its exact location may change depending on the morphology of the complex word, and the surrounding phonological context. In Chizigula, a Bantu language spoken in Tanzania, some words have all syllables low-toned, like the various forms of the verb /damany/ 'to do', whereas others have one or more syllables with a hightone, as in the syllables marked with acute accents in the forms of the verb /lombéz/ 'to request':

(3)   *Toneless verbs:*   *H-tone verbs:*
        ku-damany-a   'to do'   ku-lombéz-a   'to request'
        ku-damany-iz-a   'to do for'   ku-lombez-éz-a   'to request for'
        ku-damany-iz-an-a   'to do for   ku-lombez-ez-án-a   'to request for
                            each other'   each other'

The high tones are part of the lexical entry of certain verb roots, like /lombéz/ 'request', but they show up on the penultimate syllable of the complex verb form, and not necessarily on the verb root itself. Nonetheless, the tone is always there somewhere, and distinguishes high tone verbs from toneless verbs like /damany/ 'do'. This book is about languages like Cantonese, Dagaare and Chizigula, which are called 'tone languages', or more precisely 'lexical tone languages'.

It is not entirely straightforward to decide when a language is a tone language and when it is not. Many languages have occasional uses of pitch to change meaning. In American English, if one says 'Uh-huh' with high pitch on the first syllable and low pitch on the second, it means 'No'. If one says it with low on the first syllable and high on the second, it means 'Yes'. The only other difference between the two words is whether the second syllable begins with a glottal stop in [ʔʌʔʌ] 'No' or an [h] in [ʔʌ hʌ] 'Yes', so these words are close to a minimal pair distinguished only by tone. Nonetheless, we would not want to call American English a tone language, because in the overwhelming majority of cases pitch does not change the core meaning of a word, so that 'butter' means 'butter' whether it has a high-low or a low-high pattern. It is true that at the level of the sentence, or, more precisely, utterance, pitch can denote such things as statements, questions, orders, lists, and so on, but we reserve the word 'intonation' for this use of pitch, and it seems to be found in all languages, whether or not they have lexical tone, as we shall see in chapter nine. Using pitch like this 'to convey "postlexical" or sentence-level pragmatic meanings in a linguistically structured way' (Ladd 1997) is not enough to earn a language membership in the class of tone languages.

A subtler question is how we distinguish between what are called stress languages and tone languages. In English, the words 'guitar' and 'glitter' are pronounced with different pitches. In normal statement intonation, 'guitar' has high falling pitch on its last syllable, but 'glitter' starts the fall on the first syllable. Should we then conclude that these words have high falling tones on different syllables in the lexicon? The answer is no, because it turns out that the actual pitch of these syllables depends entirely on the intonation pattern of the utterance into which they are put. Suppose we say the following two dialogues:

(4)   A. Tom's just bought himself a guitar.

          B. A guitar? I thought he played the drums.

(5)   A. I thought I'd sprinkle glitter on her birthday cake.

          B. Glitter? You can't eat glitter.

If the second speaker in each case is incredulous about the first speaker's statement, she can say the words 'guitar' and 'glitter' with a quite different pitch pattern. 'Guitar' will have a very low then rising pitch on the last syllable, and 'glitter' will have a very low pitch on the first syllable, rising into the second syllable. There is no truly high pitch anywhere in either word in this context. So pitch does not stay in any way constant for these words. Instead, what is held constant is that in each word one of the two syllables is more prominent than the other, and attracts the intonational pitch, whether it is the statement's high fall, or the incredulous response's extra low-rise. In 'guitar', this is always on the second syllable, whereas in 'glitter' it is always on the first. English then is what is termed a stress language, not a tone language. Stress languages have one other common property, not illustrated by our sample words so far. The stressed syllable does not usually have to be identified in the lexicon, but is generally picked by a counting algorithm that starts from one end of the word, and selects, for example, the second-to-last syllable, or the first syllable, as the stressed one. Other factors, such as syllable size and morphological structure, may also affect stress placement, but in the typical stress language it is not lexically marked.

This simple typology of tone languages versus stress languages is blurred by the existence of a large group of languages called accentual languages. Such languages, which include, for example, Japanese, Serbo-Croatian, and some types of Dutch, have lexical tones, but what makes them special is that these languages have only a small number of contrasting tones (usually only one or two), and these are sparsely distributed or even absent on some words and usually belong to specific syllables, from which they are inseparable. There is no absolute division between accent languages and tone languages, just a continuum from 'accent' to 'tone' as the number and denseness of tones increase, and they become freer to move around. I shall follow many previous authors in taking the position that the so-called accentual languages are just a subclass of tone languages, and adopt a definition of a tone language from Hyman (in press) that is designed to include the accentual languages under its umbrella:

(6)   *Definition of a tone language:*
        'A language with tone is one in which an indication of pitch enters into the lexical realization of at least some morphemes.'

Although accentual languages as a subtype of tone language fall under the purview of this book, most of my examples will be drawn from those languages that everyone calls tonal, and the term accentual will still be used from time to time for convenience. For further discussion see chapters six and especially nine.

Before we look at actual tone languages, there are some important background issues that we need to discuss. First, it is essential that we understand something of the phonetics of tone, the basic mechanisms that underlie our ability to produce different pitches. Second, we need to discuss where the work of the phonology ends and that of the phonetics begins. Third, we need to think about the place of the tonal phonology in the larger grammar, including how phonology, syntax, and semantics communicate so that tonal information originating in any of these components is integrated into the larger whole. In this introduction I will give a brief overview of each of these issues, but they will arise again at various points in the book. The discussion is necessarily technical at times, and assumes a solid prior background in general linguistic theory. Some readers may prefer to skip one or more of these sections for now and return to them later. In that case the reader can proceed to chapter two, which jumps right in to the subject matter of this book, beginning with an overview of the range of tonal contrasts found in languages.

1.2   How is tone produced?

This book is a book on phonology, not phonetics, but it is still important to have some idea of how tones might be produced and perceived. An understanding of the phonetics of tone sheds light on the relationship between tone and other aspects of the phonology, such as voicing in obstruents, and also helps our understanding of the tonal phonology itself, for example in understanding some phonological processes as the phonologization of phonetic processes. In this chapter I will discuss mainly the production side of the picture, and leave perception for chapter ten, where it leads naturally into first-language acquisition. I start with a discussion of the larynx, and how pitch differences are produced. I then move on to discuss some consequences of the physiological constraints on the realization of pitch – peak delay and declination; these are important here because they have been phonologized in many languages.

There are three terms that need to be distinguished in any discussion of tone: fundamental frequency (F_0), pitch and tone. In this order, the terms move from a purely phonetic term, F_0, to a truly linguistic one, tone. F_0 is an acoustic term referring to the signal itself: how many pulses per second does the signal contain, where, in the case of the speech signal, each pulse is produced by a single vibration of the vocal folds. The frequency of these pulses is measured in Hertz (Hz) where one Hertz is one cycle per second. The next term, pitch, is a perceptual term. What is the hearer's perception of this signal: is it heard as high in pitch or low in pitch, the same pitch as the previous portion of the signal, or different? The mere existence of F_0 differences may not be enough to result in the perception of pitch differences. The F_0 changes could be too small, or be the result of segmental or other factors for which the hearer unconsciously compensates. Pitch can be a property of speech or non-speech signals. For example, music varies in pitch constantly, and we talk of a high-pitched scream, bird-call, or squeal of tyres. Tone, on the other hand, is a linguistic term. It refers to a phonological category that distinguishes two words or utterances, and is thus only a term relevant for language, and only for languages in which pitch plays some sort of linguistic role.

1.2.1   *The larynx*

The perception of tone is dependent in whole or in part on pitch perception, and thence on fundamental frequency, or F_0. For distinct tones to be perceived, the signal must contain F_0 fluctuations, and these must in turn be large enough to be perceptible as pitch differences. The fundamental frequency of a sound, which we perceive as pitch, is primarily determined by the frequency of vibration of the vocal folds inside the larynx. The following explanation of the

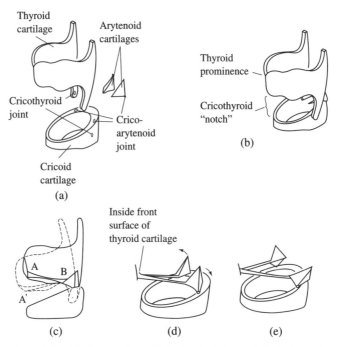

Figure 1.1   *The larynx, from Ohala 1978 (a) An exploded schematic representation of laryngeal cartilages and their movements.*
(b) Cartilages as they are normally joined. (c) Manner of rotation of thyroid and cricoid cartilages which cause vocal cords, AB, to increase in length, A'B. (d) Adducted position of the vocal cords when arytenoid cartilages are tilted inward. (e) Abducted position of the vocal cords when arytenoid cartilages are tilted outwards.

laryngeal mechanisms responsible for regulation of pitch is taken mainly from Ohala 1978 and Hirose 1997.

The larynx is composed of two rings of cartilage, the cricoid cartilage, and the thyroid cartilage; the latter is an open ring, sitting on top of the former. There are also two smaller pieces of cartilage, called the arytenoid cartilages, sitting on top of the rear rim of the cricoid cartilage. Figure 1.1, particularly (a–b), should help to visualize the anatomy. The vocal folds (often wrongly called the vocal 'cords') are two bands of muscle, the vocalis muscle, that join the thyroid cartilage and the two arytenoid cartilages. They can be seen clearly in Figure 1.1 (d). The space between them is the glottal opening (the glottis) that allows air to pass from the lungs into the mouth. Rotation of the arytenoid cartilages brings the vocal folds closer together or further apart, thus opening or closing the glottis. This can be seen in Figure 1.1 (d–e).

We are now ready to understand why the vocal folds vibrate at all. First, the vocal folds are brought rather close together by the adductor muscles. Air is forced through the narrow glottal opening from the lungs, and Bernoulli's Law exerts a sucking effect that draws the vocal folds closed. Pressure from the lungs then builds up behind the closure, and eventually bursts through, releasing a puff of air and reducing the sub-glottal pressure again. The cycle re-starts. Each burst of air is one cycle of vocal fold vibration, and this may happen from a low of around eighty times per second in normal male speech to a high of around 400 times per second for a female voice. Note that, because the vibration is caused by the pressure drop across the glottis, it will only take place if the pressure in the lungs and the oral pressure are different. If there is complete oral closure, as in a stop consonant, the oral pressure may not be sufficiently different from the sub-glottal pressure for vibration to take place, whereas during sonorants air flows out of the mouth, keeping the oral pressure low and the pressure drop high. This creates ideal conditions for vibration, and the ensuing voicing is known as spontaneous voicing.

In a stop consonant, keeping the voicing going requires particular conditions. If the vocal folds are stiff, they will only vibrate if there is a large pressure difference across the glottis. As a result stop consonants produced with stiff vocal folds are voiceless. Since the vocal folds are stiff, the following vowel is produced with raised pitch. If the vocal folds are slackened, they vibrate more readily, and thus it is possible to keep voicing going. Because the vocal folds are slack, the following vowel has lower pitch (Halle and Stevens 1971). A striking example in which this effect has become phonological is found in Songjiang, a Wu dialect of Chinese. The numbers are a way of showing pitch. 5 means highest pitch, 1 means lowest pitch, and so on. Where there are two digits they refer to the pitch at the start and the end of the syllable respectively

(7)   *Songjiang tones:*

ti	53	'low'	di	31	'lift'
ti	44	'bottom'	di	22	'younger brother'
ti	35	'emperor'	di	13	'field'

What you can see is that the words in the right-hand column, which begin with a voiced obstruent, have lowered versions of the pitches of the words in the left-hand column, which begin with a voiceless obstruent. This connection between voiceless obstruents and high pitch, and voiced obstruents and low pitch, is widely attested in natural languages, and in many cases it is possible to trace the origins of tonal contrasts back to a prior contrast in voicing on obstruents, in a process known as tonogenesis.

In vowels and sonorant consonants the rate of vibration of the vocal folds is controlled by a number of factors. Rotation of the thyroid and cricoid cartilages with respect to each other causes changes in the length of the vocal folds. By these means, the vocal folds can be deformed in several ways, and as a result they may or may not vibrate, and the frequency of vibration may be controlled.

For those readers interested in a little more detail, we know that pitch differences come from adjusting the mass and stiffness of the vocal folds (Hirose 1997). The crico-thyroid muscle contracts, and this elongates the vocal folds, decreasing their effective mass and increasing their stiffness. This increases the frequency of vibration, and raises pitch. In tone languages, it can be shown very clearly that it is the activity of the crico-thyroid muscle that is primarily responsible for raising pitch. An increase in the activity level of this muscle precedes each pitch peak by a few milliseconds. Pitch lowering has slightly more complex causes. The activity of the crico-thyroid muscle is reduced, while the thyro-arytenoid muscle contracts, thickening the vocal folds and increasing their effective mass.

Apart from internal changes to the larynx, there are some other articulatory mechanisms that have been implicated in pitch control. The main one is larynx lowering. There is some reason to think that lowering the larynx may play quite an important role in lowering pitch, presumably because it stretches and thins the vocal folds somewhat (see Ohala 1978 for discussion). One way or another, then, vocal fold vibrations are the primary source of pitch differences, although other noise sources, such as the turbulent noise produced at the narrow constriction of the fricatives [s] and [ʃ], may also differ in pitch. Nonetheless, controlled pitch differences (as opposed to ones that are automatic concomitants of other aspects of articulation) are always produced at the larynx in speech.

This very brief and over-simplified explanation of the production of tone is sufficient for our purposes. For more details, the interested reader can consult Ladefoged 1975, Ohala 1978, Stevens 1997, Hirose 1997.

1.2.2   Performance factors that affect pitch

The physiology of speech production has further effects on the speech signal, and two of these effects deserve mention here. When the brain sends a signal to produce high tone, instructions go to the appropriate muscles. The muscles configure the vocal folds suitably, and the rate of vibration then increases, resulting in high pitch. All this takes a small but finite amount of time, and as a result the full flowering of high pitch is somewhat delayed. The delay is enough that the peak is typically at the end of the tone-bearing segment, or indeed often not reached until early in the following syllable. The term 'peak delay' is usually used for the latter case. This effect has been well documented in languages as diverse as Mandarin Chinese (Xu 1998, 1999b), Chichewa (Kim 1998, Myers 1999b) and Yoruba (Akinlabi and Liberman 1995). The schematic pitch trace in Figure 1.2 from Xu 1999b shows how three different tones on a medial syllable – high (H), falling (F) and rising (R) – are realized between two low tones. First, look at the heavy dashed line, which shows the realization of a high-toned syllable in between two lows. It can be seen that the high peak is not reached until the very end of the syllable. Now look at the solid line,

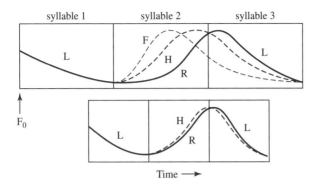

Figure 1.2 *Peak delay, from Xu 1999b. Schematic peak alignments in F, H, and R at normal speaking rate (upper panel), and in H and R at fast speaking rate (lower panel).*

which shows a rising tone between two lows. The culmination of the rise is delayed all the way into the following syllable. Finally, look at the light dashed line. The fall of the falling tone does not begin until more than half-way through the syllable. Although most of the data focusses on the delay of high peaks, it is probably true for any change in pitch movement, so that a low trough can also be delayed.

A second physiologically based phenomenon is declination, by which the pitch of an utterance falls as the utterance proceeds. This has been observed in tonal and non-tonal languages alike, but the mechanism is not fully agreed upon. One possibility is as follows. As an utterance proceeds, assuming the speaker has not paused for breath in the middle, the amount of air in the lungs decreases, and the sub-glottal pressure drops. As a result, the pressure difference across the larynx decreases, and the rate of vibration of the vocal folds slows, so the pitch lowers. This means that the same amount of muscular effort aimed at producing a high tone produces a lower-pitched version of this high tone later in the utterance than it does at the beginning. Of course, if additional effort is exerted, the pitch can be raised back up, but the overall trend is downwards. The problem with this plausible-sounding explanation for declination is that sub-glottal pressure has been measured, and it is clear that it drops very little during an utterance, and probably not enough to account for the size of the declination. See Ohala 1978 for some other possible mechanisms.

These two phenomena – peak delay and declination – are of interest here because they have been phonologized in many languages. For example, in Yoruba (Akinlabi and Liberman 2000b), peak delay has developed into a phonological process that turns a high-low sequence into a high-falling sequence by spreading the high tone. An acute accent shows high tone, a grave accent shows a low tone, and a circumflex shows a fall.

(8)   rárà (HL)   → rárâ   (H HL)   'elegy'

More generally, tone spread or shift to the right is very common, but tone shift or spread to the left is much rarer. Our second phenomenon is extremely widespread, especially in Africa, where declination has apparently given rise to a phonological process called downdrift or downstep by which high tones are drastically lowered after low tones. See chapter six for details.

I end this section with a rather obvious point. Just like segmental contrasts, tonal contrasts can be affected by co-articulation effects (Peng 1997, Xu 1994). The laryngeal articulators, as has already been observed, have their own inertia, and it takes time for change to take place. Hearers seem well able to compensate for these effects, and continue to recognize the tones, but nonetheless caution must be observed in deciding whether some particular tonal effect is phonetic or phonological, and indeed the answer is not always clear. One relatively uncontroversial diagnostic is whether the effect in question is dependent on speech rate, and is variable in extent. If it is, it is usually classified as phonetic. If, on the other hand, it takes place at all speech rates, and is an all-or-nothing categorical affair, then it is usually classified as phonological.

1.3   The structure of the grammar: Phonetics and phonology

So far we have been discussing phonetics, but the main topic of this book is the *phonology* of tone. It is not always easy to know where phonology ends and phonetics begins, nor to understand the nature of the relationship between the two. In order to keep things clear, in this section I shall spell out what I am taking to be the division of labour between phonology and phonetics, and how they communicate with each other. In recent years there has been much discussion of these questions, but it would be beyond the scope of this book to go deeply into the issues. The interested reader is referred to any of the volumes in the Papers in Laboratory Phonology series, particularly the introduction to Beckman and Kingston 1990. In what follows I articulate issues that arise again later in the book. Some readers may find it hard to grasp their significance at this point, and may wish to (re-)read this section later.

I shall assume a rather traditional model with the following properties. Phonological representations are categorical, using either binary or unary features. It is the business of the phonology to generate an output out of these elements, in which most segments are specified for most features, but some may lack specifications for certain features. In particular, some syllables may lack tones at the end of the phonology. The phonetics then interprets this phonological output, making use of all phonological information: featural, structural, phrasal, and so on. This phonetic component ultimately produces instructions to the articulators; these instructions may or may not be binary, but in any case they result in a continuous signal in which every syllable is pronounced at some fundamental frequency. In the final acoustic output, the pitch values of the successive syllables will not be limited to a few binary distinctions, but will cover the range of the speaker's voice. The phonetic output is thus often termed 'gradient'.

The interpretation may be rather simple, or quite complex. At the simpler end, suppose a syllable [ta] is specified with H tone. The phonetics must decide how to interpret [H]. It will have at least two components: the overall available pitch range for that particular speaker at that particular time and place, and where in the pitch range the tone should be produced. Since the tone is [H], the pitch will be at or close to the upper edge of the pitch range, which in my case might be about 350Hz. A third decision that must be made by the phonetics is *when* to realize this pitch. It cannot be realized on the [t], since the main characteristic of a voiceless stop is silence! It will thus be realized on the vowel, and there is usually a slight lag (peak delay, see previous section), so that the maximum frequency is not reached immediately, presumably because implementation of any instruction takes time: the articulators do not move instantaneously. See Xu and Wang 2001 for examples from Mandarin. A fourth component seems necessary in some languages, where tones have concomitant voice-quality distinctions. For example, suppose the [L] tone is always predictably breathy, and that the breathiness plays no apparent role in the phonology. The simplest assumption is then that the breathiness is supplied by the phonetic interpretation of [L], much as in some languages the phonetic interpretation of voicelessness in stops may supply aspiration.

In some cases the phonology itself will have nothing significant to say about the pitch range itself, which will be determined by extra-linguistic factors such as the speaker's sex and mood. In other cases the phonological representation may also affect the pitch range. For example, in many languages the pitch range is lowered after a L tone, so that a subsequent H tone is lower in pitch than the Hs preceding the L. This is called downdrift or downstep, and is discussed later in this book. In such cases the phonological representation of a sequence like /H L H/ remains unchanged, but at the interface with the phonetics the L has two effects. First, it causes its own syllable to have a pitch at the low end of the pitch range. Second, it causes the whole pitch range to move down. This in turn means that the second H has a lower phonetic pitch than the first H, so that phonetically we get something like [H L M]. Although downdrift is very common, it does not seem to be universal. This means that the pitch-lowering effect of the L tone must be language specific, and that the phonetic component may be divided into language-specific and universal subparts. For further discussion, see chapter six.

A more complex case arises if some syllables have no tones of their own at the end of the phonology. They are, nonetheless, pronounced with some particular pitch, but a pitch that is dependent on the immediate surroundings. A number of studies have shown that such syllables derive their surface pitch by interpolation from the surrounding tones, so that a toneless syllable between two Hs will have a fairly high pitch, one between two Ls will have a fairly L pitch and one between a H and a L will have a mid pitch. Phonologically, though, these syllables are all toneless: their pitch is an automatic by-product of the transition between the specified tonal targets, combined with a tendency to return to the mid-level pitch produced when the articulators are at rest. A good illustration is the treatment of Japanese in Pierrehumbert and Beckman 1988. They look at Japanese phrases with a phrasal H accent on some syllable, and a final boundary L tone. They show that the pitch of the intervening syllables is best explained by simple interpolation between these two targets, so that if only a small number of syllables separate the accent from the end, there is a steady steep fall across those syllables. If a large number of syllables intervene, there is still a steady fall, but with a gentler gradient because of the length of the phrase. There is no way to assign discrete phonological tones to each of these intervening syllables and derive the actual surface pitches. Instead, their pitch must be purely a surface phonetic phenomenon.

As phonologists, we have to make decisions about how much detail we can account for in the phonology, and how much is a matter for the phonetic implementation of a phonological output. On some aspects there is wide agreement. No-one would expect the phonological representation to be different for a male speaker and a female speaker just because one of them produces high tones at frequencies of around 170 Hz, and the other at frequencies of around 370Hz. Other areas are less clearly understood. Downdrift, for example, is taken by some researchers to be a matter of a change in the phonological representation, and by others to be a matter of phonetic implementation. It is entirely possible, indeed likely, that such matters vary from language to language. Downdrift is related to declination, a probably universal and clearly phonetic tendency to gradually lower pitch across an utterance. Just as phonetic co-articulation can be phonologized as rules of assimilation, applying only under certain conditions, so declination could be phonologized as downdrift, occurring only after a L tone trigger. The final stage is downstep, in which the trigger may be a phonologically present but phonetically absent floating low tone, with no phonetic realization of its own except in so far as it causes lowering of the pitch register.

1.4   The place of phonology in the larger grammar

The relationship between phonetics and phonology is not the only link that tonal phonology has to the rest of the language faculty. It also must be linked in some way to the rest of the grammar, since tone can be used to signal lexical, morphological, syntactic, semantic and pragmatic information.

Obviously, tone can signal lexical information via lexical tones (Cantonese *yau*H 'worry' vs. *yau*L 'again'); it can signal syntactic information through the use of boundary tones (Yoruba signals subjects by adding a high tone to the end of the NP: ọkọ̀ lọ → ọkọ̌ lọ 'The car went'); it can signal semantic information such as focus through tonal focus markers (Bengali puts a LH accent on focussed words); and it can signal pragmatic information through intonational melodies (Mazahua, an Otomi language of Mexico, adds a H to form a question: thṹs?ḛ 'a cigar', thṹs?ḛ́ 'a cigar, you say?'). Somehow, then, information must get passed from other components of the grammar to the phonology. How this works is clearer in some areas than in others, and here I merely touch on some of the observed interactions. For the purposes of this book what matters is that the phonological representation may contain tones that have a variety of sources. Some of them originate from the lexical entry of the morphemes themselves, some may originate from tones that are inserted at prosodic boundaries, some may be the only PF manifestation of syntactic markers such as case, tense, or [+WH], and some may come from sentence-level intonational melodies with pragmatic sources. At the end of the day we arrive at a phonological representation rich in tones, and subject to the general principles of the phonology in the language in question.

Let us start with the least controversial area, lexical information. Lexical tones are part of the phonological portion of a lexical entry, and thus part of the underlying form that is presented to the phonology. Their route to the surface is clear enough.

Secondly, let us look at syntactic information, which seems to enter the phonology by a heavily restricted route. Lexical syntactic categories and their projections can influence the proper construction of prosodic phrasing (see chapter five), and the prosodic phrasing is part of the phonological representation, and thus affects the phonology in a variety of ways. In the case of tone, for example, it may trigger the insertion of a boundary tone, or define the domain within which tonal rules apply. It seems, however, that not all syntactic information can influence prosodic structure. The presence or absence of a category or its projection can be noted by the algorithms that construct prosodic phrases, but not which type of lexical category one is dealing with. For example, Xiamen Chinese starts a new phonological phrase after the end of every XP, whether that is an NP, VP, or AP (see chapter five for details). Empty categories are also ignored. See Truckenbrodt 1999 for recent discussion.

Thirdly, let us look at semantic information. This seems to be the least studied, and yet the interactions between anaphora, scope and focus, and the prosodic phrasing, stress and intonational patterns are very striking. For example, if the question 'Do you like him?' is said with the third person pronoun unstressed it must be referring to someone in the previous discourse. However, if the third person pronoun is stressed, typically with a falling-rising pitch contour, it is usually not co-referent (unless contrastively stressed) and instead refers to a new individual, such as that smartly dressed man across the room at the crowded party. Some of the transfer of semantic information can arguably be mediated through the syntax, and thence to the prosody. Scope distinctions, for example, may be associated with different syntactic structures. Some focussed elements, most obviously those involving movement, can also be handled via structural distinctions in the overt syntax, but others such as contrastive focus may need an abstract focus marker, with stress and tonal consequences. There may be a residue of phenomena that seem to require direct communication between LF and the phonology. [+WH], for example, may have particular tonal consequences. One possibility for many cases is to assume that the lexicon has functional morphemes whose only manifestation in PF is tonal. Exploring this would take us well beyond the scope of this book, since our main concern here is lexical tone, so I leave this for future research. The interested reader can consult Blakemore 1992, Krifka 1998, Sperber and Wilson 1982 and Steedman 2000.

Lastly, the sort of information most often conveyed by sentence-level tones, or intonation, is pragmatic information. This includes contrastive stress, focus, information structure, declarative, continuation, list, astonishment, and any number of other 'tunes'. It is usually assumed that there is some sort of intonational lexicon that collects together all these tunes, and from which the most appropriate one for the situation may be selected. See chapter nine for discussion.

The overall picture that emerges is that the tonal phonology must accept input direct from the lexicon, and from the utterance after lexical insertion. At this stage, in addition to lexical items, the representation may include certain abstract markers such as focus, and also syntactic structure, which in turn influences prosodic structure. The lexical entries that contribute tones to the phonology include not only the traditional lexical items such as nouns, verbs, roots, and affixes, but also functional elements and operators such as [WH], prosodic phrases such as Phonological Phrase or Intonational Phrase, and intonational tunes such as Declarative. The phonology takes all this as input, perhaps in one go, or perhaps step-by-step, with word-level phonology preceding phrase-level phonology. I will take this as the working model for the rest of this book, without commitment to any particular formal development of how these interactions take place.

1.5   The organization of this book

In the remainder of this book I offer an overview of tonal phonology. I begin in chapter two with a descriptive summary of the distribution of tone languages, including the sorts of tonal inventories that are known and how they are recorded by field workers. The notational systems in use will be introduced next, since they are a necessary prelude to what follows. Some attention will be devoted to the dangers and difficulties inherent in relying on other people's often excellent but sometimes hard-to-interpret fieldwork, and the issue of disagreement between sources. The discussion of inventories will include the numbers of level tones that may contrast, why downstep is not an extra tone, the types of contour (rising and falling) tones, the upper bound on complexity (apparently rise-fall, or fall-rise), and whether contours are found on short vowels as well as long. The chapter will end with a section on the interaction between tone and segmental properties, continuing into a short section on tonogenesis – how tone arose historically.

Chapter three will propose a feature system for capturing all and only the observed systems. Since the clearly described systems have no more than a four-way contrast, it will propose two binary features, Register and Pitch. How to handle five-tone systems will also be covered. Contour tones will be analysed as sequences of level tones, and the reasons for choosing this over a unitary contour alternative will be explained and discussed. This will be followed by a section on the geometric relation between Register and Pitch and what sort of data bear on the choice. I will also discuss whether tonal features are entirely disjoint from segmental features, focussing mainly on Laryngeal features, but with some discussion of Pharyngeal and Tongue Root features. The last part of this chapter will introduce toneless syllables and whether they receive default tones.

From chapter four onwards, the bulk of the book concerns the phonology of tone. Chapter four itself will lay the groundwork by summarizing the arguments in favour of an autosegmental treatment of tone, particularly the mobility, stability, and one-to-many and many-to-one arguments. Next I will discuss the most common association patterns (left-to-right, one-to-one, right-edge spreading to form plateaux, right-edge clustering to form contours). I then introduce Optimality Theory (OT), and analyse the common phenomena introduced earlier within OT. No prior knowledge of OT is assumed. This chapter also includes a discussion of what is the Tone Bearing Unit (TBU). Having set the scene, these tools will then be used to look at a range of common tonal alternations: spreading, deletion, insertion, flop, dissimilation, and downstep. Final sections deal with the relationship between tone and stress, and with the Obligatory Contour Principle (OCP).

Chapter five will look at the role played by tone in morphology and syntax. It will begin with topics in word-level morphology, including tonal morphemes, and the role of morphological structure in conditioning tonal processes. I then look at tonal morphemes associated with units larger than the word, particularly the phonological phrase. The last, longest, part of the chapter discusses the influence of syntax on prosodic phrasal structure, and the role played by this prosodic structure in forming the domains for tonal processes.

Each of the next three chapters deals with a different geographical area: Africa, Asia, and the Americas respectively. Although the tonal systems of a particular area have some common characteristics, they also show very wide variation, and it is dangerous to assume that all African languages behave one way and all Asian ones another way. Nonetheless, so long as this caution is borne in mind the areal organization is useful. Chapter six, on African systems, builds on the extensive analytical work done on these systems by Clements, Goldsmith, Hyman, Kenstowicz, Kisseberth, Leben, Meeussen, Myers, Newman, Odden, Snider, and many others. It includes data from Bantu languages from different parts of Africa, and from West African families such as Chadic and Kwa. It then looks in some detail at downstep and downdrift, and also depressor consonants. I end with a more extended discussion of Igbo.

Chapter seven on Asian systems includes extensive Chinese data from the work of Bao, Chen, Duanmu, Yip, and others, as well as data from Vietnamese, Mon-Khmer, Thai, Burmese, and Tibetan. I will begin with sketches of the tonology of four very different Chinese languages from different families. Between them these sketches will illustrate left prominent systems, right prominent systems, systems with virtually no sandhi, and systems with local dissimilation. They will also bear on the relationship between syllable structure and tone, the relationship between voicing, register and tone, and the structure of tonal inventories. I will end with a selection of typologically different systems from South-East Asia.

Chapter eight on American systems devotes most attention to the relatively well-documented languages of Mexico, followed by data from North American systems like Navajo, and ending with South American languages like Bora. Here there is less generative literature but nonetheless some languages show interesting interactions between tone and stress, and tone and laryngeal features.

Chapter nine addresses the relationship between tone and intonation, pulling together issues that will inevitably have been touched on earlier. I start with a discussion of stress languages, accentual languages, and tone languages, arguing that accentual languages are just a special kind of tone language. Then I spend the bulk of the chapter on intonation, beginning with the basic mechanisms, then looking at how they are used in non-tone languages, and then in tone languages. Lastly, I look at the interaction of speech rate and tone.

Chapter ten looks at the perception and acquisition of tones. Successful perception is the first prerequisite for tonal acquisition, and that is the reason for combining in this chapter two apparently unrelated topics, perception and acquisition. I will begin with adult perception, and then move on to the child. We know depressingly little about the acquisition of tone, so this portion of this chapter will summarize our current understanding, and raise questions for future research. It is divided into five main sections. Section one discusses the earliest evidence for infants' perception of tonal distinctions. Section two looks at early production data. Section three looks at the tonal phonology proper, including tone sandhi rules and other tonal alternations. Sections four and five look briefly at child-specific phonology, and at second-language acquisition.

2

Contrastive tone

The goal of this chapter is a descriptive summary of the types of tones and tonal inventories found around the world. It begins with a discussion of notational and fieldwork issues, then moves on to consider level tones and contour tones, the interaction of tone with segmental phenomena, and the origins of tonal systems (tonogenesis). It lays the groundwork for the following chapter, in which I will develop a theory of distinctive features for the analysis of tonal systems.

2.1   Which languages are tonal?

Although those of us whose first language is English think of tone as exotic, it is in fact extremely widespread. At a very rough estimate as many as 60–70 per cent of the world's languages may be tonal. Three areas of the world have so many tone languages that I have given them a chapter each later in this book: Africa (chapter six), East and South-East Asia and the Pacific (chapter seven), and the Americas (chapter eight). In parts of these areas (such as Meso-America), tonal languages are so common that they can almost be considered the norm. The vast majority of the world's tone languages are found in these areas. Conversely, there are parts of the world where tone languages are rare or perhaps non-existent, most notably Australia and New Zealand. Many other parts of the world show a more mixed picture. Let me go into a little more detail. In what follows, bear in mind that, as explained in chapter one, languages termed 'accentual' are often analysed as a sub-type of tone language having a small number of sparsely distributed tones. They are marginal to the main focus of this book, but will occasionally feature in our discussions, particularly in chapters six and nine. Sub-Saharan Africa is the home of perhaps the largest concentration of tonal languages in the world. Many of the major language families, such as Niger-Congo, are virtually entirely tonal, although some are described as accentual in character (see Downing forthcoming for a survey). It is only when we move north of the Sahara that we find a preponderance of non-tonal languages. Moving eastwards, in the Near and Middle East, the Semitic languages, Turkic, and the Caucasian languages are not reported to be tonal. Then we reach the Indian sub-continent, where the two largest language families are Indo-Aryan and Dravidian. The former includes a few tone languages, although the majority of languages of this family are not tonal. Among the tonal ones are Punjabi (Bahl 1957, Bhatia 1993), Kalam Kohistani (Dardic branch of Indo-Aryan, Baart 1997), and Meitiri. Dravidian languages are generally not tonal.

East and South-East Asia abound in tone languages, which are pervasive throughout the Sino-Tibetan and Mon-Khmer families. Elsewhere in East Asia, Japanese is often described as accentual rather than tonal (although, as we have seen, the distinction is apparent rather than real), and Korean has pitch differences determined by the laryngeal properties (such as voicing, aspiration, and glottalization) of onset consonants, rather than lexical tones (Jun 1998). Elsewhere in the Pacific, Papua New Guinea and Irian Jaya include a number of tone languages. One of the better reported ones is Siane (James 1981), also Golin (Bunn and Bunn 1970, Hayes 1995) and Iau (Edmondson *et al.* 1992). Melanesia also has some tonal languages, such as the languages of New Caledonia (Rivierre 1980) and Jabem (Poser 1981).

Crossing the Pacific to the Americas, Central America hosts large numbers of tone languages, especially the Otomanguean family. In North America they are fairly rare, and South America has a few languages believed to be tonal (for details see chapter eight), but the area is still under-studied, and it is possible that more languages will turn out to be tonal after more extensive research.

Finally, crossing back over the Atlantic, even Europe has a scattering of tonal or accentual languages. Serbo-Croatian (Zec 2000) and Lithuanian (Kenstowicz 1972, Young 1991, Blevins 1993) are both tonal, as are some Basque dialects (Hualde 1999), some of the Scandinavian languages, such as Swedish and Norwegian (see Riad 1996 for a good summary), and the Limburgian or Franconian dialects of Dutch (Gussenhoven and van der Vliet 1999). Like Japanese, these are tonal in the broad sense of the word, but are often termed accentual instead. Typically there are either one or two tones, and each word has only zero or one tone or tonal sequence which shows up on the stressed syllable. Certain tones bear a diacritic (*), marking them as subject to alignment with the primary stress, so that H*L differs from HL* in which tone appears in stressed position. Because of this marginal status as tone languages, they will mostly be considered beyond the scope of this book.

2.2   Tonal notations

In order to publish linguistic data, it first has to be translated into visual form. In the case of tone, the phonetic facts are plots of fundamental frequency over time, but for phonological purposes a transcription is needed. In the segmental domain, the International Phonetic Alphabet provides a common set of symbols for consonants and vowels (although American linguists often use a somewhat different system), but unfortunately in the case of tone there is much less consensus. Over time linguists working in different geographical areas have developed different traditions, each well suited for the languages in question, but quite different from each other. One of the few commonalities is that tone is nearly always transcribed on the syllable nucleus, which is usually a vowel. This convention masks the fact that the tone may be phonetically realized on any voiced sonorant segments in the syllable.

I will describe the three main traditions below. Systems other than these are sometimes used, but if so they are usually clearly explained. In each case I will also discuss the orthographic traditions, if any. Many tone languages either do not write the tones at all (such as the character-based Chinese script), or have only recently developed a writing system, in which case it may or may not use the same conventions as those used by linguists.

2.2.1   Africa

Africanists have traditionally used a set of accent marks to convey tone.

(1)   High tone   acute accent   á
       Low tone   grave accent   à   or unmarked   a
       Mid tone   level accent   ā   or unmarked   a

Thus a word with a sequence of HLM tones would be shown as either *ádàmā* or *ádàma*, and in a two-tone language a word with a HL sequence would be shown as either *ádà* or *áma*. In systems with more tones, such as extra-high or extra-low, the symbols are usually explained, but a common system uses two acute accents for extra-high, [a̋], and two grave accents for extra-low.

Contour tones are shown by combinations of levels:

(2)   Fall from high to low   acute plus grave   â
       Rise from low to high   grave plus acute   ǎ

Lastly, downstep (see § 2.4) is traditionally shown by an exclamation point before the downstepped syllable or its vowel, often but not always superscripted, denoting that the following tone is downstepped. In *á'dá* the second high is downstepped.

This system is used by linguists, but also orthographically in many cases.

2.2.2   Asia

The Asian tradition is quite different. I first look at Chinese, then other language families. Among linguists, tones are shown numerically in a system known as the 'Chao tone letters', based on work by Chao (1930). These are in fact numbers, not letters, and they divide the natural pitch range of the normal speaking voice into five levels, with 1 as the lowest and 5 as the highest. Five levels seems to be the maximum used by any language, with anything beyond four being exceedingly rare. Each syllable is given zero to three digits, usually written after the segmental transcription and often, but not always super-scripted. Zero digits means the syllable has no phonological tone of its own. Most syllables are given two digits, one for the starting pitch and one for the ending pitch. This is true even for level tones, unless the syllable is very short, in which case only one digit is usually used. Three digits are used for tones which change direction in the middle of the syllable, so that the pitch of the peak or trough must be indicated.

(3)   Sample level tones:

Sample level tones:	high	ta^{55}	tak^5
	mid	ta^{33}	tak^3
Sample contour tones:	high rising	ta^{35}	
	low falling	ta^{31}	
Sample complex tones:	low falling-rising	ta^{214}	
	low rising-falling	ta^{231}	

These digits may be accompanied by small diagrams of the tonal shape, drawn next to a vertical stave showing the range of the voice, so that [-|] shows a mid level tone. In primary sources published in China, such as the journal *Fangyan*, one may see a syllable followed by two of these diagrams, in which case the first denotes the underlying tone, and the second the surface tone.

This system works well for the linguist, especially when dealing with languages with contour tones and large numbers of levels, which would need complex combinations of accents in an African-style notation. It is less well suited to orthography, but the traditional Chinese writing system uses characters, and does not necessarily show any phonemic information even of a segmental nature, so representing the tones is not considered necessary. Pinyin, the alphabetic writing system used on mainland China, shows the tones of standard Putonghua with a set of accents quite different from the African ones. The chart below shows the tones in numerical form as well:

(4)   mā   55   mǎ   21(4)   ma   toneless
        má   35   mà   41

In this book, Chinese data will normally be given with numerical tones.

2.2.3   The Americas

Central Americanists have a strong tradition of their own not unlike the Chinese one, but with a twist: the digits are reversed, so that 5 shows low tone and 1 shows high tone. For level tones only one digit is used, and contours are often shown with a hyphen between the two digits, although I will usually omit the hyphen in this book:

(5)	Level:	high	si^1
		low	si^4
	Contour:	high rising:	$si^{3\text{-}2}$
		high falling	$si^{2\text{-}3}$

2.3   Field-work issues

Having a notation system in hand does not solve all data-related problems. The chief among them is caused by the relative nature of tone. A high tone does not have a fixed F_0 – it will vary from speaker to speaker, and even for a single speaker, depending on such factors as whether the speaker is male or female, young or old, calm or agitated, whether the word occurs at the start or the end of the utterance, and so on. It thus cannot be identified in isolation by pitch alone. This is not true for vowel quality. A vowel can be accurately identified in isolation because it is distinguished from other vowels by the relative frequencies of its various formants. As a set, they may be higher or lower depending on the size and shape of the speaker's vocal tract, but so long as their relative frequencies remain constant, the same vowel will be perceived. For the trained field linguist, transcribing vowels is relatively straightforward, and the degree of agreement among different researchers is very high. For tones, the problem is more serious. For example, consider a two-tone language. All workers may agree that there are two contrasting tones, and even that they should be called high and low, but beyond that there may well be disagreement. Using the Asian system, this contrast may be given as 55 vs. 11, or 44 vs. 11, or 55 vs. 22, for example. Even calling the contrast one of high vs. low is, if one thinks about it, an unmotivated leap. The low tone may well not be at the lowest point of the speaker's range, so that one might just as well be justified in calling it a high vs. mid contrast. Data in Maddieson 1978: 339 support this view. He gives data from which Example (6) is extracted, suggesting that the distance between the highest and lowest tones is smaller in a two-tone language than in a three- or a four-tone language, and that what stays roughly constant across languages is the distance between adjacent tones. The frequencies are given in Hertz (Hz), where one Hz is one cycle per second.

(6)   Difference in Hz between each tone and the lowest tone in the system: sample
         languages only. Extracted from Maddieson 1978.

Two levels: Siswati	Three levels: Thai	Four levels: Toura
		+50
	+32	+30
+18	+16	+10
+0	+0	+0

From (6) we can see that the 'high' and 'low' of a two-tone language are in the same relationship as the high and the mid, or the mid and the low, of a three-tone language, and *not* the same as the high vs. low relationship in the three-tone language. Indeed, speakers of a three-tone language will often identify the higher tone of a two-tone language as mid rather than high. (A. Akinlabi personal communication).

Many of these divergences in the reports of a single language do not matter to the theoretician. If two level tones are reported in any of the three ways mentioned in the last paragraph, most phonologists would not hesitate to say that the crucial fact is that there is a two-way contrast between a higher tone and a lower tone, and take that as the starting point for analysis. In other cases it can have real consequences for the analysis, as we shall see when we look at the features of tone in chapter three. Looking ahead a little, in many Asian languages the tonal range can be divided into two pitch registers (which sometimes but not always also differ in their phonation type, such as breathiness vs. modal (i.e. normal) voice), and contours typically belong to one register or the other, with 3, the mid pitch, falling on the boundary between the two. Thus a 35 is an upper register rising tone, whereas a 13 is a lower register rising tone. Now suppose that one field worker reports that a language has a 24 rising tone. We do not know which register to assign this to, but if we then uncover a report by a second field worker, who calls the same tone 13, we can then feel comfortable assigning it to the lower register.

A different sort of field-work problem relates to the level of detail transcribed, and here there are parallels in the segmental domain as to whether broad or narrow transcription is what matters. In tones, the most common confusion occurs in deciding whether a tone is level or falling. Low tones in Chinese, in particular, may be given as 21 by many workers, but 22 or 11 by another. The 21 transcription pays attention to the small fall that begins many such tones, but it may not be phonologically relevant, since when producing a very low tone it may take a little time for the voice to drop to the lowest pitch. Maddieson (1978) suggests that the definition of a level tone is 'one for which a level pitch is an acceptable variant', and this will be my working definition. As a rule of thumb, any contour with a two-digit difference between starting and ending points, such as 13 or 53, is probably phonologically a contour, but the ones with only a one digit difference, like 21 or 45, should be greeted with a degree of caution. By this logic, a 213 tone may be phonologically a rise, and the initial fall may be a production effect. Given these concerns, statements such as 'This language contrasts three falling tones' should be carefully examined. Consider the following data (adapted from Edmondson *et al.* 1992; I have re-numbered the tones to make the point clearer):

(7)   Iau 'falling' tones   52   53   32

The F_0 plots for Iau confirm that the 52 and 53 tones have a considerable fall, whereas the 32 tone falls much less, and is in fact level for most of its duration, with the fall condensed in a short initial portion, and a short final downdrift. I would thus conclude that the 32 tone is not phonologically falling, and that the language contrasts two, not three, falling tones.

The last fieldwork-related issue that must be guarded against is to do with the number and location of tones. For many languages, reports tend to give a tonal transcription for each syllable. The temptation is then to turn this into a phonological representation that does the same. In a simple case, consider a word pronounced on high pitch throughout. It will be described, for an Africanist, like this: *ádámá*. Phonologically, however, it is a mistake to assume that such a word has three H tones. It could have three, two, or only one. Below I give phonological representations in which tone is shown on a separate tier, associated by vertical lines with the vowels on which it is pronounced. Such representations are explained and justified in chapter four.

(8)   ádámá   ádámá   ádámá
        | | | | |/ |//
        H H H   H H   H

A more insidious case is encountered quite often in working on Chinese. Underlyingly, each syllable is a morpheme with its own tone. In combination, tones may be deleted, but nonetheless the tradition is to transcribe a tone on every surface syllable. So we see things for a quadri-syllabic word in Shanghai like [pø33 jia55 sɛ33 kā21] 'pre-dawn', when in fact what has happened is that a /35/ rise originating on the first syllable /pø35/ 'half' has spread over onto the second syllable and the last two syllables are phonologically toneless, falling gradually down from the high pitch of the second syllable. Figure 2.1 illustrates the impression left by the syllable-by-syllable numerical notation, in (a), vs. the actual envelope over the four-syllable word, in (b). Data simplified from Zee and Maddieson 1980: 65.

This syllable-by-syllable notation biases the researcher into looking at syllable-sized windows of the utterance, instead of at the overall pitch envelope.

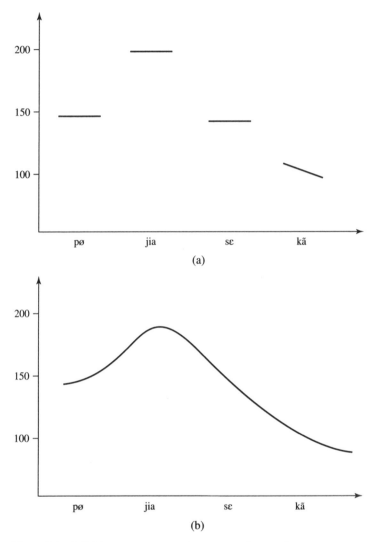

Figure 2.1   *Syllable-tone representation compared to word-tone representation. Data from Zee and Maddieson 1980.*

2.4   Contrasting level tones

The published data on a language give us an approximation of the phonetics, and inspection of the available data suggests that the preferred type of lexical tone seems to be level, or nearly so. True contour tones seem to be added to tonal inventories only in languages with large numbers of tonal contrasts.

Two-tone languages, for example, usually contrast two level tones, rather than a rise and a fall (although Maddieson 1978 gives a couple of exceptions, including Amahuaca, which contrasts a rise and a fall). The number of level tones can be quite large: there is no question that languages may have up to four level tones, and quite possibly five, even excluding downstep (see below). As for the lower bound, two contrasting surface tones is the minimum necessary to earn the name 'tone language' in the first place!

One of the first tasks for the phonologist is to establish the underlying inventory of level tones. This is not always as easy as it sounds. First, one must make decisions as to which tones are truly level, as discussed in the previous section. Then one must decide which of these levels are contrastive. In Tiv (Clements 1979), the following sentence shows three phonetic pitch heights, with the final word, *kwa*, having a mid pitch:

(9)   *i lu kwa*   ‾ _ ‑   'It was a ring of huts'

One might therefore, quite reasonably, posit three contrastive level tones. Now consider the following sentence:

(10)   *i lu kwa ga*   ‾ ‾ ‾ ‾   'It was not a ring of huts'

The same morpheme *kwa* here has a high pitch. Further investigation of Tiv shows that the high pitch is its underlyingly true pitch, and its lowered manifestation in (9) is fully predictable, happening after a low tone. Furthermore, all high-toned morphemes lower after low tones, and the lowering is iterative. This is known by a number of names, including downdrift, downstep, or catathesis, and will be discussed in chapter six. For our present purposes, the point is that a phonetic pitch distinction does not necessarily translate into an underlying phonological tone contrast.

The smallest possible underlying tonal inventory has only one specified tone, and the surface contrast necessary for us to call the language a tone language comes from the option of leaving syllables phonologically toneless. This is a very common situation, and indeed many Bantu languages have been analysed in this way. See Hyman 2000 for an excellent recent summary. In the classic cases, such as Haya (Hyman and Byarushengo 1984), there is an underlying H tone, and any syllable that is not specified as H by the end of the phonology either receives a L tone by default, or stays toneless and surfaces with a pitch determined by phonetic interpolation from one H tone target to the next. (See chapter one on the relationship between phonology and phonetics.) The reason for taking H tone to be specified and low to be absent is that H is active in a variety of ways in the phonology, whereas low is largely inert, as one expects if it is not actually there at all! There are also a smaller number of languages where L has been suggested to be the specified tone, and H the default, for example Huave (Noyer 1992), Ruwund (Nash 1992–4), and Mandinka (Creissels and Grégoire 1993). When there are zero or one Hs (or Ls) per *word*, and the location of this H is what matters, these languages are often called accentual, since the tonal contrast is reduced to a minimum: the presence or absence of H (or L) on a particular syllable.

Given a two-way surface contrast, there is an obvious alternative to analysing it as an underlying contrast between high and zero. Instead, we can propose that every syllable has a phonological tone, and the inventory contrasts two tones, let us assume H and L. In such a language both tones would be phonologically active, for example engaging in spreading. There are many languages of this type, including many African ones, such as Aghem (Hyman 1987), Bambara (Rialland and Badjime 1989, Clements 2000), Dagaare (Gur: Antilla and Bodomo 1996), and of course languages from other areas, such as Songjiang (Chen 2000). For some languages, there is no consensus on whether the contrast is one of H/L, or H/Ø. See Hyman 2000 for discussion.

Of course, if we add to an underlying H vs. L system the possibility of syllables being unspecified, and a default process that provides a mid tone, then we have three phonetic tones, but only two phonological tones. In general, (n) phonological tones may produce (n + 1) surface tones, assuming that toneless syllables persist throughout the phonology, and that when the default rule eventually inserts a tone it is distinct from the underlying tones. Thus in some languages mid is the default, so we have a /H/ vs. /L/ vs. zero underlying system, as in Yoruba (Benue-Congo; Akinlabi 1985, Pulleyblank 1986).

True underlying three-tone systems are also very common, and found in all regions, such as Huajuapan Mixtec (Pike and Cowan 1967), Nupe (Benue-Congo, Smith 1967), and Kunama (Nilo-Saharan, Connell *et al.* 2000). Punjabi (Bhatia 1993) contrasts three tones on stressed syllables. On unstressed syllables L is not found.

(11)   kòRaa   'horse'
            kōRaa   'whip'
            kóRaa   'leper'

Four surface tone levels are much rarer, but they are reported for a number of languages, including Grebo and other Kru languages (Kaye and Koopman 1982, Newman 1986), Igede (Stahlke 1977), Mambila (Connell, 1999, 2000), Mazateco (Pike 1948), Chatino (Pride 1963), Jianyang (Chen 2000), and Cantonese (Yip 1990, under certain analytical assumptions). Ngamambo (along with other W. Grassfields languages) has four phonetic levels, but Hyman (1986) analyses it as having only a two-way underlying contrast. In most cases of a phonological four-way contrast known to me, all four tones are analysed as phonological tones, rather than the logical alternative of H, M, L, and zero. However, Hyman and Magaji

(1970) analyse Gwari as a four-tone system derived from only three underlying tones, and Hyman (1972) offers a similar analysis for Fe'fe'. In both cases one of the four tones is derived from a combination of two of the underlying three tones.

After this, we enter relatively unknown territory. There are quite a number of reports of languages that contrast five level tones, but most are known only from fairly brief reports, with not enough detail to determine unequivocally whether there are actually five underlying level tones, or whether one or more are derived in some way. Hei-Miao (Miao-Yao; Chang 1953), Gaoba Dong (Shi *et al.* 1987), Dan (Bearth and Zemp 1967), Trique (Longacre 1952), and Ngamambo Bamileke (Asongwed and Hyman 1976) are some of the best-known cases. In all except Hei Miao and Gaoba Dong, it has been argued that only four level tones contrast underlyingly. See Yip 1980a for discussion.

2.5   Location, number and type of rising and falling tones

In addition to level tones, many languages have tones that change their pitch during the syllable, either rising or falling. In the next chapter I will suggest that these are best understood as sequences of level tones, but in this section I limit myself to the basic observations.

2.5.1   Location of contour tones

If a language places a heavy information load on its tonal contrasts, level tones do not suffice. There are many languages that contrast four or more tones, and, as we have seen, this number of contrasting levels is rare. Instead, a smaller number of level tones is supplemented by the addition of one or more contours. These may be simple rises or falls, or tones which first rise and then fall (convex tones) or first fall and then rise (concave, or dipping, tones). The existence of the more complex tones usually implies the existence of simple rises and falls. Falls are much more common than rises (Zhang 2000, 2001).

When a language is reported to have a contour tone, for example a falling tone, one must first ask where this contour is found. There are three main possibilities. It may be found only on polysyllables, so that each syllable is essentially level, with the first high and the second low, but the word as a whole has a fall. In such cases the language can be straightforwardly described with level tones only, assigning tone to syllables, and need not be treated as a contour tone language.

The second possibility is that a contour may occur within a single syllable, but only if that syllable is heavy (a long vowel or closed syllable). Hausa, for example, allows falling tones only on heavy syllables. The usual analytical step here is again to assume that contour tones are sequences of level tones, that tones are properties of weight units (moras), and that therefore only if a syllable has two moras can it bear two tones, giving rise to a surface contour. The need for two moras imposed by contour tones can cause vowel lengthening. In Chiang Rai (N. Thai, Gandour 1977) non-low vowels with rising tones have lengthened historically, and those with non-rising tones have shortened. Synchronically, then, we find rising tones only on long non-low vowels. A particularly interesting example of this type is Rongxian Chinese (Zhou 1987). In Rongxian syllables may end in long vowels, diphthongs, nasals, or unreleased oral stops. Syllables ending in sonorants may bear level or contour tones, presumably because the nucleus and the following sonorant each have their own mora. Stop-final syllables may only have level tones, suggesting that non-sonorants cannot be moraic. Reduplication imposes a [35] rising tone on the second syllable, as shown in (12a). In order to realize this contour, syllables must be bi-moraic, so stop-final syllables change the final stop to the corresponding nasal, which can be moraic, and thus can now bear a tone, as in (12b):

(12)　　a. taː33　　taː33 taː35　　'hit'
　　　　　liu55　　liu55 liu35　　'slide, glide'
　　　　b. wat33　　wat33 wan35　　'dig, excavate'

The third possibility is that contours may occur on any syllable, light or heavy. Such languages are less common, but many descriptions are found in the literature. Two analytical options are open to the phonologist. First, these contours too could be sequences of levels, and the language allows a syllable or mora to have more than one tone attached to it. Second, these contours are single phonological objects, and thus can show up on any vowel, mora, or syllable. Both options will be considered in the next chapter. This last class of languages are what one might call 'true contour tone languages'.

In addition to restrictions on the type of syllable on which they occur, contours are quite often restricted as to where in the word the syllable must be located. Language after language allows contours only on the word-final syllable, with Mende (Leben 1973, 1978, Goldsmith 1976, Zoll 1997b) being the classic example. We find words like *mbǎ* 'rice' or *nyàhâ* 'woman', but no words like **nyâhá*. As a further example, in Kunama (Connell *et al.* 2000) there are three level tones, H, M, L; three falls, HM, ML, HL; and one rise, MH. The contours are found medially, but always on heavy syllables. However, they may occur on short vowels, provided those vowels are word-final:

(13)　　géérê　　'tall (pl.)'　　ắkkúbê　　'camels'

Word-final syllables are, of course, often lengthened cross-linguistically, and it is highly likely that this accounts for their greater propensity to bear contour tones.

Zhang (2000) shows that rising tones in particular are usually found on longer syllables, and even for African languages often claimed to have short contours, the phonetic data shows lengthening (Ward 1944).

2.5.2   *Number and type of contrasting contours*

Just as with level tones, languages with a small number of contrasting contours are more common than languages with a large number of contrasts. Since the presence of contours implies the presence of level tones, it is perfectly possible for a language to have only one contour tone, in which case it is usually a fall, as in Hausa. Zhang (2000, 2001) in his sample of 198 tone languages finds 39 with no surface rising tones but only 3 with no surface falling tones. Languages with surface rises but no falls include Bamileke-Dschang (Hyman 1985). See Manfredi 1993 for a summary. It is also very common to find that a language has one rise and one fall. Among such languages are many African languages, such as Bambara, Mende and Ibibio, and Gao'an Chinese (Bao 1999). If the contours are composed of levels, and if the language has only two levels, then the maximum number of contours is a HL fall and a LH rise.

Languages may also contrast more than one contour of the same shape: two rises or two falls, for example. Cantonese has two rises and one fall. Grebo (Kru, Newman 1986) has two rises, Bai (Bao 1999) has two falls and one rise.

If the contours are composed of levels, the existence of two falls implies at least three levels, and then in fact we might expect to find up to three contours of the same shape. For example, from H, M, and L we can compose the falls HM, HL, and ML. However, such systems are rather rare. Reports include San Juan Copala Trique (Hollenbach 1977), Chatino (Pride 1963), and LianYunGang (Iwata and Imagawa 1982). As discussed in section 2.3, some reported contours may in fact be phonologically level. In Trique, for example, the three-way rising contrast is given by Hollenbach as [21] vs. [32] vs. [53] (1 is high, 5 is low) but at least one of the apparent rises 21 and 32 may actually be 1 and 2 level tones, since otherwise the level-tone inventory has only 3, 4, and 5, with gaps for the two highest levels. Systems with more than three contrasting contours of the same shape are extremely rare: one of the richest examples is another Trique dialect, discussed in chapter eight, which is claimed, quite convincingly, to have six falls and seven rises!

Lastly it is worth noting that contrasting contours tend to be fairly far apart in the pitch space. If there are two falls, they are more likely to be 53 and 31 rather than 53 and 52. This is hardly surprising: the perceptual advantages should be clear. See chapter seven on Min for further discussion.

2.5.3   More complex tones

Tones that fall and then rise (concave) or rise and then fall (convex) are rare in African languages, but quite common in Asia. Nonetheless, they are much rarer than levels or simple contours. C.-C. Cheng (1973) in a cross-dialect count of Chinese tones found the numbers shown in (14).

(14)	*Type of shape*	*Number found*
	Level	1086
	Simple contour: Fall	1125
	Rise	790
	Complex contour: Concave	352
	Convex	80

These numbers should be treated with caution, especially the high number of falling tones, many of which are probably level tones with an utterance-final fall since they are usually listed in their isolation forms. Still, they clearly show the lower frequency of the complex contours, and especially of the convex ones.

In many cases one portion of the contour is more dramatic than the other, and they can be analysed as a simple rise or fall, preceded or followed by a phonetic on- or off-glide. Among the concave tones, a very large number fall to the lowest level, [1], in the middle, making the preceding fall quite plausibly phonetic, and parallel to the initial fall in many low level tones. For example, the Mandarin third tone in its citation form [214] is arguably a rising tone with an initial phonetic fall. See Bao 1999 for a detailed analysis of Xining along these lines. Nonetheless, not all concave or convex tones can be reduced to simple rises or falls. Bambara has LHL on words like *baLHL* 'goat' (Rialland and Badjime 1989). Changzhi has [535] as well as [213], and although Bao tries to derive both these from simpler forms, the attempt is not entirely successful. Convex tones seem to be less common than concave tones, but they are found. Pingyao, for example, has a surface [423] tone phrase-finally, although the falling portion could be due to phrase-final lowering.

Just as some languages allow level tones anywhere, but simple contours only phrase-finally, languages with complex contours often allow simple contours anywhere, but complex contours only phrase-finally. This is true of both Mandarin [214] and Pingyao [423], but not of Changzhi, which has nouns composed of root + suffix like these, with complex contours copied from the root on both syllables:

(15)	ts'ə-tə	213-213	'cart'
	i-tə	535-535	'chair'

In many languages syllables bearing these contours are lengthened. Again, this is true in Mandarin, but for many languages the relevant data are not available.

2.6   Tone and vowel quality

Tones cannot be considered in complete isolation from the segments on which they are realized. In some languages they are indeed fully independent, so that any vowel may bear any tone, and the quality or phonation of the vowel is in no way affected. In some languages, however, different tones are associated with different laryngeal properties, such as breathiness or glottalization. In yet others there are relationships between tone and pharyngeal qualities such as the width of the pharyngeal cavity, usually characterized by the feature Advanced Tongue Root (ATR). Finally, in a few cases there are little understood relationships between tone and cavity features, primarily vowel height. Examples of each of these are discussed in the remainder of this section. Note first that this is not a random set of connections. We know that the articulatory mechanisms that produce pitch changes are not limited to laryngeal changes, but also include raising and lowering of the larynx, which in turn may affect the pharynx and the tongue root, and thence perhaps the tongue body (Trigo 1991). For further discussion, see chapter one on phonetics. Unsurprisingly, we do not usually find connections between phonetically unconnected gestures such as lip rounding, or retroflexion, and tone.

For examples of laryngeal interactions with tone, we turn to East Asian and Mexican tone languages. Jingpho (Maddieson and Hess 1986) has a contrast in breathy versus plain vowels, and the breathy vowels are significantly lower in pitch than the plain vowels. The contrast originated in a voicing contrast in onsets, now lost. This phonation contrast is overlaid on the tonal system of the language, so that the 33, 31, and 55 tones, for example, occur with both phonation types. Shanghai (Zee and Maddieson 1980), on the other hand, has retained its voiced onsets, and these induce breathy voice on the following vowel, and a lower tone. Open syllables beginning with voiced obstruents always have a LM rise, and the initial low pitch is too great, and extends too long, to be attributed to the effect of the onset consonant, but must instead be related to the vowel's breathy quality and its phonologization as lowered tone. A rather unusual interaction between voicing and tone can be found in Turkana (Nilotic, Dimmendaal and Breedveld 1986). Word-final short vowels are devoiced pre-pausally if they bear the opposite tone to the tone of the preceding syllable:

(16)   a. /à-lép-ì/   [àléphi̥]   'it (she) has been milked'

        b. /á-mòt-í/   [á!môthi̥]   'cooking pot'

If one thinks of the tonal sequence as a contour spread over two syllables, it is as if the tonal load on the second part of the contour is relatively unimportant.

Glottalization may also interact with tone: in many languages some degree of glottalization is a crucial component of certain tones, particularly low tones. See the discussion of Chinantec in chapter eight.

For examples of pharyngeal interactions with tone, we turn to East Asia again, to the Mon-Khmer languages. Although the facts here are historical rather than synchronic, they provide the clearest illustration of a pharyngeal/tonal relationship known to me, which earns them their place in this section. Mon-Khmer has a widespread distinction referred to as a 'register' difference. We have already encountered the term 'register' in connection with other Asian languages, and there it referred mainly to a pitch difference. However, the register difference surfaces in different languages in different ways, and Mon-Khmer shows a number of different manifestations in closely related languages, including vowel height differences, onset voicing distinctions, voice quality distinctions, and pitch contrasts. Gregerson (1976) argues that the difference is pharyngeal: one register has an advanced tongue root [ATR], and the other has a retracted (or non-advanced) tongue root [RTR]. The correlations are as follows; the specific vowel inventories are those of Rengao:

(17)   *First Register*   *Second Register*
        Voiceless onsets   Voiced onsets
        Modal voice   'Breathy' voice
        Higher pitch   Lower pitch
        Open, RTR vowels [e_i, o_u, ɛ, ɔ, a]   Closed, ATR vowels [i, u, e, o, ə]

Gregerson's suggestion is that the action of retracting the tongue root 'both lowers the vowel and creates conditions favorable for voicelessness'. Advancing the tongue root enlarges the pharyngeal cavity, producing deep pharyngeal resonances (sometimes misleadingly called 'breathy' voice). These resonances are further enhanced by a lowered larynx (Stevens and Keyser 1989, Stevens *et al.* 1986), which in turn lowers pitch and encourages voicing. A language may then phonologize any of these correlates of ATR, so that Vietnamese, for example, has lost the vowel height differences but become tonal.

The previous discussion of pharnygeal/tonal interaction showed us a surprising side effect: vowel height differences interacting with tone. However, more direct and unequivocal interaction between vowel height and tone is extremely rare, and the examples are controversial. If a connection exists, one would expect higher vowels to be found with higher tones, since in many languages, including English, studies have shown that higher vowels have an intrinsically higher fundamental frequency than low vowels (see Maddieson 1997 for recent discussion and references). The most studied case is Fuzhou, a Min dialect of Chinese, where there are alternations involving both tone and vowel height. The data are complex, but a simplified subset are given below (from Wright 1983; see also Jiang-King 1998):

(18)   *If tone is 12, 242, 13ʔ*   *If tone is 44, 52, 22*
        ei(ŋ), ou(ŋ), øü(ŋ)   i(ŋ), u(ŋ), ü(ŋ)
        aiŋ, auŋ, ɔiŋ   eiŋ, ouŋ, øüŋ

Roughly speaking, the tones in the second column are higher, and so are the vowels. There is much controversy over how to understand this case. For a full account, see Wright 1983 and references therein. It seems clear that the tone change must trigger the vowel change, rather than the reverse, since with other vowels the tone change is found even when the vowels are invariant. However, synchronically the correspondence between pitch and vowel height is murky: the 'low' tones include 242 and the 'high' tones include 22.

A second case is to be found in Cantonese. In syllables closed by stop consonants, there is a correlation between vowel quality and tone (Yue-Hashimoto 1972). The low [3] tone occurs with all vowel types, but the high [5] and mid [4] tones occur with lax and tense vowels respectively. The distinction may be one of tenseness or of length, since the lax vowels are shorter than the tense vowels:

(19)   a. Higher tone, short lax vowel   b. Lower tone, long tense vowel
          sɛk5 'know'   yiːp4 'leaf'
          sʌp5 'wet'   saːt4 'kill'

This sort of interaction between vowel tenseness and tone can be seen phonetically in languages like Madurese (Trigo 1991), where the so-called 'chest register' vowels seem to be ATR (tense), and also lower in pitch. For further reading on vowel quality and tone interactions, see Dimmendaal and Breedveld 1986.

2.7   Consonant types and tone

It is not only vowels that may interact with tone. The most common way in which consonants interact is that voiced obstruents are often associated with low tone. In some languages, such as Ewe, the connection extends at least to some degree to all voiced consonants, even including sonorants (see Smith 1968 for full details), whereas in others, such as historically in Punjabi, it involves only a subset of the voiced obstruents, those with breathy voice.

We have seen that a connection between obstruent voicing and low tone is articulatorily unsurprising, and in the next section we shall see that historically it has been extremely common. Synchronically, too, it is not unusual. Nearly always, consonants affect tones rather than the reverse, and in African languages this is quite common. Voiced consonants often cause lowering of neighbouring tones. Such consonants are called depressor consonants. For example, in Suma (Gbaya, Bradshaw 1999), imperfective verbs have H tone: *éé* 'leave behind' *kírí* 'look for', but if the verb begins with a voiced obstruent it has a LH rising tone: *bŭsí* 'be bland'. The lowering effects can show up in various ways in addition to straightforward lowering. Sometimes depressors cause downstep (see chapter six), or they may repel H tones, as in Siswati (Bradshaw 1999: 26ff.), where H tones, which are usually in antepenultimate position as in (20a), shift rightwards away from a depressor consonant, /z/, as in (20b).

(20)   a. *kulimísaana*   'to cause to plough for each other'

         b. *kucaɓuzeláana*   'to kiss each other for'

Depressors may also block H tone movement or spread. In Siswati, again, the rightward shift we have just seen cannot cross over another depressor, such as /d/, so the H shifts over only locally within the syllable, creating a rise: *lidădaana* 'little duck'.

Although rare, there seem to be some cases where tones affect consonant voicing. In Wuyi, for example, higher tones have voiceless onsets and lower tones have voiced onsets (Yip 1995, from Duanmu 1990, Bao 1990). If a higher tone spreads across a voiced onset, it causes de-voicing: /sa24-vuo31/ → [sa24 fuo53] 'raw meal'. This kind of example is especially striking because the effects of the tone overwhelm the cross-linguistically more common phenomenon of intervocalic voicing. Perhaps the clearest example is that of Jabem (Melanesian, Poser 1981), where the person prefixes are underlyingly high toned, but in the second conjugation a low-toned root spreads its tone leftwards into the prefixal syllable, not only causing the vowel to become low, but also voicing the onset consonant: /ká-wìŋ/ → [gàwìŋ] 'accompany, 1sg. realis'.

Schuh (1978) gives a few other cases of tone affecting consonants, including this interesting one from Jingpho. A morphological process of gemination is accompanied by voicing after a low tone, but not after a high tone:

(21)   yàk   'difficult'   yàggai   'it is difficult'
         cát   'tight'   cáttai   'it is tight'

However, the low-toned vowels in Jingpho are breathy, so the voicing may be caused by the (possibly secondary) breathiness rather than by the low tone itself. Thurgood (1980) argues that *all* cases of tones apparently affecting consonants are actually cases where the vowels differ not only in tone but also in phonation type.

Apart from this widespread interaction between voicing and tone, we find some interaction between other laryngeal properties such as aspiration and glottalization and tone. In most such cases, the laryngeal qualities are located on the vowel, as discussed in section 2.6. Cases in which truly consonantal aspiration or glottalization interact with tone are largely limited to historical cases, and I will postpone their discussion till the next section. One of the few synchronic cases is Seoul Korean (Jun 1998). Korean is not a lexical tone language, but accentual phrases have their own tonal melody which is either (LHLH) or (HHLH). The choice of H or L at the start of the phrase depends on the laryngeal features of the phrase-initial segment. If it is either aspirated or tense, the phrase begins H. Otherwise, it begins L. The class of H-inducing consonants is the [+ stiff vocal cords] class in the Halle and Stevens system of laryngeal features, as we shall see in the next chapter.

2.8   Tonogenesis: the birth of tones

To speakers of a non-tonal language, tones seem to be a rather baroque complication: why should speakers pay such close attention to the pitch of a word? There are in fact well-understood phonetic underpinnings for the development of tonal contrasts: see Hombert *et al.* 1979 for an excellent review. However, an understanding of the phonetic principles is not sufficient. When we study a modern tone language it is not always possible to reconstruct its history, but there are enough cases in which it can be done to enable us to make some general statements about where tones come from. The usual source of evidence is comparative data from closely related languages. For example, if a group of non-tonal languages contrasts [ta] and [da], and one tonal language in their midst instead contrasts [tá] and [tà] on the same pair of lexical items, we may suppose that the tonal contrast on the vowels has arisen out of the loss of a prior voicing contrast on the onsets. In the real world the data are not usually quite as clear cut, but nonetheless general patterns can be discerned.

Pitch differences are of course present in all languages, but if the language is non-tonal they are not contrastive, and not perceived by the speaker/listener. When a language becomes tonal the pitch differences come to the fore, taking on a contrastive role. The best-known source of tonal contrast is a voicing contrast in obstruents. Voiced obstruents are known to lower the pitch of the following vowel (Hombert 1978, Maddieson 1997), and voiceless obstruents may even raise it. There are various reasons for this. Voicing in obstruents is associated with slacker vocal folds, and a lowered larynx. Both these tend to lower pitch, at least at the start of the following vowel. Voiceless obstruents seem to have tenser vocal folds, and thus tend to raise the pitch on the following vowel. If the consonants lose their voicing contrast over time, the pitch difference may persist, and the burden of contrast is then shifted from a voicing contrast in the consonant to a tone contrast in the vowel. In Kammu, a Mon-Khmer language of Cambodia (Svantesson 1983, Dell 1985), the southern dialects have a contrast in onset voicing on obstruents, but the northern dialects have lost the voiced set and instead they contrast a H tone where the north has a voiceless onset, and a L tone where the north has a voiced one:

(22)   *Kammu dialects*
         South   North
         klaaŋ   kláaŋ   'eagle'
         glaaŋ   klàaŋ   'stone'

If a language is already tonal from some other source, such as final consonants (see (23)), this change may double the number of tones. For example, in Cantonese Chinese we see a six-tone system arising out of a three-tone system as the result of the influence of the historically voiced onsets, all now voiceless. Stop-final syllables underwent a secondary split probably related to vowel tenseness, and are excluded from the following table. These examples are reconstructed by Karlgren (1966) as having voiceless onsets (top row), and voiced onsets (bottom row) respectively.

(23)   *Cantonese tonal split*
         Historically voiceless onsets   si53/55   si35   sei44
                                           'govern'   'excrement'   'four'
         Historically voiced onsets   tsʰi21   tsʰi24   si33
                                           'word'   'rely on'   'serve'

This type of change is extremely widespread throughout East and South-East Asia, as documented in pioneering work by Haudricourt (1954) and Matisoff (1973). The intermediate stages in the development of tone can often be observed in related languages. For example, in Shanghai Chinese there is still a voicing contrast in the obstruents, and these consonants are followed by breathy voiced vowels with lower tones. The tonal contrasts have appeared, but the voicing contrast on the onsets has not yet disappeared. Two further points should be made. First, cross-linguistically the tonal effect is usually caused by the initial consonant (with Jingpho as a possible exception; see Hombert 1978), but the languages in question usually had no voiced obstruent codas at the stage when tonogenesis is thought to have taken place, so this apparent asymmetry may be less significant than at first appears. Second, there are some languages that reverse the usual and phonetically expected connection between voicing and low tone, having higher tones after historically voiced consonants. For example, Shan has the following tones:

(24)   *Shan tonal split*
         Historically voiceless or glottalized onsets   334   11   22
         Historically voiced onsets   55   22   44

Kingston and Solnit (1989) discuss various possible explanations for this. One option is that the original tonal split had lower tones after voiced stops, and the inversion was a later development. They point out that the problem with this idea is that some languages show the inversion at a stage when consonants still preserve their original laryngeal contrasts. Their proposal instead requires a

language-specific assignment of tonal features to consonants, itself a rather problematic idea, as we shall see when we discuss tonal features in the next chapter.

There is some reason to think that voicing alone may not be sufficient for the
emergence of a tonal contrast. If a language has more than one voiced series, they
do not necessarily all result in low tone reflexes. For example, in Punjabi (Bahl
1957, Chatterji 1969), only the historically voiced aspirates lowered the tone,
whereas plain voiced stops grouped with the voiceless stops. Interestingly, the effect is not only passed on to the following vowel, but also affects the preceding
one. In what follows reconstructed historical forms are shown with a preceding
asterisk. For example, *bɦiukh > pukh24, where the pre-vocalic voiced aspirated
[bɦ] has depressed the start of the tone, creating a rise. Conversely, in *baddɦa
> bʌdda53, the post-vocalic voiced aspirate [dɦ] has depressed the end of the
tone, creating a fall. Historically, in Thai (Li 1977) plain voiced stops caused
lowering, but pre-glottalized voiced stops did not. In many African languages today, such as Zulu, voiced implosives (which are glottalized) do not lower pitch,
but plain voiced consonants do. A further area of variation is the behaviour of
voiced sonorants, which in some languages pattern with voiced obstruents but in
others with voiceless ones.

Tones have arisen from other laryngeal contrasts in consonants, but the
effects of voiceless aspiration and glottalization on obstruents are not nearly as
consistent as those of voicing. There is often claimed to be a tendency for voiceless aspirated stops to give rise to higher tones than unaspirated stops, but while
this has happened in some languages in others the reverse is the case. Haudricourt (1972) and Kingston and Solnit (1989) discuss languages which have
three-way tonal splits caused by onset laryngeal contrasts. Plain voiced stops
form one category, as discussed earlier, and the two other categories are typically voiceless aspirated stops and glottalized stops. The plain voiceless stops
usually group with the glottalized series. The picture is confused. In some cases
the aspirated series are higher (as in the Karen language Palaychi), in other
cases the glottalized series are higher (as in Renli Kam). In (25) I use the labials to represent the entire laryngeal series.

(25)

Palaychi: aspirates higher		Renli Kam: glottalized higher			
*ph	55ʔ	*p, *ʔb	55	324	53
*p, *ʔb	22ʔ	*ph	35	213	453
*b	21	*b	11	21	31

The possible explanations here are parallel to those proposed for the behaviour of
voiced consonants in apparently raising or lowering tones. Finally, one relatively

clear development is the influence of post-vocalic glottal stop and [h]. Glottal stop raised the end of the tone, leaving a rise, whereas [h] lowered it, leaving a fall. See Haudricourt 1954.

We have seen that tones may be not only level, but also contoured (rising or falling), and one can also ask about the origins of these differences in shape. In many ways one might expect the influence of consonants to be relatively local, in which case they would create rising and falling tones by depressing or raising the pitch only at the start of the following vowel. In fact, although the greatest perturbation in pitch caused by onset voicing is certainly at the start of the vowel, in (as yet!) non-tonal languages like English the pitch of the vowel after a voiced consonant is still significantly lower 100 ms into the vowel (Hombert *et al.* 1979). In languages with breathy voiced onsets, Edmondson (1992) finds that the breathy phonation continues through up to 50 per cent of the following vowel. In tonal languages like Thai, the perturbation is more local, which obviously aids in retaining contrastive tone on the remainder of the vowel. Historically, the effects of a voiced consonant may either be to lower the entire tone (Cantonese), or to perturb only the start and thus create a contour (Punjabi).

Although the details are murky, the overall picture is clear enough: tonal contrasts developed from the loss of laryngeal distinctions, particularly voicing, in the surrounding consonants. This does not mean that modern tone languages cannot also have a voicing contrast, and indeed many do. There could be many reasons for this: for example, the voicing contrast may have re-emerged after tonogenesis took place, or tones may have arisen from an aspiration contrast instead. Often we do not know: the tones developed too long ago for us to do more than speculate.

3

Tonal features

Having described the range of tonal contrasts in the previous chapter, this chapter proposes a feature system for capturing all and only the observed inventories. A good feature system has several desiderata, which are outlined in section 3.1. The following sections deal first with how to represent the number of levels. Since the clearly described systems have no more than a four-way contrast, the system will be based on two binary features, Register and Pitch. How to handle five-tone systems if they exist will also be covered. Next we move on to how to deal with contour tones, and conclude that they should be analysed as sequences of level tones. The reasons for choosing this over a unitary contour alternative will be explained and discussed. This section will be followed by a section on the geometric relation between Register and Pitch (comparing the approaches of, among others, Bao, Clements, Duanmu, Hyman, and Yip), and what sort of data bear on the choice. The penultimate section asks whether tonal features are entirely disjoint from segmental features, focussing mainly on Laryngeal features, but with some discussion of Pharyngeal and Tongue Root features. The chapter will end with the question of whether features are binary or unary, and how we deal with unmarked tones.

3.1 Desiderata for a feature system

It has been known for years that the smallest units of phonological structure are not phonemes, or indeed 'individual sounds' (if such things exist), but the properties that make up those sounds, stated in terms of distinctive features (or elements in Government Phonology, see Harris 1990). The syllable [pa] is represented as two sounds [p] and [a], but [p] is just a symbol for a voiceless stop consonant articulated with the lips, and [a] is just a symbol for a low, back, unrounded vowel. In binary SPE feature terms, [p] is [+anterior, –coronal, –cont, –voice], and [a] is [+low, +back, –round]. The properties themselves may need more than one feature to pin them down. For example, labials are traditionally described by the two features [+anterior, –coronal]. Mid vowels are described as [–high, –low]. If the contrast implicit in the description of the sound is a two-way contrast, such as voiced vs. voiceless, then a single binary feature [+/–voice] will do the job. If the contrast is multi-valued, such as vowel height, which must distinguish at least high vs. mid vs. low, then two or more features will be needed. In the case of vowel height, the usual practice is to assume the following system, with two features giving three heights.

(1)   High vowels   [+high], [–low]
       Mid vowels: [–high], [–low]
       Low vowels: [–high], [+low]
       impossible: [+high], [+low]

This system predicts a number of things. First, it limits the number of purely height contrasts to three (although other features, such as ATR, can add to the number of phonetic vowel heights). Second, it predicts certain natural classes of vowels. The [–high] class includes mid and low vowels, and the [–low] class includes high and mid vowels. There is no class of high and low vowels only, excluding mid vowels (unless we allow statements such as [α high, –αlow], the class of vowels with opposite values of plus and minus for the features [high] and [low]). The system also makes stating certain types of changes simple, and others difficult or impossible. For example, one cannot easily state a rule which moves each vowel up one notch, since when a low vowel raises to mid, the feature [low] changes, whereas when a mid vowel raises to high, the feature [high] changes. (This made formulating the Great English Vowel Shift very difficult!)

Tones, too, are properties of sounds, and we will need to discover the right system of features to explain tonal inventories and tonal behaviour. There is no prima facie reason why tone height and vowel height should have closely similar feature systems, although they could. Note that the word 'height', used for both vowels and tone, actually refers to quite different things. In the case of tones, it refers to the acoustic entity, fundamental frequency, but in the case of vowels, it refers to the articulatory position of the tongue body in the oral cavity. We can thus use the vowel height analogy as a useful starting point, but not one that will necessarily turn out to be suitable for tone.

The desiderata for a feature system for tone include the following:

(2)   *Design criteria for a feature system for tone*
       a. Characterize all and only the numbers of level tone contrasts.
       b. Characterize contour tones, and their relationship to level tones.
       c. Characterize all and only the numbers of contour tone contrasts.
       d. Allow for simple statements of common tonal alternations.
       e. Allow for simple statements about tonal markedness.
       f. Characterize the relationship between tonal and non-tonal features, particularly laryngeal features, both synchronically and historically.

Table 3.1. *Some specific criteria for a tonal feature system*

General criteria	Specifics
a. Number of level tones	• at least four, possibly five
b. Contour tones	• rising, falling, convex, concave • sometimes result of combining two or more levels
c. Contour tone contrasts	• two, possibly three, of a given shape
d. Common alternations	• assimilation, dissimilation, contour formation and simplification, downstep
e. Tonal markedness	• In a two-tone system, low is usually unmarked • In a three-tone system, mid is usually unmarked • Level tones are less marked than contours
f. Tonal and laryngeal features	• Low tone associated with voicing, and especially breathiness • High tone associated with voicelessness

As a reminder of the previous chapter's more robust findings, and in some cases as a preview of things to come in later chapters, we can make some of these goals more explicit in Table 3.1.

There have been a number of attempts over the years at achieving these goals, none of them as yet perfect, and I begin with a review of earlier proposals. The majority have been based on research on Asian tonal systems, with African systems getting relatively little attention until the work of Hyman (1979, 1986, 1993). The reasons for this are clear. Just as we would not design a feature system for vowel height on the basis of a language with only [i, u, a], we cannot design a feature system for tone height on the basis of languages with only a two-way contrast such as we find in a large number of African languages. In such cases, there are really only two options. Either there is a single binary feature for tone, such as [+/–high], or there is one unary, privative feature, say High, and low syllables are unspecified for tone. It is only when we look at systems with large numbers of level and contour tones that we know that a single binary feature is not sufficient for all languages. Languages with the requisite rich tonal inventories are much more common in Asia and Central America, and of the two, Asia has been better studied, at least until recently. There is one less obvious reason, too. African tone languages tend to have rich morphology and very mobile tones, as we shall see, so tonologists focussing on Africa devoted most of their attention to understanding how tones ended up where they did, and kept very busy doing so. Asian tone languages often show relatively static tones, so tonologists working on those languages paid more attention to characterizing the dazzlingly complex tonal inventories in featural terms. There was also a long tradition of historical work on tonogenesis that provided a rich array of data bearing on one of our criteria, the relationship between tonal and laryngeal features.

I will start with the most basic question: what feature system do we need to characterize the number of contrasting level tones?

3.2   Numbers of level tones

3.2.1   Four levels

We have seen that it is certainly necessary to distinguish four levels, and perhaps five. Wang (1967) and Woo (1969) both propose systems for five levels, using three binary features. Three features can in principle be combined in eight ways, so the features had to be carefully defined. For example, Woo used [high tone] and [low tone] in a way analogous to [high] and [low] for vowel height to define three levels [55, 33, 11], then added a feature [modify] which could regulate the extreme tones in the system, making them less extreme [44, 22].

(3)   *Woo's feature system:*

	55	44	33	22	11
high tone	+	+	–	–	–
low tone	–	–	–	+	+
modify	–	+	–	+	–

One advantage of this system is that any language with less than four tones can be assumed not to make use of the feature [modify]. On the other hand, the many four-tone languages are slightly surprising, since they do require the feature [modify], but it apparently only combines with one of the two extreme tones, not both.

Most later researchers have concentrated on four-tone languages as being the upper limit most solidly motivated by the data. Four tones would suggest two features, each binary, but this gives rise to a problem: the combination [+high tone, +low tone] makes no sense, and thus the two binary features only define three levels, just like the features for vowel height. But there is a way to use only two features to define four tones, and this move was first made in Yip 1980a. In various guises it is now the most widely used feature system for level tones. Yip proposes that one feature, [+/–Upper], called a 'Register' feature, divides the pitch range of the voice into two halves. A second feature, [+/–high], referred to somewhat confusingly as a 'Tone' feature, sub-divides each register into two again, creating four tones. All four combinations of these features are entirely interpretable, as follows:

(4)   +Upper   +high   55   extra-high
                 –high   44   high

        –Upper   +high   33   mid
                 –high   11   low

This system has some surprising qualities. One of the most striking is that it defines discontinuous natural classes: the [+high] tones are non-adjacent in the pitch space, as are the [–high] tones. Astonishingly, there is some evidence that this is correct. Odden (1995) gives an Ewe example from Clements 1978, in which a mid is claimed to become extra-high (not high) when surrounded by high tones. If we have the tonal system in (4), where extra-high is [+Upper, +high], high is [+Upper, –high], and mid is [–Upper, +high], then the change from mid to extra-high is a change from [–Upper] to [+Upper] as a result of spreading the [+Upper] of the surrounding high tones onto the mid. The [+high] feature of the underlying mid tone remains unaffected. The diagram below shows this in action, with the centre syllable undergoing raising from mid to extra-high.

(5)   +U –U +U
        [̲ ̲ ̲]
        σ   σ   σ   H M H → H XH H
        | | |
        –h +h –h

A second interesting property of the system in (4) is that the treatment of the middle tone in a three-tone system is often underdetermined. It could be either [+Upper, –high] or [–Upper, +high], on the assumption that [–high] means 'at the lowest pitch of the register', and [+high] means 'at the highest pitch of the register'. This again seems to be correct, but the best cases depend on an understanding of contour tones, so I will defer presentation of the data until section 3.3.1.

The register model has been widely adopted, with some refinements. Pulleyblank (1986) renames the Tone feature [high] as [raised]. Clements (1981), Snider (1990), and Hyman (1993) use unary H and L, not binary [+/–high]. Although these latter three authors differ in many details, some of them important, they have in common the use of the *same* feature for both Register and Tone, arranged in a hierarchical structure so that they are interpreted differently depending on whether they are on a superordinate node, called a Tonal Root Node, in which case they denote Register, or on a subordinate node, called a Tonal Node, in which case they denote Tone. We will return to this issue in detail below in section 3.2.3 and again in section 3.4, when we discuss the geometry of tonal features. Lastly, Duanmu (1990) and Bao (1990, 1999) both identify the tonal features completely with particular laryngeal features. We will return to this in section 3.5.

3.2.2   A fifth level

Some of these models can be more easily extended than others if it turns out that five levels must be accommodated. One rather general move is available to all theories: allow for the option of a completely unmarked tone in addition to the four defined levels. This unmarked tone then either receives a different phonetic value from the other four tones, or its pitch is contextually determined (and thus variable). If we want to define a featurally specified fifth level, the hierarchical models, such as Clements' and Hyman's, could add further levels of structure, but the non-hierarchical models will need an additional feature along the lines of Woo's [modify]. Five or more phonetic levels are certainly needed, but this is not necessarily a problem (any more than it is for vowel height). First, other features could cross-cut the purely tonal ones and have consequences for phonetic pitch. For example, if tonal features and laryngeal features are distinct, then a vowel could be specified for both low tone and glottalization, and this vowel could be phonetically lower than a low-toned vowel with no glottalization. The analogy here would be the interaction of vowel height features and ATR, resulting in a greater number of surface vowel height contrasts than that provided for by the height features alone:

(6)   [+high]   [+ATR]   i
                           [−ATR]   ı
         [−high, −low]   [+ATR]   e
                           [−ATR]   ɛ
         [+low]   æ

Secondly, it is commonly suggested that, although phonological representations are binary, phonetic realizations are n-ary. It is entirely possible, then, that a tonal specification could be translated into a different n-ary value depending on context, such as the voicing of surrounding consonants. There has been one recent attempt to make the phonological feature system n-ary, Tsay 1994. Tsay posits a single feature, called [P] for pitch, which may have any value from one to infinity, constrained only by extra-linguistic factors. For example, a three-tone system has [1P], [2P], and [3P], where 1 is the lowest. A five-tone system is then [1P], [2P], [3P], [4P], [5P]. The first problem is that there is no upper bound to the number of tones. The second problem with this system is that it defines no natural classes defined solely in terms of tone. Consider a simple assimilation in Yala (Nigeria; Bao 1999, using data from

Armstrong 1968). In Yala, H becomes M after M or L. If M and L are both [–Upper], this is simply explained as the spreading of [–Upper] in a binary Register system, but for Tsay the conditioning environment of M and L must be simply the list [1–2P].

3.2.3   An infinite number of levels?

Feature systems are usually assumed to assign absolute properties to a segment. For example, a vowel is a high vowel or a low vowel, and it may or may not be higher or lower than the neighbouring vowels: it depends on the neighbouring vowels' own absolute specifications. For features that are articulatorily based, this is inevitable; [+high] in vowels specifies the position of the tongue body. For tones, things could be different. A lexically high-toned vowel has a tone that is greatly influenced by its surroundings, the particular speaker's voice, and so on. One person's high tone could be another person's low tone. In African languages the phenomenon of downstep lowers high tones iteratively, and a high tone late in the utterance can be as low as or lower than a low tone early in the utterance. Obviously a set of features designed to distinguish exactly four levels cannot deal with the potentially infinite number of levels in a series of downsteps like in this Igbo sentence from Pulleyblank 1986, which shows six different levels. I have inserted down-arrows to show where the register lowers under the influence of the preceding L tone.

(7)   ó nwèrè àkọ́ nà   úchè   'she was clever and sensible'

H   L L L↓H L↓H L

For this reason some people such as Clark (1978) have proposed features that effect a change in pitch relative to the preceding pitch, rather than assigning an absolute value. Hyman (1993) uses H and L tones at two levels in a geometric structure. At the higher structural level, called the Tonal Root node, H and L define Register, but not in the same way as the [+U] and [–U] of Yip. Instead, a L at the Register level lowers the register relative to the previous tone, and if a second Register-level L occurs later in the utterance it will further lower the register. This is exactly what Hyman wants for downstep, and will provide for an infinite number of phonetic levels, but it does not provide for four invariant levels that can occur in sequence without iterative lowering or raising. In comparing the two models, keep in mind that Yip's [+U] and [–U] are roughly equivalent to Hyman's H and L on the Tonal Root Node, whereas Yip's [+h] and [–h] are equivalent to Hyman's H and L on the Tonal Node.

(8)   *Sequence of H L L register syllables in two different models*

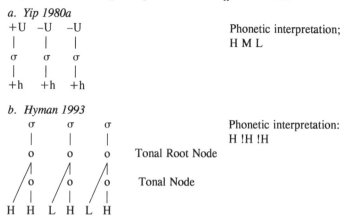

a. *Yip 1980a*

```
+U   –U   –U                    Phonetic interpretation;
 |    |    |                    H M L
 σ    σ    σ
 |    |    |
+h   +h   +h
```

b. *Hyman 1993*

```
 σ    σ    σ                    Phonetic interpretation:
 |    |    |                    H !H !H
 o    o    o    Tonal Root Node

 /o   /o   /o   Tonal Node
/ |  / |  / |
H H  L H  L H
```

The low register syllables (with [–U] or L on the Tonal Root Node) are realized as invariant in Yip's model, but steadily declining in Hyman's.

A further issue that arises with respect to downstep is whether a downstepped high tone is to be identified with a mid tone. Hyman's 1993 feature system allows one to keep them distinct, because a L and H under the same Tonal Node merge into Mid, whereas a L under the higher Tonal Root Node lowers the overall register.

(9)   Mid: σ   !H: σ

```
             |            |
             o            o     Tonal Root Node
             |           /|
             o          / o     Tonal Node
            /\         L |
           L H           H
```

Hyman argues that Yala Ikom motivates this distinction, but other languages do not; see Snider 1999 for evidence that in Bimoba (Gur) mid and downstepped H are identical. For a more thorough discussion of some approaches to downstep, see chapter six.

So where does this leave us? One possibility is that the interpretation of 'register' is language specific, held constant in some languages but shifting steadily downwards in others. Another possibility is that Yip's and Hyman's 'registers' are quite different things, in which case they could co-exist, so that Yip's features could be used to denote four constant levels, and Hyman's register could be overlaid on this to achieve downstep. The rarity of downstep in languages with more than two level tones could be attributed to some extra-linguistic perceptual factors. In this book, I will often, in common with most phonologists, duck the issue of tonal features and couch my analyses in terms of atomic tones H, M, and L, but ultimately the reader should bear in mind that these are shorthand for some set of tonal features yet to be authoritatively determined.

We now move on to looking at contour tones, using Yip's model for four levels as our starting point.

3.3   Contours

The most fundamental question about contour tones is whether they are single curves whose crucial feature is their rise or fall, or whether they are sequences of level tones realized on a single segment, and the contour is simply the inevitable by-product of the transition from low to high or vice-versa. Both positions have been espoused by phonologists (see Wang 1967, Woo 1969, Yip 1980a, Yip 1989), but a great weight of evidence has built up in favour of the latter position. We begin by looking at some of this evidence.

3.3.1   *Evidence for contours as sequences of level tones*

It has been known for a long time that some contour tones have a very transparent origin in sequences of level tones. Consider a language with vowel deletion. In Hausa (Newman 1995, Jagger 2001), some words have two variants, bisyllabic and monosyllabic. If the bisyllabic word is HL, then the monosyllable has a fall. If the fall is simply a HL on a single vowel, then we can understand this as vowel deletion, with retention and reassociation of the remaining tone:

(10)   mákà   'to you'
       mátà   'to her'
       másà   'to him'   *or*   mâr̃
       mínì   'to me'   *or*   mîn

For a rather different sort of example, consider Yoruba (Akinlabi and Liberman 2000b). As in many Benue-Congo languages, bisyllabic words never surface with H on one syllable and L on the other. Instead, the transition from one tone to the other shifts to half-way through the second syllable, so that the surface pattern is either [H HL] or [L LH], with a contour on the second syllable: /àlá/ 'dream' → [àlǎ]; /rárà/ 'elegy' → [rárâ]. If the contour is viewed as a sequence of level tones, this is simply tone spreading from the first syllable onto the second.

A similar case with an interesting twist is found in Gao'an Chinese (Chen 2000: 78). Here the tone of the second syllable spreads back onto the first, creating a contour, but we can clearly see that it is only the Tone feature [–high] that spreads, and not the register feature [Upper]. This is because the result of spreading from a low tone, [11], onto a preceding [55] is not [51], but [53], where the original register of the first syllable, [+Upper], is unchanged, and the syllable now has the sequence of tone features [+high, –high], giving a fall. The data are as follows; the Register feature [+Upper] is abbreviated as uppercase H, and the Tone features are abbreviated as [h, l].

(11)   *Gao'an leftward spreading of [–high]*
       song tçi   'bi-seasonal'   tçi han   'egg'
       55.33 → 53.33   55.11 → 53.11

In rule terms, these changes can be successively abbreviated as follows:

(12)   a. 55 → 53   / _____ 33   *and* 11
          [H, h]   [H, hl]   [H, l]   [L, l]

       b. [H, h] → [H, hl] / _____ [l]

       c.   σ   σ
                         |\ /|
                         h   l

These Gao'an data thus provide evidence both for contours as sequences of levels, and for the particular feature system argued for above.

Some further evidence for contours as sequences comes from tonal affixes. Returning to Hausa, the definite article is a suffixal nasal, with a low tone which surfaces on the preceding vowel. If this vowel is underlyingly high, a falling contour results: /gídáa-ǹ/ 'house-the' [gídân]. (The vowel shortening is required to avoid a super-heavy syllable.)

For my last piece of evidence, I look at tones that cannot be shown to arise by concatenation of level tones, but that nonetheless appear to be decomposable to the native speaker. In modern Cantonese songs with several stanzas (Chan 1987), each line has requirements on the tones that can occur on each syllable. The first line of one song must have the following tones in each stanza: 13 and 33 are interchangeable, as are 35 and 55.

(13) σ_1 σ_2 σ_3 σ_4 σ_5 σ_6 σ_7 σ_8
       22   11   22   13/33   35/55   35/55   13/33   35/55

The pairs 13/33 and 35/55 are clearly paired because they share an end-point. In other words, the speaker (or the singer!) is aware that the two contour tones 13 and 35 end with a tone that is the same as a level 33 or 55 respectively.

If contours are composed of levels, the representation of a tone would look something like this, with two (or more) tones associated with one syllable (or perhaps vowel or mora).

(14)   53 σ   13 σ
          ∧   ∧
         H M   L M

More precisely, the tones would be feature matrices:

(15)   53 σ   13 σ
          ∧   ∧
        [+U] [+U]   [−U][−U]
        [+h] [−h]   [−h][+h]

Notice, interestingly, that the pitch of the endpoint of the [53] fall, featurally [+Upper, −high], is the same as the pitch of the endpoint of the [13] rise, featurally [−Upper, +high]. This is entirely typical, and confirms the speculation in section 3.1 that mid-tones are featurally ambiguous, being either the lowest tone of the upper register, or the highest tone of the lower register.

One striking fact about contour tones is that there aren't as many of them as one might expect there to be. If a feature system can distinguish four levels, and if contours are the result of concatenating four levels, then one might expect to find six underlying falls and six underlying rises, a point first made by Pike (1948). In Chinese languages, underlying contours seem typically to remain within either the upper or the lower half of the pitch range, so formally we may capture this by suggesting that underlyingly a syllable may not have more than one occurrence of the feature [Upper], but it may have more than one occurrence of the feature [high]. Thus we can replace (15) with (16):

(16)   53 [+Upper]   13 [−Upper]
              | |
              σ   σ
              ∧   ∧
           [+h] [−h]   [−h] [+h]

Derived contours, on the other hand, are clusters of two tones formed by reassociation of stranded tones. They may thus be composed of any two levels. In African languages, in fact, contours tend to fall from the top to the bottom of the pitch range (Akinlabi personal communication), as one might expect if they are formed by the concatenation of the H and the L of a two-tone system.

The reasons for supposing that the tones are represented on their own separate tier, linked to the syllable by association lines, will be discussed in the next chapter. For now, note that a perfectly reasonable alternative would be to treat tonal features on a par with segmental features like Place, or vowel height, so that high-toned [á] would be:

(17)   [+low, +back, −round, +Upper, +high tone]

However, when a vowel has two sets of tone features, as we need for contour tones, this option starts to look a bit tricky, although there are segmental precedents, such as the representation of affricates as being sequentially [−cont, +cont].

3.3.2   Evidence for contours as units

Given the extensive evidence for the view that contours are sequences of levels, one might wonder why any voices would ever be raised in support of a unitary analysis of contour. There are three reasons. Firstly, there are many languages that lack clear evidence (or indeed any evidence at all!) for decomposing contours into levels. Looked at in isolation, the question is thus an open one for the linguist working on such languages, and this includes many Asian languages with rich contour systems. However, for the theoretical linguist committed to universal grammar, if contours in one language are sequences they are presumably sequences in all languages, in the absence of evidence to the contrary. It is not that a typological difference cannot exist, it is just that the burden of proof is on those who wish to complicate universal grammar by allowing not just one but two sorts of contour tones.

The second reason relates to the overall inventories. If contours are composed of levels, we would expect that they would be composed of the exact levels used on their own in that language. If a language has [H, L], we would expect contours like [LH] and [HL], but not [MH] or [ML], since M is not part of the level tone system in that language. Pike (1948) used this as a major diagnostic to distinguish between languages with contours that are composed of levels, and ones where they are not. In the first category he put languages like Mixteco. Mixteco has three levels, and long vowels may have level or contour tones. The end-points of the contour tones can be clearly identified with the three level tones of the system. Four of the six logical combinations occur in monomorphemic forms:

(18)   *Mixteco contour tones*

HM   káā   'climbing'   MH   –
ML   kōò   'snake'   LM   kàā   'metal'
HL   náà   'mother'   LH   –

In Pike's second category of tone languages he puts those with contours whose endpoints cannot be identified with the level tonemes of the system. For example, Mandarin Chinese has a [35] rising tone, but no [33] level tone. He also points out that 'the basic tonemic unit is gliding instead of level'. I take this to mean that in such languages a morpheme is at least as likely to have a contour as a level tone, and indeed in many cases more likely. The Mandarin inventory, for example, includes only one clearly level tone, the high level tone, but it has a fall, a rise, and falling-rising tone (although this last may be phonologically level). Lastly, Pike says that in such languages the contours behave morphologically like units, being monomorphemic.

The third reason for questioning whether all contours are composed of levels is that in some languages contours really do seem to behave phonologically like indivisible units. Newman points out that contours are avoided in many languages, and rising tones are particularly scarce – recall that Hausa has falls but no rises. If contours are just sequences of level primitives, we can describe a level-tone-only language as one that never allows two tones on a single syllable or vowel, but it is harder to explain why HL (i.e. a fall) on one vowel should be fine, but LH (i.e. a rise) on one vowel should be out. If we can refer explicitly to the notions 'rise' and 'fall', there is no particular problem, and we can then draw directly for our explanation on our knowledge of phonetics, which tells us that rises are quite generally harder to produce, and take longer than falls. The phonetic basis of this restriction is confirmed by the fact that some languages rule out rises even on long vowels, while allowing falls.

More strikingly, in some languages contours seem to copy or spread as units. Changzhi has a diminutive suffix /tə(ʔ)/, with no tone of its own. It acquires its tone by the copying or spreading of the entire complex tone of the preceding root (but see Duanmu 1994 for a dissenting view):

(19)   *Changzhi whole tone copying*
        tsə213 tə213   'cart'
        paŋ535 tə535   'board'
        xæ24 tə?24   'child'
        çiaŋ53 tə?53   'fillings'

Identity is also sometimes computed across the entire tone. In Tianjin (Yip 1989) sequences of two identical tones dissimilate. If both have the same contour, the first one simplifies to level. If both are L, a H is inserted between them. (If both are H, nothing changes, for reasons that are unclear.)

(20)   *Tianjin whole tone dissimilation*
        LH.LH   → H.LH
        HL.HL   → L.HL
        L.L   → LH.L

These data are interesting because they show the possibility not only of perceiving the contour as a unit, but also of simultaneously accessing its component tones. The outputs in (20) satisfy two conditions: (1) the two syllables do not have identical tones, when viewed holistically, and (2) at the level of the component tones, there are no sequences of identical tones either. The Obligatory

Contour Principle (the OCP, see chapter four), which disallows sequences of identical tones, is thus satisfied at both the level of the complete tonal contours, and the level of their component tones.

How then can we explain this schizophrenic behaviour of contour tones? In the following section we see how the internal feature geometry of the tonal features can solve the conundrum.

3.4   Feature geometry

In the early 1980s it was suggested that distinctive features were not just a list, but the terminal nodes in a structured tree. For example, the features relating to place of articulation formed a constituent called Place, and this constituent was a phonological entity which could spread, delete, or enter into identity calculations. For an overview, see Kenstowicz 1994, and for specific proposals see Halle 1983, Sagey 1986, McCarthy 1988, and Clements and Hume 1995. In these early works tones were largely ignored. Yip's original feature proposal had explored the possibility that tonal features could spread independently of each other, situating Upper and [high] on different autosegmental tiers (see chapter four on autosegmental phonology), but this left no way for them to spread as a unit, so that the complete tone spreads. There was clearly a need for both options, and feature geometry provided the necessary framework.

Let us start by looking at some possible models. The toughest testing ground is the representation of contour tones, so I will use a high rising tone which is [+Upper] Register, here for convenience shown by an upper-case H, and which has the Tone features [–high][+high], shown here by [l, h].

(21)   *Models in which the features are entirely independent of each other, and there is no tonal node dominating them both: Yip 1980a, also Hyman 1993: 81 (8a).*

(22)   *Models in which the two features are sisters under a Tonal Node, and each half of the contour tone is entirely independent: Duanmu 1990, 1994, Clements 1981, Snider 1990.*

(23)   *Models in which the Register feature is the Tonal Node, dominating the Tone features: Yip 1989, also Hyman 1993:81 (8d).*

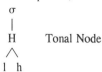

σ
|
H   Tonal Node
∧
l   h

(24)   *Models in which Tone features are dominated by a node of their own, called Contour, which is a sister to the Register feature, and where both are dominated by a Tonal Node: Bao 1990, Snider 1999.*

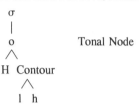

σ
|
o   Tonal Node
∧
H Contour
    ∧
    l   h

These models make different predictions about which tonal features can spread independently, and which can spread together. In all cases the terminal features can spread independently, but in Yip's 1989 model in (23) register cannot spread without bringing the contour tone features along with it. The whole tone can only spread as a unit in the last two models in (23) and (24). The Contour – the property of being rising or falling – can only spread as a whole, and independent of register, in the last model, Bao's model in (24). These differences are tabulated in (25).

(25)

Models	Register free to spread alone	Whole tone able to spread as a unit	Contour able to spread independent of register
21	✓		
22	✓		
23		✓	
24	✓	✓	✓

Clearly the most powerful model is Bao's in (24), but it seems that it may well be necessary. Although it is good analytic practice to adopt the most parsimonious theory, we must never forget that, no matter how elegant and restrictive a theory may be, if it cannot account for the range of natural language data it is either wrong, or only partially right. Let us review some of the relevant evidence that suggests Bao's more permissive theory may be correct.

3.4.1   Evidence for register spread

To find clear evidence of register spread, we must look for a language with two rises or two falls, and where under the assimilatory influence of an adjacent register the rise/fall in one register changes to the rise/fall in the other register, without its shape being affected. Clear instances of this are hard to find, and until recently alternative explanations for the putative cases were available, throwing doubt on the existence of the phenomenon. However, Bao (1999) gives a persuasive case from Chaozhou Chinese, where the register of the final syllable determines the register of the initial syllable. The focus here is on the first syllable in these compounds. The words for 'goods' and 'fire' in (26) have the same segmental content, but different tones: 'goods' is falling but 'fire' is rising. Their contours remain invariant, but their register is determined by the register of the following syllable: in the (a) examples they are [+Upper], and in the (b) examples they are [–Upper], with the register spread from the second syllable. The shape of the second syllable has no effect: in 'torch' the second syllable is falling, but the first syllable persists in being rising.

(26)   *Inputs to register spreading, after earlier rules have applied*
        /hue, hl/   'goods'   /hue, lh/   'fire'

   a. goods ship   fire handle
        hue lung   'cargo ship, freighter' hue ba   'torch'
        HM.H   MH.HM
        [+U, hl] [+U, h]   [+U, lh] [+U, hl]

   b. goods storage   fire arrow
        hue ts'ng   'warehouse'   hue tsi   'rocket'
        ML.L   LM.LM
        [–U, hl][–U, l]   [–U, lh] [–U, lh]

The model in (23), of Yip (1989), cannot accommodate register spreading, and is thus out of the running. Note also that if, as most Africanists believe, downstep is a kind of register spreading, it also constitutes counter-evidence to Yip 1989.

3.4.2   Whole tone spreading or copying

In section 3.2 we saw the example of Changzhi affixation, in which the whole tone of the root was spread or copied onto the suffix, giving words like [tsə213 tə213] 'cart'. This is by no means the only example of a complete tone functioning as a phonological unit. Danyang Chinese associates its tonal melodies to the edges of longer words as units, and although details of the analyses vary (see Bao 1999 for a useful survey) this central point seems unassailable. I will give one further example, from Lalana Chinantec (data from Mugele 1982, analysis from Yip 1989). There is a Tonal Harmony rule which spreads the Low 2 tone and the Falling 31 tone onto a following syllable if the next syllable is stressed. In the following examples stress is on the final syllable.

(27)   a. ri31 gwiːn2   'he goes to sleep'
          mĩ2 ri2 gwiːn2   'when he goes to sleep'
     b. mĩ2 kin2   'he takes care of it'
          ri31 mĩ31 kin2   'he will take care of it'

In the (a) examples, we see the spreading of a level [2] tone. The (b) example is the telling one; here the entire [31] complex spreads, giving [31][31]. Delving a little deeper here, this rule has more to tell us about features. The two tones that spread are the two that end on a low tone, a [–high] featurally. All other tones in the language are high level, or rising of some sort. However, it is not just the [–high] that spreads, and nor is it just the 'contour' portion in Bao's sense. The register feature must spread too, in order to ensure that the output is a low fall, not a high fall. There is thus no question that this rule spreads the entire tone.

Only two of the models we started with can accommodate whole tone spreading, and one of those has been eliminated because it fails to allow register spreading. We are left with only one model that can do both, that of Bao (1990, 1999). Before we conclude that this is the final truth, however, let us recall that Bao's model predicts one further possible type of spreading, that of a contour without its register. In the next section I show that this indeed happens.

3.4.3   *Contour spreading*

The clearest example here comes from Zhenhai (Chen 2000). In Zhenhai bisyllables, the tone of the first syllable determines the tone of the compound, but it shows up not on its own syllable, but on the second syllable, because this second syllable is stressed, and attracts the tone (a common phenomenon in tonal languages, as we shall see later). The first syllable receives a default low tone, [–high]. The interest of the data here lies in the fact that what is attracted to the stress is not the entire tone, but exactly all and only the Tone features [+/–high], which in Bao's approach are dominated by the node Contour. Zhenhai contrasts two rising tones on the final syllable, a relatively high [+Upper] [334], and a relatively low [–Upper] [24]. Which of these surfaces depends on the register of the final syllable, combined with a rise that originated on the first syllable. Crucially, the register of the first syllable does not move with its contour, and is irrelevant to the outcome on the final syllable, although it does control the pitch of the first syllable, so that after default [–high] is inserted we get [33] if the first syllable is upper register, and [11] if it is lower register. Note that the linear order on the paper of register and contour within the tonal complex is irrelevant, and the arrangement here is simply the most typographically perspicuous.

(28)   'bedroom'

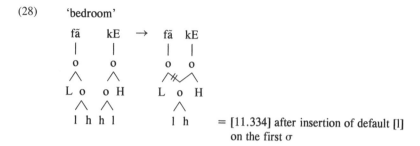

= [11.334] after insertion of default [l]
on the first σ

I conclude that the powerful model of feature structure suggested by Bao may well be needed to account for the full range of spreading, copying, and association facts.

3.5   Relationship to laryngeal features

Thus far we have looked at tone features in isolation from segmental features, but one of the desiderata for a feature system was that it should allow for a statement of the known relationships between laryngeal properties and tone, such as voicing and low tone. With this goal in mind, there have been various attempts to identify tonal features with laryngeal features, usually by appealing to the articulatory mechanisms involved. This was very much in line with the overall bias towards articulatorily based features that strongly influenced distinctive feature theory from SPE until the end of the twentieth century. The following section is quite technical, and can be skipped without detriment.

The best-known attempt (and one of the earliest, along with Maran 1971) to combine tonal and laryngeal features is that of Halle and Stevens 1971. One of the major physiological correlates of pitch change is variation in the tension in the vocal folds. Increased tension raises pitch, just as it does in tuning a viola or a guitar. But there are other effects of tensed vocal folds. In particular, if the pressure across the glottis is low, as it is when the airflow out from the lungs is blocked in the production of an oral stop, allowing the pressure in the mouth to approach that of the pressure in the lungs, the vocal folds are less likely to vibrate if they are stiff than if they are slack. There is thus an association between vocal fold tension and voicelessness in obstruents. Pursuing this idea, Halle and Stevens proposed a set of laryngeal features, two of which are particularly important to us here. The same features are realized as voicing if they are features of a consonant, and tone if they are features of a vowel, as follows:

(29)

[stiff vocal folds]	–	–	+
[slack vocal folds]	–	+	–
Realization on C	contextually voiced C	voiced C	voiceless C
Realization on V	mid tone V	low tone V	high tone V

This feature system can do some things very elegantly. If voiced consonants lower tone, as the depressor consonants do in Zulu, it can be seen as the spreading of the feature [+slack vocal folds] from consonant onto vowel. The core cases of tonogenesis (see section 2.8) could also be handled straightforwardly.

Noble though the goals of this model were, it was not without problems. The most obvious is that it only allowed for three levels of tone, and we have seen that this is not enough. A further problem was that the features had a third function, voice quality differences in vowels, so that voiceless vowels were distinguished from breathy vowels by the same features as those used for mid tone versus low tone. This meant that languages with tonal contrasts on breathy vowels could not be represented in this system. See Yip 1980a and Anderson 1978 for a detailed critique.

In 1990 two direct successors of this model were proposed independently by Bao (1990) and Duanmu (1990). Both Bao and Duanmu retain the Halle and Stevens features and try to incorporate them into Yip's 1980a tonal feature proposal. Duanmu uses both [stiff] and [slack] for register, and adds two pitch features [above] and [below]. This provides for three registers, and three pitches in each register, giving nine level tones:

(30) *Duanmu's 1990 model:*

| +stiff | [+above, –below] |
| –slack | [–above, –below] |
	[–above, +below]
–stiff	[+above, –below]
–slack	[–above, –below]
	[–above, +below]
–stiff	[+above, –below]
+slack	[–above, –below]
	[–above, +below]

The problem has now been shifted from a model that cannot specify enough levels, to a model that predicts more tonal contrasts than languages appear to use. Duanmu is aware of this problem, and he deals with it by insisting that his register features are not purely tonal, but should show accompanying phonation contrasts, so that, for example, [+slack] denotes breathiness; as a result he predicts only three purely tonal contrasts arising from the features [above] and [below]. We have already seen, however, that this is not sufficient – languages may have four tones without any phonation differences.

Bao uses just [+/–stiff vocal folds], equating this with Yip's [+/–Upper], but in Bao 1999 he takes a different tack. He suggests that since we do not really know what muscles are used to stiffen and slacken the vocal folds, and indeed two different sets may be involved, it is entirely possible that both sets can be activated simultaneously. In that case the combination [+stiff, +slack] becomes possible, and the two features combine to give four levels. So Bao uses [+stiff] instead of [+Upper], and [+slack] instead of [+high], and proposes a model with all the properties of Yip's plus the Halle and Stevens' connection to obstruent voicing.

(31)   *Bao's 1999 model*

| +stiff | –slack |
	+slack
–stiff	–slack
	+slack

This move is clever, but it has two problems. First, we do in fact have a reasonable idea of what causes the vocal folds to stiffen and slacken: one of the major muscles, the cricothyroid, appears to contract to increase stiffness, but relaxes to decrease stiffness (Hirose 1997, cited in chapter one). If the same muscle is indeed involved, and must act differently in each case, then obviously contra Bao [+stiff] and [+slack] are *not* compatible. Secondly, Bao's proposal appears to cause problems if one now returns to the facts that motivated Halle and Stevens in the first place. Register splitting in tonogenesis is not caused by all [–stiff] consonants, but only by contrastively voiced consonants, which are [+slack] as well as [–stiff]. This does not fit well with the fact that in Bao's proposal one of the [+slack] tones is higher than one of the [–slack] tones.

Duanmu (2000) has also returned to this question, and draws a quite different conclusion from phonetics work on the musculature that controls the vocal folds. He cites Zemlin's (1981) claims (largely supported by Hirose 1997) that the cricothyroid muscles control the elongation and thickness of the vocal folds, while the vocalis muscles control the 'isometric tension'. Duanmu suggests that Register is caused by the vocalis muscle, stated as a featural distinction between [stiff] and [slack]. [slack] is associated with murmur, or breathiness, which is indeed a common accompaniment of lower register. Pitch on the other hand is caused by the cricothyroid muscle, stated as a featural distinction between [thin] and [thick] (vocal folds).

(32)

	Register	Pitch	
Muscle	Vocalis	Cricothyroid	
Effect	Vocal cord tension	Vocal cord thickness	
Features	stiff	thin	(non-murmured H)
		thick	(non-murmured L)
	slack	thin	(murmured H)
		thick	(murmured L)

For Duanmu, as in his earlier work, [slack] register vowels are explicitly murmured (breathy), so that register is not a purely pitch distinction. This leads to an
interesting consequence, which he states like this: 'there is no specific prediction
as to whether slack and thin vocal cords will give higher or lower F_0 than stiff and
thick vocal cords'. What this means is that a tone that is featurally [stiff, thick]
might be phonetically *lower* in pitch than a tone that is featurally [slack, thin]. As
a result, unlike Yip's model, Duanmu allows for overlapping contours. To be precise, a fall in the upper register might be [52], and a rise in the lower register
might be [24], because there is no particular prediction as to the relative level of
the lower tone in the upper register, and the higher tone in the lower register.

(33)   Upper register fall: [stiff]   [53] or [52]
                              [thin][thick]

         Lower register rise: [slack]   [13] or [24]
                              [thick][thin]

This is a nice consequence of his proposal, since such tones are quite common,
and pose a small, little-discussed challenge to Yip's 1980a theory and many of its
subsequent variants.

   One last topic needs touching on here. Is there any connection between the feature
geometry of segmental features, and the feature geometry of tonal features? Can one
construct a single feature tree incorporating both? Theories of feature geometry suppose that features are not an unstructured set, or list, but are grouped into constituents
under a root node. While there is disagreement on many details, some commonly
agreed-upon constituents would be Place – which dominates Labial, Coronal, and
Dorsal – and Laryngeal, which dominates [voice], [spread glottis], and [constricted
glottis]. Feature geometric trees are heavily influenced by articulatory phonetics, so
that features implemented by the same articulator are under the same node. For

example, [round] is usually under the Labial node. A full exposition of the arguments for supposing that features are grouped into constituents would take us too far afield; any reader unfamiliar with these ideas might consult Kenstowicz 1994 and the other references at the start of section 3.4.

We should note that just because tonal features enjoy considerable independence does not mean they cannot also be linked under the larger structure. By way of analogy, consider the vowel features again. Many languages have vowel harmony that involves backness, and yet the feature [back] is usually assumed to be part of the feature tree under the segmental root node. The same point can be made with reference to labial or nasal harmony. So where then would tonal features belong? It would seem reasonable to suppose that if the tonal features are to be incorporated into this tree, be they purely tonal or along the lines of Halle and Stevens, then they would belong under the Laryngeal node, since tones are implemented at the larynx. It is possible to imagine many different ways in which the details might be arranged: if the tonal features are distinct from the other laryngeal features, there might be a Tonal Root Node under the Laryngeal node, for example:

(34)

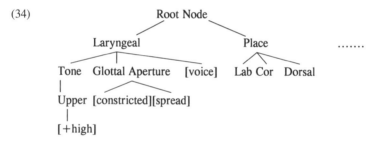

The Tone node dominates a constituent, so the whole tone can still spread. Different arrangements would have different implications, by embedding any of the approaches to tone outlined above into this larger tree.

If tone is treated in this way, then it is, on some level, part of the segment, although it would still enjoy autonomy. Another view is that tone is special because it is never truly segmental, and associates not to a feature tree under a segmental Root Node, but directly to prosodic structure, the structure in which syllables group into feet, feet into prosodic words, words into phonological phrases, and so on. In chapter four we will explore this approach further. Before we leave the discussion of laryngeal and tonal features, we must also look at the other types of interaction that we have observed.

We saw earlier in this chapter that there is also some interaction between tone and ATR, and perhaps tone and vowel height. We must then ask if these interactions are also to be incorporated into our larger theory of tonal features. I will take the position that they are not, for two reasons. Firstly, a simple interaction does not necessarily imply that the same features are responsible, or even that the features are geometrically related. In many languages front vowels are unrounded and back vowels are rounded, but few people have suggested that the *features* [back] and [round] are related (although SPE connected them in markedness statements, and see Odden 1991 for a proposal in which they form a constituent in the feature tree). Instead, most people assume that vowel systems have evolved this way for perceptual reasons, to produce vowels that are maximally distinct from each other. Gregerson's 1976 suggestions for the enhancement relationship between low pitch, voicing and ATR are somewhat similar, and do not need us to identify tonal features with ATR in any way. The second reason is less noble and more theory-internal: in our current theories of feature geometry each feature is uniquely assigned to a single superordinate node. If this is correct, it seems clear that Laryngeal is a more plausible home for tonal features than the Tongue Root or Tongue Body (or V-Place) node, so that is where I shall assume they belong.

This concludes the discussion of laryngeal and tonal features. From now on I will use the features [Upper] and [high] as my working features, frequently abbreviated to [+/–U], or [H/L], for Register, and [h/l], for Tone.

3.6   Binarity, markedness, and underspecification

Distinctive features are either binary, like the feature [+/– back] for vowels, or unary, like the feature Coronal in consonants (for discussion, see Kenstowicz 1994). If the feature is unary, some segments simply lack the feature entirely. So labial and velar consonants are not [–coronal] in most recent approaches, they just lack the feature Coronal. The justification for this approach is essentially that generalizations that refer to Coronal are common, but nothing seems to refer crucially to [–coronal]. If Coronal is unary, then [–coronal] does not exist, and no generalization *could* ever refer to it. For many features the question of whether they are unary or binary remains unsettled. Some authors, for example, take [voice] to be unary, and voiceless segments just lack [voice]. Other authors believe [+/–voice] to be a binary feature. Further confusing the picture, even if a feature is binary it can be the case that only one value is present underlyingly, and the opposing value is inserted late, or perhaps not at all. With this as background, what about tone? I have implied above that the features are binary, but is this necessarily true, and if it is, are all values specified underlyingly? In what follows I assume that we want our feature system to be universal, so that any given feature is either unary in all languages, or binary in all languages.

If we look at simple systems with a two-way high vs. low surface contrast, the most natural assumption is that a single tone feature is being used contrastively, probably [+/–high], and that both values are present. However, there are many languages in which only one tone seems to play any sort of role in the phonology, and it is usually the high tone. In Chichewa, for example (Myers 1999a), there are restrictions on the placement of high tones, but not on low tones. High tones dissimilate under the influence of the Obligatory Contour Principle, but low tones do not. High tones may not be doubly associated. In fact, the entire tonal phonology can be described without reference to low tones, and this is true in many Bantu languages. By contrast, consider a language that differs from Chichewa in that it has contour tones arising from vowel deletion, such as Yoruba (Akinlabi and Liberman 2000b). Contours (assuming they are sequences, and ignoring the additional power introduced if we allow empty tonal nodes) cannot even be represented without reference to two tone levels, and tonal stability like that involving the survival and reassociation of the low tone on /i/ in the following example after deletion of its host vowel shows clearly that the low tone is phonologically present: /muH + iweLH/ → muwe H.LH 'take a book'. (See Hyman 2000 for a useful discussion of why empty tonal nodes should be prohibited.)

Returning to the Chichewa-type languages, we could therefore either say that only [+high] is present in Chichewa, or that [high] is unary. In either case, syllables without [+high] or [high] surface phonetically as low. In either case high syllables are specified and can be active, and low syllables are unspecified and inactive. Once we move to Yoruba, however, only one of these feature systems can be adopted unchanged. If we choose the binary proposal, then Yoruba uses both binary values, so both [+high] and [−high] are present and active. If we choose the unary proposal, however, then in Yoruba we must introduce a second unary feature [low] in addition to [high]. In both proposals, syllables without either feature in Yoruba will be mid, as indeed they are. The differences between the binary and unary accounts here are usually almost impossible to detect. They become easier to distinguish as one looks at larger tonal inventories, because they make different predictions about natural classes. For example, the binary system can define natural classes that invoke negative values for a feature, such as [−high], including both mid and low, but it is common to find no evidence bearing on the question one way or another. Even when such evidence is found, the committed unary aficionado can simply add another unary feature to the list to cover the necessary category. In practice, most linguists duck the issue by using H, M, and L instead of features, and allowing unspecified syllables if the data warrant it.

When high is the specified tone, low is of course the default. In a much smaller number of languages, such as Mandinka (Creissels and Grégoire 1993), Ruwund (Nash 1992–4), Gernika Basque (Hualde 1991), and Huave (Noyer 1992), low has been claimed to be specified, and high to be the default. In a third set of languages, such as Yoruba, high and low are both specified and mid is the default. The difference between high-marked and low-marked languages is somewhat surprising. One way to understand it, jumping ahead a little to the idea of output constraints (see chapter four), is as follows. Cross-linguistically, low tones are preferred and high tones are less preferred, perhaps for reasons to do with articulatory effort. This suggests a tendency towards low-marked languages. However, this is counter-balanced by an opposing preference for high tones on stressed syllables, and by the requirement that each lexical word contain a stressed syllable. This second preference leads one to expect high-marked languages. Depending on which preference is deemed more important, we get either a high-marked language like Chichewa, or a low-marked language like Basque. I should note, however, (Myers personal communication) that this explanation fails to explain languages with H tone marked, but in which tone is entirely independent of stress, and thus it cannot be the whole story.

The possibility of languages in which only some syllables are supplied with tonal features raises the question of their ultimate fate: do they receive tonal features at some point in the phonology, perhaps at the very end, or do they enter the phonetics toneless and receive their pitch by some purely phonetic mechanism such as interpolation or a return to the resting position? In Chichewa Myers (1999a) has argued that toneless syllables never receive a phonological low, but take their pitch from their surroundings, but comparable data are not available for languages in which low is marked and high unmarked.

It is worth spending a little more time on the treatment of toneless syllables. It appears to be necessary to distinguish at least the following three types of 'low' syllables:

(35) a. Low tone specified throughout the phonology and phonetics; phonetically low.

      σ
      |
      L

    b. Toneless throughout phonology and phonetics, pitch acquired by phonetic interpolation only.

      σ

    c. Toneless during phonology, but L tone specified at phonology/phonetics interface.

In type (a), low tones are active in the phonology, doing such things as spreading, deleting under the Obligatory Contour Principle (see chapter four), and forming contours. In the phonetics, they act as L tone targets, surfacing as reliably and consistently low. This type almost certainly needs further sub-division into languages that have underlying L, versus languages that specify it at some stage during the phonology, particularly the post-lexical phonology (see Hyman 2000 for details). Type (b) syllables are tonally inert in the phonology, and surface with a highly variable pitch determined entirely by the surrounding syllables. They seem to have no target tones at all. Finally, in type (c) syllables, low tones appear to be absent during the phonology. While high tones participate in spreading and so on, the other syllables are passive, and are best understood as toneless. However, they surface as phonetically low, as if they had low targets, suggesting that somewhere after the phonology and before assignment of pitch values they have acquired L targets. Types (a) and (b) are straightforward enough (although internal to the phonology they raise issues of underspecification), but type (c) needs further discussion.

The major question is where and how these toneless syllables acquire their L tone targets. One possibility is that the last act of the phonology, so to speak, is the insertion of L on all toneless syllables. This was the approach taken in rule-based theories of underspecification, and such rules were called default rules or context-free redundancy rules (see Steriade 1995 for useful discussion). They were apparently language-specific, within certain bounds, so that, for example, languages could vary as to their default vowel. This approach is problematic in Optimality Theory, the theory used in this book, with its commitment to a non-derivational analysis, although it otherwise seems to be the most natural way to handle such cases. A second possibility is that the phonetics component contains a language-specific subcomponent that in some (but not all) languages fills in all missing tones with L's, thus supplying every syllable with a tonal target. However, the nature of this operation seems more phonological than phonetic, since it acts to insert categorical featural information, not the gradient values more often associated with phonetic representations. The final possibility is that the insertion is an interface operation, happening at the point of transition from phonology to phonetics, and presumably driven by a requirement in such languages for full specification at the start of the phonetics. The output of the OT phonology would still be underspecified, but the input to the phonetics would be fully specified. It is not clear what kind of empirical data would bear on the choice among these three options, so I leave the question open, but I will use the third, interface, option as my working hypothesis.

As we proceed to the analytical portion of this book, our task will usually be limited to the phonological analysis, with much phonetic detail not accounted for. Unsatisfactory though this may be, it is forced upon us partly by the limits of the available data. We will often find ourselves positing 'outputs' in which syllables described in the literature as 'low' remain unspecified, and whose ultimate fate – receive a default tone, or remain forever toneless – will be left open.

I end this chapter on a reassuring note. Although I have left unresolved many of the complex issues bearing on the choice of a feature system, in much of the rest of this book it will not be necessary to look closely at the features of tone. Instead, we will use just H, M, L, or tone numbers, unless extra insights are to be gained by formulating the analysis in featural terms.

4

The autosegmental nature of tone, and its analysis in Optimality Theory

The focus of this chapter is on the appropriate tools for the analysis of tonal phonology. Before we study the behaviour of tone in any detail, we need a common framework in which to couch our analyses. In section 4.1, I will begin by identifying five properties of tone that any analytical framework must be able to capture. Section 4.2 shows that an 'autosegmental' representation nicely deals with these properties. Section 4.3 introduces the Optimality Theory framework, and section 4.4 extends it to tonology. Section 4.5 applies the framework to the five central properties of tone, and sections 4.6–10 flesh out a full working model of tonal phonology within Optimality Theory.

Tone differs from many other phonological features in the following ways, rarely or never observed in more familiar consonantal or vocalic features:

a.   Mobility: Movement away from point of origin
b.   Stability: Survival after loss of original host segment
c.   One-to-many: A single tonal feature shared by two or more segments
d.   Many-to-one: Multiple tonal features surfacing on a single host segment
e.   Toneless segments: Potentially tone-bearing segments that never acquire phonological tone

The only non-tonal features that regularly exhibit any of these characteristics are harmonizing features like nasality and certain vowel features, which may spread over large domains from their source segments. Features like consonantal place features, or laryngeal features like aspiration and voice, do not usually show these behaviours. Indeed, tone seems to have more in common with stress than with anything else. Stress, for example, can move around, as it does in the well-known English Rhythm Rule that retracts stress away from an adjacent stress in phrases like *fífteen mén* (contrast *fiftéen*). The singular behaviour of tone has led to a long tradition of treating it distinctly in the phonology, as can be seen at least as far back as Firth (1948), and more recently Leben (1973) and Goldsmith (1976).

Let me give some brief illustrations of each of the unusual characteristics of tone, drawn from a wide range of languages.

4.1   Characteristics of tone

4.1.1   Mobility

Unlike most segmental features, tone may move a long way from its lexical source. In Chizigula (Bantu: Kenstowicz and Kisseberth 1990), H tone migrates from the verb root to the penultimate syllable of the word. It may thus end up three or more syllables away from its source. The reader should be aware that in many languages, including many Bantu languages, only H tones are specified, and unspecified syllables end up L on the surface. In the data below, the source of H is underlined, and its surface position is shown by the usual acute accent. We can discern the source of the H by observing that certain verbs, such as /lómbez/ 'to request', always contribute a H to the output, but the H need not necessarily surface on the verb root itself (as in the second and third examples below). Conversely, the H seen on the morpheme -ez/-iz in 'to request for' does not originate there, because the same morpheme in the verb 'to do for' shows no H tone anywhere.

(1)   *Toneless verbs*   *H-tone verbs*
       ku-damany-a   'to do'   ku-lombéz-a   'to request'
       ku-damany-iz-a   'to do for'   ku-lombez-éz-a   'to request for'
       ku-damany-iz-an-a   'to do for   ku lombez-ez-án-a   'to request for each
                             each other'   other'

In Sukuma (Bantu: Sietsema 1989), H tone again moves rightwards, but here the target syllable is exactly two syllables to the right of the source (again, underlined).

(2)   aka-bon-aníj-a   'he saw at the same time'
       ku-tonolá   'to pluck'
       tu-ku-sól-a   'we will choose'
       a-ku-ba-sol-á   'he will choose them'

In Sierra Juarez Zapotec (Otomanguean: Bickmore and Broadwell 1998), H tone moves leftwards to the first free syllable. In this language H and L tones are present underlyingly, and toneless syllables eventually surface as M. In these examples the verb /-xuʔnì-/ has a toneless first syllable, which surfaces as M in the form for 'you will wrinkle'. The first person subject suffix has a floating H tone, which shows up on the first toneless syllable to its left, so that the same verb now acquires a H on its first syllable in the form for 'I will wrinkle'.

(3)   gú-xuʔnì-luʔ   'you will wrinkle'
       gú-xúʔnì-ʔàʔ   'I will wrinkle'

In Somali (Cushitic: Banti 1988), a final H moves back to the penult phrase-finally. Consider the word for 'crow', /tukḗ /. There are two possible word orders for the

sentence below. If the second word order is used, so that 'crow' is phrase-final, the
H on the last syllable of /tuk$\underline{é}$ / retracts:

(4)   sháley   b-úu   tuk$\underline{é}$ arkey   'Yesterday he saw a crow'
        yesterday FOC-he crow saw
but: sháley   b-úu   arkey túk$\underline{e}$

4.1.2   Stability

Unlike most segmental features, when a segment deletes, moves, or
reduplicates, tone may stay behind or fail to copy. In Haya (Bantu: Hyman and
Byarushengo 1984), segments copy, but tones do not. The verb 'to tie up' has a
H(L) tone on its penultimate syllable, but the reduplicated form shows no H tone
at all on the second copy:

(5)   okukôma   'to tie up'   vs. okukómaakoma   'to tie up here and there'

In Thai secret languages, segments exchange places, with the rhyme of the first
and second syllables being interchanged. However, the tones stay behind. In the
first examples below, the /HL/ sequence from /uay/ stays behind on the first syllable, and surfaces on [ɔɔm]. /uay/ on the other hand surfaces with the /LH/ that
originated on /ɔɔm/.

(6)   klúày hɔ́ɔm   >   klɔ́ɔm hùáy   'banana'
        ténrām   >   támrēn   'dance'

In Pirahã (Everett, 1986), vowels delete in hiatus, but the tone remains behind. In
this example, first the /x/ elides, leaving a three-vowel sequence /òí - o/. Then the
/i/ deletes, but its tone remains behind and surfaces on the adjacent /o/, giving
[ŏo]:

(7)   sitòí - xogabagaí   >   sitŏogabagaí   'egg-want'   'I want eggs'

In Cantonese there is a widespread phenomenon known as changed tone (Yip
1980a). In one sub-type, there are alternations between certain specific morphemes with high tone, and forms in which the morpheme deletes, but the tone remains behind and attaches to the preceding morpheme. If that morpheme has a
low or mid tone, as here, the result is a rise from low or mid to high. I remind the
reader that in the Chinese tradition 1 is low and 5 is high. The sequences of interest are underlined.

(8)   a. yat5 <u>tiu21 yat5</u> tiu21   'one-strip-one-strip'   'strip by strip'
           ~ yat5 <u>tiu25</u> tiu21
        b. <u>sik3 tsɔ35</u> ~ <u>sik35</u>   'eaten-PERF'   'have eaten'

4.1.3   One-to-many

Unlike most segmental features, tone may spread to cover a long span. In Chilungu (Bantu: Bickmore 1996), there is unbounded H spread from the infinitival prefix /kú-/, clearly visible when this is attached to toneless roots. The H spreads to all except the last syllable:

(9)   kú-vúl-à   'to be enough'
       kú-víímb-à   'to thatch'
       kú-fúlúmy-à   'to boil over'
       kú-sáákúl-à   'to comb'
       kú-sóóbólól-à   'to sort out'

The origin of these H spans is clearly a single H-toned vowel, and yet the output shows H pitch across a long polysyllabic sequence. If this is spreading of a single H, rather than the creation of multiple H copies, then it is one tone associated with many vowels or syllables, as shown below:

(10)   ku -soobolol-a
        H

Indeed, in many cases it is clear from the rest of the phonology that we are dealing with a single tone that has spread. For example, Odden (1986) discusses a rule in Shona that lowers a H tone after the H-toned associative prefix /né-/. If there is more than one adjacent H-toned syllable, they all lower: /né-hóvé/ > [né-hòvè] 'with a fish', /né-mbúndúdzí/ > [né-mbùndùdzì] 'with worms'. If these sequences of high-toned syllables in fact contain a single high tone associated with several syllables, this is exactly what we would expect:

(11)   H   H   →   H   L
        | ∧ | ∧
        ne hove   ne hove

On the other hand if each syllable had its own H tone only the first should lower, since the rule is triggered only by the associative prefix, not just any H tone, and it applies only to an adjacent H, as Odden shows.

In Chiquihuitla Mazatec (Jamieson 1977), we see unbounded spread of the two highest tones, shown as /1, 2/ in the Meso-American tradition. In these examples the last tone of the first morpheme spreads rightwards, obliterating all other tones except the last:

(12)   kih31 'went' + -nka3 'again' + mu3su34 → kih31 nka1 mu1su14 'hired worker'
        nku2 'one' + nta3?nka34   → nku2 nta2?nka24   'corncrib'

In the South American language Barasana (Gomez-Imbert and Kenstowicz 2000), we see unbounded spread of both H and L. In compounds, the last tone of the first half spreads to the second half; the first two examples show H spreading, and the last shows L spreading. (The tilde in front of a word shows that all its voiced segments are nasalized.)

(13)	héá + ~gɨtá-a	→	héá~gɨtá-á	'flint stone'
	~ɨdé + ~bídi	→	~ɨdé~bídí	'Guilielma (sp.) bird'
	hée + jáí	→	hée jai	'shaman (ancestor-jaguar)'

Also very common is bounded spreading, most commonly just one syllable over. This is sometimes called 'tone doubling', and we find it in many African languages. The following examples come from Vai (Welmers 1976) and Bade (Schuh 1978):

(14)   *Vai: Low spreads one syllable to the right*
         /mùsú náánì/   →   mùsù náánì   'four women'

         Bade: High spreads one syllable to the right
         /nɔ́n kàtáw/   →   nɔ́n kátáw   'I returned'

4.1.4   Many-to-one

Unlike most segmental features, more than one feature may appear in sequence on a single segment, producing contour tones. In the previous chapter I presented the evidence for analysing contours as sequences of levels.

In Ibibio (Benue-Congo: Urua 1995), contour tones have a limited distribution. They can all be derived from underlying level sequences. For example, unlike most monosyllabic verbs, [CrV] monosyllabic verbs can have LH tones. Urua suggests that these are underlyingly bisyllabic, /CVdV/, and that first the /d/ lenites to an [r], giving /CVrV/, then the first vowel deletes, leaving its tone behind [CrV]. Anticipating slightly by using an autosegmental representation, the derivation looks like this:

(15)   tVdV   →   tVrV   →   trV   'stop'
          | | | | ／|
         L H   L H   L H

Evidence that these verbs are underlyingly bisyllabic is of three types. (1) They take the same allomorphs of suffixes as bisyllabic verbs, not other monosyllables. (2) In reduplication, LH is copied onto the CVV prefix as a sequence: bèébrě. (3) In a closely related language, Anaaŋ, the bisyllabic forms are actually attested, suggesting that historically at least these verbs were bisyllabic in Ibibio too.

In Siane nouns (Highlands, Papua New Guinea: James 1994), contours are formed only when excess tones have nowhere else to go. A monomoraic noun with two underlying tones shows up with only one tone on the noun root, and the second tone on any suffix. Only if there is no suffix do the two tones surface on the noun itself, forming a contour.

(16)   /yoLH/   yo + te   →   yòté   'fire, 1sg.poss'
                 yo   →   yǒ   'fire'

In Mende nouns (Leben 1978), we see exactly the same phenomenon:

(17)   /mbuHL/   mbu-ma   →   mbúmà   'owl-on'
                   mbu   →   mbû   'owl'
        /mbaLH/   mba-ma   →   mbàmá   'rice-on'
                   mba   →   mbǎ   'rice'

In Cantonese changed tone (Yip 1980a), we saw earlier that deletion of a morpheme (or perhaps syllable) left its tone behind and that this tone re-attached to the preceding morpheme. In other examples of changed tone, there is no segmental morpheme as the source of the tone, which instead seems to be entirely composed of a high /5/ tone. This tonal morpheme, here used to create familiar names, freely attaches to syllables that already bear a tone of their own, creating contours. If the syllable already begins high, /5/ or /53/, the addition of the new high gives a [55] output.

(18)   a. *Surnames*
           /ts^{h}an^{22}/   a^{33} ts^{h}an^{25}
           /yip^{22}/   a^{33} yip^{25}

        b. *Family Relations*
           a^{33} kuŋ^{55} 'grandfather (mother's side)'
           a^{33} yi^{55} 'mother's younger sister'

        c. *Names based on birth order*
           /yi^{22}/   a^{33} yi^{25} 'No. 2'
           /ŋ^{24}/   a^{33} ŋ^{25} 'No. 5'
           /sei^{33}/   a^{33} sei^{35} 'No. 4'

        d. *Nicknames*
           /pai^{53}/   a^{33} pai^{55} 'the lame'
           /fei^{24}/   a^{33} fei^{25} 'the fat'

4.1.5   Toneless syllables

Unlike most segmental features, tonal features may be missing both underlyingly and at the surface. In segmental phonology, underspecification has often been suggested at early levels of representation, but nonetheless by the surface, with rare exceptions, each segment has its more-or-less full specification.

For example, even coronal consonants are clearly supplied with the feature Coronal by the phonetic stage, since their place of articulation is not completely dependent on the surrounding environment. For tones the picture is rather different. Some syllables may lack tonal targets even in the phonetic component, taking their pitch from surrounding specified syllables. And examples of syllables that are toneless throughout the phonology, only to receive a late L specification, abound. See chapter one for a discussion of the relationship between phonetics and phonology.

In Chichewa (Bantu, Myers 1999a), only H is specified, and low is the absence of tone. Only H is a tonal target, and other F_0 values are assigned in the phonetic component by interpolation. Myers gives two kinds of argument in favour of these claims. Phonologically, only H tone is 'active'; there are restrictions on its placement, and it shows dissimilation effects. Phonetically, low is not a phonetic target: its precise value is predictable from the surrounding Hs, and the timing of the low trough depends on the inter-peak interval. In fact, it looks remarkably similar to Japanese, an accentual language thoroughly investigated by Pierrehumbert and Beckman 1988.

In Sekani (Athapaskan, Rice 1999a), only L is specified. L tone is consistently retained after V deletion, while H is lost:

(19)   sə-chu-è-azi → [səchuàzi] 'my dear daughter'

Further, L tone acts as a possessed morpheme, but H does not:

(20)   chu 'water'   -chù   'water, possessed'
        da 'eye'   -dà   'eye, possessed'

(Of course, H might be present, but not used as a morpheme in its own right, just as English has the phoneme /p/, but no morpheme consisting of /p/ alone. Strictly speaking, then, this is more evidence for the presence of L in underlying forms than evidence for the absence of H. Nonetheless, it is certainly consistent with the lack of underlying Hs.)

In Mandarin (Shih 1987), both H and L are specified, but some morphemes are toneless, such as /-de/ 'POSS' and /-ge/ 'Classifier'.

(21)   *Preceding tone*   *Toneless syllable*
        55   H   high level   ta -de '3p.sg-POSS'   starts high, then falls
        35   LH   high rise   shei-de 'who-POSS'   starts high, then falls, but not as low
        21   L   low   wo-de '1p.sg.-POSS'   starts fairly low, then rises
        53   HL   high fall   nei-ge 'that-CL'   starts fairly low, falls even lower

The descriptions of the phonetics of the toneless syllable make it clear that its pitch is determined by that of the preceding syllable, and that it has no phonological tone of its own, and probably enters the phonetic component still toneless.

In Shanghai (Duanmu 1993), non-initial (i.e. non-head) morphemes become toneless, but then the two tones of the initial morpheme readjust themselves to cover the first two syllables (as in Mende above):

(22)   se52 + pe52   →   55 21   'three cups'
        se52 + bø23   →   55 21   'three plates'
        sz34 + pe52   →   33 44   'four cups'
        sz34 + bø23   →   33 44   'four plates'

Any subsequent syllables also lose their tone, and do not acquire any from the initial syllable. They surface as low, no matter what the tone of the preceding second syllable. Since they are invariantly low, it seems best to assume that they are supplied with a phonological L tone before the phonetics, so that in this respect Shanghai is unlike Mandarin.

We now turn to a representational system that will allow us to capture these five properties.

4.2   Autosegmental representations

4.2.1   The basics

The model I will describe here is called Autosegmental Phonology, and originates in the work of Goldsmith (1976), building on work by Leben (1973). Goldsmith's work revolutionized our thinking about tonal phonology, and has never been seriously challenged in its fundamentals. Tone is on a separate 'tier' from the segmental and prosodic material, like a musical melody. A tone is only realized on the surface if it is 'associated' with some segment or prosodic entity such as the syllable or the mora, on which it is eventually pronounced. These associations are denoted by lines connecting the tiers. σ stands for the syllable, and T for any tone.

(23)   σ σ σ σ
        | | | |
        T T T T

In underlying representation, tones may not necessarily be associated to specific syllables, because the tones are simply a property of the morpheme, and not of any particular segment or syllable in that morpheme. In other languages, particularly accentual languages, the associations must be underlying, because they are lexically distinctive. If tones are unassociated underlyingly, in order for them to surface associations must be supplied by the grammar. The mechanisms responsible for this will be discussed shortly, but in the unmarked case the associations will be one-to-one, as shown in (23), with no left-over tones or syllables.

It is not always clear whether tones associate to segments, syllables or moras. In the case of a language with only mono-moraic, open CV syllables, where each syllable bears exactly one tone, the Tone-Bearing Unit (TBU) could be the vowel, mora or syllable. I have put the tone to one side here for typographical clarity.

(24)   C V --- T *or* C V   *or* C V
           | | |
           μ   μ --- T   μ
           | | |
           σ   σ   σ ---- T

If the language has syllabic nasals which bear tone, but onset nasals which do not, we can rule out the segment as TBU, since the prosodic affiliation of the segment determines its TBU status. This leaves the mora or the syllable as the possible TBU in such cases, and I show the mora option here. Nasals that have moras will bear tone, but mora-less onset nasals will not:

(25)   N C V   *and* N V   *not* *T---N V
           | | | |
       T--- μ   μ---T   μ --- T   μ
           | | | |
           σ σ   σ   σ

If the language has both light mono-moraic and heavy bi-moraic syllables, and if these differ in the number of tones they can bear, so that mono-moraic syllables can have only one tone but bi-moraic syllables can have two, then it must be the case that the TBU is the mora, not the syllable.

(26)   C   *and* C V   *and* C V V   *and* C V C
       | | | | | |
       μ ---T   μ --- T   T --- μ μ ---T   T --- μ μ ---T
       | | V   V
       σ   σ   σ   σ

There are languages in which the TBU is not just any mora, but vocalic or sonorant moras only. See Zec 1988 and Steriade 1991 for discussion.

Lastly, if the two different syllable weights can bear the *same* number of tones, then the syllable must be the TBU.

(27)   C V   *and* C V V
       | | |
       μ   μ μ
       | V
       σ ---T   σ ---T

Since there are cases in which the TBU *must* be the mora or the syllable, and no cases in which it *must* be the segment, it seems that tone always associates to prosodic entities. Languages can differ in whether the syllable or the mora is the TBU. Note that for brevity I will often show tones as if they were associated directly to segments, but the reader should be aware that the TBU is strictly speaking the intervening but unshown prosodic element.

4.2.2 Autosegmental representations of the five tonal properties

4.2.2.1 Mobility

Autosegmental phonology can simply characterize mobility as a change in association.

(28) $\sigma\,\sigma\,\sigma\,\sigma \;\to\; \sigma\,\sigma\,\sigma\,\sigma$
|||||||||||||| |
T   T

There is no representational limit on the distance that a tone may travel from its source, unless it is blocked by other tones in the representation. If tone were a segmental feature, this kind of tonal shift would require copying of the tonal feature at a distance, followed by deletion of the tonal feature on the original segment – a phenomenon with no known counterparts among other features.

4.2.2.2 Stability

Since tones are on a separate tier, and are associated to prosodic structure, there is no particular reason to expect them to be affected by segmental deletion rules. Tonal stability under deletion is thus the norm, and re-association will follow from other properties of the grammar to be discussed later. In this example the two vowels come together in hiatus, and the second one deletes, in order to avoid an onsetless syllable and allow the preferred CV syllabification:

(29)   CV - VCV → C V C V → C V C V
   | | | | | \ |
   T T T   T T T   T T T

One might add that associating tones with syllables, not segments, makes the step of re-association unnecessary (and the direction of re-association predictable), since the tone-syllable associations are undisturbed throughout.

(30)   C V - V C V → C V C V
   \/ \   \ \
   σ σ   σ σ
   /\ | /\ |
   T T T   T T T

The snag is that this requires assuming that the two original vowels are syllabified initially into the same syllable, and yet vowel deletion usually happens because without it proper syllabification is not possible.

Lastly, note that other features occasionally show this sort of behaviour, but it is quite rare outside nasality. For example, in Japanese verbal morphology, voicing survives deletion of the segment on which it originates, and reassociates to the suffixal consonant: /kog-ta/ > [koi-da]. This is unusual: in the more standard case, when segments delete they usually do so *in toto*.

4.2.2.3 One-to-many

Tonal plateaux, where one tone spreads onto many syllables, is straightforwardly represented as multiple association. If on the other hand features were not separated out, but remained inextricably bundled within the segment, then any spreading behaviour would have to be shown as copying. In some cases it can be shown that a single multiply-linked tone is essential, because subsequent processes still treat it as an entity, and affect the entire plateau. (See section 4.10 for examples.)

$$(31) \quad \begin{array}{ccc} \sigma\,\sigma\,\sigma & \to & \sigma\,\sigma\,\sigma \\ | & & \swarrow\!\!\!\diagdown \\ T & & T \end{array}$$

4.2.2.4 Many-to-one

We saw in a previous chapter that many contour tones are indubitably sequences of levels. This is simply represented as many-to-one association:

$$(32) \quad \begin{array}{ccc} \sigma\,\sigma\,\sigma & \to & \sigma\,\sigma\,\sigma \\ |\;|\;| & & |\;|\;\diagdown \\ T\,T\,T\,T & & T\,T\,T\,T \end{array}$$

Some languages do not allow this at all, and very few allow more than two tones per TBU, although three are attested in some languages. If tone were purely segmental, there would be few non-tonal precedents for more than one value of a feature on a single segment: only affricates, which have been argued to be [−cont][+cont] (Lombardi 1990), and pre-nasalized stops, which might be [+nasal][−nasal], come to mind.

4.2.2.5 Toneless syllables

A toneless syllable is simply a syllable associated with no tone:

$$(33) \quad \sigma \quad or \quad \begin{array}{c} \sigma\,\sigma\,\sigma\,\sigma\,\sigma \\ \;\;\;|\;| \\ \;\;\;T\,T \end{array}$$

The inverse of this, a tone associated with no syllable, is also found, and such tones are called floating tones. They will be encountered often in the following pages. Their eventual fate can be association, and thus surface realization, or failure to associate, in which case they are not pronounced, but may have effects on surrounding tones, particularly downstep (see chapter six).

4.2.3   Well-formedness conditions

I said earlier that associations are not always underlying. I now turn to the conditions that control a well-formed association. Goldsmith proposed that association was accomplished by, and subject to, the following conditions.

(34)   *Well-formedness conditions*
         1. Every TBU must have a tone.
         2. Every tone must be associated to some TBU.
         3. Association proceeds one-to-one, left-to-right.
         4. Association lines must not cross.

We will view these as violable constraints in Optimality Theory, as we proceed.

Consider the effect of (34) on three types of input. In the first case, there are equal numbers of tones and TBUs. Here are some possible associations.

(35)   a. σ σ σ   b. σ σ σ   c. σ σ σ   d. σ σ σ   e. σ σ σ
            | | | / /   V | \   X |
            T T T   T T T   T T T   T T T   T T T

Only (a) satisfies all the clauses of (34). (b) violates all of (1–3). (c) violates (2) and (3). (d) violates (1) and (3), and (e) violates (3) and (4).

So far, as the alert reader will have noticed, clause (3) does no essential work, but it comes into its own in the next two cases. Consider a case with more syllables than tones. In such cases many languages show spreading of the final tone onto the last syllable, giving a plateau at the right edge, as in (a) below. (36) shows three possible association patterns.

(36)   a. σ σ σ   b. σ σ σ   c. σ σ σ
            | V | | V |
            T T   T T   T   T

Only (a) satisfies all the clauses of (34). (b) violates (1), and (c) violates (3). Only the left-to-right stipulation in (3) accounts for the preference for spreading at the right edge, not the left edge. (I ignore here the additional possibility that the language might satisfy (34) by inserting an additional tone associated to the excess syllable.)

Lastly, consider a case with more tones than syllables. Here languages prefer to stack up the excess tones at the right edge to give contours, as in (a). (37) shows three possible association patterns.

(37)   a. σ σ   b. σ σ   c. σ σ σ
         | ∧ | | ∧ |
         T T T   T T T   T T T

Again, only (a) satisfies all clauses of (34). (b) violates (2), and (c) violates (3). It is the left-to-right stipulation of (3) that gives the preference for contours on the right edge, not the left.

Goldsmith viewed his well-formedness conditions as both causing and controlling initial association, and as inviolable universals. The problem is that this is too strong. Some languages associate all excess tones, creating contours, but others do not, leaving them floating and unrealized. Some languages spread tones out so that every syllable gets a tone, but others do not, leaving some syllables toneless. Some languages limit contours to the right edge, but others allow them non-finally. For example, Hyman and Ngunga (1994) draw attention to several ways in which the Bantu language Ciyao, spoken in Mozambique, Tanzania, and Malawi, fails to observe the putatively universal conventions, ranging from free tones that do not re-link to idiosyncratic tone associations that do not conform to the left-to-right pattern. A second problem is that the well-formedness conditions have to operate at every level of the grammar, not just as one-time rules, and yet each language will have to stipulate at which levels they do and do not apply, given the cross-linguistic variation. A third problem is that their effects are often replicated by phonological rules, such as rules of spreading or rules that de-link part of a contour. Here the conditions seem to act like output goals, not as initial associations. See also Tranel (1995) for discussion of similar issues in Mixteco tonal analysis.

With the advent of Optimality Theory a different perspective has become available, in which they are indeed universal, but violable under certain circumstances. Instead of operating at many levels of the grammar, they operate once only, as constraints on outputs, but ones that cannot always be satisfied because of conflicting pressures elsewhere in the phonology. In the next two sections I first lay out the basics of OT, then show how Goldsmith's ideas can be understood within OT.

4.3   The bare bones of Optimality Theory

The standard phonological theory for a generation of phonologists was the rule-based derivational theory most fully laid out in *The Sound Pattern of English* (Chomsky and Halle 1968). In 1993 Prince and Smolensky proposed a very different, non-derivational approach called Optimality Theory, or OT, and this has proved enormously influential, particularly in the United States, where it has supplanted the SPE model and become the new standard. For this reason I have chosen OT as the framework in which to couch the analyses in the remainder of this book. I assume no prior familiarity with OT, so the basics are explained in this section. Readers already comfortable with OT may skip directly to section 4.4.

It is beyond the scope of this book to compare and contrast different phonological theories, although the elegance of OT will I hope emerge by example as I proceed. The interested reader should consult first three excellent textbooks on OT, Archangeli and Langendoen (1997), Kager (1999), McCarthy (2002), and then McCarthy and Prince (1993, 1995), or the extensive readings in Kager's and McCarthy's bibliographies. A number of papers are available for download on the Web at http://roa.rutgers.edu.

In recent years there have been several proposals for grammars in which the output is selected by direct evaluation by various criteria or constraints. This should be contrasted with the SPE model, in which the output was derived by applying a series of rules to an input, and the output itself was simply the product of those rule applications. Like other declarative phonologies, such as Bird's (1990) computational phonology or Scobbie's (1991) attribute value phonology, OT is thus an output-based grammar. The term 'output' as used by most OT practitioners (but see Kirchner 1997 and Flemming 1995 for a different view) refers to something short of the fully-fledged phonetic output, being rather the output of the phonological component, which in turn serves as an input to a phonetic component. Phonetically, every syllable is pronounced on some pitch, with a frequency that depends on a vast array of factors, including but by no means limited to the sex of the speaker, whether he or she is excited or calm, whether he or she has laryngitis, whether the syllable is near the beginning or end of the utterance, and last but not least the phonological tone features associated with that syllable, such as H, L, or perhaps nothing. By contrast, the outputs that concern us here look only at this last factor – the featural and structural information. They are at a more abstract level, and they are categorical, not gradient. For more on the relationship between the phonology and the phonetics, see chapter one.

Assuming this sense of output, then, all possible outputs for any given input are considered, and the best is selected as the actual output. This output may not be perfect, but it will be the best possible output in a sense to be described below. There are no constraints on inputs, a hypothesis known as The Richness of the Base Hypothesis. The grammar that selects the optimal output consists of a set of ranked, universal constraints, which assess the desirability of each output candidate. Violations of higher-ranked constraints are fatal, and the winner is the output candidate that survives this winnowing. The constraint set is the same in all languages; language variation comes from the ranking only. Constraints are of two types: markedness constraints, and 'faithfulness' constraints. Markedness constraints may concern features (e.g. *[constricted glottis]), feature combinations (e.g. *[–back, +round]), or structures (e.g. NoCODA). Faithfulness constraints penalize changes to the input form (insertion, deletion, or featural change). If FAITHFULNESS >> MARKEDNESS, where C_1 >> C_2 means C_1 outranks C_2, marked segments/structures are found. If MARKEDNESS >> FAITHFULNESS, they are not. For example, if *DELETE >> NoCODA, codas will not be deleted, and closed syllables will be found. If NoCODA >> *DELETE, codas will not surface, and all syllables must be open. The aspect of this theory that makes it so appealing to many phonologists is the universal nature of the constraints, which directly encode well-established cross-linguistic preferences for particular classes of sounds and types of structures. All alternations are seen as the result of pressure from these well-formedness constraints to produce 'better' words, but conflicts between irreconcilable constraints are resolved in different ways in different languages depending on the relative importance given to each constraint, here encoded through rankings.

I should emphasize that OT shares with SPE the notion of an underlying form, or input, and of course both theories produce outputs. The difference is that SPE moves from input to output in a series of stages, or a derivation, whereas OT simply selects the optimal output. Within the OT phonology proper, there are only two stages: the input and the phonological output. This commitment to a non-derivational approach means that certain phenomena, such as opacity, which have traditionally been analysed as making crucial reference to intermediate stages in the derivation, pose a serious challenge to OT, but one that is beyond the scope of this book. The interested reader should consult McCarthy 1999, 2002.

Let me give some examples of the types of constraints that have been posited in OT. We start with faithfulness constraints. In a rule-based theory these have no direct equivalent. Inputs remain unchanged unless a rule applies, so faithfulness is just what you get when there is no applicable rule. In OT, however, the faithful output is just one of many candidates, and frequently it is quite marked, and thus fails on one or more markedness constraints. We thus need a family of constraints that encourage underlying forms to resist change at the expense of markedness violations, and these are the faithfulness constraints

(38)   *Some faithfulness constraints*
- *No deletion:* MAX-INPUTOUTPUT (MAX-IO): Every input segment/tone has an output correspondent
- *No insertion:* DEP-IO: Every output segment/tone has an input correspondent
- *No changes:* IDENT-IO: Correspondents are the same.
            *ASSOCIATE: Do not insert new association lines
            *DISASSOCIATE: Do not delete association lines
- IO-INTEGRITY: Each input segment has no more than one output correspondent
- FAITH-BR: Similar set of constraints that relate a reduplicant to its base.

The terminology is unfortunately not always transparent. The 'no deletion' constraints are named MAX as shorthand for the preference for 'maximal' realization of input material. The 'no insertion' constraints are named DEP as shorthand for the preference for output material to be 'dependent' on input material rather than *sui generis*. The suffixes IO and BR stand for Input-Output and Base-Reduplicant respectively. Faithfulness constraints can compare the output to the input (the usual case), or, in reduplication, the reduplicant to the base. Unless it is necessary to distinguish these, I will omit these suffixes. Simple MAX, DEP, and IDENT should be understood as referring to input-output relations. (Note that even reduplicated forms can be handled in a single step from input to reduplicated output, without intermediate steps. See McCarthy and Prince 1993, McCarthy and Prince 1995.)

What about markedness constraints? The markedness constraints that pertain to tone will be introduced shortly, but in general markedness constraints can concern features, structure, or what one could term structural matching. My examples are restricted to ones relevant to tonal issues, and are only a sample of what we will encounter later.

(39)   *Markedness constraints that pertain to features*
   • *H: No high tones
   • *CONTOUR: No contour tones
   • *[VOICE]: No voicing specifications
   • *[–SON][TONE]: No tones on obstruents

(40)   *Markedness constraints that pertain to structures*
   • FT-BIN: Feet must be binary
   • OCP: Obligatory Contour Principle: No adjacent identical elements
   • *FLOAT: No floating tones

(41)   *Markedness constraints that pertain to matching*
   • *HEAD/L: Heads may not have L tone
   • ALIGN-R (H, STEM): Align every H tone with the right edge of some stem
   • NON-FINALITY: Do not align tones with the right edge of the prosodic word
   • ALIGN-L (X", PHPH): Align the left edge of every X" with the left edge of some phonological phrase

Many of these constraints represent families of constraints specific to particular tones. For example, the OCP might apply only to Hs, in which case we write OCP(H). Or *FLOAT might apply only to Ls, so we have *FLOAT(L). NOCONTOUR might be broken up into *FALL and *RISE, and so on (Akinlabi 1996).

Given an input, and some set of constraints, how do they select an output? In any particular language, the constraints have a language-specific ranking. This ranked set is the grammar of that language. The set of possible outputs is first checked by the highest ranked constraint. Any that violate this are discarded, and those that satisfy it are then passed on to the next constraint down. This continues until only one output survives. At any stage, if all candidates fail, then the decision is passed down to the next constraint in the hierarchy. The procedure is displayed in tableaux, and we will go through the first example step-by-step. The constraints head the columns, with the highest-ranked on the left. The candidates begin the rows, and the violations are shown by asterisks below the relevant constraints. The key to reading the tableaux is as follows:

(42)   *Key to tableaux*
- * = violation
- ! = fatal violation
- Shaded cells no longer matter because a higher-ranked constraint has made the decision
- ☞ shows the winner

Consider tableau (43), which uses three constraints, two faithfulness constraints MAX-T, which bans deletion of tones, and IDENT-T, which bans changing tones from H to L or vice-versa, and the markedness constraint *H, which dislikes H tones. The input is in the top-lefthand cell, and the actual output in this language is unchanged, candidate (a).

Taking each candidate in turn from the bottom up, candidate (c) is first checked against MAX-T, which it fails, because the underlying H has been deleted. Since both the other candidates pass on this constraint, the violation is fatal, as shown by the exclamation point. (c) is now out of the running. Candidate (b), which passed MAX-T, is now checked against IDENT-T. It fails, because the underlying H has been changed to L. Since candidate (a) passes on this constraint, (b)'s violation is fatal, and it is discarded. Candidate (a) thus wins, even though it too violates a constraint, *H, but *H is the lowest ranked of these constraints, and thus by the time it gets a chance to have an influence, the decision has been made.

(43)   Tableau for MAX-T, IDENT-T >> *H: marked H tone survives

/ta/ | H	MAX-T	IDENT-T	*H
☞ (a) ta | H			*
(b) ta | L		*!	
(c) ta	*!		

In theory, all possible outputs should have been considered. In practice, one selects the most plausible options in order to keep things manageable, but the reader should bear in mind that an infinite number of candidates exist in theory. (On the issues that this raises for acquisition and computability, see Tesar and Smolensky 2000.) For example, in the particular case under discussion I did not consider outputs in which a L had simply been added, so that we get *[taHL], or outputs with lots of extra H's, as in *[taHHHH]. These could easily be ruled out by DEP-T, of course.

Before we get down to specifics, two other points are worth making. OT is committed to the view that the difference between grammars is a difference in constraint rankings, and that the set of constraints is universal. By extension, then, it follows that the difference between dialects is also a difference between constraint rankings, and presumably since two dialects are more similar to each other than two distinct languages, the ranking differences should be relatively minor, with most rankings the same. Along the same lines, the grammars of a single language at two points in time must also differ only in constraint rankings, so the process of historical change also results in the re-ranking of constraints. This book is largely limited to discussion of synchronic phonology, but the implications for historical phonology are clear.

This completes the overview of OT. Further subtleties will be introduced as they are needed.

4.4   An OT treatment of the central properties of tone

The final step is to take the theoretical machinery of autosegmental representations and OT and apply them to tonal phenomena. We begin by developing a set of constraints that pertain to tone. This constraint set will be fully exemplified and enlarged as the book proceeds. Note that in the tonal domain there is no standardized consensus on the names and precise formulation of the constraints; for four previous versions, see Bickmore 1996, Pulleyblank 1997, Myers 1997, and Cassimjee and Kisseberth 1998.

Recall Goldsmith's Wellformedness Conditions. Although these represent well-motivated generalizations about tone, they are not always surface true. The following list reinforces this point:

(44)   *Some striking properties of tonal morpho-phonology*
         • Tones are usually associated with syllables, but not always (cf. floating tones).
         • Syllables are usually associated with tones, but not always (cf. toneless syllables).

- Association is preferably one-to-one, but not always (cf. contour tones, spreading).
- Tone (especially H tone) is attracted to prominent positions (beginnings of things, edges, accented or stressed syllables), but not always.

Each of these is observable – i.e. surface true – in some but not all languages. Each can be stated as a markedness constraint. The names are chosen to be easy to remember, or because they are prevalent in the literature. The choice of No-X versus *X is not significant.

(45)   • *FLOAT: A tone must be associated with a TBU.
       • SPECIFY T: A TBU must be associated with a tone.
       • NOCONTOUR: A TBU may be associated with at most one tone.
       • NOLONGT: A tone may be associated with at most one TBU.
       • ALIGN-TONE: Align the specified edge (L/R) of a tone span with the head or edge (L/R) of a prosodic or morphological unit.

(A tone span is a string of TBUs associated with a single tone.) This might be a good place in which to point out that it is sometimes important to distinguish the degrees of constraint violation. The idea, called 'gradient assessment', is that a constraint like NOCONTOUR is violated once for each excess tone that is associated with a single TBU, or a constraint like ALIGN-R is violated once for each 'empty' TBU that intervenes between the tone and the right edge of the word: the greater the mismatch, the worse it is.

In addition, tone is subject to general faithfulness constraints, which preserve underlying contrasts of tone quality and placement:

(46)   *Tonal faithfulness constraints*
       • DEP-T: No insertion of tones
       • MAX-T: No deletion of tones
       • Tone usually stays in its original position, but not always (cf. flop, spreading).
         *ASSOCIATE: No new association lines
         *DISASSOCIATE: No removal of association lines
       • NOFUSION: Separate underlying tones must stay separate.
       • IDENT-T: Correspondent tones are the same.
       • LINEARITY: Preserve underlying linear order.

Next, we need a way to capture Goldsmith's observations about the preference for contours and plateaux at the right edge of the word, which he attributed to left-to-right association. In OT these can be dealt with by alignment constraints. Like all OT constraints, they are violable, so languages like Ciyao which do not show left-to-right alignment are unsurprising.

(47)   *Left-to-right association effects result from*
       • ALIGN-L: Each T should align with the left edge of the domain (gradiently assessed).

- Align-R Contour: Contour tones should align with the right edge of the domain.

Zoll 1997b argues for this treatment of contours by means of the positional markedness constraint, Align-R Contour, which may override the leftward pressure of the more general Align-L. The preference for contours at the end of the word is probably the phonologization of a phonetic fact: word-final syllables are frequently longer, and thus there is more time to realize a complex tone in that position. See section 4.7 and Zhang 2000, 2001 for further discussion.

Finally, tone is also subject to more general phonological conditions such as the Obligatory Contour Principle (OCP) (Leben 1973, 1978, McCarthy 1986, Yip 1988; see Itô and Mester 1998 for a markedness view of the OCP; also de Lacy 1999a) and locality and markedness constraints:

(48)   • OCP: Adjacent identical elements are prohibited.
        • NoGap: Multiply linked tones cannot skip TBUs.
        • Local: Spread only to the adjacent element.
        • General markedness: *H >> *L

NoGap is familiar from vowel harmony systems. Local prefers maximally binary associations, and like many binary phenomena is perhaps more fundamentally a foot-bound restriction. The relative markedness of H and L tones will be discussed in detail later.

In its purest and strongest form OT claims that *all* constraints are universal and present in the grammars of all languages. Any constraint should therefore be a plausible universal, and postulation of obviously language-specific constraints should be avoided if at all possible, and never undertaken without comment. If a constraint is sufficiently low ranked, its effects may be invisible, and in that case it will not be mentioned in the discussion of that language. Nonetheless, the reader should always remember that it lurks beneath the surface.

4.5   Tonal behaviour and its OT treatment

I now return to the five special properties of tone with which I began this chapter, and give each of them a treatment within OT.

4.5.1   Mobility

Recall that tones may move far from their source, so that the underlying high tone of the Chizigula verb root /lómbez/ 'request' actually surfaces three syllables to the right on the penultimate syllable in [ku-lombez-ez-án-a] 'to request for each other' (section 4.1.1). How can such mobility effects be handled in OT?

When tones move, association lines are deleted and inserted. These changes are faithfulness violations, and must be caused by some dominating constraint or constraints. Let us for the moment restrict our attention to real tonal shift, not spreading. In what follows I assume that the tones are prelinked to some TBU in underlying representation. In the most common cases, tones migrate away from their host towards either a toneless syllable, a word edge, or a prominent, stressed syllable. In the case of toneless syllables, the output leaves every syllable with a tone, satisfying SPECIFY. In the case of word edges, the output succeeds in aligning the H tone with the word boundary. In the case of stressed syllables, it is well known cross-linguistically that there is an affiliation between H tone and stress. I will use attraction to the final syllable as my example. The relevant constraints for tonal shift to a final syllable can be formulated as follows:

(49)   ALIGN-R(H, PRWD): Every H tone should be aligned with the right edge of a Prosodic Word.

(50)   HEAD = H: Head syllables should be H.

At least one of these constraints will outrank *ASSOCIATE and *DISASSOCIATE and result in tonal shift to the right. Here I assume that ALIGN-R is the relevant constraint. SPECIFY must be ranked below *ASSOCIATE to ensure that we get shift, not spreading.

(51)

σ σ σ | H	ALIGN-R	*ASSOC	*DISASSOC	SPECIFY
☞ a. σ σ σ | H		*	*	**
b. σ σ σ ⊬ H		**!		
c. σ σ σ | H	**!			**

Candidate (c), which leaves the tone in place, violates ALIGN-R twice, because two toneless TBUs intervene between the H and the right edge of the prosodic word. Candidate (b), with spreading, violates *ASSOCIATE twice, because two new association lines have been added. Candidate (a) also violates *ASSOCIATE, but once only, so it prevails over (b) to win even though it violates both the lowest ranked constraints. In passing, I have introduced one other convention in this tableau. The dashed line separating the last two columns tells us that the relative ranking of these two constraints with respect to each other cannot at present be determined.

Exercise 1.   Think of other candidates for the above tableau. Will this grammar still give the right result? If not, what changes/additions are needed? (Answers to exercises are to be found at the end of this chapter.)

Exercise 2.   Work out grammars for Chizigula and Zapotec from section 4.1 of this chapter. Assume that Chizigula words end in a trochaic foot, so that the penult is stressed.

4.5.2   Stability

Stability is the survival of tone after deletion of segmental material. For example, consider Pirahã, from section 4.1.2, in which the high tone of /í/ survives after the vowel itself deletes in hiatus, and joins the low on /ò/ to create a rise: sitòí - xogabagaí > sitǒogabagaí. How will this be handled in OT?

Resistance to deletion is captured in OT by the faithfulness constraint MAX-T, which must be high ranked, outranking the constraints on reassociation, *ASSOC, and in some cases outranking NOCONTOUR. A vowel deletes in hiatus, presumably because the constraint requiring onsets, ONSET, is high ranked, and instead of the tone deleting or floating, it reassociates to form a contour tone with the existing tone on the preceding vowel. The necessary ranking is *FLOAT, MAX-T >> *ASSOC, NOCONTOUR. I consider only candidates that satisfy ONSET through vowel deletion.

(52)

/...oi.../ || LH	*FLOAT	*MAX-T	*ASSOC	NOCONTOUR
☞a. ...o ... ∧ L H			*	*
b. ...o... | L		*!		
c. ... o... | L H	*!			

Candidate (c) retains the tone, but does not reassociate it. This violates *FLOAT, which is high ranked. Candidate (b) deletes the tone, in violation of MAX-T. Candidate (a) wins, because it only violates the low-ranked *ASSOC and NOCONTOUR.

4.5.3 One-to-many

In Barasana (section 4.1.3), after deletion of the tone on the second half of a compound, the tone spreads from the first half, héá + ~gitá-a → héá~gitá-á. The result is one tone linked to several TBUs in a one-to-many relationship. How will this be handled in OT?

When there are more TBUs than tones, for any reason, including as a result of tone deletion as in Barasana, the final tone frequently spreads to all the excess TBUs, forming a plateau. This is a result of the preference for all TBUs to receive tonal specifications, in OT stated as SPECIFY >> *ASSOC, NOLONGT.

(53)

/σ σ σ σ/ | | L H	SPECIFY	*ASSOC	NOLONGT
☞a. σ σ σ σ | ⋁ L H		**	**
b. σ σ σ σ | | L H	**!		

In candidate (b), no spreading takes place, leaving two unspecified syllables, and violating SPECIFY. Candidate (a) wins, despite violating the two lower-ranked constraints.

Exercise 3. Consider Chiquihuitla Mazatec in section 4.3.2. What might be behind the spread of the /1, 2/ tones here? Will SPECIFY alone do it? If not, why not? Suggest an alternative. Construct a mini-grammar.

4.5.4 Many-to-one

When there are more tones than TBUs, many languages associate the excess tone(s) to the final vowel to form a contour. We saw some examples in section 4.1.4, such as Siane /yoLH/ > [yǒ]. The alternative is to let the excess tones delete or float.

In OT, this type of many-to-one association is captured by assuming that MAX-T and *FLOAT >> NOCONTOUR, *ASSOC, exactly as we already needed for the stability effects in section 4.5.2. Here is another example from Cantonese, this time with an underlying floating tone:

(54)

/a -yip- / | | 3 2 5	MAX-T	*FLOAT	NOCONTOUR	*ASSOC
☞ a -yip- | \ 3 2 5			*	*
b. a -yip- | | 3 2 5		*!		
c. a -yip- | | 3 2	*!			

The preference for these contours to be at the right edge will be discussed in the next section, but to set the scene, and without looking at the next section, think about this:

Exercise 4. Assume that left-to-right tone assignment is achieved by ALIGN-L. Where would we expect to find most contours? In answering this question it will help to consider inputs with three syllables and four tones.

4.5.5 *Toneless syllables*

In some languages, such as Chichewa, some syllables remain toneless throughout the phonology, and never receive phonological tone. In other languages, underlying tones may delete for some reason, but the remaining tones step in and spread onto these syllables, as in Barasana (§4.1.3 and 4.5.3), or Shanghai (§4.1.5). How is this handled in OT?

Surface tonelessness, where some tone, usually low tone, is never specified, can be achieved if the markedness constraint *L dominates both SPECIFY and MAX-T.

Even underlying /L/ (inevitable in a theory like OT that has no way of restricting underlying forms) will not survive in such a grammar.

(55)

/σσ/ | L	*L	SPECIFY	MAX-T
☞ a. σ σ		**	*
b. σσ | L	*!	*	

Since these toneless syllables stay toneless even in the presence of surrounding H tones, it is also necessary to assume that no underlying H can spread just to satisfy SPECIFY, so NoLongT >> SPECIFY. This does not mean of course that they could not spread in response to some other imperative, such as alignment.

For toneless syllables created by tone loss, the usual analysis is that some sort of positional faithfulness dominates markedness, which in turn dominates general faithfulness. For example, in Shanghai (§4.1.5), the positional faithfulness constraint HEAD-MAX-T ensures that head tones survive. This dominates the markedness constraint *T, which in turn dominates MAX-T, so all other tones will delete. For the accompanying spreading of the head tone, the usual mini-grammar of SPECIFY >> *ASSOC will suffice. Note that spreading does not increase markedness, because the number of tones remains the same. For a full treatment, see chapter seven.

4.6   Some Bantu phenomena in OT

The extreme mobility of tone so well-illustrated by Bantu languages poses one of the most interesting challenges to phonological theory. After all, languages in which tone more or less stays put can be handled by ranking the faithfulness constraints highly, but when tone starts to move, spread, and delete all over the place, as it does in Bantu, we must ask exactly what constraints are causing such deviations from the underlying form.

I start with tonal shift, or displacement. In many languages an input H moves off its host towards the right edge of the word. The shift may be to the final syllable

(Digo), the penultimate syllable (Chizigula) (and, rarely, to the antepenult (Xhosa)), just one syllable to the right (Kikuyu), or, rarely, some other specified number of syllables to the right (two in Sukuma). Some sample data follow; as usual the source of H tones is underlined.

(56) Shift to final syllable: Digo (simplified from Kisseberth 1984, Goldsmith 1990)

Toneless verbs		*H-tone verbs*	
ku rim a	'to cultivate'	ku n<u>en</u> á	'to speak'
ku ambir a	'tell'	ku <u>a</u>ruk á	'begin'
ku gandamiz a	'press'	ku <u>go</u>ngome á	'hammer'

Object marker has own H tone, again shows up on final vowel

ku <u>a</u> rim á	'to cultivate them'
ku <u>a</u> ambir á	'to tell them'
ku <u>a</u> gandamiz á	'to press them'

(57) Shift to penult: Chizigula (Kenstowicz and Kisseberth 1990)

Toneless verbs		*H-tone verbs*	
ku-guh-a	'to take'	ku-l<u>o</u>mbéz-a	'to request'
ku lagaz-a	'to drop'	ku-l<u>o</u>mbez-éz-a	'to request for'
ku-damany-a	'to do'	ku l<u>o</u>mbez-ez-án-a	'to request for each other'

(58) Shift one syllable to the right: Kikuyu (Clements 1984)

to-mo-rɔr-aɣa	'we look at him/her'
to-mo-t<u>o</u>m-áɣa	'we send him/her'
to-m<u>a</u>-rór-aɣa	'we look at them'
to-m<u>a</u>-t<u>ó</u>m-áɣa	'we send them'

(59) Shift two syllables to the right: Sukuma (Sietsema 1989)

aka-b<u>o</u>n-aníj-a	'he saw at the same time'
ku-t<u>o</u>nolá	'to pluck'
t<u>u</u>-ku-sól-a	'we will choose'
a-ku-b<u>a</u>-sol-á	'he will choose them'

This rightward pull is usually captured by a constraint already mentioned above, which we will call ALIGN-R:

(60) ALIGN-R: Every H tone should be at the right edge of the prosodic word.

For the movement to take place, represented as a change in association lines, ALIGN-R must dominate *ASSOC and *DISASSOC. In the absence of any other constraints, this will successfully shift the H to the extreme right edge. To stop it short of the right edge, something else must override it. For the case of a penult target, we can assume that NONFINALITY selects the result that comes closest to satisfying ALIGN-R without also violating NONFINALITY. ALIGN-R must of course be gradiently assessed:

(61)

/σ σ σ/ ⎮ H	NonFinality	Align-R

☞ a. σ σ σ
      ╱
    H
		*

b. σ σ σ
    ⎮
    H
		**!

c. σ σ σ
    ╱
   H
	*!	

An alternative approach to the case of attraction to penult is to postulate a trochaic foot at the right edge, and assume that the H is attracted to the head of that foot. This is the tack taken by Kenstowicz and Kisseberth 1990. See Bickmore 1996 for discussion of the two approaches.

For the case of movement only one syllable to the right, most people have assumed a constraint like LOCAL (Myers 1997). For our purposes the following informal statement will suffice.

(62)   LOCAL: An output tone cannot be linked to a TBU that is not adjacent to its host.

If LOCAL dominates ALIGN-R, we will correctly characterize the case of one-syllable shift:

(63)

/σ σ σ σ/ ⎮ H	LOCAL	ALIGN-R

☞ a. σ σ σ σ
       ╱
     H
		**

b. σ σ σ σ
    ⎮
    H
		***!

c. σ σ σ σ
       ╱
      H
	*!	*

Finally, the trickiest case is the two-syllable shift of Sukuma. One possibility, suggested by Sietsema (1989), is to suppose that we are dealing with binary feet, and that the two-syllable shift is a shift from the head of one foot to the head of the next: (σ̱σ)(σ́σ). This proposal is not without problems, among them that it will require allowing for monosyllabic or monomoraic feet in the case of odd-numbered words: (σ̱σ)(σ́). See Roberts 1991 for an alternative account.

Each of these types of tonal displacement also has a spreading variant, in which the tone remains anchored to its host, and spreads to the targeted syllable and all syllables in between. The same alignment constraint can be used to trigger the spreading. The difference is that *DISASSOC is high-ranked, and stops detachment of the tone from its host. NOGAP will disallow skipping of any TBUs. In languages with spreading, NOLONGT must be ranked below *DISASSOC. Tableau (64) shows only candidates that satisfy ALIGN-R.

(64)

/σσσ/ | H	*DISASSOC	NOGAP	NOLONGT

☞ a. σσσ
     \\/
     H
			*

b. σσσ
     \\/
     H
		*!	*

c. σσσ
     /
     H
	*!		

Before leaving our discussion of spreading, I should add that there are other types of motivation beyond alignment pressures. In the case of simple initial association, where there are more syllables than tones, the final tone often spreads to form a plateau. This is presumably the result of high-ranked SPECIFY, dominating both NOLONGT and *ASSOCIATE. A different type of spreading prolongs a contour into the next syllable, even when this already has a tone of its own, as in Comaltepec Chinantec (Silverman 1997b):

(65)   kwaLH to:L   →   kwaLH to:HL   'give a banana'
        kwaLH ku:M   →   kwaLH ku:HM   'give money'

We can picture this as follows:

(66)   kwa toː

$\bigwedge$

L HL

Silverman suggests that this is functionally motivated, because of the difficulty of finishing a rise within a single syllable. Zhang (2000) has accumulated a considerable body of data showing that cross-linguistically rising tones are longer than other tones, and proposes an OT analysis along these lines.

Cases of spreading from a level-toned or falling syllable cannot be explained in this way, however. In Yoruba and other Benue-Congo languages (Hyman and Schuh 1974, Akinlabi and Liberman 2000b), level tones are prolonged into the next syllable, as shown below:

(67)   àlá (L.H)   →   àlǎ (L.LH)   'dream'
          rárà (H.L)   →   rárâ (H.HL)   'elegy'

Akinlabi and Liberman offer a two-step explanation. First, they suggest that tones 'naturally form binary prosodic complexes', so that rises and falls are as natural as diphthongs. Second, they suggest that the rightward direction of spreading is preferred because it allows each F_0 target to remain at the end of its segment, rather than at the beginning, in line with a known preference for tonal targets to be placed at the end of their segments. Hyman (personal communication) points out, however, that this cannot be the full story, because there is also a rightward bias in tone absorption: LH-H is more likely to become L-H than L-LH is to become L-H.

Returning to the OT treatment of straightforward spreading and displacement, we can summarize with the following typology:

(68)   • Unbounded displacement: ALIGN-R, NoLongT >>*DISASSOC
          • Bounded displacement: LOCAL >>ALIGN-R, NoLongT >>*DISASSOC
          • Unbounded spreading: ALIGN-R, *DISASSOC >> NoLongT
          • Bounded spreading: LOCAL >>ALIGN-R, *DISASSOC >> NoLongT

4.7   Initial left-to-right association

One of the central findings of Goldsmith's pioneering work was that tone association seems to proceed from left to right across the word. This mechanism immediately offers an explanation for the very common pattern in which languages only allow contours at the ends of words: left-over excess tones associate to the final syllable, creating contours. However, in a non-derivational theory like OT, we cannot resort to a step-by-step left-to-right procedure. Instead, the obvious counterpart is to use left alignment, but while this works fine in the case of fewer tones than TBUs, it fails when there are more tones than TBUs. Tableaux (69) and (70) illustrate this point; note that each tone is assigned an asterisk for each TBU that intervenes between the one it is associated to, and the left edge of the word. The sad face ☹ marks the winner as chosen by the grammar, but wrongly so.

(69)   ALIGN-L correctly chooses (a), with a plateau at the right-edge

/σσσ/ LH	ALIGN-L

☞ a. σ σ σ
  | V
  L H
	*

b. σ σ σ
  \ |
  L H
	**!

(70)   ALIGN-L incorrectly chooses (a), with a contour at the left edge:

/σ σ/ HLH	ALIGN-L
☞ a. σ σ ☹ Λ \ HL H	*

b. σ σ
  | Λ
  HLH
	**!

Zoll (1997b) points to a further empirical problem with attributing the distribution of contours solely to left-to-right association. In many languages contours can arise from other sources, such as vowel deletion, and even these contours may be disallowed and eliminated non-finally. Let us look at Mende, a language first studied theoretically in influential work by Innes (1969) and Leben (1973). Consider these basic noun patterns, simplified from Zoll's work:

(71)   *Mende Nouns*

H	kó	'war'	pɛ́lɛ́	'house'	háwámá	'waistline'
L	kpà	'debt'	bɛ̀lɛ̀	'trousers'	kpàkàlì	'tripod chair'
HL	mbû	'owl'	ngílà	'dog'	félàmà	'junction'
LH	mbǎ	'rice'	nàvó	'money'	lèlèmá	'mantis'
LHL	mbʼâ	'companion'	nyàhâ	'woman'	nìkílì	'groundnut'
HLH	-		ndéwě	'sibling'	yámbùwú	'tree (sp)'

The majority of these nouns follow the expected left-to-right pattern. Zoll suggests that the avoidance of non-final contours be attributed to a licensing requirement on contour tones stated as ALIGN-R(CONTOUR), requiring any contours to be final. Provided this constraint plus MAX-T and *FLOAT dominate ALIGN-L, we will achieve the desired results.

Exercise 5.   Give tableaux for the words for 'woman' and 'junction'.

Zoll's proposal has the further advantage that, unlike left-to-right association, it explains the contour shift that happens in cases like this:

(72)   mbu-i → mbu-i
         ╱│ ╱╱│
         H L H H L H

Based on other data, Zoll argues that tone association is cyclic, so that /HL/ must be associated with /mbu/ before the suffix is added. After suffixation, the contour is non-final, in violation of ALIGN-R(CONTOUR), which triggers reassociation.

   Lastly, she points out that left-to-right association, and also ALIGN-L, make the wrong prediction for /LH/ on trisyllables. We expect LHH, but actually get LLH. Zoll attributes this to a constraint against adjacent H-toned syllables, *CLASH:

(73)   *CLASH: No adjacent syllables linked to prominent tone, i.e. H

Crucially for Zoll, *CLASH does not care whether there are two H tones (one per syllable), or only one shared tone. It is thus much more powerful than the OCP. SPECIFY and DEP-T dominate *CLASH, so a single /H/ survives, and can spread to all syllables. For further details of the analysis the reader is referred to Zoll's work.

Exercise 6.   Complete this analysis by deciding the ranking of *CLASH and ALIGN-L, as well as SPECIFY and DEP-T. Give tableaux for the words for 'mantis' and 'house'.

I have now laid out a theory that will deal with the basic patterns of association, shift, and spreading, but there are still a few more tools we will need before moving on to look at the range of tonal languages found around the world. The remaining sections look at extrametricality, the interaction of tone and stress, and the OCP.

4.8   Extrametricality

Although the usual association pattern starts at the left edge of the word, this is not always the case. In Kikuyu (Clements and Ford 1979), tonal melodies are shifted one syllable to the right when compared to closely related Bantu languages. The first syllable is always low.

(74)   Kikamba: ŋgíŋgɔ́   Kikuyu: ŋgìŋgɔ́   'neck'
              mòté   mòtě   'tree'

If we assume that the first syllable (and indeed any other syllables that for some reason or other fail to be associated with a phonological tone) receives its low tone by default at the end of the phonology (or in the phonetic component), and is phonologically toneless up until then, we can explain these patterns by somehow excluding the first syllable from the initial tone association process:

(75)   Kikamba: mote   Kikuyu: (mo)te
                        | | /\
                        L H   L H

A second piece of evidence for this proposal comes from the behaviour of downstep. Downstep (see chapter six) is frequently caused by a floating low or extralow tone. Kikuyu is the only language of this family with non-automatic downstep, and it is found exactly when related languages have an extra-low tone that gets pushed off the end of the word in Kikuyu. In these data, I use a notation in which underlining indicates extra-low, and ! shows downstep.

(76)   Mwĩmbĩ: èkálà̱   Kikuyu: ìkàrá!   'charcoal'

If downstep is caused by a floating extra-low, this is explained.

(77)   Mwĩmbĩ: ekala   Kikuyu: ikara
                        | | | / /
                        L H XL   L H XL

The inability of the first syllable to receive tone in Kikuyu is a type of extrametricality that we can call NONINITIALITY, the mirror-image of NONFINALITY in Chizigula. More formally, these can be viewed as non-alignment constraints such as *ALIGN-L(WORD, T), banning any word from beginning with a tone, in counterpoint to the lower-ranked ALIGN-L(T, WORD).

(78)

mote LH	*ALIGN-L(WORD, T)	ALIGN-L(T, WORD)
☞mote ⟋\ L H		**
mote | | L H	*!	*

As with Chizigula, an alternative is to view the phenomenon as accentual. This is the tack taken by Clements and Ford, who suggest that Kikuyu has a fixed accent on the second syllable, and tones are attracted to this accent: ALIGN-L(T, ACCENT). As we shall see in the next section, there is considerable cross-linguistic evidence for an attraction between stress and H tone, or indeed any tone.

4.9   Relation between tone and stress

De Lacy (1999b) has proposed an interestingly restrictive theory of the interaction between tone and prominence based on two universal hierarchies of negative markedness constraints, one of which regulates the appearance of tones in heads, and one their appearance in non-heads. The first hierarchy deals with the preference for H over L in head syllables by positing constraints that bar certain tones in Head position. So *HD/L means 'No L on head syllables'. The full hierarchy is given below:

(79)   *Prominence prefers H, avoids L*
        *HD/L >> *HD/M >> *HD/H

It can be used to explain phenomena such as the insertion of H on stressed σ (Lithuanian), the movement of H to stressed σ (Zulu, Digo), and the tendency for stress to avoid L σ (Golin, Mixtec).

Phenomena such as the deletion of H on unstressed σ (Vedic Sanskrit), the movement of H off unstressed σ (Digo), and the avoidance of unstressed H σ (Golin, Mixtec) are dealt with by the second hierarchy, which deals with the preference for L tone on non-heads:

(80)   *Non-prominence prefers L, avoids H*
         *NonHd/H >> *NonHd/M >> *NonHd/L

De Lacy develops this proposal in detail, and his analysis of a Mixtec dialect is given in detail in chapter seven. We have already seen cases in Bantu that can be analysed as attraction of H tone to a stressed syllable. Here I give only some additional brief examples.

Consider the well-known rule of Mandarin third-tone sandhi, in which the OCP-violating input /L̲.L/ (where the dot shows the syllable boundary and the head is underlined) is broken up by the insertion of a H, giving /L̲H.L/. The placement of the H tone on the head syllable rather than on the non-head can be understood as the result of *Hd/L and *NonHd/H, as shown in tableau (81). The preference for (a) [L̲H.L] over (b) [H̲.L] can be attributed to Max >> *Hd/L, and the triumph of [L̲H.L] in (a) over [L̲.HL] in (c) follows directly from *NonHd/H:

(81)

/L.L/	OCP	*NonHd/H	Max	*Hd/L
☞ a. (L̲H.L)				*
b. (H̲.L)			*!	
c. (L̲.HL)		*!		*
d. (L̲.L)	*!			

In many languages (e.g. Mandarin, Shanghai), *all* underlying tones are lost on unstressed syllables (and they receive either a default tone at the end of the phonology, or phonetic pitch by interpolation), and *all* underlying tones are retained on stressed syllables. While de Lacy's account allows for discrimination between H and L tones, it does not require it. So languages of this type are what we get when the entire *NonHd/T hierarchy from (80) dominates the entire *Hd/T hierarchy from (79), with Max-T intervening:

(82)   *Ranking for languages with all tones retained on all and only head syllables*
         *NonHd/H, M, L >> Max-T >> *Hd/H,M,L

In the rest of this section I briefly discuss some implications of de Lacy's work, suggesting that it may need some amendments. See Yip 2000 for details. This section may be skipped without detriment.

De Lacy explicitly limits the constraint inventory to negative markedness constraints, but it may be necessary to admit also positional faithfulness constraints, positive markedness constraints, and sequential markedness constraints. In Zhuang, the first syllable of a bisyllable of certain types acquires an initial H tone. This tone combines with the underlying tone on the first syllable, so that toneless syllables become H, /H + TH/ (where T stands for any tone) becomes HH, and /H + TL/ becomes HL. It seems likely that the first syllable of these bisyllables is the head, and the H is inserted in response to a positive markedness constraint HEAD = H. *HD/L does not suffice, because outputs may be HL, with the L still present. Mandarin Chinese presents a second argument for positive constraints: contrastive stress avoids L syllables, but is freely allowed on H, MH, and HL syllables. The requirement for a H tone must be stated positively.

In Shanghai Chinese, all tones of a phonological phrase are deleted except those of the head. The surviving tones are then re-distributed over the first two syllables, so that a /LH.HL/ input produces a [L̲.H] output, violating both *HD/L and *NONHD/H. De Lacy's grammar would lead us to expect that the H of the head, and the L (if any) of the non-head would be retained. Clearly, the origin of the tones still matters, and there is thus no alternative to a positional faithfulness constraint such as HEAD-MAX-T. See chapter eight for further details.

A further case in which de Lacy's approach is overly restrictive concerns downstep. I defer discussion of this more complex case to chapter six, where I will argue that we need a sequential markedness constraint, contra de Lacy: PROMTONE-MATCH. Prominence profiles and tonal profiles cannot contradict one another.

4.10 The Obligatory Contour Principle

Leben (1973) proposed that tone was governed by a principle he called the Obligatory Contour Principle, usually referred to as the OCP:

(83) *Obligatory Contour Principle (OCP)*
      Adjacent identical elements are prohibited

This means that words with sequences of high-toned syllables must be represented as in (a), not as in (b):

(84) a. σ σ σ   NOT   *b. σ σ σ
         ↘↙ | | |
          H   H H H

Since Leben's original proposal, it has become clear that this principle covers more than tone, and also that it is perhaps best viewed as a constraint on outputs, a conception that fits very naturally into OT. As an output constraint, it can block changes to the input if those changes would produce an OCP violation (McCarthy 1986), or force changes if the input itself violates the OCP (Yip 1988). OCP violations can be avoided in a variety of ways, such as deletion of one tone, movement of one tone away, blocking of spreading if it would cause adjacency, or fusion of two tones into one. Furthermore, like any constraint in OT, the OCP is violable, so surface violations will be observed, as pointed out by Odden (1986).

Myers (1997) gives an elegant overview of the way the OCP influences tonal phonology, and the remainder of this section is taken from his work. We shall see that the OCP may be observed (Shona), or violated (Kishambaa); the OCP may force a change in the input, a faithfulness violation (i.e. trigger a rule), or the OCP may block an otherwise expected change (i.e. block a rule).

The first case is one where the underlying form contains a sequence of H tones, and the OCP causes deletion of the second one. This rule, known as Meeussen's Rule, is widespread in Bantu tonology, and these examples come from Shona. Underlining draws attention to underlyingly H toned vowels.

(85)   *OCP-triggered deletion* (Shona: Meeussen's Rule)
        bángá   'knife'   í-banga   'it is a knife'

The noun 'knife' has one doubly-linked H tone underlyingly, and the copula prefix also has a H tone. Attachment of the copula causes deletion of the H on the noun.

The deletion can be captured by the ranking OCP >> MAX-T, and the preference for deleting the second of the two tones by including ALIGN-L in the grammar.

(86)

/i banga/ \ | \ \/ \ \ H_1 H_2	OCP	MAX-T	ALIGN-L
a. i banga \ \ | \ \/ \ \ H_1 H_2	*!		*
b. i banga \ \ \ \/ \ \ \ H_2		*	*!
☞c. i banga \ \ \ | \ \ \ H_1		*	

Our second case shows the OCP blocking the usual spreading from a clitic if doing so would create an OCP violation:

(87)   *Failure to spread H from clitic* (Shona)
        Normal spreading: sadza   'porridge'   í-sádza   'it is porridge'
        Spreading blocked: badzá   'hoe'   í-badzá   'it is a hoe' (*í-bádzá)

Let us assume that the spreading is caused by pressure from SPECIFY, and that SPECIFY dominates *ASSOCIATE. The blocking effect will then be caused by the OCP outranking SPECIFY. Lastly, since we do not get spreading followed by deletion (candidate (b)), MAX-T must also dominate SPECIFY. The ranking OCP >> MAX-T was justified in the previous tableau.

(88)   OCP>>MAX-T >> SPECIFY-T >> *ASSOCIATE

/i-badza/ H₁ H₂	OCP	MAX-T	SPECIFY-T	*ASSOCIATE

a. i -badza
    ⟋ |
  H₁   H₂
	*!			*

b. i-badza
    ⟋⟋
  H₁
		*!		**

☞c. i-badza
    | |
  H₁   H₂
			*	

The final way OCP violations are avoided in Shona is by fusion, which is limited to applying within the part of the verb Myers calls the macrostem, made up of the root and any suffixes, the object prefix, and subject prefixes in the subjunctive, negative, and participial forms.

(89)   *Fusion* (Within macrostem only)
        a. tí-téng-és-é   'we should sell'
        Evidence for fusion: whole sequence deletes by Meeussen's Rule after a clitic
        b. há-ti-teng-es-e   'let us sell'   (*há-ti- téng-és-é)

In (a), we see that in this environment two adjacent underlyingly H syllables remain high-toned, in apparent violation of the OCP. However, Myers points out that it can be shown that these two syllables are now associated with a single H tone, because if the word is placed in the environment of Meeussen's rule, as in (b), both of them lose their high pitch. The two underlying tones of /tí-téng/ have thus fused into one. Fusion is a faithfulness violation, usually stated as a constraint we can call NoFusion, so clearly the OCP dominates NoFusion. Since fusion is preferred to deletion, we must also say that Max-T dominates NoFusion:

(90)   *Fusion:* (Macrostem)   OCP >> Max-T >> NoFusion

/ti-teng-es-e/ | | H_1 H_2	OCP	Max-T	NoFusion

a. ti-teng-es-e
   | ↙
  H_1 H_2
	*!		

b. ti-teng-es-e
   |
  H_1
		*!	

☞c. ti-teng-es-e
   \\ ↙
   $H_{1.2}$
			*

Lastly, note that the difference between the macrostem grammar, where fusion removes OCP violations, and the phonological word grammar, where deletion is used, is only in the relative ranking of NoFusion and Max-T. Before we leave fusion, it is worth noting that one very common tonal process, tonal absorption, can be viewed as a sub-case of OCP triggered fusion. Hyman and Schuh (1974) note that in many languages, including Bamileke, Mende, Kikuyu, Hausa, and Ngizim, sequences of /HL.L/ become [H.L], and sequences of /LH.H/ become /L.H/. They view this as rightward shift, followed by loss of one of the two identical tones on the second syllable, but it could equally well be fusion of the two tones. No matter which, the OCP is clearly at work here too.

We have seen that Shona and many other languages carefully observe the OCP, but not all languages rank it so highly, as noted by Odden in an influential 1986 paper. For example, in Kishambaa, spreading is not blocked by the OCP (Odden 1982, 1986):

(91)   *Surface OCP violations (Kishambaa)*
    /ní-ki-chí-kómá/   [níkí-!chíkómá]   'I was killing it'

Quite generally in Kishambaa H tones are downstepped after another H tone.

Since there is downstep between [kí] and [chí], these must be associated to two different H tones. Since the OCP violation is not fixed up by deletion, fusion, or by the blocking of spreading, the OCP must be ranked below all the constraints discussed earlier. We see then that, like any other constraint in OT, the OCP is violable if it is outranked by other conflicting constraints.

(92)   MAX-T, SPECIFY-T, NOFUSION >> OCP

/niki-[chikoma]/ H_1 H_2	MAX-T	SPECIFY-T	NOFUSION	OCP
a. niki-[chikoma] H_1	*!	***		
b. niki-[chikoma] H_1 H_2		*!		
c. niki-[chikoma] $H_{1,2}$			*!	
☞d. niki-[chikoma] H_1 H_2				*

This has been a long and dense chapter, but we have now got in hand the major tools we need as we continue to explore the behaviour of tone in the world's languages.

Answers to exercises for chapter 4

Answer to exercise 1

σσσ will wrongly win, so we must add NOGAP to the tableau, ranked
H above *DISASSOCIATE.

Answer to exercise 2

Chizigula: Replace ALIGN-R by HEAD = H in the above tableau.
    Zapotec: SPECIFY >> *ASSOCIATE, LINEARITY

Answer to exercise 3

The spreading is on to syllables that already have tones of their own, so SPECIFY cannot be the motivating force. The simplest alternative, given that /1, 2/ are both high tones, is to assume that the constraint ALIGN-R(H, PRWD) plays a role, and that NONFINALITY stops it short of the last tone. The ranking we need is NONFINALITY >> ALIGN-R >> *DISASSOC, *ASSOC.

Answer to exercise 4

ALIGN-L will try to keep *all* tones to the left, including excess tones, so we will get contours on the first syllable, not the last.

Answer to exercise 5

/nyaha/ LHL	ALIGN-R(CONTOUR)	MAX-T	*FLOAT	ALIGN-L
☞a. nyàhâ				**
b. nyàhá (L)			*!	*
c. nyàhá		*!		*
d. nyăhá	*!			*

/felama/ HL	ALIGN-R(CONTOUR)	MAX-T	*FLOAT	ALIGN-L
☞a. félàmà				*
b. félámà				**!
c. félámá (L)			*!	
d. félámá		*!		

Answer to exercise 6

SPECIFY, DEP-T >> *CLASH >> ALIGN-L

5

Tone in morphology and in syntax

In the previous chapter we looked at the pure phonology of tone, or how tones are influenced by their phonological surroundings, but we must not forget that phonology interacts with both morphology and syntax. That interaction is the topic of this chapter. The goal here is to draw attention to the types of interaction between tonology and other components of the grammar commonly found in natural languages, and illustrate them with brief examples. In chapters six to eight we will encounter and analyse many additional instances.

The dividing line between morphology and syntax is not always clear. I will classify as syntactic anything that somehow requires reference to the phrasal level, including tones that mark specific types of syntactic phrasal boundaries – such as complementizers – and tones that mark any phonological phrase, where phonological phrasing is partially or wholly conditioned by the syntax. Tonal morphemes or processes that participate in word-formation but do not seem to play a phrase-level role will be considered purely morphological. I start with morphology, and distinguish three types of interaction. Firstly, tone may be a morpheme in its own right. Such purely tonal morphemes are then subject to the general phonology of the language, associating, deleting, spreading, and so on. Secondly, certain morphological constructions may manipulate tone in particular ways. This is especially true in reduplication, where tone may be copied or not copied, or where a new tone may be supplied as part of the reduplicative process. Thirdly, the internal morphological structure of a word may affect the tonal phonology.

Then I turn to syntax, and ways in which the tones may interact directly with the syntax. We may distinguish two subcases. As in word-level morphology, tone may be a lexical morpheme in its own right, an X_0, typically a functional category supplied by a particular syntactic construction, such as a complementizer, question particle, possessive, or associative marker. Secondly, syntactic phrasing may affect prosodic structure, and thus the domains within which tonal rules apply. This is a particularly rich area of research, and will be the longest part of this chapter.

5.1   Morphology

5.1.1   *Tonal morphemes*

Although we usually begin by thinking of a morpheme as something with segments, purely tonal morphemes abound. It is useful to divide them into two types based on where the tones surface in the word. Type one are tonal morphemes that affix to the beginning or end of a word, and thus precede or, more commonly, follow the tones of the root. Type two are tonal morphemes that overwrite the tones of the root, if any, replacing them entirely. I should add that languages with morphemes of the second type are often analysed as having an *underlying* affix of the first type, that starts as a prefix or suffix, and that the larger surface manifestation of the tone can be derived from the general phonology. Nonetheless, the descriptive division is a useful one.

A simple example of the first type is the high tone affix of Cantonese familiar names. A monosyllabic family name can be turned into a familiar name by the addition of a prefix /a:33/, and a tonal suffix, as in /yi:p22/ → a:33 yi:p25. The addition of this affix produces a word that begins with its own underlying tone, but ends high. Using 5 for high and 1 for low, the changes can be listed as follows:

(1)	*Underlying*	*After affixation*
	21	25
	24	25
	33	35
	53	55
	35	35

These patterns can be derived by positing a simple 5 high-tone suffix, accompanied by some simplification of excessively complex tones. See chapter eight for more details.

In Hausa (Chadic; Newman 1992), monosyllabic verbal nouns formed from high-toned verbs show a falling tone.

(2)	sháa	'to drink'	shâa	'drinking' (N)
	cí	'to eat'	cîi	'eating' (N)

One common way to analyse these is as the addition of a L tone, with concomitant lengthening of the final vowel to accommodate the extra tone, but see Newman for a different explanation, at least as far as their historical origin is concerned.

The second type of tonal affix, in which the tones overwrite any pre-existing root tones, is perhaps best exemplified by the verbal morphology of Bantu, where an entire verb may change its tone as the result of the addition of a tonal morpheme. For example, in N. Karanga (Hewitt and Prince 1989) the assertive and non-assertive forms of the verb differ in their overall tonal melody. I have used Hewitt and Prince's examples; for some reason they use different roots to illustrate the assertive and non-assertive of H-toned roots. Note also that prefixes are omitted.

(3)
		Assertive		*Non-assertive*	
H-toned roots	téng-es-a	'sell'	tór-es-á	'didn't make take'
	téng-és-ér-a	'sell to'	tór-és-er-á	'didn't make take for'
Toneless roots	bik-is-a	'make cook'	bik-ís-a	'didn't make cook'
	bik-is-ir-a	'make cook for'	bik-ís-ír-a	'didn't make cook for'

Hewitt and Prince analyse the non-assertive morpheme as a H-tone suffix, but nonetheless its effects are felt throughout the word. See chapter six for further details and analysis.

A very different example comes from Cantonese, where historically noun-verb pairs were formed by tonal change. There is more than one pattern, and most of them are not productive these days; see Tak 1977 for details. The important thing to note here is that the pattern below cannot be simply analysed as the addition of a particular tonal prefix or suffix, since the entire tone changes.

(4)
Verbs: /53/		*Derived nouns: /44/*	
taːm	'to carry'	taːm	'a burden'
sow	'to count'	sow	'a number'

Finally, let us look at some facts from Iau (Tor Lakes-Plains-Stock, spoken in Irian Jaya; Edmondson *et al.* 1992). Verbal aspect is signalled by tone, overlaid on monosyllabic verbs. Although the major pitch differences come on the later portions of the verb, they can cover at least two-thirds of the syllable. For example, /baui/ 'come to' has a mid-level tone in the Resultative Durative, a high-to-mid falling tone in the 'Inter-goal' aspect (with the meaning 'finally came to X'), and mid-to-low falling tone in the Process aspect. It would appear, then, that aspectual tones associate with the syllable as a whole, and not just one edge.

5.1.2 Construction-specific tonology

Leaving tonal affixes, let us now see how specific morphological constructions may have their own particular tonal phonologies, especially reduplication. In some languages tones are copied in reduplication, in others the reduplicative morpheme supplies its own tone, and in yet others the reduplicative morpheme remains toneless or receives a default tone. One language may have more than one reduplicative construction, and they may differ in these regards. For example, Mandarin Chinese (Chao 1968) has several types of reduplication, three of which I mention here. Kinship nouns reduplicate without their tone, producing a phonologically toneless reduplicant. Classifiers reduplicate with tones intact. Adjectives, in the type of vivid reduplication that turns adjectives into pre-verbal or resultative adverbs, reduplicate with a fixed high tone on the second half of the reduplicant (for some speakers). The last two types also add a retroflex ending /-r/ in Beijing Mandarin.

(5)	T-0	Nouns:	ge55 ge	'older brother'
			jie21 jie	'older sister'
	T-T	Classifiers:	chu53 chur53	'everywhere'
			tian55 tiar55	'every day'
	T-55	Adjectives:	(chi55de) bao21 baor55de	'(eaten until) good and full'
			kuai53 kuar55de	'quickly'

In OT treatments of reduplication, base-reduplicant identity is produced by faithfulness constraints relating base to reduplicant, such as MAX-BR (McCarthy and Prince 1995). MAX-BR(TONE) is a B-R faithfulness constraint that requires all tones in the base to be present in the reduplicant. When base material is not copied, this is attributed to markedness dominating MAX-BR(TONE). When base material is copied, MAX-BR(TONE) dominates markedness (McCarthy and Prince 1994). In both cases high-ranked input-output faithfulness, MAX-IO(TONE), ensures survival of the input tones on the base syllable. The first two types of reduplication will thus need construction-specific constraint rankings, with *TONE >> MAX-BR(TONE) for the toneless verbal reduplication, and MAX-BR(TONE) >> *TONE for tone copying reduplication with classifiers. Tableau (6) shows the case of noun reduplication, with no copying of the tone. The interested reader can construct the appropriate grammar and tableau for the case of classifiers.

(6)

/ge55-RED/	MAX-IO(TONE)	*TONE	MAX-BR(TONE)
☞ a. ge55 ge		*	*
b. ge55 ge55		**!	
c. ge ge	*!		

The third type of reduplication, for adjectives, is presumably like the first since the reduplicant has lost the base tones, but with the addition of a H-toned suffix.

A very interesting case is found in the Khoisan language Juǀ'hoansi (Miller-Ockhuizen 1999). Roots are minimally bi-moraic, consisting of at least one heavy bi-moraic syllable or two light mono-moraic syllables, and may have a single tone shared by both moras or two different tones. For bisyllabic roots, the form of the reduplicant is determined by the number of tones on the root. If the root is mono-tonal, as in (7a), only the first vowel reduplicates. If the root is bi-tonal, as in (7b), both vowels reduplicate:

(7)   a. L   gkʰù.rì 'to become visible'   gkʰù.gkʰù.rì   'to cause to be visible'
       H   xɔ́.βɔ́ 'to sting (of skin)'   xɔ́.xɔ́.βɔ́   'to cause to sting'

       b. LH   tsxɔ̀.βí 'to grab'   tsxɔ̀í.tsxɔ̀.βí   'to grab forcefully'

Apparently the TBU is the mora and reduplication requires full reduplication of both tones, while observing the NoCONTOUR constraint that limits moras to one tone, and also limiting the reduplicant to a single syllable in size.

(8)

/RED-tsxɔ̀.βí/	RED=σ	MAX-BR(TONE)	NOCONTOUR
☞ a. tsxɔ̀í.tsxɔ̀.βí			
b. tsxɔ̀.tsxɔ̀.βí			*!
c. tsxɔ̀.tsxɔ̀.βí		*!	
d. tsxɔ̀.βí.tsxɔ̀.βí	*!		

I end this section with a more complex case from Chichewa (Myers and Carleton 1996). In Chichewa, tones are sometimes copied in reduplication, as in (9a), and sometimes not, as in (9b). When they are copied, they sometimes move onto a different syllable, as in (9c). The reduplicant is underlined in each case.

(9)   a. nda-namizá-<u>namizá</u>   'I have deceived repeatedly'

       b. ndima-sángalatsa-<u>sangalatsa</u>   'I used to please repeatedly'

       c. chigawénga-<u>wengá</u>   'a real terrorist'

Myers and Carleton argue that tone copying is blocked in cases like (b) because the tone in question originates not on the verb stem, but on the preceding auxiliary element (although it is realized on the stem). Reduplication, then, only copies stem elements. In cases like (c), the tonal movement is caused by the OCP, which dislikes H tones on the heads of two adjacent feet. Feet in Chichewa are left-headed, so if the H tone were copied but not moved we would have *chiga(wénga)(<u>wénga</u>), with H tones on both heads. The prohibition on such sequences outweighs the copying requirement. The authors work out the rather complex analysis in an OT framework that would take up too much space here, and the interested reader is referred to their paper for details.

This completes the summary of tonal processes specific to certain constructions. In the final part of this section on morphology, we look at morphologically defined domains for tonal processes.

5.1.3   *Morphological structure, tonal domains, and cyclicity*

It is very common for morphological structure to determine how tones behave. In Bantu languages, for example, verbs have a complex morphology, and tonal processes may apply within sub-constituents of the verb only. Myers (1997, 1999c), following Meeussen (1967) and Barrett-Keach (1986), argues that the verb in five Bantu languages has two main constituents. The Verb Stem consists of the root, its suffixes ('extensions') marking things like causation, passive, reciprocal and so on, and a terminal vowel. It is immediately preceded by any object marker, and these join together in the Verbal Macrostem. The Inflectional Stem, which precedes the Macrostem, consists of the morphemes marking subjects, tense, and/or modality. Here is an example from Shona:

(10)   nd-a-ká-mu-tár-ís-ir-a   'I looked for him/her (yesterday or before)'
SM/1sg-past-remote- OM/3sg-look-caus-appl-term
[Inflectional stem   ] [Macrostem [Verbal Stem   ]]

Myers gives a number of arguments for this bi-partite structure. What concerns us here is its effects on the tonal phonology.

Meeussen's Rule deletes the second of two adjacent H tones. However, it only applies across the boundary between Inflectional Stem and Verbal Macrostem, as in (11a), where the H tone on /téngésá/ deletes under the influence of the preceding H. The surface form is shown directly underneath, in italics. The deletion does not apply within either constituent, as shown by the contrasting examples in (11b–c). The square brackets show Inflectional Stem and Macrostem.

(11)   Meeussen's Rule applies: Meeussen's Rule does not apply:

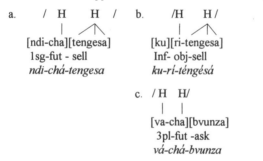

Without reference to the word-internal structure these facts cannot be explained.

In segmental phonology the phonological effects of word structure have been used as arguments for the cycle. In rule-based approaches, rules apply to the innermost constituent of a word, then re-apply to each larger constituent in turn. Tonal phonology is no different. For my first case, I turn to Margi (Chadic; Hoffman 1963, Pulleyblank 1986). Margi spreads tones onto toneless vowels, satisfying the constraint SPECIFY, which requires every TBU to have a tonal specification. This spreading must take place on each morphological cycle, before association of any tones supplied by a morpheme added on the next cycle. For example, the bisyllabic L-toned root in (12) takes a suffix with a H tone. The root L spreads onto both root-syllables on the first cycle, and the suffixal H then links to the final, suffixal syllable on the second cycle, as shown in (13a). If on the other hand all association took place after the entire word was formed, then the H would associate to the second root syllable, as shown in (13b):

(12)   /dza'u/ - / ba/   dzà'ùbá 'to pound well'
        L   H

(13)   a. *Cyclic association and spreading* b. *Non-cyclic association*
           (correct)   *(incorrect)*

        [[dza'u]-ba]   *[[dza'u]-ba]
          ⋁ | | ⋁
          L   H   L H

This argument, the reader should note, goes through only on the assumption that the tones are underlyingly unlinked to their hosts.

For my second example of cyclic tonal phonology, I will look at Shanghai Chinese (Duanmu 1997). Like all Chinese languages, Shanghai makes rich use of productive compounding. Within these compound words, binary left-prominent prosodic domains are built up from left-to-right, and in a prosodic domain all tones except the first are deleted. The domains are clearly stress domains, since they can be affected by contrastive stress, and are subject to clash avoidance. In long polysyllabic mono-morphemic words, or if the compound has no internal structure, such as a string of digits, the binary structure is very apparent. In words with an odd number of syllables the final foot may be trisyllabic, so a five-syllabled word has the pattern (T0)(T00), where T stands for a syllable that retains its tone and 0 for one whose tone is deleted. For details of how the surviving tone associates, see chapter eight.

Most compounds have internal structure, and this structure affects the domains. Look at the examples in (14), from Duanmu 1997. They are both trisyllabic compounds, but the tonal outputs differ, and the difference correlates with (but is not isomorphic to) differences in their internal morphological structure. Square brackets show morphological structure and parentheses enclose tonal domains.

(14)   a. [[bi   fia] tsʰã̄]   (T 0) (T)
              leather shoe factory
        b. [ha' [bi   fia]]   (T 0 0)
              black leather shoe

Two simple assumptions derive the facts. First, domains are built cyclically. Second, stress clashes are eliminated by deletion of the second stress. In the first example, shown in (15), a left-headed binary foot is built on the first cycle, and on the second cycle only one unfooted syllable is left, so this forms a unary foot. There is no stress clash, so nothing further happens.

(15)   [[ha'   bi]   fia]
        (T   0)   First cycle: build left-headed feet.
        (T   0)   (T)   Second cycle: remaining free syllable forms monosyllabic foot.

In the second example, shown in (16), after footing on the second cycle there are two adjacent stresses, so the second is deleted, resulting in a single stress and thus a single surviving tone:

(16)   [ha'   [bi   fia]]
                    (T   0)   First cycle: build left-headed feet.
        (T)   (T   0)   Second cycle: remaining free syllable forms monosyllabic foot.
        (T   0   0)   Deletion caused by stress clash, and refooting.

The full range of data when one looks at longer compounds confirms the cyclic character of the domains. However, in OT, with its commitment to a non-derivational approach, cyclic phenomena demand a different analysis. Duanmu proposes the use of output-output constraints that compare the compound to its constituent words and prefer identical stress placement, producing the effects of cyclicity without the need for derivations. Here I call this constraint OUTPUTOUTPUTMATCH:

(17)   OUTPUTOUTPUTMATCH: In an XY compound, surface stress locations should be the same as in the independent words X and Y.

These constraints can be overridden by the more highly-ranked *CLASH, as in the example (16), shown in the tableau in (18), where /bi fia/ 'leather shoe' has a different stress pattern as part of the larger compound than it does in isolation, in order to satisfy *CLASH. The input is /ha' # bi fia/, where # shows the word boundary. The two output words whose stress patterns should be matched if possible are (ha') and (bi fia), where the stressed syllables are underlined. In candidate (a), the stress locations match those of the independent words, but at the cost of an unacceptable stress clash. It therefore loses to candidate (b), despite the fact that (b) does not preserve the stress locations.

(18)

/ha' #bi fia/ CONSTITUENT OUTPUTS: (ha'), (bi fia)	*CLASH	OUTPUTOUTPUTMATCH
a. (ha') (bi fia)	*!	
b. ☞ (ha' bi fia)		*

The role of OUTPUTOUTPUTMATCH is crucial in cases where a monosyllable combines with an odd-numbered word. Consider a compound like nø # yī-du-ñi-çi-ya 'South Indonesia', which has the output (T00)(T00), but whose constituent words have the outputs (T) and (T0)(T00) respectively. Without appeal to the stress patterns of the component words, candidate (19b) with binary footing would win. Although their stress patterns cannot be perfectly matched without violating *CLASH, which rules out (19a), the minimum disruption compatible with avoiding stress clash correctly produces (19c) as the winner.

(19)

(T), (T0)(T00)	CLASH	OO-MATCH	FTBIN
a. (T)(T0)(T00)	*!		**
b. (T0)(T0)(T0)		*!***	
☞ c. (T00)(T00)		**	**

The reader is referred to Duanmu's paper for full discussion. See also Kager 1999 and McCarthy 2002 on output-output constraints.

This completes the section on the interaction of word-level morphology and tone. I now move on to discuss syntax.

5.2   Syntax

5.2.1   *Tones supplied by particular syntactic constructions*

I am including in this section tones that can be viewed as functional morphemes and that interact with the syntax. In a non-tonal language like English functional categories can be independent words or segmental affixes. For example, the comparative marker is either the word *more* or the affix *-er*. It is associated with a particular syntax 'X is more -adj than Y'. In tonal languages the tone can be applied to the entire construction, or to one edge of it, or to a particular word such as the head. The decision as to whether to include something here or in the earlier sections on morphology is not always straightforward: since tones must attach to segments to be realized, there is a sense in which all these are affixes, and thus come under the heading of morphology. Nonetheless, the syntactic function of many of these earns them a place in this section.

5.2.2   *Final particle tones*

In non-tonal languages, we sometimes find words that, for want of a better term, get called particles. The most common kind are sentence final, and are used for particular constructions, such as questions or imperatives. In some cases they occupy a different position, such as after the first constituent (Wackernagel's position). Tonal languages may have such particles too, and they may be segmental, but they may also be purely tonal. Consider Cantonese (Law 1990, Yip and Matthews 1994). Cantonese adds a sentence-final particle *ma33* for questions (with segments and tone) but it also has particles where the segments and tone are distinct morphemes:

(20)   ɛ   'suggestion'
        55   'echo question' attaches to final syllable of utterance
        ɛ55   'suggestion' *plus* 55 'weakener; tentative'
        ɛ11   'suggestion', *plus* 11 'strengthener, expecting agreement from hearer'

The segment [ɛ] carries the semantics of suggestion, but the tones 55 carry an echo question meaning. The combination conveys a questioning, or weak, suggestion, not unlike the Canadian English 'eh?'.

The line between final tonal particles and what we usually call intonation is extremely fuzzy. Intonation is sometimes still thought of as an add-on, an optional extra, that adds nuances but does not change meaning, but of course every sentence has to be pronounced with some sort of intonational contour, even if it has no easily identifiable function, and furthermore it is clear that many of the things we call intonation are not optional at all. In many languages question intonation is obligatory, and is the only way in which questions are distinguished from statements. For example, Kinande has two intonational phrase (IP) tones: L for assertions and H for question/list intonation. These tonal morphemes must then be considered just as much functional categories as the Russian *li* or English tags like '...won't you?'. There is an extensive literature on intonation, and the interested reader should consult Bolinger 1986, Cruttenden 1986, Ladd 1986, 1997, and Pierrehumbert 1980. Intonation is discussed further in chapter nine.

The way in which such tonal particles are realized is quite variable. One common way is for them to attach to the end of the utterance, either to the last TBU or to the last stressed syllable. In some cases they attach to both ends, as in Japanese (Pierrehumbert and Beckman 1988). Another possibility is that the entire utterance may be affected, by moving all the tones up a notch in pitch. This is attested in Dangme (Kwa; Kropp Dagubu 1986), where all tones are raised throughout to show a Yes/No question, and it also seems to be quite common in languages with large tonal inventories, such as Mandarin (Chao 1933, 1968).

Although the most common tonal syntactic morphemes are those associated with complete sentences forming single utterances, we also find cases in which they are used to single out particular syntactic constructions that are embedded sentence-internally and are therefore usually smaller than the full utterance.

In many African languages, the associative construction (a sort of possessive) is conveyed by means of a tonal affix: these data come from Igbo (Williamson 1986), where the affix is a H tone which links to the left:

(21)   àgbà   ènwè   →   àgbá ènwè   'jaw of monkey'
       L   L + H + L L

In Burmese, the nominal modifier marker is tonal (Bernot 1979). Clause-final particles, like the realis verb marker /tɛ/ in (22), have unmarked tone in non-modifying position, as in (a), but acquire a creaky tone in modifying position, as in (b). The added tone is shown by an acute accent following the particle; I do not show the voicing of /t/ to [d] that happens after vowel-final syllables.

(22)   a. sɛɴ   `θi   ne   tɛ   'She is covered in diamonds'
       b. sɛɴ   `θi   ne   tɛˊ   θɘ̀mi   'a girl covered in diamonds'
          diamond produce AUX PART girl

In Yoruba, subject noun phrases are marked with a H tone clitic. Akinlabi and Liberman (2000a) suggest that syntactically it is a sort of auxiliary, and it cliticizes to the preceding NP host. It is only found on NPs followed by a VP:

(23)   Ø + H → H   ọmọ lọ   →   ọmọ́ lọ   'The child went'
       L + H → LH   ọkọ̀ lọ   →   ọkǒ lọ   'The car went'
       H + H → H   adé lọ   →   adé lọ   'Ade went'

It is extremely common to find tone used inflectionally, to mark case, definiteness, or referentiality (see Blanchon (1998) on Kongo), and of course tense and aspect all over Bantu. An interesting example can be found in Olusamia (Bantu; Poletto 1998). This language has no tonal contrast in verb roots, but H tone is used in combination with segmental affixes to convey a collection of tense/aspect/modality distinctions. It is the positioning of the H that varies, and it may appear on any of the first three moras of the verb stem, as shown in (24a–c), where the left edge of the stem is marked by '['. From its host mora, it may or may not spread – contrast the first two examples in (24b). See Poletto for an OT account of these facts.

(24)   a. [μ́   xu[déexere   'we will not cook (today)'
       b. [μμ́   ota[deéxa   'you should not cook'
                    n[deéxá   'I am cooking' (constructed by analogy)
                    ndaxá[deéxá   'I have cooked'
       c. [μμμ́   oná[deexá   'you will cook'
                    oxú[deexá   'to cook'
                    oxú[deexáná   'to cook each other'
                    oxú[deexéráná   'to cook for each other'
                    muta[deexérana   'you should not cook for each other'

The way in which these various tones arrive at their proper positions, be it the attachment to the edges of phrases, an overlay on the entire phrase, or positioning on specific moras, poses some interesting puzzles in OT. It is useful to distinguish three cases:

(25)   (1) Tones whose positioning can be attributed to the general word-level tonology of the language;

    (2) tones whose positioning can be attributed to the general phrase-level tonology of the language;

    (3) tones whose positioning depends on the choice of one particular syntactic feature or combination of features.

The first case has been dealt with in chapter four, and will also be the topic of extensive discussion in chapters six to eight. A major influence on positioning is alignment constraints, but I will not address it further here.

The second case, exemplified by Cantonese final tonal particles, is the phrasal counterpart of the regular word-internal cases, and the tones can presumably be positioned by alignment, either with edges or with stressed syllables or both.

The third case is exemplified by Olusamia, in (24). The different tense/aspect/modality semantics each supply a H tone, but whether this tone appears on the first, second or third moras is apparently a property of the morpho-syntax. General alignment constraints could pick out the first mora, and perhaps the second (by NON-INITIALITY), but the constraint ranking would have to differ for each construction, rather as suggested for three different types of reduplication in Mandarin. For example, for the data in (24a), with H tone on the stem-initial mora, ALIGN-L >> NON-INITIALITY. For the data in (24b), with H tone on the pen-initial mora, NON-INITIALITY >> ALIGN-L. Presumably the lexicon would have to provide a constraint ranking as part of the lexical entry for the morphemes in question. The case in (24c), with high tone on the third mora, is more complex, needing reference to both NON-INITIALITY and the head of an iambic foot: [μ (μμ́). The alternative to lexicalized constraint rankings is for the lexical entry to state directly which mora the H tone must attach to, in which case it would, rather surprisingly, have to count at least to three!

In this section we have seen examples of tonal morphemes at the phrasal level. We now move on to less direct interactions between syntax and phonology in which syntax contributes to defining the domains for tonal processes.

5.2.3 Syntactically influenced tonal domains

5.2.3.1 How are domains determined?

Tone sandhi (tone rules that apply across word boundaries) often take place between not just any two words, but only between words that are in the same 'domain'. The domain is usually taken to be prosodic, for example a phonological phrase, but this prosodic phrasing may be at least partly syntactically defined, so that indirectly the syntax conditions the tonal rule. This mediation via the prosody is a more limited theory of syntax–phonology interaction than one in which the full array of syntactic information is available directly to the phonology. It is more limited in at least two ways. First, once the prosodic structure is in place it cannot change to suit different phonological rules. One single prosodic structure must be able to deal with all types of phonological phenomena, be they stress-related, tonal, or segmental. Second, most researchers would claim that only certain types of syntactic information can be passed on to the prosody, perhaps only the placement of X_0 and XP boundaries. In a theory in which syntax influences only prosody, this restriction will apply via the prosody to all phonological phenomena. In a theory in which syntax directly influences phonological processes, different processes could in principle access different types of syntactic information. The issue is still very much under review. For discussion, see various papers in Inkelas and Zec 1990, especially Hayes.

Assuming for now that all the syntax can do is influence prosodic structure, and that this in turn then provides domains for phonological rules, we need to know what we mean by prosodic structure. A common view is that utterances are organized into a hierarchy of prosodic categories that looks something like (26); the term utterance subsumes not only full sentences, but also utterances composed of grammatical fragments or even single words.

(26)

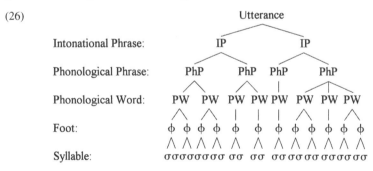

By the Strict Layer Hypothesis (Selkirk 1984, Nespor and Vogel 1986), a larger category is strictly composed of one or more of the next category down. Although this hypothesis is no longer an article of faith to all linguists, most phonologists still take it as a working hypothesis, at least in the form of a universal but violable OT constraint. If it is true, one particularly important consequence is that each prosodic word must contain at least one foot: the foot is the minimal word. Feet are preferably binary, as shown here.

Most of the literature on syntactic influence concerns its role in building the phonological phrase, an entity larger than the word but smaller than the utterance, within which tonal rules may apply, but across which they are often blocked. We shall see shortly, however, that there are some problems in equating tonal domains with the phonological phrase.

Before looking at tonal cases in detail, let us look at how syntax can influence prosodic phrasing. In general, work in this area uses a theory of syntax without functional categories, and where these *are* included they are usually stated to have no prosodic effects. I shall largely follow this custom and ignore them in this chapter. One might expect that there would be an isomorphy between syntactic and prosodic phrasing, so that, for example, each NP was a phonological phrase, and so on. The reality is more interesting, as discovered by Selkirk (1986). It turns out that only one edge of the syntactic phrase usually matters, and which edge is used is language-variable. For example, consider two Chinese languages, Shanghai (Selkirk and Shen 1990) and Xiamen (also called Taiwanese or Southern Min; Chen 1987). They both build tonal domains that are syntactically influenced. In Shanghai, within a domain the first syllable is the head and keeps its tone. All other tones are deleted. In Xiamen, the last syllable is the head and keeps its tone. All other tones change to different allotones, as we shall see in section 5.2.3.2.

Both Shanghai and Xiamen have very similar syntax, with [P [NP]] prepositional phrases, and [V [NP]] verb phrases, like English. This means that after the P or the V there is the left edge of an NP, in both languages. It turns out that this triggers the building of a new phonological phrase, and thus a tonal domain, in Shanghai, but it does not in Xiamen. In the data below, # marks the boundary between two tonal domains.

(27)   *V-NP*
         Taiwanese: One tonal domain
                 [pang]$_V$ $_{NP}$[hong-ts'e]   'fly kite'
                 fly   kite

         Shanghai: Two tonal domains
                 [taN]$_V$ # $_{NP}$['niN]   'hit people'
                 hit   people

These facts suggest that left edges of XP matter in Shanghai, but not in Xiamen. Instead, right edges turn out to matter in Xiamen. Very often, of course, the two coincide. In both languages subjects precede verbs, so we have the structure [NP][VP]. The subject–verb boundary has both a right edge and a left edge, and sure enough it begins a new tonal domain in both languages, as shown in (28).

(28)   *NP-VP: Separate tonal domains in both languages*
        Taiwanese: [tsit   e   gin-a]$_{NP}$ # $_{VP}$[k'un-lat tak-ts'eq]
                    This CL boy   diligent study   'This boy studies hard'

        Shanghai: [lisz]$_{NP}$ # $_{VP}$['zaw # poqtsiɴ tsou]   'Lisi walks towards Beijing'
                    LiSi   towards Beijing walk

In some languages, the phrasing seems to be highly variable, with more than one option available depending on such matters as focus, speed of speech, and style of speech. In Mandarin there are often several different acceptable phrasings, as shown by the operation of third-tone sandhi rules (see below, section 5.2.3.3). In Chichewa (Kanerva 1990), a simple sentence with a verb, object, and instrumental phrase has three possible phrasings, with focus being the additional significant factor. Here are the three possibilities, plus a fourth that is not acceptable.

(29)   a. (Anaményá nyumbá ndí mwáála)   'He hit the house with a rock'
           pro-hit   the house with a rock

        b. (Anaményá nyumbá) (ndí mwáála)

        c. (Anaményá) (nyumbá) (ndí mwáála)

        d. *(Anaményá)(nyumbá ndí mwáála)

These are appropriate answers to the following questions, with (30a–c) corresponding to (29a–c) above:

(30)   a. What did he do?/What did he hit the house with?

        b. What did he hit with the rock?

        c. What did he do to the house with the rock?

The basic generalization is that a focussed constituent ends a phonological phrase. In the answer to (30a), either nothing is focussed or the last word *rock* is focussed, so only one domain is used. In (30b), *house* is focussed, so two domains are needed. In (30c), *hit* is focussed, so the verb must be its own domain, and it turns out that post-focal constituents must also each form their own domain, so we get (29c) and not (29d).

Although in many cases simple algorithms do a good job of defining prosodic phrases that can in turn be used to control tonal domains, there are other cases that do not succumb to this treatment. In Kimatuumbi (Odden 1990b), for example, a H tone is placed on the final word of an XP (Odden uses X'') that is followed by a sister XP, both of which are dominated by an XP. This configuration includes the end of a subject NP before its sister VP, and the end of all but the last of a string of conjoined NPs. It excludes an NP that precedes an adjunct clause, since the adjunct is not the sister of the NP. For example, no H is inserted on the NP Mamboondo in the sentence below, because the following XP is not its sister:

(31)   [naamwéni Mamboondo [[[paáapangité kaási]$_{VP}$]$_S$]$_{AP}$]$_{VP}$
        I-him-saw M.   when-I-did work
        I saw Mamboondo when I worked

If we assume that the H tone is placed at the edge of some prosodic phrase, defined by the right edge of XP, we still have to explain the fact that it only defines a phrase edge if another *sister* XP follows. Such examples remain a challenge for constrained models of syntax–phonology interaction. The reader is referred to the extensive literature for discussion of these interesting issues. See particularly the papers in *Phonology Yearbook* 4, Inkelas and Zec 1990, and Kager and Zonneveld 1999.

We have seen that tonal processes may be corralled by syntactically influenced domains. We now turn to examples of the types of changes that display these effects. I shall distinguish four types. Firstly, there are tonal changes that depend on whether something is or is not at the edge of a domain. Secondly, there are changes that apply between syllables if and only if the two syllables are domain partners. Thirdly, there are boundary tones inserted at the edges of domains. Fourthly, downstep may apply only within a domain. I take each of these in turn.

5.2.3.2   Rules that depend on whether something is at a phrase edge or not

Many Chinese languages allow underlying tones to surface only at the edge of a domain. All other syllables either lose their tones (as in Shanghai) or use a different allotone (as in Taiwanese). The syllable that retains its tone is usually taken to be the head of the domain, and languages vary as to whether the domains are head-final or head-initial. Consider the Min dialect Taiwanese, which has a much-discussed chainshift of tonal changes known as the famous Min tone circle (Chen 2000):

(32)   *Taiwanese tonal changes: Min tone circle*

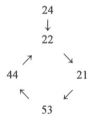

In final position, on sonorant-final syllables, there are five tones. In non-final position each underlying tone changes as shown by the arrows, so that, for example, a syllable which is /24/ becomes [22] non-finally. There is some neutralization, so that only four tones are found non-finally. Every morpheme (= syllable) has two tones, one in final position and one in non-final position. These changes are very difficult to state in any formal way. There have been many attempts over the years, particularly Wang 1967, Yip 1980a, Kirchner 1996, and Moreton 1999, but the chainshifting nature of the pattern, and especially its circular nature, remain very problematic. In chapter eight some similar facts in Chaoyang are given an OT treatment, and the reader is referred there for further discussion. Our focus here is on the domain within which the changes take place.

The syntax and the phonological phrasing are not isomorphic. In the following sentence, the domain boundaries are marked by #. The subject NP is its own domain, but the VP breaks into two domains, and the break comes half-way through the sentential complement, after 'parrot'.

(33) $_{NP}$[lao tsim-a-po]$_{NP}$ #$_{PredP}$ [m $_{VP}$[siong-sin $_S$[$_{NP}$[ying-ko]$_{NP}$
        old lady   not believe   parrot
        #$_{PredP}$ [e $_{VP}$[kong-we]$_{VP}$]$_{PredP}$] $_S$]$_{VP}$]$_{PredP}$ #
             can talk
        'The old lady doesn't believe the parrot can talk'

The syllables just before # – *po, ko, we* – bear their original citation tones. All others have the changed sandhi tones. Chen 1987, following Selkirk 1986, proposes that domains are constructed by the following algorithm:

(34)   Mark the right edge of every (non-adjunct) XP with #.

All lexical XPs behave the same in this regard: the domain-construction algorithm ignores the differences between NP, VP, AP, and PP. Other than syntactic phrasing, it seems that the only information that passed from the syntax to the phonology is this rather messy 'non-adjunct' requirement. In later work, Lin (1994) shows that a more elegant and precise statement of the condition that Chen formulates as 'if not an adjunct' can be had in terms of lexical government: the right edge of any XP that is not lexically governed ends a tone group. This formulation has the advantage that it appears necessary for phrasing in other languages, especially Papago (see Truckenbrodt 1999).

Exactly what these tone groups are in terms of the prosodic hierarchy is controversial. Being larger than the Phonological Word, the most obvious candidate is the Phonological Phrase. However, Chen (1987) says that they may cross-cut Intonational Phrases, and thus cannot be identified with the phonological phrase, since the Strict Layer Hypothesis says that phonological phrases are strictly contained within intonational phrases. For example, the sentence in (33) above may be divided intonationally after *siong-sin* 'believe', and the tone sandhi facts remain unchanged. *siong-sin* is then final in the IP, but has a non-final sandhi tone, showing that it is not final in the tonal domain.

A different type of domain-internal tonal alternation is exemplified by Shanghai. As I noted above, Shanghai marks the left edge of domains, not the right edge.

Once the domain is constructed, Shanghai simply erases all except the head tone, and this head tone then spreads out over the rest of the domain. For details, see chapter eight. Note particularly that in addition to the syntax, binary rhythmic considerations play a major role in Shanghai sandhi, as discussed in connection with compounds in section 5.1.3 above. Lastly, let me note that it may not be chance that where the left edge of the syntax determines the domains, it is the left-most syllable of the domain that keeps its tone, and is arguably the head of that prosodic phrase. For right-edge domains, the reverse is the case.

For my next example of a process specific to a domain edge, I turn to Kikamba (Bantu; Odden and Roberts-Kohno 1999). Kikamba has a super-low tone, SL, which can only surface at the ends of phrases, where it contrasts with plain low. It is found on nouns in isolation (35a), and on nouns that are final in their own NP (35b) even though they are not sentence final, but not on nouns that are followed by modifiers within the NP (35c). SL tone is shown here with a grave accent.

(35)   a. kalolò   'little leg'
          andò   'people'

       b. andò némábálókilê 'people fell'

       c. kalolo ká-ángé   'another leg'
          kalolo káatólékilé 'leg that broke'

Odden and Roberts-Kohno give an OT analysis of these facts, which I have slightly modified here to bring it into line with the constraint set used in this book. First, note that in Kikamba the right edge of every XP is the right edge of a phonological phrase. We now need four constraints, the first of which requires any SL tone to be at the right edge of a phonological phrase; this dominates three faithfulness constraints, and forces deletion of SLs that are not at the right edge.

(36)   Align-R (SL, PhPh) >> *Disassoc, *Assoc >> Max-T

If a SL tone is not right-aligned, it cannot be moved or spread because of the constraints on deleting and adding association lines, so in order to satisfy Align-R it will be deleted, in violation of lowest-ranked Max-T.

One last phenomenon in Kikamba is worthy of our attention. All assertive verbs (affirmative, main clause verbs) end in a SL tone, either on its own or as the second half of a fall. This SL does not necessarily show up on the verb itself, however. Instead it shifts to the end of any following complement; the SL is underlined:

(37)   a. nétó.otálelà   'we are counting for'

       b. nétó.otálela maiò   'we are counting bananas for'
          nénénaatálie moɛmà namwɛɛndé 'I counted Moema and Mwende'

It can shift over an arbitrarily long string of words until it comes to rest on the end of the first phrasal complement, no matter how long that may be. Odden and Roberts-Kohno propose that in addition to ALIGN-R(SL, PHPH) there is a constraint aligning the SL with the verb, ALIGN-R(SL,VERB), and that ALIGN-R(SL, PHPH) >> ALIGN-R (SL,V). This second constraint will ensure that the SL shifts no further to the right than to the first PHPH boundary after the verb.

5.2.3.3   Rules that apply between syllables in the same domain

We frequently encounter cases where tonal changes take place in some context, but where the context must be contained within some domain. I begin with a rather extended look at the famous Mandarin third-tone sandhi rule, and follow this with briefer looks at two other cases.

Mandarin takes a sequence of two low tones ('third tones') and turns the first one into a high rising tone ('second tone'). This is usually attributed to an OCP-driven avoidance of low sequences. However, this only happens if the two low tones are in the same domain. The domains are largely prosodic, with a strong preference for binary units, but syntax still intervenes. For example, the three sentences (38), (39), and (40) are each composed entirely of underlyingly low-toned syllables, and in each case some of these undergo sandhi, shown here by 's'. Which syllables undergo sandhi is determined by the syntax (examples from Chen 2000). L, H denote unaltered underlying tones. Square brackets show the morphosyntactic structure, and parentheses enclose tonal domains. Other phrasings are also possible, depending on such things as focus, speech rate and style, but these are the unmarked phrasings at normal speed.

(38)   which kind   wine   good
        [[nei   zhong] jiu]   hao   'Which kind of wine is better?'
        (s   L)   (s   L)

(39)   paper tiger   run
        [zhi   [lao-hu]] pao   'The paper tiger is running'
        (L   s   s   L)

(40)   I   think buy book
        wo xiang [mai shu]   'I plan to buy books'
        (s   L)   (L   H)

Note especially that in the last example adjacent low third tones survive unchanged, because they are in different domains. It is clear that the domains are not isomorphic with the syntax. For example, in (38) the prosodic tonal domain bracketing, shown by (), has (jiu hao) as one domain, and yet they are not a syntactic constituent. This interaction between prosodic and morphosyntactic structure has been the object of extensive study, which merits a closer look.

The phrasing is determined by two things: the syntax and a preference for binary constituents. The account that follows is substantially that of Chen 2000, with minor changes, and this is in turn largely an OT formalization of Shih 1986, 1997. Chen notes that Mandarin has a very strong preference for words to be at least two syllables long. Cross-linguistically this is a common situation, and is usually attributed to a minimal word effect in which prosodic words should contain at least one prosodic foot, and in which prosodic feet prefer to be binary.

Consider the following strings of the number 'five', *wu21*, in which there is no syntactic or morphological structure to muddy the prosodic waters. Notice that although each syllable is underlyingly L – and thus all but the last precede another L and might be expected to change to LH – something more interesting goes on in longer strings: the strings are divided into shorter units, shown with parentheses, and sandhi takes place only within those units.

(41)   wu wu   (s L)
        wu wu wu   (s s L)
        wu wu wu wu   (s L)(s L)
        wu wu wu wu wu   (s L) (s s L)

Chen calls these units Minimal Rhythmic Units (MRUs), and I will use his term here to avoid a discussion of whether they are in fact feet or phonological phrases or some other sort of beast. Clearly there is a preference for MRUs to be two to three syllables long. Longer sequences are subdivided into smaller chunks, but no chunk is ever monosyllabic: (wu wu)(wu) is not a possible grouping. He posits two constraints, called here BinMin and BinMax; BinMin is undominated.

(42)   BinMin   MRUs are at least binary.
        BinMax   MRUs are at most binary.

Chen also points out that MRUs stack up to the left: $(\sigma \sigma)(\sigma \sigma \sigma)$ is preferred to $(\sigma \sigma \sigma)(\sigma \sigma)$ because although in both candidates the first MRU is at the left edge, the second MRU is further left in $(\sigma \sigma)(\sigma \sigma \sigma)$. We may posit a constraint Align-L(MRU, PPh).

The picture gets more complicated and more interesting when one examines strings with syntactic structure. To make the data easier to scan quickly, I will use 's' for 'sandhi' for syllables that change to LH, and those that remain unchanged are shown by L as before. In all examples each syllable is underlyingly L.

(43)   a. strike-down governor
           [da-dao] [sheng-zhang]   'Down with the governor!'
           (s   L) (s   L)

b. which kind wine good
  [[nei zhong] jiu] hao   'Which kind of wine is better?'
  (s   L) (s   L)

c. gou [yao [xiao-mei]]   'The dog bit Xiaomei'
  (s L) (s   L)

d. zhi-[lao-hu]] pao   'The paper tiger is running'
  (L s   s   L)

e. look-for cowardly devil
  zhao [[dan-xiao] gui]   'Look for the coward'
  (L   s   s L)

In (43d–e) there are no binary prosodic constituents, and the reason is simple: morphemes that are sisters under the same terminal node, like [lao-hu] in (d) and [dan-xiao] in (e) cannot be separated into two MRUs. Chen calls such morphemes 'immediate constituents'. If they are placed in one MRU, and if monosyllabic MRUs are prohibited, then the only option is to create a single large MRU containing the entire string. I give Chen's constraint below:

(44)   NoStraddling: Immediate constituents must be in the same MRU.

This constraint is one of a family of constraints that have been proposed to govern the influence of syntax on prosody, including alignment of syntactic boundaries and prosodic boundaries (Chen 1987 on Xiamen, Selkirk and Shen 1990 on Shanghai), and, most specifically, containment constraints that block splitting an XP between two prosodic phrases, such as the Wrap-XP constraint of Truckenbrodt (1999). Tableau (45) shows how things work.

(45)

/zhao[[dan-xiao]gui]/	NoStraddling	Bin-Min	Bin-Max
☞ a. (zhao dan-xiao gui)			*
b. (zhao dan)-(xiao gui)	*!		
c. (zhao)(dan-xiao gui)		*!	
d. (zhao)(dan-xiao)(gui)		**!	

NoStraddling is an interface constraint: it allows syntax to influence phonology. Nonetheless, examples like (44b), in which the phrase [[nei-zhong] jiu] is split into two MRUs (nei-zhong)(jiu hao), show that there is not a complete match between larger syntactic constituents and MRUs. In particular, so long as immediate constituents are not split binarity takes precedence, choosing (nei-zhong)(jiu hao) over *(nei-zhong jiu)(hao).

The effects of syntax go beyond those encapsulated in the NoStraddling constraint. Consider one last bit of data:

(46)   that kind wine harmful
        [[nei zhong]jiu][you-hai]   'That kind of wine is harmful'
        (nei zhong jiu) (you-hai)

So far, we would expect the parse *(nei zhong) (jiu you-hai), since it ties with the actual winner on NoStraddling and BinMin/Max, and better satisfies the Align-L constraint. The actual parse better matches the syntax, so Chen posits a constraint Congruence, which outranks Align-L; X stands for any constituent, from a single terminal element to a phrase.

(47)   Congruence: Group X with its closest morphosyntactic mate to form an MRU.

In (46), this constraint will prefer a parse in which *jiu* is grouped with *nei zhong*, matching the syntax. The complete ranking of these constraints is NoStraddling, BinMin >> BinMax >> Congruence >> Align-L.

This is the bones of the analysis. The remaining interesting twist is that all of this machinery must be applied cyclically, and it is this that accounts for a piece of data that I have so far ignored, but which will have been bothering the alert reader! In (43d–e), a single MRU spans all four syllables, and yet the sandhi pattern is not (s s s L), as we might expect, but (L s s L). Under cyclic application, this falls out straightforwardly, since an application of sandhi on an earlier cycle removes the context for application to its left on a later cycle, as in cycle 2 below:

(48)   [zhi [lao-hu] pao]   'the paper tiger runs'
            (s   L)   1st cycle, sandhi applies
        (L   s   L)   2nd cycle: first L not in front of another L, sandhi
                             cannot apply
        (L   s   s   L)   3rd cycle: sandhi applies

Since OT in its strictest form is committed to a single stratum of 'derivation', apparently cyclic phenomena are problematic. Even though Chen ultimately argues that cyclic application is limited to the lexical level of MRU formation, and is across-the-board at the phrase level, data like these nevertheless suggest that at some level cyclicity may still be required. For OT approaches to cyclic phenomena, see Kager 1999. Before we leave Mandarin I should also note that, in addition to the sandhi outlined here, at faster and more casual speech rates sandhi may apply across MRUs, giving more than one pronunciation for many forms. I now move on to other examples of domain-bound processes.

In Kinande (Bantu; Hyman 1990), we find an example of a common domain-internal process, spreading. Phonological phrasing in Kinande is defined as follows:

(49)   Each daughter of S' or S preceding the verb constitutes a PhPh. The verb and all following material constitutes another PhPh.

We might surmise that this is an instance of the right edge of X'' defining the right edge of a phonological phrase. Be that as it may, within the PhPh H tone spreads one syllable to the left. This is the type of bounded spreading discussed in chapter four, and attributed to ALIGN-L.

(50)   e-ki-ryatu 'shoe'   e-ki-ryatú   kí-néne   'big shoe'
                               shoe   big

Between phonological phrases, spreading does not take place, as shown by the failure of the H tones on /ká/ and /á/ to spread leftwards.

(51)   o-mu-tututu#   ká-tsuba#   á-lya-w-â
         in the morning# Katsuba#   fell

When spreading happens only within a domain, the simplest explanation is that the pressure for spreading is alignment with the edge of that domain:

(52)   ALIGN-L (H, PHPH): Every H tone should be aligned with the left edge of a phonological phrase.

If a H tone is already at the edge of a PhPh, there is no reason for it to spread further. Rather than describing this as the blocking of spreading, it is thus better thought of as the absence of any pressure to spread.

A slightly different example comes from Kiyaka (Kidima 1990). In Kiyaka, tone is attracted to a following prominent syllable within the same phonological phrase. In Kidima's analysis, Kiyaka has both accented syllables and tone. Tones float and may be attracted to the accent of the *next* word, provided both are in the same phonological phrase. Contrast the following two examples: in the first complex NP, we have a single phrase and the H tone of the first word links to the accent (shown by an asterisk) of the second word. In the second example, although the lexical items are the same the syntax is different, and there the two words each form their own phrase, and the H tone stays with its host.

(53)   * *   *   *
         [beto [tusuumbidi]]   'we who bought'

           H   H
          we   bought

(54)   * *   *   *
    [beto] [tusuumbidi]   'we bought'
      | |
     H   H
    we   bought

Phonological phrasing here seems to be roughly the same as in Xiamen: the right edge of X" is the right edge of the phonological phrase.

5.2.3.4   Insertion of tone at prosodic boundaries, conditioned by syntax

It is extremely common to find rules that insert tones at the boundaries of prosodic constituents. These are not lexical tonal morphemes associated with one particular morpho-syntactic construction and its semantics, but tones marking some type of prosodic boundary. In non-tonal stress or accentual languages, this is one of the major components of intonation, but in tonal languages it happens too, and these tones may interact with the lexical tones.

Luganda (Bantu; Hyman 1990) inserts an optional boundary high tone, shown conventionally by H//, at the right edge of the IP; the H// carries a completive meaning (Hyman personal communication):

(55)   bá-gùl-à   OR   bá-gùl-á   'they buy'

In Kinande interrogatives, the intonational phrase boundary H// is obligatory, and can override a lexical L, so that the word for 'bush' /e-kí-sákà/ becomes [è-kí-sáká/ at the end of a question. In other cases, a boundary L// is inserted at the end of IP, to mark a completed assertion. This L// does not cause a H to delete, but either displaces it one syllable over, or if there is no suitable displacement site combines with it to form a falling contour. To demonstrate this, we first need to introduce one other fact about Kinande phrasal phonology.

Kinande also inserts an obligatory phrase boundary H, shown conventionally by H%, onto toneless moras at the end of a PhPh. In the example below the final vowels of *kyo* and *langir-a* are toneless, and the surface H on each is the boundary H%. This phrasing is determined by the syntax, as given earlier.

(56)   [è-kì-ryàtù è-kyó] [tù-ká-làngìr-á]   [kì-kâ-w-â]
     shoe   that   we see   is falling

Now note that the end of an IP is also of course always the end of a PhPh as well. Consider a completed assertion. The final mora will get a H% from the PhPh, and a L// from the IP, in that order, since the PhPh is inside the IP. The effect is that the inner H% is pushed leftwards onto the penultimate mora. If the penultimate mora has a lexical tone of its own, this will be shifted left to make room for the boundary tone.

(57)   e -ki-ryátù   'shoe'
        H% L//

If there is no room for the displaced tones, the H% and the L// form a final fall, as shown on the last syllable of *kì-ryâ* before a PhPh H% followed by an IP L//, where the penultimate syllable already has a low tone and no room to host any boundary tones that could have been displaced from the final syllable (Hyman 1990: 114).

5.2.3.5 Prosodic phrases as domain of downstep

Most literature on downstep says that tones are downstepped across the utterance. However, it seems likely that this is an oversimplification. In the few cases where the issue is addressed, the domain may be smaller than the entire utterance. In Chichewa (Kanerva 1990), the intonational phrase is the domain of downstep. This is true even if the intonational phrases are not separated by a pause. Within the IP, a H tone following a L tone has a lower pitch than the Hs preceding the L. This chain is broken at the IP boundary, and the first H of the new IP is higher than any lowered Hs at the end of the previous IP. IPs are of course composed of PhPhs, which are themselves the domains of two rules of local H tone doubling, but Kanerva argues that no single syntactic algorithm uniquely determines the phrasing at this level, as mentioned in section 5.2.3.1 above.

5.3   Summary

This brief chapter has drawn our attention to the rather obvious fact that tonal phonology does not take place in a vacuum, but is frequently affected by the morphology and syntax of the language. As a result, the tonal output may provide the listener with cues that signal, directly or indirectly, such things as phrase boundaries, compound structure, or syntactic category, as well as grammatical information such as tense or mood and of course lexical information!

6

African languages

6.1 Classification

The languages of Africa display an astonishing variety of complex tone systems, and a correspondingly large body of literature has grown up in an attempt to understand them. Together with East Asia, Africa has probably the highest ratio of tonal to non-tonal languages, with tonal languages found in just about every language family with the exception of Semitic and Berber. In particular, the Niger-Congo family, which subsumes most of the sub-Saharan languages, including the Bantu group, is almost entirely tonal (or occasionally accentual). Table 6.1, based largely on Bendor-Samuel 1989, shows the affiliation of the major tonal languages of Africa, including all those discussed in this chapter.

6.2 Common or striking characteristics of African tone languages

By most estimates Africa contains well over a thousand languages, with the Niger-Congo group alone having more than 900; among the Bantu languages, at least fifteen are spoken by more than three million people, and at least six are spoken by more than five million. As one might expect in such a huge group of languages covering such an enormous geographical area, there is great diversity in their tonal systems. Nonetheless, one can identify some characteristics that are particularly widespread in Africa, and much less common in Asia or Central America, which we shall look at in later chapters.

The theoretical literature on tone has been dominated by studies of African languages, and as a result an understanding of African systems is a foundation for a study of other areas from a theoretical perspective. An excellent summary can be found in Odden 1995. The machinery developed on the basis of African data can be tested on the data from other areas, and, interestingly, different though these systems often are superficially, the same machinery by and large does a good job of characterizing them as well. In some ways this is not surprising, since the African languages

Table 6.1. *Classification of modern African languages (roughly following Bendor-Samuel 1989)*

Afro-Asiatic	Chadic		Bade, Hausa, Margi, Ngizim
	Cushitic		Oromo, Somali
	Berber		
	Semitic (non-tonal)		Arabic, Hebrew
Nilo-Saharan	Nilotic		Alur, Dinka, Kalenjin, Luo, Nuer, Shilluk
	Other		Kunama
Khoisan			Hadza, Nama, !Xóõ, !Xũ, Juǀhoansi
Niger-Kordofanian	Kordofanian		

Niger-Congo	Atlantic			Fulani (=Fula), Temne, Wolof
	Mande			Bambara, Dan, Mandinka, Mende, Vai, Kono
	Gur (Voltaic)			Dagaare, Konni Lama, Moore, Mossi, Supyire, Bimoba
	Kwa			Akan (Asante, Twi, Fante), Ewe, Krachi
	Adamawa Eastern			Suma (Gbaya)
	Kru			Kru, Grebo, Guere
	Defoid			Yoruba
	Edoid			Engenni
	Igboid			Igbo
	Nupoid			Nupe, Gwari (Gbari)
	Idomoid			Yala (Ikom), Igede
	Benue-Congo	Cross-River	Delta-Cross Bendi	Efik, Gokana, Ibibio
		Bantoid	Northern	Mambila
			Southern, non-Bantu	Tiv, Mbe, Mbam, Grassfields[a] (Ngamambo, Dschang-Bamileke, Bafut)
			(Narrow) Bantu	See next section of the table

Table 6.1. *(Continued)*

(Narrow) Bantu[b]	Bemba M42, Chichewa N31B, Chiluba L31, Chilungu M14, Ciyao P21, Chizigula G31, Digo E73, Kikuyu E51, Kimatuumbi P13, Kinande D42, Kishambaa G23, Luganda E15, Nguni (Zulu S42, Xhosa S43), Rwanda D61, Kinyarwanda D62, Ruwund K23, Shona S13, Sukuma F21, Swahili G42, Tembo, J57.

[a] Grassfields languages are sometimes called 'Grassfields Bantu', but they must be distinguished from the true Bantu languages, known as 'Narrow' Bantu.
[b] Guthrie (1967–71): Numbers refer to Guthrie's classification, and are taken from the CBOLD page at the University of California, Berkeley website: www.linguistics.berkeley.edu/CBOLD. Note also that I have for the most part followed the traditional practice in retaining the prefixes 'Chi-', 'Ki-', on language names to permit easier cross-reference to the literature. Thus Chizigula is the same as the more recent Zigula, Chiyao is the same as Yao or Ciyao, Kinande is the same as Nande, and so on.

turn out to display some of the most complex tonal phonologies we know of, so any theoretical framework that is up to the task of dealing with them has a good chance of also coping with 'simpler' systems. The one area in which Africa is less rich appears to be in tonal inventories, with both Asia and the Americas having many languages that offer larger arrays of both level and contour tones.

I begin by listing some issues of interest that one encounters when studying tone in African languages.

(1) The most striking property of African tone is its mobility. In the earlier survey chapters we have, time and time again, seen tone that starts life on one morpheme, but either spreads to a chain of adjacent morphemes or surfaces on a different morpheme altogether. This property is closely tied to the fact that many of these languages have complex, largely agglutinative, morphology. This is especially true of Bantu, and has given rise to a huge literature. Tonal association is often controlled not by lexical association to a TBU, but by general phonological constraints such as alignment with word edges, prominent syllables, or phrasal boundaries, or by the OCP in its most common African incarnation known as Meeussen's Rule. Tonal rules of flop, spreading, deletion, and even metathesis abound, and in combination give rise to extraordinarily rich tonal phonologies that have stretched the ingenuities of phonologists to their limits. The mobility of tones in turn has given rise to systems that are often described as more accentual rather than truly tonal, with sparse distribution of H tones, and where the positioning of H is contrastive.

(2) The second factor that blurs the distinction between systems called 'tonal' and systems called 'accentual', and which makes the development of an 'accentual' system likely, is that many languages have only a two-way contrast in tone: phonetically high versus low, but phonologically often H tone versus the absence of tone. Only the H tone is 'active' in such systems, and L is apparently supplied at the end of the phonology to supply any still toneless syllable with a tonal specification. Some languages have L marked and H as default (Ruwund, Chiluba, Tembo).

(3) Nonetheless, richer tonal inventories are found in Africa. Some languages do have a three-, four-, or even five-level contrast, although the last two are quite rare. Contour tones are also fairly rare and are often limited to the ends of words or to heavy syllables. In many cases it can be clearly shown that contours are composed of two level tones, but in other cases we see contour tones that could be primes, not sequences. Some languages with underlying level tones even seem to show a preference for contours over levels in the output.

(4) The tone bearing unit, or TBU, varies from language to language. It may be the mora in some languages, but the syllable in others. Often the facts are compatible with either view, most obviously if all syllables are mono-moraic.

(5) Downdrift (the lowering of a H tone after a L tone) and downstep (the lowering of H in the absence of an overt L tone, but usually caused by a floating L) are extremely common. Upstep is also found. Because these phenomena are so prevalent in African languages I will devote a lot of attention to their analysis.

(6) The most frequent form of interaction between tone and laryngeal features in African languages is the presence of 'depressor' consonants. This term describes a subset of consonants, usually voiced, which lower the tone of neighbouring high tones, and may also block high spreading across them. This is a departure from the usual inertness of consonants in tonal systems, and therefore of some interest here.

(7) Finally, we will look at polarity. This term describes affixes whose tone is the opposite of that of the root, and the phenomenon is quite common in this region.

I will take each of these in turn in the following sections.

6.2.1 Tonal mobility

As I observed earlier, the most striking property of African tone is its mobility. When morphemes are concatenated into words or even phrases, the tones of one morpheme may migrate some distance from their point of origin. We have seen numerous examples of this behaviour in African languages in earlier chapters, and by now the reader should have a good sense of the kinds of constraints that cause these changes. Just to refresh your memory, movement and/or spreading may be caused by attraction to particular strong positions, such as domain heads or domain edges, by the OCP or simply by the need to provide each syllable with its own tone. Movement may be unbounded or constrained by a locality require-ment, in which case it is usually binary, but occasionally ternary. Deletion may be caused by the OCP, by a shortage of TBUs, or by a loss of head status, which re-duces the permissible tonal specifications and thus allows markedness to exert its influence. Insertion may be caused by the need for tones in prominent positions, by the OCP, or just by SPECIFY. These do not exhaust the possibilities, but they cover the major ones. I have picked two languages to illustrate some of the possi-bilities here, but I also refer you back to the discussion of Chilungu, Chizigula, Kikuyu, Sukuma, and Shona in chapter four.

6.2.1.1 Digo

Consider these data from Digo (Bantu; Kisseberth 1984); in chapter four I touched on Digo, and there I used a simplified version of the data for expository reasons, following Goldsmith 1990. Here I revert to the more complex data in the original source. Bantu verbs can have a rich variety of prefixes on the root includ-ing, most importantly, the subject marker, tense marker, and (optional) object marker in that order. This complex may also be preceded by other prefixes and various pro-clitics. In Digo the object marker is particularly closely attached to the verb root, so that Kisseberth argues for a macrostem constituent containing [object marker-root-terminal vowel]. The first set of data are infinitives, with the structure [ku-verb root-terminal vowel].

(1)   *Toneless verbs*   *High-tone verbs*
       ku-rim-a   'to cultivate'   ku-arŭk-â   'to begin'
       ku-ambir-a   'to tell'   ku-furukŭt-â   'to move restlessly'
       ku-gandamiz-a   'to press'   ku-fukíz-a   'to apply heat'

The low-toned verbs in the first column show no H anywhere. In the second col-umn, we see two types of H-toned verbs. If the root ends in a voiceless consonant (or voiced sonorant), as in the first two examples, we get a sequence of rising-falling over the last two syllables. If the root ends in a voiced obstruent, as in the last example, we get a high tone on the penultimate vowel. I will assume that in both cases a H tone appears on the final binary foot. If this foot has a voiceless consonant in the middle, the H surfaces centred on the foot, so to speak, giving a rise on the first part of the foot and a fall on the second part. If the foot has a voiced obstruent consonant, on the other hand, the H tone is blocked from straddling it, and must stay on the penult syllable only. The voiced obstruent is here seen exer-cising the blocking effect common to depressor consonants; we will return to this below. In any case, whether this is exactly the right way to view things does not affect the central point at issue here: both these surface forms involve a H tone located near the end of the word.

Now it turns out that *any* underlying form with a H tone realizes it on the last two syllables in the same way, and it does not matter whether the H originates on the root, as above, or on an object-prefix, as in (2b), or on a subject prefix, as in (2c). The H tone moves away from its source (underlined) several syllables to the right to the final foot. The following data show only toneless roots.

(2)   a. ku-vugur-ir-a   'to untie for'   ku -raʙiz-a   'to insult'

        b. ku-a̲-vugur-ǐr-â   'to untie for you pl./them'   ku-a̲-raʙíz-a   'to insult you pl./them'

        c. a̲-na-vugŭr-â   'he is untying'   a̲-na-raʙíz-a   'he is insulting'

It also does not matter whether the syllables on which the H tones surface are themselves root syllables or instead those of some affix. All that matters is its position in the word. In the first example in (2b), /-ir-/ is the applicative affix with the meaning 'for/with', and the Hs show up here. A H-toned root tone may also move entirely off the root onto an affix, as in this example:

(3)   ku-bundúg-a 'to pound'   ku-bundug-ǐr-â 'to pound for/with'

Notice here another effect of the shift: the consonant internal to the final foot in the simple infinitive is a voiced obstruent, so we get a plain high on the penultimate syllable, but in the affixed form the foot internal consonant is a sonorant, so we get the rise-fall pattern.

In OT this sort of movement, common in Bantu languages, is usually handled by alignment constraints that require any H tones to line up with some prominent element, here the head foot. We can thus formulate the constraint ALIGN-R(H, HEADFT), and this will outrank any faithfulness constraints that attempt to preserve underlying affiliations.

There are two further aspects of Digo that interest us here. Consider inputs with two adjacent high tones, such as arise when a H-toned root is directly preceded by a H-toned object prefix, underlined.

(4)   ku-pu̲pǔt-â 'to beat'   ku-a̲-pu̲pǔt-â 'to beat you pl./them'

Here the object prefix has no tonal effects at all. Its H tone appears to have been deleted, and this is in fact something we see frequently in Bantu languages: in a sequence of two adjacent H tones, one deletes. In its most common form, where the second high deletes, it was dubbed Meeussen's Rule by Goldsmith (1984); it has been called Anti-Meeussen's Rule if the first of two Hs deletes, (as here). It can be seen as an instance of the OCP. The OCP was discussed at length in chapter four, and in a large number of cases we have seen that viewing the OCP as an output constraint along the lines of Myers (1997) offers a straightforward account of the facts. However, the Digo data raise a serious issue in output-based theories like OT, and one that is beyond the scope of this book to resolve. The problem is that the OCP seems to care here about the *underlying* adjacency of the tones, even though the standard alignment constraints of the language would in fact allow the Hs to surface on non-adjacent vowels. To see this, look at the second example in (4). Here the two Hs originate on the adjacent object marker and first root syllable, but the alignment constraint pulls the second H onto the final foot, so that on the surface it is no longer adjacent to the object marker. Nonetheless, it causes deletion of the first H. In a moment we will see a second problem: OCP violations seem to be possible on the surface in Digo, suggesting that the OCP cannot be very high ranked in the language.

To see this, we first need to look at cases with two non-adjacent Hs underlyingly. This arises in the case of a high-toned subject prefix, separated by a toneless object marker from a high-toned verb root. Here both Hs clearly survive, since the pattern is distinct from the pattern with a toneless subject marker, as shown in (5). Since the two Hs are non-adjacent underlyingly, and the OCP only penalizes adjacency, this is not surprising. What we find is a high plateau that begins on the first syllable of the macrostem (object-marker + verb stem), and continues to the penultimate syllable, as shown in (5a–b).

(5)   *Toneless subject marker*   *High-toned subject marker*
      a. ni-na-p̲u̲pu̠t-â   'I am beating'   a̲-na-p̲ú̲pu̠t-â   'he/she is beating'
      b. ni-na-t̲anyiríz-a 'I am driving off   a̲-na-t̲ányíríz-a   'he/she is driving off
                           predators'   predators'
      c. ni-na-v̲u̲rúg-a   'I am stirring'   a̲-ná-v̲u̲rúg-a   'he/she is stirring'

Given what we have seen earlier, this pattern appears to combine the familiar movement of one H to the final foot, just as in our earlier examples, movement of the prefixal H to the first syllable of the macrostem, and then construction of a plateau between the two Hs. This plateau is interrupted if any voiced obstruents intervene, as shown in example (5c). The details are fairly complex: see Kisseberth 1984.

Looking at these facts in OT terms, it would seem that a secondary preference for positioning a H tone is to align it with the start of the macrostem morphological constituent. We can call this ALIGN-L(H, MACROSTEM). This will be outranked by ALIGN-R(H, HEADFOOT), so a single H tone will move to the end, but a second H tone will go to the left edge of the macrostem. We saw earlier that underlyingly adjacent Hs undergo Meeussen's Rule (OCP), and further that this is a problem in an output-based theory. The problem is compounded by the fact that surface OCP violations are tolerated fine. Consider a form like

/a̱-ka-[i̱giz-a]/ > [a-ka-íɡíz-a], with a H subject prefix and a trisyllabic macrostem. On the surface, the H that is initial in the macrostem, shown by the square brackets, is adjacent to the H that is on the final foot, and yet they both survive. One possible way out is to suggest that the two Hs have in fact fused into one, and thus there is no surface OCP violation. In support of this idea, Myers (personal communication) points out that there is no downstep between the two surface highs, as one might have expected if they were indeed two separate H tones. This is an interesting challenge to OT, or for that matter to the ambitious reader!

To complete this section, we need an explanation for the plateau between the two surface Hs. If no plateau were formed, the pitch contour would have a dip. Let us suppose that Digo abhors such dips or troughs, and write a constraint *Trough. If this is ranked below the various alignment constraints so that it does not block tone mobility, but above *Associate, then a plateau can be formed. This plateau can be of any length, so the spreading is unbounded.

Exercise 1.   We have developed the following grammar. AlignR(H, Head-Foot) >> Align-L(H, Macrostem) >> *Trough >> *Associate. Test it on these inputs: /ku-[pu̱put-a]/ > [ku-[pupǔt-â]], and /a̱-na-[a-pu̱put-a]/ > [a-na-[ápúpút-â]], where the underlined tones have underlyingly linked H tones, and the square brackets in the inputs mark the macrostem. Do you see problems in addition to the OCP issues raised earlier? Where do the various faithfulness constraints fit in? Do you wish to add to it or amend it? (The answer to this and all other exercises can be found at the end of the appropriate chapter.)

This fairly extended example is designed to remind the reader of the extreme tonal mobility of Bantu languages. It has also introduced the way in which consonants can interfere with tonal processes, a topic to which we will return in section 6.2.5. I now move on to another illustration of mobility, this time from a language in which (1) tonal melodies are used as markers of different verb forms and (2) spreading is bounded, not unbounded.

6.2.1.2 Edge-in association in N. Karanga

N. Karanga is a dialect of Shona, a Bantu language spoken in Zimbabwe. The analysis in its essentials is based on Hewitt and Prince 1989. As in Digo, roots and affixes are H-toned [ku-téng-a] 'to buy' or toneless [ku-bik-a] 'to cook'. The verb root can be followed by a range of suffixes conveying such things as causative, reciprocal, intensive, and so on, allowing for the formation of very long words. Focussing on the portion of the verb usually called the stem, consisting of the root plus suffixes plus the terminal vowel, Karanga has two verb forms known as the Assertive and the Non-assertive which differ in their tonal patterns. Rather than giving the data, I will give the patterns in schematic form, due to Odden (1984: 259). In (6) I give the two types of verbs (H and toneless) and the patterns on words of steadily increasing length as suffixes are added.

(6)   *H-Toned Roots*

a. Assertive	*b. Non-assertive*
H	H
H H	H L
H H H	H L H
H H H L	H H L H
H H H L L	H H H L H
H H H L L L	H H H L L H
H H H L L L L	H H H L L L H

L-Toned Roots

c. Assertive	*d. Non-assertive*
L	H
L L	L H
L L L	L H L
L L L L	L H H L
L L L L L	L H H L L
L L L L L L	L H H L L L
L L L L L L L	L H H L L L L

Clearly the assertive and non-assertive have different tonal patterns. The first observation is that the non-assertive seems to introduce its own H tone. For H-toned roots, this results in two H tones, one located at each end of the stem, and for toneless roots it results in just one H, near the beginning. In fact, whenever there is just one H – the assertive of H-toned roots and the non-assertive of toneless roots – it always surfaces at or near the start of the stem. The OT account, then, would have ALIGN-L(H, STEM) dominating ALIGN-R(H, STEM).

Exercise 2.   In principle, alignment may be assessed absolutely or gradiently. Absolute assessment assigns a single asterisk if alignment is not perfect, disregarding how far from the edge the tone is. Gradient assessment cares about degrees of violation, so one asterisk is assigned for each TBU intervening between the TBU associated to the tone, and the edge of the domain. In N. Karanga, ALIGN-L(H, STEM) and ALIGN-R(H, STEM), as stated here, would have to be non-gradiently assessed: Why? Is there any alternative?

Returning to our analysis, the second thing to notice about the N. Karanga verbal patterns is that the longest sequence of H-toned syllables is three. Hewitt and Prince suggest that this is because spreading in N. Karanga, unlike in Digo, is bounded (i.e. spreads only to the immediately adjacent syllable), and that there are two types of spreading. One spreads a root tone rightwards by one syllable, and one spreads any tone rightwards by one syllable. The combination of the two thus leads to three-syllable spans of H tone, and this can only occur if a root H tone is present. This is confirmed by the fact that toneless roots never show more than two Hs in succession. Spreading, as in my earlier analyses, can result from either alignment pressures, or from SPECIFY, and when spreading is bounded, as here, these must be kept under control by a dominating constraint LOCAL. I should note that Hewitt and Prince's analysis, in which root-spreading feeds the more general spreading, cannot translate directly into a non-derivational theory like OT. For a discussion of triplication in general, see chapter four. A final note on spreading: the normal spreading processes can be curtailed if they would bring one H into contact with a second H. In the non-assertive of H-toned roots, a buffer toneless (i.e. L) syllable is always retained between the initial H span and the final H, so the full three-syllable H sequence cannot surface until we get to words of five syllables or more [HHHLH]. This can be attributed to the OCP dominating the constraints responsible for spreading.

Thirdly, there are two types of extrametricality at work, both applying only to toneless syllables, and in particular verb forms. Extrametricality is the name for the phenomenon in which marginal constituents are ignored by the phonology. For example, trochaic foot construction may skip the final syllable in many languages, with the result that stress is antepenultimate. The extrametrical element is shown surrounded by angled brackets. In N. Karanga, in all non-assertives final toneless vowels are extrametrical. They therefore cannot undergo spreading, so we get H<L> instead of HH, and LH<L> instead of LHH. Secondly, initial toneless vowels are always extrametrical, so that low-toned verbs in the non-assertive have the H on the second syllable, not the first. In OT, the fact that only toneless vowels are extrametrical can be captured by assuming that the faithfulness constraint *DISASSOC dominates NONFINALITY and NONINITIALITY, so that underlyingly linked root H tones can remain on initial and final syllables.

This completes the discussion of N. Karanga. I now digress marginally to discuss so-called accentual systems.

6.2.1.3 Accentual systems

Many African languages are described as accentual rather than tonal (Downing forthcoming). See discussion in chapters one and two, and also Odden 1995 for a useful summary of accentual vs. tonal analyses of African languages. The distinction is a subtle one, and in fact possibly a spurious distinction. It dates back to the days when accentual systems were analysed as having underlying abstract markers, or diacritics, usually asterisks, which marked lexically specified prominent syllables. On the surface, tones were associated with these syllables, but the phonology manipulated the asterisks, not the tones, deleting, inserting, or moving them in various ways. An excellent example of such an analysis is Goldsmith's (1976) analysis of Tonga (Bantu: Zambia). Nowadays, most linguists analyse these languages as having underlying tones linked to the syllables or moras that formerly had asterisks, and the phonology directly works on the tones. A good example of this approach is Pulleyblank's 1986 re-analysis of Tonga. Under this view, accentual languages are just a subclass of tone languages, with certain characteristics. Typically, they have only one type of tonal melody, either H or HL. Morphemes may or may not have this melody, and if they do its position may be specified. Finally, it is common for an output constraint, perhaps the OCP, to eliminate all but one of these melodies. On the spectrum of tonal languages, this makes them relatively impoverished: few tonal melodies both underlyingly and at the surface, and relatively little tonal mobility because of the underlying associations. Nonetheless, they are tonal, and I will give one simple example here.

Somali (Cushitic; Hyman 1981, Banti 1988) uses tone in its nominal declensions to mark case, as in the first declension data in (7), where a H is placed on certain moras.

(7)

	Absolutive	*Genitive*	*Nominative*	*Vocative*		
	penult mora	*final mora*	*no h*	*initial mora*		
	rág	rág	rag	–	m.co.	'males'
	órgi	orgí	orgi	órgi	m.sg.	'billy-goat'
	hooyoóyin	hooyooyín	hooyooyin	hóoyooyin	m.pl.	'mothers'
	xáas	xaás	xaas	–	m.so.	'family'

We may analyse this as a H tone placed on a specified mora, perhaps plus a default L. No spreading seems to take place except, optionally, leftward within the syllable: hoóyo ~ hóóyo. One final detail: the presence of contours on bimoraic words such as [xáas] and [xaás], and the absence of contours on monomoraic words such as [rág] shows that the mora is the TBU in Somali.

I end this section with a language in which tone is not mobile, to make the point that not all African languages are typologically uniform in this or any other regard.

6.2.1.4   Tonal immobility

In Kunama (Nilo-Saharan, Eritrea; Connell *et al.* 2000), unlike in Bantu languages, tone largely stays on its own morpheme. Consider the morphologically complex word in (8): there is no evidence of tones being attracted to edges, or of one-to-one association with the word as domain. Instead, association is strictly morpheme-by-morpheme. The mora is the TBU, as will be shown in the next section.

(8)   agud-am- a- mme   waterpot-this-NV-dual
       ╱ │ │ ╱
       M   L M L

This said, there are, however, several purely tonal affixes, and certain syntactic constructions supply a tonal template. In possessor-possessee constructions there is L#MH melody across the syntactic boundary. For class one nouns, the L replaces the tone of the final morpheme of the first noun, and the MH replaces the tone of the first morpheme of the second noun. In nouns, the final vowels are both affixes.

(9)   M M L   M   M L MH M

          agud-a + ukun-a   →   agud-a ukun-a
          'waterpot'   'ear'   'handle of waterpot'

            aguda   ukuna
            ╱ ╲   │ │ ╲
            M   M L#M H L-M

6.2.2   Tone-Bearing Units: Syllable or mora

6.2.2.1   Syllable as TBU

In languages like Digo, Shona, and Chichewa there is no vowel-length distinction, and syllables tend to be open and mono-moraic, so it is often hard to tell whether the syllable or the mora is the TBU. However, when we look at other languages, it is quite clear that there is variation in this regard. In the Gur language Dagaare (Ghana; Antilla and Bodomo 1996), the syllable can be shown to be the TBU. They suggest it may be an areal characteristic. Consider these Dagaare words:

(10)   LH   bààlá   'sick person-sg.'
               yùòní   'year-sg.'
        HL   núórì   'mouth-sg.'
               páárì   'vagina-sg.'

The first syllable has a long vowel or diphthong, but the tone melody associates one-to-one left to right with syllables, disregarding the bi-moraic content of the first syllable. If the mora were the TBU, we would expect instead *[yùóní]. There is an alternative to supposing that the syllable is the TBU in languages like these. Suppose that only head moras may carry tone, or that two tautosyllabic moras must agree in tone. The same effects would be derived.

6.2.2.2   Mora as TBU

The Nilo-Saharan language Kunama (Eritrea; Connell *et al.* 2000) provides a good contrast here. Kunama has three level tones (H, M, L), three falls

(HM, ML, HL), and one rise (MH). Unlike Bantu, H, M, L are all specified, and the contours are found medially, but always on heavy syllables, whether CVV as in the first example in (11), or CVC as in the second and third examples. In final position, they are found on short vowels.

(11) gēérê   'tall (pl.)'

táĪl   'rock'

ā′kkúbê   'camels'

This distribution is exactly what we would expect if the mora is the TBU, tone associates one-to-one left-to-right, and then excess tones stack at the end. The first example below shows how contours on single moras will occur at word ends:

(12) a t a l i   'woman's name'
      | | |\
      L M H L

The second example shows how if the mora is the TBU contours can occur medially:

(13) m o   d a   [mōódā]   'quarrel'
      \\ \|
      μ μ   μ
      | | |
      MH   M

Finally, note that it is not only vocalic moras that are counted as TBUs but consonantal ones also (as in the first syllable of the word for 'camels' [ā′kkúbê]), something we have not seen so far in Bantu. Connell *et al.* observe that, although the consonant counts as a TBU, obstruents do not bear phonetic tone: all the tones of the syllable are realized on the sonorants, including vowels, nasals, and liquids. (This is of course not surprising in the case of stops, which being silent cannot manifest tone.) So in [ā′kkúbê] the mid high sequence is actually realized on [ā′]. Nonetheless, word-medially vowels only have contours when the syllable contains a closing consonant, which must therefore count as a TBU for phonological purposes. Sonorants as tone-bearing moras are quite common, particularly when they are syllable nuclei, as in the first syllable of the Dschang word [ŋ̍ká] 'monkey', but also when they are codas, as in the Tiv word [!dzááǹ] 'used to go'.

6.2.3 Contrast and contour

The discussion in the preceding section sets the scene for a more extended look at tonal contrasts and also contours. We saw that in Digo, typically for Bantu languages, there are only two tones on the surface, H and L, and L is completely inert in the tonal phonology, and best analysed as simply absent.

Contour tones are very restricted in their distribution, appearing only on the final foot in the form of a rise-fall profile. Common though it is, this is not the only type of tonal inventory we find in Africa. Among two-tone systems, we also find languages in which L is specified and H is default (Igbo, for example, according to Clark 1990), but more commonly we find many systems with a two-way H vs. L contrast that must nonetheless have both H and L specified underlyingly. Consider the following facts from the Gur language Konni (more properly Kɔnni) (Cahill 1999). Cahill shows that the syllable is the TBU in Konni (as it is in Dagaare, also a Gur language). Final syllables may bear any of H, L, HL or LH tones, as shown in (14); all except LH can occur on short vowels too.

(14)　　H　　dáán　　'alcoholic drink'
　　　　 L　　kàgbà　　'hat'
　　　　 HL　 chîàŋ　　'chair'
　　　　 LH　　dǎán　　'stick, day'

The simplest analysis of these facts is to specify L as well as H underlyingly. A second fact makes this essential. Konni has downstep, caused by a floating L. If there are no Ls, downstep would have to be marked by a diacritic of some kind, and the fact that it occurs exactly when a syllable that is usually L is changed to H would be unexplained. Consider these data:

(15)　　ɲúrà　　　 'chests'
　　　　 ɲú'ráhá　 'the chests'

H spreads leftwards from the suffix /-há/ by a general process, displacing the L from the final syllable of the root. This floating L then causes downstep:

(16)　　ɲʊ　ra　ha　　　　ɲʊ　ra　ha
　　　　 |　　|　　|　→　　 |　　↘
　　　　 H　 L　 H　　　　 H　 L　H

Similar facts hold if the associative morpheme for third person possessors, which consists of a floating H tone, displaces a root L /bà-H -dàáŋ/ > [bà-dá!áŋ] 'their stick'. The L floats, and downsteps the next H tone.

(17)　　ba- daaŋ　→　ba daaŋ
　　　　 |　　||　　　 |　╱╲
　　　　 L HLH　　　 L H L H

　　Elsewhere in Africa, we find languages that have more than two specified tones. Three is fairly common, with the maximum reported being Dan with five (Mande; Bearth and Zemp 1967). Nupe (Smith 1967, George 1970) has a fairly rich inventory of H, M, L, rise and fall. George claims that the rise and the fall are derived, not underlying, in the sense that the language does not contrast H, L, and HL melodies underlyingly on a single vowel. The rise is argued to come from L spreading across a voiced consonant onto a following H, and the fall is claimed to come from vowel deletion, leaving a contour on a long vowel. Let us look at some data:

(18)   bá 'to be sour'   èdĕ 'cloth'

         ba 'to cut'   dê 'outside'

         bà 'to pray'

Rising tones, George notes, are in complementary distribution with H in that rises are found only after voiced consonants preceded by a L tone, and H only after voiceless consonants (if a L precedes):

(19)   ètú 'parasite'
         èdŭ 'taxes'

He argues that L spreads to H across a voiced consonant only, producing a rise. There are no rises after voiceless consonants because voiceless consonants block L spreading. This L spreading even produces alternations, as in the tone on /gi/ below, which changes from high to rising if the preceding tone is L:

(20)   etsú gí nākā   'A rat ate the meat'
         vs. etsú à gǐ nākā   'A rat will eat the meat'

This is parallel to the more common depressor consonant effect, in which voiced obstruents block H spreading (but see Bradshaw 1999 for a different analysis). Finally, I should add that there are also *initial* rises in Nupe, but these can be shown to come from deleted L vowels, in much the same way as the falls to which I now turn.

According to George, falls typically arise from vowel deletion, as in the following example, where the mid stranded after the /a/ deletes reassociates to the remaining vowel to form a mid-low fall.

(21)   musa egi > mus egi   mus[ê']gi   'Musa is eating'
         | | | | | / |
         M M L H   M M L H

He suggests that some apparently simplex falls are loans from Hausa, as in words like *bâ*, 'defamation', from Hausa *baʔa*, where glottal stop deletion has turned a bisyllable into a monosyllable with a falling tone. However, while this is plausible as a historical account, and for rises it is plausible synchronically as well, in many dialects synchronically the falls do seem to be underlying, since the 'deleted vowels' never surface in any context. See, for example, the word *dê* 'outside', cited earlier.

We are left then with a language with a three-way contrast between H, M, and L, all specified, since they can combine into derived contours. In general, a TBU may bear only one tone, but under certain circumstances double association is allowed, so that some contours can be created as a result of spreading or vowel deletion. If there is an excess tone in the underlying form, then we get a non-derived contour.

Before we leave three-level languages, Harrison (1999) has some interesting evidence that Yoruba, usually analysed as having H and L tones, and with toneless syllables realized as M, might have only a H tone underlyingly. It seems that adult speakers can reliably discriminate between H and the other two tones on single nuclei in the absence of contextual information, but that they cannot distinguish between M and L in isolation. He suggests that both M and L syllables are underlyingly toneless, with their surface manifestation determined by their phonological context. Harrison's work is hard to square with other facts about Yoruba, however, including the active behaviour of L tones (but, crucially, not M tones) in creating contours. I return to Yoruba shortly.

Our next example comes from the Kru language Grebo (Liberia; Newman 1986), which has an even richer tonal inventory. Grebo has four levels, and two rises, all of which can occur on short vowels, which we can convey numerically, as follows, where 1 means H:

(22) to1 'store'   ni 21 'water'
      na 2 'fire'   gbe 32 'dog'
      mɔ3 'you(sg.)'
      fã 4 'herring'

However, on most roots we get only the two levels [2] and [4], and the two rises.

I have argued in earlier chapters that contour tones can usually be understood as sequences of level tones, but Newman argues that Grebo's contours are unitary objects. He considers three hypotheses:

(23) *Three different hypotheses about the nature of contours in Grebo*
      (1) Rises are phonologically levels, and the rise is phonetic.
      (2) Rises are sequences of two levels.
      (3) Rises are phonological primes, [+rise, –low], [+rise, +low]
          (Newman's choice).

He gives one argument against hypothesis (1), noting that, when a rise spreads, its rising character is always maintained and spread. For example, the past tense suffix loses its own tone after a /21/ rise, and instead receives the second part of the rise: /la21 da2/ > la2 da1 'killed' (after deletion of suffixal tone). This contrasts with the facts for the same suffix after indubitably level tones, where the suffix keeps its own tone /2/: mlɛ̃4na2 'jumped'.

He gives three arguments against hypothesis (2). Firstly, when a rise spreads out over a longer domain, it does not behave in the expected one-to-one left-to-right way. For example, on three syllables we get [2.2.1], not [2.1.1]:/ yidi2.1-da/ → yi2di2da1 'stole'. Secondly, he notes that the first person pronoun has two allomorphs: [na2] before [1] or [21] tones, but [na1] before [2], [3] or [4]. As a context, for allomorph selection, it thus appears that [21] does not behave as if it starts on /2/, contra what would be expected if it were truly a /21/ sequence. Thirdly, he reports that phonetically, [2] surfaces as [3] after 4, but [21] is unaffected. Again, then, it fails to behave as if it starts on /2/. He thus plumps for hypothesis three, the unitary contour proposal.

Another explanation is, however, plausible. Suppose that contours are indeed sequences, as in hypothesis (2), but aligned with the right edge, not the left edge. Although left-to-right association is indeed the norm, and is captured in OT by a high-ranked ALIGN-L constraint, there is no reason why this should be an unviolated universal. Indeed OT predicts that ALIGN-R could be higher ranked, and Grebo may be such a language. This disposes of his first argument against a level-tone analysis. The second argument, based on first person allomorphs, may be a historical relic of days when [21] was indeed [1]. The third argument, the phonetic lowering of [2] but not [21] after [4], may simply be because the /2/ of a /21/ in this context is sandwiched between the preceding /4/ (L) and the following /1/ (H), and the H may counteract any lowering tendency since the end of the syllable has to reach a high pitch. I conclude that Grebo is not a conclusive case of a unitary contour language.

Taking the contours to be sequences, the final question is: What exactly are they? To distinguish two rises, something fairly common in Asian languages, I have argued for a register system in which they would be [+Upper, lh] and [–Upper, lh] respectively. The four level tones can also be captured straightforwardly in such a system.

What we see in Grebo, then, is a tonal inventory that looks very similar to various Asian inventories, except for the apparent absence of falling tones. In other respects, too, Grebo resembles Asian languages. The contour tones are not restricted to final position, and their behaviour before toneless affixes is also interesting. We shall see in chapter seven that there are two common outcomes in Asia if a toneless affix is added to a toned root. Either each morpheme remains tonally distinct, with some sort of default tone on the affix, or the root tone spreads onto the affix. In the latter case it may in fact completely re-associate, so that a LH root becomes L, with the H portion shifting to the affix. Interestingly, Grebo allows both options for monosyllabic verbs before the agentive suffix /-ɔ/:

(24)   /plɛ32 -ɔ/   plɛ-ɔ [32.3]   or   plɛ-ɔ [3.2]   'bather'
       /blu21-ɔ/   blu-ɔ [21.3]   or   blu-ɔ [2.1]   'digger'

I end this section with a very interesting process that creates contour tones. This process is common in Benue-Congo languages, and the data and analysis here come from Yoruba (Akinlabi and Liberman 2000b). Yoruba, as we have already seen, has H and L tones. Toneless vowels surface as mid. Bisyllabic words that are /H.L/ or /L.H/ surface not with two level-toned syllables, but as [H.HL] and [L.LH] respectively. Clearly the tone of the first syllable has spread rightwards onto the second syllable to create a contour. The effect is much greater than can be accounted for by simple coarticulation, and it is clear that what probably started as simple perseveratory coarticulation has been phonologized. The underlying rationale for this spreading can be understood as follows. It is well known that tonal targets tend to occur late on their TBU. We also know from languages with true underlying contour tones that TBUs must have two tonal targets, one for each of the tones that make up the contour. Akinlabi and Liberman suggest that, when only one level tone is present underlyingly, it always associates to the second of these two target positions. The first target position then lies vacant, and is available for spreading. If the first of two tones spreads, we get the contours we see in Yoruba. In the diagram below, * stands for a target position:

(25)   * *   * *   →   * *   * *
        | | ╱ |
        H   L   H   L

The authors call the two positions a 'tonal complex', and suggest that languages have a tendency to form these tonal complexes. In their view, the resulting HL (or LH) sequences are thus in some sense units, and can indeed be treated as such in many languages. For example, many accentual languages have a HL complex as the accentual melody, and of course Asian languages treat such sequences in many ways as units.

It should be clear from this section that African languages, like Asian languages, make extensive use of contour tones, although it is true that they are not as widespread as in Asia.

6.2.4   Downdrift and downstep

6.2.4.1   Data and introduction

It might seem that deciding how many level tones a language has is a simple matter, but the picture is often complicated by the existence of tones that are intermediate in phonetic pitch between H and L, as a result of downdrift and/or downstep. As we saw in chapter two, these terms refer to the lowering of H tones in certain contexts, typically after a L tone. When H lowers after an overt L tone, I will call this downdrift (confusingly sometimes called automatic downstep). When it lowers in the absence of a surface L, I shall use the term downstep (sometimes called non-automatic downstep). (I will also use the term downstep as a cover term for both processes when there is no need to distinguish between them; see Connell and Ladd (1990) for a good discussion of downstep terminology.) In many cases it can be shown that this lowering in the absence of an overt L is caused by a L tone that is present underlyingly, but fails to surface. In that case the two types of lowering can thus be unified as happening after L, whether overt or covert. This analysis is particularly convincing for languages in which the phonetic data show the same amount of lowering after an overt low (downdrift) or after the posited floating low (downstep), as is the case in Bimoba (Snider 1998). In Igbo on the other hand, according to Liberman *et al.* 1993, downdrift seems to cause greater lowering than downstep.

There is some uncertainty as to whether low tones lower in the same environment as high tones. To put it another way, do only high tones undergo downstep and downdrift, with lows retaining a constant pitch, or do all tones in the relevant environment lower? Schuh (1978) concludes that low tones lower little if at all, but Laniran (1993) on Yoruba and Snider (1998) on Bimoba find that low tones also lower significantly.

A third context in which downstep is found is the lowering of a H after another H, as in Kishambaa or Supyire (Odden 1995, Carlson 1983). At first glance this seems quite distinct, but if we assume that a L is inserted between two Hs, under the influence of the OCP, then this lowering too is caused by a covert L. I should point out, as does Clark (1990), that the floating tone analysis of downstep has the disadvantage that there is no segmental precedent for a floating, phonetically unrealized, feature exerting ongoing phonological effects. Another potential disadvantage is that some languages (e.g. Dschang, Hyman 1985) have downstep but no downdrift, and under a floating L analysis of downstep this requires that floating Ls have *different* effects from overt Ls – in other words it casts doubt on any account that tries to unify downstep and downdrift.

There are various ways in which downstepped Hs can be distinguished from mid. First, the tone never returns to the pitch of the Hs earlier in the utterance. Second, the contrast between high and downstepped high is most often found only after high, because a L will usually cause *all* Hs to downstep. However, Dschang contrasts H and !H after L as well, presumably because Dschang does not have downdrift, so ordinary H after L is not lowered, but !H after L is lowered.

Downstep and downdrift are recurrent processes, re-applying every time a new L is encountered. As Hs get progressively lower across the phrase they may end up as low as or lower than Ls early in the phrase, as in Kono (Hogan and Manyeh 1996). There is no principled limit to the number of levels, but this raises questions for our feature system, because obviously infinitely extending the feature system wrongly predicts the possibility of huge numbers of *contrastive* levels. It should be noted that downstepped H, for which we usually use the symbols [!H], differs from a M in that a subsequent H will be at the same level as a !H, but higher than a M, as shown in the following picture:

(26)   H L !H H   vs.   H L M H
         -              -   -
             - -   -
         -              -

Downstep and downdrift are most often found in two-tone languages, and apply only to Hs, but Bamileke-Dschang has a !L, and Ngamambo has a !M (Hyman 1986). Finally, I should note that some instances of downstep are apparently lexically determined. These are often then attributed to a lexical floating L, so as to unify all downstep phenomena.

Let me give examples of the various types of downdrift and downstep that I have identified in the preceding paragraph. My examples are drawn from Clements 1979. For an example of simple downdrift I turn to Efik. The following phrase has three Hs, with a medial L. The final H is realized lower than the first two Hs, and this drop is caused by the preceding L:

(27)   ídíɤ(e) ùbóm   'It isn't a canoe'   - -   _
        | | | | -
        H H   L H

Downstep of the classical kind, where the lowering can be seen to be caused by an underlying L that fails to surface, is also found in Efik. When a vowel deletes, a L tone may be set loose to float. However, although it fails to surface it causes downstep of the following H:

(28)   akamba + ubom   →   àkámb úb!óm   'large canoe'
        | | | | | | | ∕ |
        L H H L H   L H H L H

Lexical downstep can be found in Tiv (Clements 1979), where words with a H tone are of two types, depending on their pronunciation after a preceding H tone. The former class are simple H nouns; the latter have a floating lexical L that causes downstep:

(29)   *Isolation*   *After H*
                     or after L
      a. H   kwá   í lú kwá gá   [– – – –] 'It was not a ring of huts'
      b. (L)H   kwá   í lú !kwá gá   [⁻ ⁻ _ _] 'It was not a leaf'

Some languages show the inverse of downstep, upstep. This is much rarer, and less often recurrent. It is often followed by downstep on the following TBU, but not always. In Engenni, for example, H becomes ↑H before a L tone, and this happens before both surface and floating Ls:

(30)   /únwónì/   → ú↑nwónì   'mouth'
        /únwónì ólíló/ → ú↑nwón ólíló 'mouth of a bottle'

The final vowel of /unwoni/ deletes, leaving its L tone behind, and this floating L still causes upstep before [won]. See also Snider 1990 for a detailed description of upstep in the Kwa language Krachi, spoken in Ghana, where a H tone is upstepped if the preceding H is doubly linked as the result of H-spread. H-spread creates a floating L, so here too it may be the floating L that causes the upstep, but, unlike in Engenni, in Krachi linked lows do not cause upstep.

6.2.4.2 Theoretical approaches

There are a number of proposals for the analysis of downstep (or upstep), and they can be divided into phonological and phonetic approaches. I will first summarize several contrasting approaches, then look at each one in more detail. A useful collection of proposals can be found in van der Hulst and Snider 1993. See also Ladd 1990.

Setting aside proposals that simply add a new feature [±downstep], such as Ladd 1983, phonological analyses proceed by turning the possibly infinite number of levels into either embedded structural binarity or embedded featural binarity. By embedded structural binarity I mean taking a single feature and using it to label binary tree structures at multiple levels, much as the labels S(trong) and W(eak) are used in stress trees. By embedded featural binarity I mean using more than one binary feature and allowing one feature to dominate the other in a featural tree. Clements (1981) and Huang (1980) take the first approach and propose metrical structures grouping each (H L) tonal pair into a foot, and feet into higher level (H L) constituents. This higher-level labelling has the consequence that each foot is lower than the preceding one. Hyman (1985, 1993) and Inkelas, Leben and Cobler (1987) take the second, feature geometric, approach, where a L feature attached at a higher 'register' level lowers pitch. Finally, one can imagine an analysis based *very* loosely on Clark 1978 in which tonal primitives are *movements*, not levels. If the movement down occasioned by a low is larger than the movement up produced by a high, then downdrift will result.

Phonetic approaches such as Beckman and Pierrehumbert 1986 do not perform any phonological operations; instead they leave the downstep effects to the phonetic interpretive component. Truckenbrodt (1998) suggests that downstep is the result of the undershoot of a target L register. In downstep languages, L register is non-contrastive, so the target is never really achieved, but the register gets gradually lower with each new L register. H register is contrastive, and thus the target is reached exactly, causing re-setting at phrase boundaries, as explained in more detail below.

How can we determine whether downstep (upstep) is phonological or phonetic? Contrastive downstep is common, and contrastive upstep, or an upstep 'phoneme', can be found in Engenni (Hyman 1993). Even if these morphemes can be analysed as floating tones, they are never phonetically present, so calling their downstep/upstep effects 'phonetic' seems at first sight implausible. However, it is possible that they could nonetheless be the result of phonetic interpretation of a phonological representation that does include these tones, since we know that phonetics pays attention to abstract information, such as metrical foot structure (Harris 1999). Under the assumption that phonetics cannot feed phonology, if the output of down/upstep (not its floating tone origins) fed some other clearly phonological process, we would have decisive evidence that downstep is phonological, not phonetic, but I know of no such examples. I will now spend a little more time on the four approaches outlined above.

Clements (1981) builds metrical trees in which the labels h, l (I have continued his practice of using lower-case for the labels) can be applied to TBUs and to larger constituents. A l heading a constituent lowers the pitch of the whole constituent, so in the following structure, the second h will be lower than the first h, and the second l will be lower than the first l.

(31)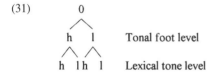

The structures are built by the following algorithm:

(32)   a. Start a new tonal foot between each /lh/ sequence.
       b. Gather any remaining tones into a tonal foot.
       c. Group feet into a right-branching tree, labelled [h, l].

This algorithm builds tonal feet, of the shape $(H_1^n L_1^n)$, and gathers them into trees as shown below, where clause (a) inserts the left brackets in line (a) below, clause (b) gathers all the tones into feet, as shown in line (b) below, and clause (c) builds and labels the higher structure.

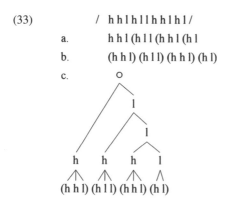

(33)   / h h l h l l h h l h l /
a.   h h l (h l l (h h l (h l
b.   (h h l) (h l l) (h h l) (h l)
c.

In Kishambaa, where downstep happens between any two Hs, clause (a) will be re-written to start a new tonal foot at each /h/ tone. For upstep, we reverse the process, building a left-branching tree labelled [l, h].

In OT, a derivational step-by-step approach is not available, so we must consider alternatives. De Lacy (1999b) has taken the familiar observation that there is a strong connection between head position and H tone, and non-head position and L tone and instantiated this as a set of constraints that ban certain tones in certain positions. For present purposes, all we need is the constraints *Hd/L and *NonHd/H. These constraints will prefer left-headed feet that are of the form (HL...L), and will disallow (HH..L). However, in downstep languages under Clements' account, the middle positions are free to be H or L, as can be seen by looking at the first two feet in (33c). Obviously these medial syllables are not heads, so we would expect H to be disallowed, but in fact feet like (hhl) are fine. If we rank *NonHd/H low, so as to admit such feet, then we will also admit feet such as (hhlhl), but such feet are absolutely out. No foot may contain within it a /lh/ sequence. To put this another way, note that *NonHd/H can never distinguish between the following two footings of a /hlhhl/ string: the good footing (hl)(hhl) and the bad footing *(hlh)(hl). In de Lacy's system this is a general problem with n-ary feet: it cannot distinguish between allowing medial Hs and disallowing terminal Hs, since both are non-heads. So the good foot (hhl) and the bad foot (hlh) will tie in all cases. De Lacy (personal communication) has proposed an analysis in which unbounded feet have a head at one edge, a non-head at the other, and the medial positions are neither. This accounts directly for their tonal freedom. The lack of long feet containing (lh) sequences is achieved through the use of FtBinMin and FtBinMax. The problem with this interesting idea is that it expands the types of metrical distinctions from two (Head/NonHead) to three (Head/NonHead/Neither), a rather powerful move.

Let us try a different approach. The defining characteristic of these feet is that they are left-headed, and may not contain a (...lh..) sequence. A (lh) sequence is tonally speaking right-prominent, and thus fights the left-prominence of the foot's own requirements. Let us then assume that tonal prominence cannot undermine prosodic prominence: tonal reversals inside a foot are prohibited, so that a (SW..) foot cannot contain (LH..) tones, nor a (..WS) foot (..HL) tones. Re-phrasing this: a tonal upturn signals an increase in prominence, and thus a new foot boundary. This reasoning underlies Clements' original first step: insert a foot boundary between every lh sequence. We may state this as a sequential constraint; it will be violated every time a head-initial foot contains a rising tonal sequence, or a head-final foot contains a falling tonal sequence.

(34)   PROMTONEMATCH: Prominence profiles and tonal profiles cannot contradict one another.

Finally, ALIGN-L will enforce the minimum number of feet consistent with this requirement:

(35)

/hlhhl/	PROMTONE MATCH	ALIGN-L (FOOT, PHRASE)
a. ☞ (hl)(hhl)		**
b. (hl)(h)(hl)		*****!
c. (hlhhl)	*!	

(36)

/hllhl/	PROMTONE MATCH	ALIGN-L (FOOT, PHRASE)
a. ☞ (hll)(hl)		***
b. (hl)(lhl)	*!	**
c. (hllhl)	*!	

The second phonological approach I will discuss here makes use of the possibilities opened up by feature geometry. Hyman (1993) allows distinctive features to be attached at more than one level in a tree structure, and their phonetic interpretation varies depending on where they are attached. Specifically, tonal features are contrastive in the usual way on the tonal plane, but on the register plane they denote upstep or downstep. He defines two unary features as follows:

(37)   H: At or above neutral pitch
          L: At or below neutral pitch

These definitions allow the combination of [H,L] to signify a tone at the neutral pitch, that is, a mid tone. He then sets up a feature tree like this:

(38)   Structure of tones:

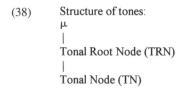

Every tone has a tonal root node, and so contours in African languages which are made up of sequences of tones have two tonal root nodes, as in (39b). Tones attached under the lower tonal node are interpreted in the obvious way, but tones attached to the higher tonal root node as in (39c) downstep (or upstep) the basic tone. (39) shows some possible structures involving L and H tones; the final one is a possible structure for Asian contour tones, and thus is not relevant to this chapter.

(39)   (a)   (b)   (c)   (d)
        [M]   [LH] (Afr.)   !H   [LH] (Asian)

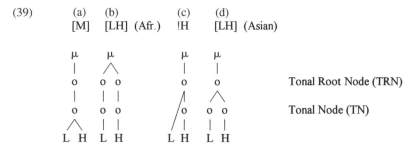

Within this theory, downstep is then phonologically spreading of L from a preceding tonal node onto a following TRN, creating the third representation above.

One nice consequence of Hyman's approach is that he can easily deal with languages like Dschang with downstep but no downdrift. Downstep is caused by association of an otherwise floating L, but downdrift is caused by spreading of an already associated L. Their similarity lies only in their common outputs, and each can exist without the other.

Although Hyman views his feature system as similar to Yip 1980a, it is not. For Hyman, L 'register' at the TRN causes *all* following Hs to be lower, but for Yip this is not so. For example, an Asian 33 tone may be featurally L register, [L, h], and yet be followed by either a true H tone [H, h], or another 33 tone at the *same* level [L, h]. A second difference: for Hyman each L register downsteps the register further, with no limit on the number of downsteps. For Yip there are only two register levels. In other words, for Yip the interpretation of L register is absolute, whereas for Hyman it is relative.

To complete this discussion, I should note that, to derive upstep, a floating H attaches to the TRN. The oddity is that upstep is frequently caused by a neighbouring L, not a H, so the H has to be inserted by rule. A second oddity of upstep is that whereas downstep affects all subsequent Hs, so that !HHH has all highs at the same downstepped level, in upstep this may or may not be the case. In Mankon, in a ꜛH H H sequence they are all upstepped, but in Engenni only the first is, and the second returns to the original level.

How can we tease apart these two phonological accounts? One piece of evidence in support of Hyman's approach is that it allows a language to have both upstep and downstep, as we find in Mankon. This is impossible under a Clements-style analysis, which must surely commit to either the (hl) feet needed for downstep, or the (lh) feet needed for upstep, but not both.

The third phonological account is loosely based on the work of Clark (1978). She proposes that the primitives of tone are movements up and down, not level targets. An up arrow instructs the articulators to raise the pitch, and a down arrow instructs them to lower it. So [↑σ↓] shows a syllable that is raised above neutral mid pitch, then drops back down after the syllable ends. Simplifying and extending her ideas, but in their spirit, suppose that tones are represented as follows; crucially, high tones are followed by an instruction to drop back down in pitch, but low tones are *not* followed by an instruction to rise back up.

(40) High tone: ↑σ↓
       Low tone: ↓σ

Downstep is then caused by the combination of the return to neutral at the end of a high, plus the drop of the low, and the fact that the low has no instruction to return back up to neutral at its right edge. For example a /H L H L H/ string will look like this. The first syllable starts raised, then drops back down. the second syllable drops below mid pitch, and stays there. The third syllable goes up, but from the new low level, so it never reaches as high as the first syllable, and so on.

(41) H   L   H   L   H
     ↑σ↓ ↓σ ↑σ↓ ↓σ ↑σ↓

H sequences will stay level, since the down arrow is canceled by the up arrow that follows it.

(42) H   H   H   H
     ↑σ↓ ↑σ↓ ↑σ↓ ↑σ↓

It remains to deal with strings of identical low tones, which would be expected to downdrift.

(43)   L L L L   ↓‾
        |σ|σ|σ|σ   ↓‾
                         ‾↓‾
                              ↓‾
                                ↓_

Such downdrift is not always reported, and where it seems to be absent perhaps one could suppose that L sequences hit the floor so early that any downdrift is not noticeable? I leave this topic for future research.

In contrast to these three phonological approaches, Truckenbrodt proposes a phonetic account. In his analysis, in downstep languages every l tone gets an automatic L register. L register lowers the whole register, as for Hyman. h tones do not necessarily get a H register (in downstep languages, anyway), so they do not cause register raising (or resetting). H register is a boundary tone introduced at phrasal boundaries, causing re-setting. Contrastive targets, such as this phrasal H register, are more accurately realized than non-contrastive ones (such as the default value for l tone, L register) (Flemming 1997). Thus the L register target is never actually reached, just aimed for in a succession of steps across the utterance. The H target is reached directly. In Asian languages, the large tonal inventories show that both H and L register are contrastive, so both will be accurately realized, and we will get no downstep. let us draw a picture of this proposal in action:

(44)   ‾   ‾
                                ‾
                    ‾   ‾

Syll. #   1   2   3   4   5   6
Tones: h   l   h   l   h   % h
           | | | |
Register: H   L   L   H

The first and last Hs are phrase-initial, and get a phrase-initial H register. The ls get the default L register. Syllable 1 has a h at the top of the H register. Syllable 2 shifts into L register, but fails to get all the way down to the lowest register because the L target is non-contrastive. Syllable 3 is h, but still in this semi-low register. Syllable 4 repeats the L register target, so it manages to get closer to the ideal L register, and stays down in that register for the h on syllable 5. Syllable 6 has its own H register, so it shifts back up to the top of the range and the process begins again.

6.2.5 Tone and laryngeal features

The final topic under the general heading of tonal inventories has to do with interactions between tone on vowels, and other features, particularly laryngeal ones. In African languages (unlike in Asia) we do not seem to find languages in which vowels themselves use laryngeal contrasts alongside pitch contrasts, but what is quite common is an interaction between the laryngeal features of consonants and the tone on neighbouring vowels. The most common situation is to find a class of consonants, usually voiced obstruents, that behave as if they had low tone. This low tone can lower the tone of a vowel (hence the name 'depressor consonants') or block the spreading of high tone across the consonant. Let me start with Zulu (Nguni language of Bantu group, S. Africa; Laughren 1984, Cassimjee 1998, Cassimjee and Kisseberth 2001, Downing 2001). The depressor consonants are the breathy, voiced obstruents, often described as [+s.g., +slack v.c.]. Voiced lenis ejective stops and fortis voiceless aspirated non-ejective stops do not act as depressors. In my examples /z/ is a depressor. I abstract away here from some complications, including the low/extra-low distinction. Examples are from Laughren 1984, but Cassimjee and Kisseberth 2001 show that these effects (with minor variations) are extremely widespread in the Nguni languages.

Consider the minimal pair in (45) and (46). In the singular the prefix has a voiceless /s/. The H of the prefix is attracted to the antepenult by an extremely regular process in the Nguni languages. In the plural, the prefix has a depressor /z/. As a result the antepenultimate syllable has a depressor consonant as its onset, and this lowers that syllable, so the H shifts onto the penult instead; depressor consonants are underlined.

(45)   i - si - hla:lo 'seat'   →   isi - hla:lo
         H   /
                                          H

(46)   i - zi - hla:lo 'seats' →   izi - hla:lo   [izihlá:lo]   *[izíhla:lo]
         H   /
                                            H

This rightward shift of the high tone off the antepenult to the penult is blocked if the penult itself has a depressor onset, as in this Zululand Zulu example from Cassimjee and Kisseberth: u-ku-vímbe:la: 'to obstruct'. Note also that the shift to the penult survives the deletion of a depressor consonant, suggesting that the consonant itself has a tonal feature, and that this feature stays behind. Hence Laughren shows the tone on the consonant itself. Further support for this view comes from the fact that some prefixes consist only of the depressor features, with no segments (Laughren 1984: 215).

There is a second phonological effect of the depressors: they block an effect that Cassimjee and Kisseberth call H tone plateauing. Consider first the normal operation of this rule. A form with two Hs can undergo rightward spreading of the first H all the way up to the second H. (The origins of downstep between the two Hs cannot be discussed here for reasons of space.)

(47)   ámàkhòsánà → ámákhó!sánà (no gloss given)
          | | ╱‾ |
          H   H   H   H

Now look at a similar word with a depressor consonant /zw/. H-spread can only penetrate onto the single vowel before the consonant, but no further:

(48)   ínsízwànyánà   'a tiny youth'
          ╱‾ |
          H   H

If we look across a wider range of African languages, we find that such effects are common. The set of depressor consonants may include all voiced consonants, or often only non-glottalized, non-implosive voiced obstruents. In some languages, such as Ewe, we find a three-way split, with voiced obstruents most active as depressors, voiceless obstruents as non-depressors, and voiced sonorants having some depressor effects, but fewer than the obstruents.

Bradshaw (1999) in a recent survey lists the following effects of depressor consonants:

(49)   1. L tone insertion or downstep insertion
        2. Conditioning of L spread and docking
        3. Blocking of L docking
        4. Conditioning of H tone shift
        5. Blocking of H shift, H-docking, or H-spread

Her examples of all of these are drawn entirely from African languages, suggesting that tonal effects caused by voiced obstruents are rare elsewhere. She does, however, point out that the inverse – voicing caused by L tone – is found in other parts of the world, and indeed all her examples here come from either Asia or Austronesia. One of the clearest cases is Jabem (Poser 1981), an Austronesian language spoken in Papua New Guinea. Jabem has a voicing contrast in stops, but not in fricatives or sonorants. Monosyllabic verb stems have voiceless consonants if H-toned, and voiced consonants if L-toned. These tones also condition voicing on a prefix, which alternates between [ká-] and [gà-] depending on the tone of the root:

(50)   ká-púŋ   'I plant'   gà-bù   'I insult'
        ká-táŋ   'I weep'   gà-gùŋ   'I spear'
        ká-kó   'I stand'   gà-dèŋ   'I move towards'

In roots beginning in fricatives, which have no voice contrast, both tones are found, showing clearly that the tonal contrast is underlying and the voicing contrast in stops derived, rather than the reverse: ká-sóm 'I speak' vs. gà-sùŋ 'I shove'. Finally, the prefix only alternates before a monosyllabic verb, when it is in a binary foot with the root. Before longer verbs it shows up with its underlying tone, H, even before L-toned verbs: ká-dàbìŋ 'I approach'. Clearly, then, in the monosyllabic voiced-initial words like gà-bù 'I insult' the L tone of the root spreads onto the underlying prefix /ká-/ and causes voicing, rather than H tone causing de-voicing.

Facts like these suggest that in some languages consonants are able to bear tone, and that in particular voiced obstruents may bear L tone. It is well known that voiced consonants lower the pitch of the following vowel, and that in many languages this lowering effect became phonologized as a tone contrast on the following vowel, frequently accompanied by loss of voicing contrasts on the preceding consonants. Languages in which the tones still reside on the consonants themselves can be seen as hybrids, possibly way-stations en route to a system in which voicing contrasts are lost and only tonal contrasts remain. See chapter two for discussion.

6.2.6   Polarity

I now change tack completely and turn to an interesting morphophonological effect known as polarity. In some languages, certain affixes have tones that are fully predictable from the tone of the foot to which they attach, but instead of receiving their tone by spreading in the usual way they show a tone that is the opposite of the neighbouring tone. Words that end in L take H affixes, and words that end in H take L affixes. This is termed 'polarity', and for an early theoretical treatment the interested reader can consult Pulleyblank's 1986 analysis of Margi. Polarity is widespread in Africa, including in Bantu, but it is particularly common among the Gur languages, from which I will take my illustration of the various approaches to this phenomenon. Cahill (1999) gives the following facts from Konni:

(51)	*singular*		*plural*	*root tone*	*pl suffix tone*	*gloss*
	/tà-ŋ́/	tǎŋ	tàná	L	H	'stone/s'
	/sí-ŋ́/	síŋ	sìà	H	L	'fish/es (sp.)'

The high-toned root takes a L-toned plural suffix, and the low-toned root takes a H plural suffix. There have been a number of proposals to explain polarity. Hyman (1993b) suggests that such suffixes are underlyingly H. After L roots, they surface unchanged. After H roots they dissimilate by the OCP. Finally, if there are toneless roots, the affixal H spreads back onto the root. Cahill points out that for Konni this analysis fails, because Konni already has a set of H affixes, including the singular velar-nasal shown above, and these do not show any polarity effects. After showing that they cannot be L either, he entertains an analysis in which they are toneless, along the lines of Antilla and Bodomo's 1996 analysis of another Gur language, Dagaare, from which the next set of data are taken. Consider the nominal singular suffix -ri:

(52)	H-L yí-rì	'house, sg.'	but	H-H lúg-rí	'prop, sg.'
	L-H wì-rí	'horse, sg.'			

Antilla and Bodomo analyse these roots as /yi, H/, /wi, L/, and /lug, ø/. H is the default tone (so *L >> *H), but the OCP is active in the language, so an underlying H will block the insertion of another H next-door (OCP >> *L >> *H). SPECIFY requires syllables to have a tonal specification, but spreading of underlying tones is avoided (ANCHOR-R(T, SPONSOR)), so this triggers insertion of the default tone, H (i.e. ANCHOR-R(T, SPONSOR), SPECIFY >> DEP-T). Tableau (53) shows two typical inputs.

(53)

/yi-ri/ | H	OCP	SPECIFY	ANCHOR-R (T, SPONSOR)	DEP-T

☞a. yi-ri
  | |
  H L
				*

b. yi-ri
  V
  H
			*!	

c. yi-ri
  |
  H
		*!		

d. yi-ri
  | |
  HH
	*!			*

/lug-ri/				

☞a. lug-ri
  V
  H
				*

b. lug-ri
  | |
  H L
				**!

c. lug-ri
  |
  H
		*!		

d. lug-ri		**!		

e. lug-ri
  | |
  H H
	*!			*

The H-toned root /yí-/ cannot take a second H on the suffix as in candidate (d) because of the OCP. Candidate (c) is ruled out by SPECIFY. Candidate (b) violates ANCHOR-R(T, SPONSOR), which says that sponsored tones must be at the right edge of their span, and therefore stops root tones spreading rightwards. Candidate (a), with a default L inserted, thus wins. The second input in the tableau is a toneless root /lug-/. Insertion of H on each syllable, as in (e), violates the OCP. Leaving one or both syllables toneless, as in (c-d), violates SPECIFY. Inserting opposite tones on the two syllables violates DEP-T twice, so the winner is (a), which inserts only one tone associated with two syllables. Since this tone is not a sponsored tone, it can spread without violating ANCHOR-R(T, SPONSOR).

Returning to Konni, this analysis does not transfer because it can be shown that in Konni the default tone is unambiguously L. Strikingly, Cahill shows that the polarity requirement is in fact an *output constraint* in that if the input already ends in a H-L or L-H sequence, it seems to satisfy the requirement without any further modification. In particular, another tone is not added, so we do not get /L-H/ > *L-H-L, as shown by nouns like /yɪɪm-HL/ 'arrow' > [yíímà] 'arrows'. He thus formulates a morphologically specific output constraint requiring a polar output. We might note that these Konni data are a nice argument for the advantages of an output-based system.

I end this section with a particularly striking example of output-based OCP-driven polarity from Yoruba (Akinlabi and Liberman 2000a). The first syllable of Yoruba clitics must have a different tone, H or L, from the last syllable of the adjacent host. This is achieved in five different ways: deletion of the clitic tone, deletion of the host tone, insertion of a buffer toneless vowel, failure to link a floating tone, or failure to delete an otherwise optional toneless vowel. Yoruba has underlying H and L tones. Toneless syllables surface as mid. I start with the object clitics, which are always H after low or mid (toneless) verbs, as shown in (54a). After high verbs, however, their H tone is deleted, as in (54b), leaving them mid, or a buffer mid vowel is inserted, as in (54c):

(54)	a. Mid toned /pa/:	ó pa mí	'he/she/it killed me'
		ó pa yín	'he/she/it killed you-all'
	Low toned /kò/	ó kò mí	'he/she/it divorced me'
		ó kò yín	'he/she/it divorced you-all'
	b. High toned /kɔ́/	ó kɔ́ mi	'he/she/it taught me'
	c.	ó kɔ́ɔ yín	'he/she/it taught you-all'

The above examples illustrate two of the five strategies for avoiding an OCP violation. The third strategy is deletion of the host tone, shown with the vocative clitic /ò/. This surfaces unchanged after high or mid nouns, in (55a), but after bisyllabic low-low nouns, in (55b–c), there are two options: (55b) shows vowel insertion just like that in (54c), and (55c) shows deletion of the final host tone.

(55)   *Vocative*
    a. High toned /adé/:   Adé ò
        Mid toned /akin/:   Akin ò
    b. Low toned /r̀gbà/:   R̀gbà o ò
    c.   R̀gba ò

The facts illustrating the remaining two strategies are more complex, and the interested reader is referred to Akinlabi and Liberman for details.

6.3   An extended example: Igbo

I end this chapter with a somewhat more extended discussion of some aspects of the tonal phonology of a single language, Igbo (Kwa; Clark 1990). The data and many of the insights are drawn from Clark's book, but the OT analysis is new. Unavoidably, I have been able to touch on only a few of the topics dealt with by Clark in her very thorough book; the interested reader should consult her work and the references cited therein.

6.3.1   Basics

Morphologically, Igbo roots are monosyllabic, but there is extensive compounding and affixation which creates long polysyllabic verbs and nouns. Different verb forms may be conveyed by purely tonal prefixes/suffixes. The nouns all have noun-class marker prefixes, which are semantically empty. Syllables are (C)V, or syllabic nasals. There is no contrastive vowel length. Igbo has two tones, H and L. There are virtually no contour tones, the only exceptions apparently being on certain syllables followed by moraic nasals (Clark 1990: 270).There is downstep between two adjacent Hs, as in Kishambaa, so that we have /-zó-/ 'hide' but [ǹ-zú!zó] 'hiding'. There is also downstep of both H and L after L. Clark therefore combines these into a single rule inserting downstep after every H that is followed by another tone. An alternative that she dismisses would be to insert a L between every pair of adjacent Hs, and then have downstep apply after L. I shall not address this issue further here.

Clark argues that verb roots are L or toneless, with H as the default tone – an unusual but not unprecedented situation (cf. Bora (Weber and Thiesen 2000), Huave (Noyer 1992), Ruwund (Nash 1992–4)). However, H cannot be completely ignored: it exists as a floating affixal tone, and some segmental morphemes seem to have it too. Furthermore H becomes active at the phrasal level, surviving under vowel deletion and contour simplification, participating in downstep contexts, and perhaps being subject to the OCP.

The evidence for L as the specified tone and H as the default comes from a collection of phenomena which show that L is active in the early phonology, but H is not. There are at least three lines of argument supporting this view. First, L-tone roots are stable, and surface as L in nearly all environments. The L tone normally stays put on its sponsor. 'H tone' roots on the other hand are quite variable, a fact that is compatible with their being toneless. Secondly, L tone is dominant, being the tone that spreads bi-directionally (except to the initial syllable). Thirdly, L can be seen to delete under the influence of the OCP at all levels of the phonology, whereas H, if it is ever affected by the OCP, is so only at the phrasal level.

6.3.2   Data

I will start with a set of verbal patterns that show both compounding and segmental affixation, as well as purely tonal affixes. I will use the following morphemes:

(56)   *Toneless*   *L-Toned*
       chi   'close'   fụ̀   'go out'
       tụ   'throw'   wè   'pick up'
       me   'make'   kpù   'cover'

In four different forms of the verb (Table 6.2) we get different tonal melodies, and in the case of toneless roots these melodies can affect the root itself. I posit the tonal affixes in the second column, which will be justified shortly; sometimes there are also segmental suffixes, as shown. The third column shows the surface forms of a toneless root /chi/ 'close' plus suffix. The fourth column shows the surface forms of a L-toned root /fụ̀/ 'go out' plus suffix. For full glosses see Clark 1990: 24–6.

Table 6.2

Verb forms	Affixal tones	Toneless roots		L roots	
		øRoot+suffix		LRoot+suffix	
a. Affirmative Factitive	L-	L -L	chì-rì	L -L	fụ̀-rụ̀
b. Aff. Imperative	L-...-H	L - H	chì-é	L-H	fụ̀-ọ́
c. Aff. Consecutive	-H	H - H	chí-é	L-H	fụ̀-ọ́
d. Negative Consecutive	ø	H - H	chí-yí	L-L	fụ̀-γì

I begin with the descriptive observations lurking in these data, since these will allow us to justify the tonal affixes posited in column two. As Clark points out, L roots like /fʉ̀/ in the right-hand column are always L, in all forms, supporting the view that they are lexically specified as L. Roots like /chi/, on the other hand, vacillate between H and L, as can be seen simply by inspecting Table 6.2 (a–b) vs. (c–d). I will therefore accept Clark's claim that they are toneless. Now consider the forms in (d). The affix has no perceptible tonal effect, since the surface forms for toneless roots and L roots share no output tones at all, being HH and LL respectively. This suggests that the affix itself is toneless. If that is so, then when attached to a toneless root there are no tones at all in the input, and any surface tones must be the default ones. Since what we get is [HH], H must be the default tone. In the case of the L root, the root L must spread rightwards onto the toneless affix. So far then, we have established the following:

(57)   (1) H is the default tone.
        (2) L spreads rightwards.
        (3) The Negative Consecutive affix in (d) is toneless.

Consider the L root in Table 6.2c. Since the root is L, any Hs that appear must be suffixal, so the Affirmative Consecutive affix must have a H tone, which is attached at the right edge. Next, consider Table 6.2a. Toneless roots surface with a L initial syllable, which must be supplied by the affix, and which spreads. The remaining affix is the Affirmative Imperative, in Table 6.2b. The toneless roots surface as [LH], and the L must originate from the affix. The L-toned roots also surface as [LH], and here the H must come from the affix. So we conclude that the Affirmative Imperative is tonally /L...H/. To summarize:

(58)   (1) The Affirmative Factitive in (a) is /L-/.
        (2) The Affirmative Imperative in (b) is /L-...-H/.
        (3) The Affirmative Consecutive in (c) is /-H/.

I will defer discussion of how these associate until after we see further data. In Table 6.3 I show the same four verb forms, but with compound verbs formed by a toneless root /me/ 'make' or /tʉ/ 'throw' in front of the forms from Table 6.2.

The final set of data shows forms when the first verb in the compound is low toned, either /wè/ 'pick up' or /kpʉ̀/ 'cover' (Table 6.4).

We are now ready to look at how the tones associate in these short forms in Table 6.2, but also in the more complex forms in Tables 6.3 and 6.4.

I start with spreading. In forms with a single L tone, whether from the root or from an affix, the L spreads out over the word. This can be seen in L roots in Table 6.2d, last column, and in Table 6.4d, third column. We see the same if there

Table 6.3

Verb forms	Affixal tones	Toneless roots øRoot+øRoot+suffix		L roots øRoot+LRoot+suff (+suff)	
a. Affirmative Factitive	L-	L -L-L	mè-chì-rì	H-L-L-L	tʉ́-fʉ̀-tà-rà
b. Aff. Imperative	L-...-H	L-H-H	mè-chí-é	H-L-H	tʉ́-fʉ̀-tá
c. Aff. Consecutive	-H	H-H-H	mé-chí-é	H-L-H	tʉ́-fʉ̀-tá
d. Negative Consecutive	ø	H-H-H	mé-chí-ɣí	H-L-L-L	tʉ́-fʉ̀-tà-ɣì

Table 6.4

Verb forms	Affixal tones	Toneless roots LRoot+øRoot+suffix		L roots LRoot+LRoot+suff (+suff)	
a. Affirmative Factitive	L-	L-L-L	kpʉ̀-chì-rì	H-L-L-L	wé-fʉ̀-tà-rà
b. Aff. Imperative	L-...-H	L-H-H	kpʉ̀-chí-é	H-L-H	wé-fʉ̀-tá
c. Aff. Consecutive	-H	L-H-H	kpʉ̀-chí-é	H-L-H	wé-fʉ̀-tá
d. Negative Consecutive	ø	L-L-L	kpʉ̀-chì-ɣì	H-L-L-L	wé-fʉ̀-tà-ɣì

is a single L from an affix, as in Tables 6.2a and 6.3a. The one exception to this pattern is if the L tone arises on the second of two roots, as in Table 6.3a–d, last column. Here the spreading does not include the preceding syllable, suggesting that the spreading is blocked from including the initial syllable. This is confirmed by more complex forms with three roots, followed by a suffix, in which a L tone on the third syllable spreads bidirectionally, but stops short of the first syllable, as in /zà-cha-fʉ̀-ɣi/ > [za-chà-fʉ̀-ɣì] 'sweep-be clean-go out-NEG'. Assuming that spreading is caused by pressure from SPECIFY, which requires that each TBU have a tone, we can conclude that the grammar has the ranking NONINITIAL >> SPECIFY >> *ASSOC. (Recall that NONINITIAL bars tones from the first TBU, and *ASSOC penalizes the addition of association lines.) Tableau (59) shows how this works; the role of the OCP will be discussed more fully shortly.

(59)

/za-cha-fụ-ɣi/ L L	OCP	NonInitial	Specify
a. za-cha-fụ-ɣi/ 　　L　　L	*!		**
b. za-cha-fụ-ɣi/ 　　　L		*!	
c. za-cha-fụ-ɣi/ 　　　L			***!
☞ d. za-cha-fụ-ɣi/ 　　　L			*

Candidate (a) is ruled out by the OCP, to be discussed below. Candidate (b), in which spreading covers the entire word, violates NonInitial. Candidate (c), with no spreading at all, violates Specify three times. Candidate (d), with the maximum spreading, short of the initial syllable, is the winner.

I should add that since Ls which originate on an initial root (as in Table 6.2a–d, last column and Table 6.4a–d, third column), or as a prefix (as in Tables 6.2a–b or 6.3a–b, third column), can be initial, some sort of anchoring faithfulness constraint must dominate NonInitial, such as Anchor -L (Tone, Sponsor), which requires that a tone remain associated to the first TBU of the morpheme from which it originates.

I have mentioned earlier that the OCP plays a role in Igbo, and indeed it played a role in tableau (59) above. To see this more strikingly, compare the L roots in the last column of Table 6.3a–d with the last column of Table 6.4a–d. The forms in Table 6.4 compound two L roots, so they have one more underlying L than the forms in Table 6.3, which have one L and one toneless root, but the outputs are tonally identical. In fact, the first root in Table 6.4a–d, which is /L/, loses its L entirely. We can conclude that the OCP is active in Igbo, and the OCP >> Max-T. (This is true in verbs, but not in nouns: see Clark 1990: 223.)

Exercise 3.   What is odd about using the OCP for these data? You might want to consider inputs like /zà-cha-fụ̀-ɣi/ > [za-chà-fụ̀-ɣ̀i], and a range of possible outputs including *[zà-cha-fụ̀-ɣ̀i].

Lastly, consider the imperative of the three-verb compound /L-zà-cha-fʋ̀-H/ 'sweep-clean-go out, IMP', which surfaces with the affixal H on the final syllable, and the only L on the originally toneless root /cha-/: [zá-chà-fʋ́]. The suffixal H tone must be associated to a TBU either because of pressure to realize the purely tonal imperative morpheme or because of *FLOAT. However, the final TBU already has an underlying L tone. Association of the H to this TBU would thus create a contour, but Igbo has no contours, showing that *CONTOUR is high ranked. In the resulting competition for a TBU, the affixal tone wins, and pushes the L off the final root, /fʋ̀/; it then flops leftwards onto the medial syllable. The prefixal L (not shown here for clarity of exposition) and the first root L delete because of the OCP. Tableau (60) tells the tale.

(60)

/za-cha-fʋ/ L L Ⓗ	OCP	MAX-T	*CONTOUR	*FLOAT	*DISASSOC
a. za-cha-fʋ L L H	*!				
b. za-cha-fʋ L		**!			
c. za-cha-fʋ L H		*	*!		
d. za-cha-fʋ L Ⓗ		*		*!	*
☞ e. za-cha-fʋ L H		*	*		*

Candidate (a) with both L's retained violates the OCP. All the others violate MAX-T at least once, but candidate (b), in which the affixal tone is lost, violates it most and is thus thrown out. Candidate (c) has an illicit contour, and the choice between (d) and (e) is made by *FLOAT (the constraint which penalizes unassociated tones), which prefers (e) where the root tone has been flopped leftwards to accommodate the affixal tone. The first syllable eventually gets H by default, giving the correct surface form [zá-chà-fʋ́].

Exercise 4.   Construct tableaux for all the examples in Tables 6.2, 6.3, and 6.4, using the constraints posited. Do you need to add any further constraints? Are there any problems not discussed above?

This analysis works fairly well, but it raises a couple of serious issues. Given the Richness of the Base hypothesis, and H tones playing a role later in the phrasal phonology, /H/ root inputs are inevitable. How can we exclude them? One possibility is to rank *H above *L, and *H >> MAX-T, but REALIZE-MORPH >> *H. REALIZE-MORPH is a constraint that stops a morpheme from disappearing altogether, and thus affixes consisting only of H tones will survive. Obviously, this will have to precede default H insertion, posing a level problem.

The second issue concerns full specification. There is much evidence that at some point in the phonology of Igbo all syllables receive a tonal specification, if necessary by a H-tone default rule. H must be specified by the end of the word-level for the following reasons:

(61)   *Reasons for specifying H*
    (1) To give the downstep facts
    (2) Because in phrase-level vowel deletion or assimilation, H beats L: Adhá àkhwa > Adháákhwa.
    (3) More generally, what might be expected to be falling tones simplify to H, and so do some rising tones: nà-Kánò 'in Kano' but /nà-úlò/ > [núlò] 'in the house'.
    (4) Once H's are specified, the OCP applies and causes fusion at phrasal level, hence the lack of phrase level downstep (Clark 1990: 118).

    zutaɣi anu   > zutaɣi anu   'and didn't buy meat'

These data raise two discussion questions: (1) Suppose we have two grammars, one at the word level, with no fusion, and a different one at the phrase level, with fusion. How would they have to differ formally? (2) Strictly speaking, OT does not countenance different levels. How could we deal with these facts without them? If we have levels, how could we restrict them? I will leave these issues for the interested reader to ponder.

This fairly extended study of Igbo verb forms completes the chapter on African languages. In a book of this nature with a commitment to breadth of coverage it is impossible to do justice to the extraordinary richness of African tonal phonology, but my hope is that some of the flavour of the central role of tonal alternations in these languages has come through during this exposition.

Answers to exercises

Answer to exercise 1

We will need to add something to stop multiple Hs all going to the final foot, and also something to stop tonal deletion, or tonal merger. These are not shown here. Faithfulness constraints governing association are generally low, especially *DISASSOCIATE, which is extremely low-ranked, and also not shown. The most complex tableau using just the existing constraints looks like this; () shows foot boundaries, and the H associated with the foot is shown on the first syllable of that foot:

/a-na-[a-puput-a)]/ | | H H	ALIGN-R(H, HDFT)	ALIGN- L(H,MACROSTEM)	*TROUGH	*ASSOCIATE
a-na-[a-pu(put-a)] | | H H	*!	*	*	
a-na-[a-pu(put-a)] ⤢ | H H	*!			*
a-na-[a-pu(put-a)] ⤢⎯⎯ | H H		*!		***
a-na-[a-pu(put-a)] | | H H			*!	
☞ a-na-[a-pu(put-a)] ⤢ | H H				*

Answer to exercise 2

Otherwise *all* tones would cluster as close to the left edge as possible, since it would, for example, be better to be one syllable from the left edge than three syllables from the left edge.

Alternative: DEP-H>>ALIGN-L(STEM, H)>>ALIGN-R(STEM, H). Hs cannot be inserted, but stems attract exactly one available H, with a preference for the left edge.

Answer to exercise 3

The two Ls are not adjacent, and yet apparently any sequence of two Ls violates the OCP in Igbo. It is as if Igbo limits outputs to one L per word, looking rather accentual in nature. Accentual systems, however, usually ban more than one H per word, so Igbo is typologically interesting.

Answer to exercise 4

One case not explained is the toneless root in the third column of Table 6.3b, where a medial toneless syllable is sandwiched between a prefixal L and a suffixal H. The initial L must not spread, since the output is LHH, either because the final H covers both syllables, or by default. A larger issue is discussed in the text after the exercise.

7
Asian and Pacific languages

Asia and the neighbouring Pacific regions are rich in tone languages, including as they do the Chinese language family, Tibeto-Burman, Tai-Kadai (which includes Thai), Vietnamese, and Papuan languages, as well as register-based languages like most of Mon-Khmer, and accentual languages like Japanese. There are of course also non-tonal languages, most prominently the Austronesian languages of Malaya and Indonesia, and the languages of the Indian sub-continent (although even here we find the occasional tonal language, such as Punjabi). The best-studied tone languages of this region are, not surprisingly, the urban languages of China, including Mandarin, Shanghai, Cantonese, and Taiwanese, and also Standard Thai, Vietnamese, and Japanese. No textbook on tone would be complete without a survey of the main characteristics of these systems, which between them illustrate both the commonalities and the diversity of the region. The remaining language families are less well studied from the point of view of their synchronic tonal phonology, although a great deal is known about their history. Nonetheless I will sketch out some of their most notable properties. Japanese is scarcely touched on, since its accentual nature puts it beyond the strict purview of this book, and it is thoroughly treated elsewhere. See especially Haraguchi 1977, Poser 1984, Beckman and Pierrehumbert 1986, Pierrehumbert and Beckman 1988, Vance 1987, and Kubozono 2000.

The following classification of the tonal languages in this region is rather coarse-grained, based on the following sources: Chen 2000, Matisoff 1973, Edmondson and Solnit 1988, Ladefoged and Maddieson 1996, and Grimes 2000. There is fairly general agreement at this level, but much disagreement if one tries for more detailed subdivisions. There are three main families. The first two, Sino-Tibetan and Austro-Tai, include large numbers of tonal languages, and Sino-Tibetan languages are almost entirely tonal.

Within the Chinese portion of Sino-Tibetan, some remarks of clarification are needed. Confusingly, the names Cantonese and Mandarin are often used both for the language families, and also for the main urban dialect within that family. I will try to use the terms Yue and Mandarin for the families, and Cantonese and Beijing Mandarin for the dialects. Although commonly referred to as dialects, Cantonese, Shanghai, Mandarin, Taiwanese, and the other four main sub-divisions of Chinese are more properly called distinct languages: they are not mutually intelligible, and have different phonologies and lexicons, and to some extent different syntax too. Within each of these groupings there are subdialects – for example, Yue includes Cantonese, Taishan, and Kaiping. The subdialects may differ greatly in their tone systems, but they share enough common elements in their overall phonologies to be considered dialects rather than members of a different language (see Tables 7.1 and 7.2).

The third, Austro-Asiatic, is mainly non-tonal, but includes Vietnamese and the Mon-Khmer register languages like Cambodian (see Table 7.3).

A few languages come from quite different families: Punjabi is Indo-Aryan, and Siane is Papuan.

By comparison with the African systems we looked at in the previous chapter, the true tone systems of Asia generally have a much richer tonal inventory including a set of contour tones in addition to several levels. Like African languages, they have quite simple syllable structures, but, unlike African languages, they tend to have simple morphology. The addition of tonal contrasts enlarges the otherwise fairly small syllable inventory substantially. (In Mandarin, for example, there are 406 segmentally distinct syllables, but 1256 when tonal contrasts are included.) As in African languages, sometimes there is an interaction between consonant types and tones, here most commonly showing up when voiced obstruent onsets are associated with lower variants of each tone. In many of these languages morphemes are entirely or mostly monosyllabic (Mon-Khmer is an exception to this, with many longer morphemes). Contrary to popular myth, however, words may be of any length (according to Chen,

Table 7.1. *Sino-Tibetan family*

Chinese	Mandarin	Beijing, Tianjin
	Wu	Shanghai, Suzhou, Chongming, Songjiang, Danyang, Wenzhou
	Min	Xiamen (Amoy), S. Min, Taiwanese, Chaoyang, Chaozhou, Fuzhou
	Yue	Cantonese, Taishan
	Jin	Pingyao, Changzhi
	Hakka	Meixian, Pingdong, Changting
	Gan	Nanchang
	Xiang	Changsha
Tibeto-Burman	Tibeto-Kanauri	Lhasa Tibetan, Tamang
	Lolo-Burmese	Burmese
	Kuki-Chin-Naga	Zahao Chin
	Other	Mpi, Meithei, Jingpho, Bai

Table 7.2. *Austro-Tai*

Tai-Kadai	Tai	Standard Thai, Lao, Wuming Zhuang
	Kadai	
	Kam-sui	
Miao-Yao		Black Miao, White Miao
Austronesian (Malayo-Polynesian)	Melanesian	Jabem, Cemuhi
	Malay (non-tonal)	
	Polynesian (non-tonal)	

Table 7.3. *Austro-Asiatic*

Mon-Khmer	non-tonal	Cambodian, Chong, Sedang, and most others
	tonal	Vietnamese, Kammu (some dialects)
Other	mainly non-tonal?	Assam, Nicobarese, Munda . . . .

85 per cent of the words in a list of 3000 high-frequency expressions in Mandarin are polysyllabic) and are frequently formed by a rich use of compounding. Morphemes in such combinations may undergo tonal change of various kinds. The interest of the tonal systems lies in (1) understanding the changes that take place when morphemes are combined into words and words into phrases, and (2) looking at the tonal inventories. It is the first of these that will provide the main focus of this chapter, since the second point has already been discussed in earlier chapters. Nonetheless we will return to it in section 7.4. A third but perhaps less central point of interest lies in examining the interaction between voicing and low tone.

When morphemes are combined into words or phrases, one or more of the following happens:

(1) a. No tonal change to either syllable

b. Limited tonal change only when certain particular tones are adjacent to each other

c. Loss or major reduction of tonal contrasts on all non-initial syllables

d. Loss or major reduction of tonal contrasts on all non-final syllables

e. Spreading of the remaining tone onto the newly toneless syllables

f. Chain-shifting of each tone to another tone in the system, usually on the non-final syllable

(1f) needs a little explanation. Chain-shifting systems are ones in which in some phonological context each tone changes into another tone in the system, so that A changes into B, B changes into C, and so on. Sometimes they are circular, so that C also changes into A.

The conditioning for changes (c–f) is arguably prosodic: prosodic heads retain their underlying tones, non-heads lose them or change them. By 'prosodic' I mean controlled by prosodic structures such as phonological phrases or foot structures, and by the difference between head position and non-head position. Heads are positions of prominence, and in stress systems this prominence is manifested as stress. In tone languages it may be manifested in other ways, particularly by retention of the full set of tonal contrasts, even though these may be lost in non-head positions. The analogy to vowel reduction may help: in many languages, including English, unstressed (non-head) vowels are reduced to a neutral vowel such as schwa, but stressed (head) vowels retain their underlying features.

Returning to the tonal changes summarized in (1), left-headed systems show tone loss to the right (c), and right-headed systems show tone loss to the left (d). Many of these processes also take place across words within the phonological phrase, which in turn is determined indirectly by the syntax and by a preference for binarity, so that 'head' may be the head of phonological word, phonological phrase, or foot. In the following sections I will illustrate each of the scenarios in (a–f) above with examples from Chinese languages, starting with an (a)-type system. For a much more detailed and comprehensive study of Chinese tone systems, the interested student should consult Chen 2000. I will then expand the field of inquiry to include non-Chinese tone languages.

7.1   Cantonese Chinese

7.1.1   Background

Standard Cantonese as spoken in Hong Kong and Canton (Guangzhou) is a Yue dialect of Chinese. The reader should note that the discussion of the tones of Cantonese in this section is specific to Standard Cantonese, and not to be taken as true for the rest of the Yue family. The best overview of Cantonese phonology is still Yue-Hashimoto 1972.

Cantonese has seven surface tones on sonorant-final syllables, and three on stop-final syllables, as illustrated below. Stop-final syllables in those dialects which have them usually have only level tones underlyingly, presumably because they are substantially shorter than sonorant-final syllables. Often only a single digit is used to show such tones; all other tones are conventionally shown with two digits, but of course the 44 tone on [siː] and the [4] tone on [siːp] are phonologically one and the same. Note that for many speakers 55 and 53 are not distinct tones, in which case the language has only six tones, not seven. In stop-final syllables, tones 5 and 4 are in complementary distribution depending on vowel quality. (Length is predictable from vowel quality, or vice versa; in open syllables only long vowels are found.)

(2) siː 55   'poem'   sɪk 5   'style, type'
     siː 44   'to try, taste'   siːp 4   'to wedge'
     siː 33   'affair, undertaking' sɪk 3   'to eat'
     siː 22/21   'time'
     siː 35   'to cause, make'
     siː 24   'market, city'
     siː 53   'silk'

A few comments: the notation used here and throughout this chapter has 5 for the highest pitch and 1 for the lowest pitch, following normal practice in Asian tonology. Where the features of tone are not at issue I may continue to use this notation during the analysis as well, since it succinctly conveys five levels. (H, M, L is well suited to systems with no more than three levels, but will not suffice here.) Unless accurate segmental transcription is relevant, or unless otherwise noted, segments will be shown in a standard romanization for that language.

7.1.2   Words in combination

When morphemes are concatenated into words and then phrases, the tones remain unchanged. Each of the words in the following sentence still has its underlying tone.

(3)   Ngo24 yiu44 ng24 ga:44 da:i33 hei44-che53   'I want five big cars'
      I   want five-CL big   gas-vehicle

Languages of this type, (type (a)), in which each syllable keeps its underlying tone, have been called syllable-tone languages. Generally speaking, if a language has n tones then a word of m syllables has n^m possible tonal patterns. In OT terms, then, faithfulness dominates markedness and any positional or positional markedness licensing constraints, so that all tonal contrasts may surface in any position.

7.1.3   Contextual sandhi

There is one place where tones do change in combination. Even for those speakers that have both 53 and 55 underlying tones, the high falling 53 tone becomes high level 55 before another tone that begins H, i.e. 53, 55, or 5. This is clearly a process of assimilation of the 3 to the surrounding 5s, but it must be stated so that it does not apply to the 3 in a sequence of a rising tone after a high tone, /x5.35/ (where the dot denotes a syllable boundary and the x denotes any tone), or to a mid level tone sandwiched between two highs in the sequence /x5.3(3).5x/. I suggest that within the syllable the first (or only) tone is the head tone, falling as it does on the nuclear vowel, and the second tone is the non-head, and thus more susceptible to change. The /53.5/ configuration is the only one in which a non-head, non-high tone is sandwiched between two highs, and thus the only one available for change. In OT terms, then, FAITHNUCLEARTONE >> *535 >> FAITH.

(4)

/53.5/	FAITHNUCLEARTONE	*535	FAITH
☞ 5.5			*
53.5		*!	
/5.35/			
☞ 5.35		*	
5.5	*!		*

*535 is of course an unsatisfactory candidate for a UG constraint, but it should be seen as a special case of a more general aversion to complete reversals of pitch within too short a span, with a clear grounding in considerations of minimizing articulatory effort.

The pattern we see here will recur in other languages. General faithfulness dominates general markedness, ensuring that by and large tones remain unchanged. One specific markedness constraint, *535, dominates faithfulness, forcing change in that environment. However, change is in turn limited by a specific even more highly ranked positional faithfulness constraint, FAITHNUCLEARTONE.

7.1.4   The Tone-Bearing Unit

I now move on to the issue of identifying the Tone-Bearing Unit. In Cantonese all sonorant-final syllables have two characteristics: they are always long (CVV or CVN, but not *CV), so presumably they are bimoraic, and they may carry either level or contour tones. Since we are committed to the view that contour tones are sequences of levels, we may say that the mora, denoted by μ, is the TBU, and thus bimoraic syllables may carry contours. (Recall that the mora is a weight unit. Light syllables have one mora; heavy syllables, such as those with long vowels or with codas that contribute to syllable weight, have two moras.) Obstruent-final syllables may have only level tones (something that is true in many dialects), so the obvious move to make is to say that they are mono-moraic, presumably because only sonorants may be moras (cf. Zec 1988 on Kwakwala). This works up to a point, but there is one problem: there is a length distinction in the low vowels /kam/ vs. /kaːm/, and this is also true before obstruents: /kap/ vs. /kaːp/. If long vowels occupy two moras, then surely /kaːp/ should be able to bear a contour tone, and yet it cannot. One possible answer to this conundrum is that these vowels also have a quality difference, with the short /a/ being a lax central [ʌ] and the long /aː/ being a further back [ɑː], so we might wriggle out of the problem by saying that the length distinction is purely phonetic, and that both vowels are mono-moraic. See Gordon 1998 for discussion.

7.1.5   Changed tone

The last tonal phenomenon of interest in Cantonese and other Yue dialects is the so-called 'changed tone'. I will illustrate this first with data from Taishan (Cheng 1973). In certain morphological environments tones have a set of alternants called changed tones (biàn yīn). Cheng uses a seven-point scale to draw attention to the exact spacing of the tones, and the very high ending pitch of the changed tone. The mid 4 tone is, according to Cheng, exactly half-way between the low 1 and the extra-high 7.

(5)

	Basic tone	*Changed tone*
	66	no change
	44	447
	22	227
	52	527
	31	317

These alternants are used to denote a familiar or diminutive, including many household objects. In this context they must be listed in the lexicon, since not all such nouns appear in changed tone. In Cantonese the tone is used productively in the formation of the familiar version of names, a kind of hypocoristic. The prefix [a33] is attached, and the following name goes into changed tone:

(6) a. *Surnames*
   /tsʰan22/   a33 tsʰan25
   /yip22/   a33 yip25

   b. *Family Relations*
   a33 kuŋ55   'grandfather (mother's side)'
   a33 yi55   'mother's younger sister'

    c. *Names based on birth order*
| /yi22/ | a33 yi25 | 'No. 2' |
| /ŋ24/ | a33 ŋ25 | 'No. 5' |

  d. *Nicknames*
| /pai53/ | a33 pai55 | 'the lame' |
| /fei24/ | a33 fei25 | 'the fat' |

We can understand these changes if we note that they all end with high tone, and posit a suffix consisting solely of high tone, which attaches to the end of the last syllable and creates a new tone beginning at the starting point of the old tone, and ending high. In the majority of cases this directly produces the correct result. The attachment of the floating tone will result if we assume that *FLOAT is highly ranked in Taishan and Cantonese.

There is one interesting difference between the two languages. In Taishan, according to Cheng's detailed pitch tracks, the changed tones are the shape of the basic tones, with an added rise to a very high tone at the end. In Cantonese, on the other hand, they are smoothed out: they start at the starting point of the base tone, and end high, but any intervening complexity is lost. So /52/ ends up as [525] in Taishan, but /53/ becomes [55] in Cantonese.

Exercise 1. Discuss how the Cantonese changed tone variant of 53 as 55 can be produced by the constraints introduced in this section. Give a precise OT account.

Exercise 2. How would the grammar of Taishan, which allows [525], differ from Cantonese?

Exercise 3. Changed tone also occurs in Cantonese as an option after deletion of the morphemes yat5, tsɔ35, hai35, a5. For example huŋ21 a5 huŋ21 → huŋ25 huŋ21 'very red' faan53 tsɔ35 lai21 tsɔ35 → faan55 lai25 'to have returned'. Provide an analysis of these facts.

7.2   Mandarin Chinese

7.2.1   *Background*

The largest family within Chinese is Mandarin, and it includes Putonghua, the national language, and also Beijing Mandarin and Taiwanese Mandarin. The term Mandarin is confusingly used both for the family and for the standard language. Here I will be discussing two dialects: Tianjin and also Beijing Mandarin. These dialects provide an instance of a type (b) language, with limited tonal change only when certain particular tones are adjacent to each other.

7.2.2 Words in combination

The Mandarin dialects tend to have fewer tones than the Yue dialects, and they also lack stop-final syllables. Tianjin, a N. Mandarin dialect, has four tones (segments in *pinyin*). (Data from Li and Liu 1985; analysis from Yip 1989. See also Chen 2000 for an extensive discussion which differs in detail from that offered here.)

(7) H nan45 'male'   HL re53   'hot'
     L fei21 'fly'   LH xi213 'wash'

By and large, syllables in combination retain their underlying tones, as in Cantonese. Again, then, faithfulness dominates both positional and general markedness.

7.2.3 The OCP

When two syllables with identical tones come together, the first one changes; only sequences of two Hs remain unchanged, a somewhat mysterious fact that suggests the possibility that H is the default tone in Tianjin, and that level H syllables are phonologically toneless.

(8) L.L   → LH.L   /feiL/   feiLH.jiL   'airplane'
     LH.LH → H.LH   /xiLH/   xiH.lianLH   'wash one's face'
     HL.HL → L.HL   /jingHL/ jingL.zhongHL 'net weight'

This looks like a typical example of the OCP in tonal systems, something that was, as we saw, widespread in African languages. In Chinese it is relatively rare (low-ranked, in OT terms), but occasionally rears its head. The interesting twist is that it clearly identifies complete contours as units: it is the identity of the LH complex that causes tonal change, not the identity of its subunits. Indeed, sequences like LH.HL with adjacent H remain unchanged. One might then be tempted to say that analysing a fall as being composed of a HL sequence is just wrong in Tianjin, but in fact in just one case the decomposition can be shown to play a role: a /HL.L/ sequence is simplified to [H.L]. Setting this aside for now, OCP(WHOLE TONE) >> FAITH >> OCP(CONSTITUENT TONE). As a coda, let me point out that this OCP activity involving L tones shows that the L tone in Tianjin (and in Mandarin) is clearly present underlyingly, unlike in many African languages, where it seems to be the unmarked tone.

There are a number of further details that need to be explained. I will deal with one here, and leave two more as exercises for the reader. Throughout, I restrict the discussion to sequences of two syllables only. We must explain why the first tone changes, not the second. Let us suppose that in Tianjin syllables are grouped into right-headed prosodic units. In that case, in the sequences where change takes place the second syllable is the head and will resist change because of a high-ranked positional faithfulness constraint. The grammar we need, then, will have the following ranking: FAITHPRWDHEAD, OCP >> FAITH >> *T. The outstanding questions concern the precise form of the changes that take place.

Exercise 4. Consider the change LH.LH → H.LH. How can you explain the choice of H for the first syllable instead of L, HL, or retaining LH? Make sure that your answer correctly predicts that underlying /L.LH/ surfaces unchanged.

Exercise 5. In the sequence L.L → LH.L, why is this output preferred to H.L? Make sure that your answer does not cause problems for your answer to Exercise 4.

7.2.4   *Beijing third-tone sandhi*

Beijing Mandarin resembles Tianjin in that most tonal combinations remain unchanged. Also like Tianjin, there is one well-known exception to this, the so-called 'third-tone sandhi' rule. (Sandhi is a term that refers to phonological changes that take place across word boundaries; in the Chinese tradition it is used for all systematic tone changes, even when they take place word-internally across morpheme boundaries.) There is a huge literature on this rule because its application is conditioned by prosodic and syntactic factors, and in chapter five I discussed the prosodic and syntactic conditioning for the rule. Here I add some detail on the nature of the tonal change itself. Finally, I will look at Mandarin 'neutral tone', the traditional term for toneless syllables.

Mandarin has four tones; the transcription here is *pinyin*, not IPA:

(9)   H   jiao55   'teach'
       LH   jiao35   'chew'
       L   jiao21(4) 'mix'
       HL   jiao53   'call'

For present purposes I will assume that the system has only two tones, H and L, since this is the most parsimonious account, but nothing significant that follows is affected by this decision. The HL tone falls all the way to 51 phrase-finally. The

21(4) tone is low falling 21 in non-final position, but acquires a rise, shown here by (4), phrase-finally. In what follows I shall ignore the final rise. This is the 'third tone' of the rule. When two of these tones come together, the first changes to the high rising 'second tone': lao21 li21 → lao35 li21 'Old Li'. The change is clearly dissimilatory, and in fact is identical to one of the Tianjin changes shown above: L.L → LH.L. If we allow the OCP to specify which feature it applies to, then the grammar will include a high ranked OCP(L) >> FAITH >> OCP-GENERAL, *T. The account of why the particular selected output is LH will be the same as for Tianjin, that is your answer to Exercise 5 above, given at the end of this chapter.

7.2.5   Neutral tone

I now leave the topic of sandhi, and move on to 'neutral tone'. Earlier I said that every syllable in Chinese languages has its own lexical tone, but that is not entirely true. A small subset of syllables, mainly affixes but also non-initial syllables of some bisyllabic words, are shorter than toned syllables, and have no tones of their own. These are traditionally called 'neutral toned' syllables. In some cases the syllables never have their own tone, in other cases they may or may not have a tone depending on context. For example, the suffix -de used to mark possessives has no tone of its own in any context. On the other hand, personal pronouns have lexical tones, normally obvious in subject position, but in object position they may lose their tone. Reduplicated forms may reduplicate without their tone in some instances: jie21jie 'older sister' has neutral tone on the second syllable; the complete lack of a copy of the underlying 21 tone on the second syllable is shown by the failure of the first syllable to undergo third-tone sandhi.

Since all syllables are of course pronounced with some phonetic pitch, we must ask what happens to these syllables. In many African languages, toneless syllables surface as L, and L is the unmarked tone. In Mandarin, however, we have seen that L tone must be considered to be present underlyingly, and in any case these toneless syllables surface with a variety of tones depending on the tone of the preceding syllable. Shih (1987), in a careful phonetic study, reports the following facts:

(10)	Preceding tone			Toneless syllable
	55	H	high level	starts high, then falls
	35	LH	high rise	starts high, then falls, but not as low as after 55
	21	L	low	starts fairly low, then rises
	53	HL	high fall	starts fairly low, and falls even lower

After a L, the rise is usually taken to be related to the prepausal rise of this tone. Just as 'horse' is pronounced [ma214] pre-pausally, so 'horse's' is pronounced [ma21 de4], with the rise showing up on toneless /de/. The tone of the first syllable is thus being spread over both syllables. A similar approach will explain the low fall after the high falling tone. The high fall on its own falls very low prepausally, so that it is often given as [51], not [53]. If this same fall is spread over two syllables, we get the right facts for a sequence of fall followed by toneless syllable. The other two cases pose more of a puzzle. There seems to be a tendency to return from a H at the end of the first syllable to a lower pitch in these two cases, consistent either with phrase-final lowering or with a lower target tone on the 'toneless' syllable, but this is hard to reconcile with the rise after the L tone. Yip (1980a) offers a proposal in which neutral-toned syllables have [–Upper] register, accounting for their generally lower pitch. The case of the final rise, under this view, is just the realization of the feature [+high] on the [−Upper] syllable. See Yip 1980a for details.

The neutral tone facts are our first real encounter with the role of stress in Chinese. There is considerable disagreement as to whether there are any stress distinctions among fully toned syllables, but all researchers agree that toneless syllables are unstressed. Toneless syllables are not possible words: they can only appear in non-initial position preceded by at least one syllable with a tone of its own. They are substantially shorter (according to Shih, about half as long as a fully toned syllable in final position), and there are some losses of vowel contrasts. They show all the symptoms of being unstressed. This means that in those cases where a syllable loses its underlying tone we may attribute the loss to the inability of stressless mono-moraic syllables to bear tone, a topic that will play a role in the next section, where I discuss Wu dialects with wholesale tone loss and spreading.

The general thread of the analysis that follows goes like this. Neutral-toned syllables lose their tones because they are unstressed (non-heads), and they are unstressed because they are short, mono-moraic syllables. I now flesh out this idea.

In OT, facts like these where a contrast is preserved in stressed syllables but lost in unstressed syllables have been analysed as involving positional faithfulness constraints requiring more diligent preservation of contrasts in privileged positions such as prosodic heads (see Beckman 1997, but cf. Zoll 1998b for a dissenting view). Here I will use the positional faithfulness constraint HEAD-MAX-T:

(11)   HEAD-MAX-T: Preserve the underlying tones of head syllables.

This will outrank general markedness, which penalizes any tonal specification (and thus assigns one * for a level tone and two * for a contour tone):

(12)   *T: Each tone incurs a markedness violation.

However, since tones are lost in non-heads, markedness must dominate the simple faithfulness constraint MAX-T:

(13)   MAX-T: Preserve all underlying tones.

To see how this works, consider the reduplicated [jie21jie] from /jie21jie21/. I underline the head syllable.

(14)

/jieL jieL/	HEAD-MAX-T	*T	MAX-T
☞ <u>jieL</u> jie		*	*
<u>jieL</u> jie L		**!	
<u>jie</u> jie	*!		**

The second analytic step is to show how the grammar selects which syllables are heads and thus keep their tones, and which are non-heads and thus lose theirs. In words with fully toned syllables we must assume that each syllable is the head of its own binary foot, and this can be attributed to the influence of two highly ranked constraints, the WEIGHTTOSTRESSPRINCIPLE (WSP, Prince 1990), and FOOT-BINARITY, FT-BIN:

(15)   WEIGHTTOSTRESSPRINCIPLE (WSP): Heavy syllables must be stressed.
       BINARITY (FT-BIN): Feet must be minimally binary at the moraic level.

This will select the footing (μ́μ) (μ́μ) over the alternative (μ́μ.μμ), since these normal syllables in Mandarin are bi-moraic and can legitimately form their own binary trochaic feet, satisfying FT-BIN. However, monomoraic syllables cannot, and must thus group with a preceding heavy syllable to form a foot. We must also assume another member of the family of faithfulness constraints, stipulating that underlying weight cannot normally be altered:

(16)   PRESERVEWEIGHT (PRESWT): Retain underlying weight distinctions.

Tableau (17) shows how these constraints operate to force bi-moraic syllables to form independent feet, and to force mono-moraic syllables to attach to the preceding syllable, from which they eventually will derive their phonetic pitch. It is this phonetic fact that justifies the assumption that monomoraic syllables are footed with the preceding syllable, rather than left unparsed. Formally, this shows that PARSE-σ must be high-ranked.

(17)

/μμ.μ/	WSP	FT-BIN	PRES-WT
☞ (μ́μ.μ)			
(μ́μ) (μ́μ)			*!
(μ́μ) (μ́)		*!	
/μμ.μμ/			
☞(μ́μ)(μ́μ)			
(μ́μ.μ)			*!
(μ́μ.μμ)	*!		

Finally, consider an input with one bi-moraic syllable followed by two or more monomoraic syllables, such as [wo21mende] 1stperson-plural-poss 'our'. Monomoraic syllables cannot group together to create their own foot, but must still attach to the left, since mono-moraic syllables are never possible heads. We thus also need the constraint STRESSTOWEIGHTPRINCIPLE (SWP, Prince 1983, Prince and Smolensky 1993, Myers 1987b).

(18)   STRESSTOWEIGHTPRINCIPLE (SWP): Stressed syllables must be heavy.

This will select (μ́μ.μ.μ) over (μ́μ) (μ́.μ). So far, all successful candidates perfectly satisfy all the constraints, SWP, WSP, FtBin, PresWt so no ranking can be detected. One detail suggests, however, that PRESWT is low ranked and violable. Consider cases where full-toned syllables have neutral-toned variants. This can happen either for morphological reasons (such as reduplication), lexical reasons (as in some particular compound), or phrasal reasons (as with object pronouns). In the phrasal case it must surely be the result of a change in prosodic structure (syntactically, pragmatically, or intonationally influenced), such that the syllable is no longer a head. Let us assume the same is true in the other cases, that the change involves demotion of these syllables to non-head status, shown here by a constraint *FINALSTRESS. Then we must ensure that our analysis correctly reduces these syllables to toneless single moras. This can be done by ranking WSP >> PRESWT, so that a non-head syllable must become short:

(19)

/µµ.µµ/	*FɪɴStʀ	WSP	PʀᴇsWᴛ
☞ (µ́µ.µ)			*
(µ́µ.µµ)		*!	
(µ́µ)(µ́µ)	*!		

This argument for low-ranked PʀᴇsWᴛ is confirmed by a further observation. Consider inputs with initial mono-moraic syllables. Although such inputs are not found in Mandarin, because all roots are at least bi-moraic, and the language is suffixing, the Richness of the Base hypothesis in OT forces us to consider them, and indeed we shall see shortly that they are found in Shanghai. Mandarin feet are always left-headed, Hᴇᴀᴅ-Lᴇꜰᴛ, but we must ensure that outputs like (µ́.µµ) or (µ́.µ) with stressed initial short syllables never surface. This will be the case if SWP >> PʀᴇsWᴛ in Mandarin (tableau 20).

(20)

/µ.µµ/	Hᴇᴀᴅ-Lᴇꜰᴛ	WSP	SWP	FᴛBɪɴ	PʀᴇsWᴛ
☞ (µ́µ)(µ́µ)					*
(µ́)(µ́µ)			*!	*	
(µ́.µµ)		*!	*		
(µ.µ́µ)	*!				
/µ.µ/					
☞ (µ́µ.µ)					*
(µ́.µ)			*!		

7.3 Wu Chinese

7.3.1 Background

The Wu dialects are spoken in the South, in the area around Shanghai, and include Shanghai, Suzhou, Chongming, Danyang, and Wenzhou. They have three properties of interest to us. First, they retain voiced obstruents, and syllables with voiced obstruent onsets have a lower-pitched set of tones than those with voiceless onsets. (The Yue and Mandarin dialects discussed earlier have lost their voiced obstruents, which conditioned tonal splits historically.) Secondly, they have rather simple syllable structures, with no post-nuclear glides, and Duanmu (1993) has argued that all Shanghai syllables are light. Thirdly, polysyllabic words retain only the tone of the head syllable, which is realized over two or more syllables. This last property means that these dialects should be classified as word-tone languages, not syllable-tone languages. These terms refer to the unit which carries the tonal specification on the surface. In Mandarin, each full syllable has a tone, and a word may have as many tones as it has syllables. In Shanghai only one tone per word survives, and so that one surviving tone, although originally the underlying tone of the first syllable, is ultimately a property of the entire word. These dialects illustrate types (c–e) of the typology in (1), with loss of non-head tones and spreading left or right from the remaining head tones.

7.3.2   Onset voicing and tone

To illustrate the effect of voicing in onsets, look at the following data from Songjiang dialect (Chen 2000):

(21)   HL ti 53 'low'   di 31 'lift'
        H   ti 44 'bottom'   di 22 'younger brother'
        LH ti 35 'emperor'   di 13 'field'

Although there are six surface tones here, one need only posit a three-way contrast between H level, HL fall, and LH rise; the lower variants after voiced onsets can be predictably derived. In featural terms, Songjiang has [+/–Upper] conditioned by onset voicing, and [+/–Raised] is the only contrastive tonal feature. This situation pertains to some degree, not always quite as regularly and simply, in most Wu dialects, including Shanghai. The voiced obstruents are frequently murmured or aspirated, increasing the pitch depressive effect (see Yip 1980a). It is not clear to what extent the relationship between voicing and low register is active synchronically in conditioning alternations; in most cases it is probably now just a relic of the historical origin of the tones. I return to this point in the next section. We will see later that in some other Asian languages voice quality distinctions such as creaky or breathy voice may co-exist with pitch distinctions.

7.3.3   Shanghai tones in combination

I now turn to syllable structure, which interacts with tone sandhi in an interesting way in Shanghai. In what follows I draw heavily on two rather different analyses of Duanmu (1993, 1999), but the details of the analysis differ from his in several respects. Duanmu (1993: 8) draws attention to a difference between Mandarin and Shanghai. Consider the following inventories of rhymes found in each of the two languages, excluding pre-nuclear glides:

(22)   *Mandarin*
        a. z r i u ü a ɣ
        b. ai ei au ou in an ən iŋ aŋ əŋ oŋ er

        Shanghai
        a. m n z i u ü r a ɑ o ɔ ɣ ɛ ø ã ã̄
        b. ən in ün oŋ aʔ oʔ əʔ ɪʔ

Clearly Shanghai, unlike Mandarin, has relatively few bi-segmental rhymes, and no Place contrasts in the post-nuclear material, since the choice of [n] vs. [ŋ] depends on the quality of the nuclear vowel. Duanmu shows that even these few may be more properly transcribed as being simple vocalic nuclei with nasalized or glottalized vowels, so that [in] is actually [ĩ], for example. He concludes that these syllables are light, monomoraic syllables, and that just like the light 'neutral tone' syllables of Mandarin they lose their tones. (In certain positions they may be lengthened, and then the nasalization and glottalization may indeed surface as separate segments.)

This difference in syllable structure has widespread tonal consequences. Monomoraic syllables prefer to be unstressed, and therefore tend to be vulnerable to tone loss. This is exactly what we see in Shanghai – each word has initial stress, and only that stressed syllable keeps its tone. The retained tone then spreads out over the whole word.

(23)   se52 + pe52   →   55 21   'three cups'
        se52 + bø23   →   55 21   'three plates'
        sz34 + pe52   →   33 44   'four cups'
        sz34 + bø23   →   33 44   'four plates'

Note that when the tone changes, according to Zee and Maddieson (1980: 67), onset voicing is unaffected. For example, when the tone of /pe52/ lowers to [21] in the first example, the onset does not become voiced. Conversely, when the tone of /bø23/ raises to [44] it does not become devoiced. This is the reason for saying that the correlation between voicing and low register may no longer be phonologically active.

Let us now see how prosodic structures are selected by the grammar. If Shanghai syllables are all monomoraic, then we must consider a type of input that never actually arose in Mandarin: sequences composed entirely of light syllables. If PRESERVEWT dominates the STRESSTOWEIGHTPRINCIPLE (SWP), then we will correctly foot such sequences; note that this is the reverse of the Mandarin ranking justified above.

(24)

/μ.μ/	PresWt	SWP
☞ (ǵ.μ)		*
(ǵμ.μ)	*!	

Because stressed monomoraic syllables violate the STRESSToWEIGHTPRINCIPLE, as few syllables as possible will be stressed, so in longer strings only the first will be stressed, in response to the requirement that every prosodic word must have a head somewhere. So (ǵ.μ.μ.μ) will beat both (ǵ.μ) (ǵ.μ) and the unheaded (μ.μ.μ.μ). Since there is only a single head, only its tones will be preserved. In Mandarin, in contrast, each heavy syllable is a foot, and keeps its tones.

The last point of interest here concerns the placement of the surviving tones. In Shanghai, if the input has a contour tone on the first syllable, it 'splits' and shows up on the first two syllables. In the first example the fall becomes high followed by low, and in the second example the rise becomes low followed by high:

(25)   se52 pe52   55 21   'three cups'
        sz34 pe52   33 44   'four cups'

This is quite different from what happens in Mandarin, where the contour remains intact on the head syllable, although it then may spread (for details see previous section): si53 ge → 53 21 (*55 21) 'four-CL'. We can understand this if we assume that the TBU is the mora, not the syllable, and that the contour tones are composed of two level tones. Since Mandarin has heavy syllables, each mora can carry a tone. In Shanghai, on the other hand, the syllable is monomoraic, and can carry only one tone. Final syllables (including of course all monosyllables) lengthen, and may thus carry a second tone:

(26)   *Mandarin   Shanghai*
        si ge   se pe   se#
        μ μ μ   μ μ   μμ
        | ⩘ | | ||
        HL   H L   HL

7.3.4   Right-dominant Wenzhou

The last section concentrated on the left-dominant system of Shanghai, with the loss of contrasts on non-initial syllables. The mirror-image, although less common, also occurs among Wu dialects, and my data here come from Wenzhou (Zhengzhang 1964). Only the tone of the final syllable matters; all else is neutralized. (With certain final tones, the penult also matters; see Yip 1999 for details.) In the examples below, both strings underlyingly end in a 45 toned syllable, preceded by a variety of other tones. The output strings have identical patterns controlled only by the final tone. The origins of the exact surface pattern will not concern us here. Using pinyin:

(27)		*Citation*	*Surface*	*Gloss*
san chang liang duan	44 31 34 45	(2 4 43 34)	'3 long 2 short'
tong hang tong zou	31 31 31 45	(2 4 43 34)	'together walk together walk'

In the next section we will see a quite different type of right-dominant system involving a chain-shift effect.

7.4   Min Chinese

7.4.1   *Tonal inventories*

The last type of sandhi commonly found in Chinese is best known from the Min dialect group, which includes Xiamen (sometimes called Taiwanese, Southern Min, or Amoy), Chaoyang, Chaozhou, and Fuzhou. This type, type (f) from the introduction, shows a chain-shift effect whereby every tone changes to a different tone from the basic inventory when in non-head position. Each tone has two variants. One is found in final, pre-pausal position, or before a toneless syllable, and the other is found elsewhere. The changes are not easily stated in any natural phonological way, since a tone that is pre-pausal for one syllable may be the non-final variant for a different syllable. This is because the changes often create a chain (sometimes a circular one). For example, in Chaoyang (Zhang 1981) we get the data shown in Table 7.4, looking only at sonorant-final syllables. The tone in the first column is the citation, pre-pausal form, and the one in the second column is the non-final variant. So a pre-pausal /53/ becomes a non-final 31, but a pre-pausal /31/ becomes a non-final 55, and so on. The final column shows what happens when a syllable is completely unstressed.

Table 7.4. *Chaoyang tone inventories in different contexts*

Final/citation		Non-final sandhi		Post-tonic, unstressed	
55	H	11	L		
31	ML	55	H		
33	M			11	L
313	LM	33	M		
11	L				
53	HM	31	ML	31	ML

At first glance these changes are mysterious phonologically. It has been suggested for Taiwanese that they may not be productive: psycholinguistic experiments by Hsieh (1976) and Tsay and Myers (1996) suggest that if speakers are given a nonce form in citation tone, and then asked to use it in a sandhi context, they answer more or less at chance. Tsay and Myers thus suggest that all lexical items come in pairs, and that a lexical insertion rule controls the choice. The problem here is that any pairing could be learnt, but in fact all words, including loans, conform to the standard pairings of allotones. Sometimes the changes are more easily stated historically (Chen 2000). I shall explore a partially phonological account, based on the observation that usually (but not always; see for example Tsay 1996 on Taiwanese short tones) there is some degree of neutralization in non-final position (leading most researchers to take the citation tones as basic), and, more importantly, that the inventory of tones in each position is progressively less marked as the stress reduces. Some readers may wish to refer back to chapter two for an overview of tonal inventories before reading this section. Because it requires considerable OT background, it is included in this chapter rather than in chapter two.

To begin, note that markedness cannot explain the individual tonal changes. For example, in Chaoyang, suppose 55 becomes 11 in non-head (non-final) position because 55 is marked and 11 is unmarked. Then we must ask why 31 becomes the 'marked' 55 in the same context and why the 'unmarked' 11 becomes the presumably more marked 33? However, as I have said, the inventory as a whole *is* usually less marked: it has fewer tones, and the tones that are lost are typically marked, especially rising tones. I propose then that the individual pairings are indeed lexical, but they must be picked from the inventories appropriate for the position in question. What remains for the phonologist is to explain the particular inventories found in each position.

The following markedness facts will play a role; all of these are clearly underpinned by a tendency to minimize articulatory effort, and can be thought of as constraints

(28)   a. Contour tones are more marked than level tones: *CONTOUR.

   b. High tones are more marked than low tones: *H >> *L.

   c. Rising tones are more marked than falling tones: *RISE >> *FALL.

These articulatorily based constraints are balanced by a set of perceptually based ones. Lindblom (1986, 1990) observes that vowel inventories tend to spread out to occupy the available phonetic space, with clear functional advantages. For tones, this would mean that inventories with few tones have those tones as widely spaced as possible at the edges of the pitch space and inventories with more tones have them closer together. Although not entirely true (see discussion in chapter 2, section 3 of Maddieson 1978), for Chinese languages at least this seems to be a promising line of attack on defining what is or is not a possible tonal inventory, and I shall explore it here.

Flemming (1995) develops Lindblom's idea in OT as a way of explaining segmental inventories, and the following account is heavily influenced by his work. In what follows you will see tableaux that compare tonal inventories, not different output candidates for a given input. Suppose that Lindblom's Dispersion Theory is formulated as constraints that require spacing the tones some given percentage of the pitch range apart:

(29)   SPACE-100%: Level tones must be 100 per cent of the pitch range apart. (Can only be satisfied by systems with two or fewer evenly spaced tones: [H, L], or any single tone.)

SPACE-50%: Level tones must be 50 per cent of the pitch range apart. (Can only be satisfied by systems with 3 or fewer evenly spaced tones: [H, M, L], [H, M], [H, L], [M, L], or any single tone.)

Different languages have different numbers of tones, for no apparent reason, so this must be stipulated. In Chaoyang, the number changes with context, from 6T to 4T to 2T, instantiated here as constraints:

(30)   6T/4T/2T: Distinguish 6/4/2 tonal distinctions.

The ranking of the different instantiations of this constraint is universal, with nT >> (n+1)T. Given the spacing requirements, sufficient distinctions are not always possible with level tones only. *RISE exacts a price for adding rises, so, if possible, falls are added instead. *H exacts a price for adding H, so any contours will if possible be ML or LM.

The general idea is that in different positions the inventory is defined by different OT mini-grammars. In each position, different numbers of contrasts are required, which means formally that one of the constraints 6T, 4T or 2T is ranked above tonal markedness constraints. In unstressed syllables, tones must be widely spaced in order to be perceptible during the brief syllable, so SPACE-100% is high ranked. In stressed syllables SPACE-100% is demoted, leaving only the less stringent SPACE-50% visible. The tonal markedness constraints *RISE and *H (the only ones which will matter here) have a fixed ranking for the whole language, with *RISE >> *H. As prominence decreases, minimizing articulatory effort gets more important and keeping any contrasts as distinct as possible becomes more important. Both these priorities have their roots in functional considerations: less prominent syllables are often shorter (giving less time to articulate distinctions and less time to perceive those distinctions) and quieter (also making them harder to perceive) (Zhang 2000). Here, then, MINARTICEFFORT (the markedness constraints *RISE >> *H with an invariant ranking) and SPACE-100% both move up the hierarchy. Chart (31) shows the three grammars associated with different degrees of prominence.

(31)   *Maximal prominence: citation*
SPACE-50% >> 2T >> 3T >> 4T >> 5T >> 6T >> MINARTICEFFORT >> SPACE-100%

Medium prominence: sandhi
SPACE-50% >> 2T >> 3T >> 4T >> MINARTICEFF >> SPACE-100% >> 5T >> 6T

Minimal prominence: neutral/post-tonic
SPACE-50% >> 2T >> MINARTICEFF >> SPACE-100% >> 3T >> 4T >> 5T >> 6T

Let us start with the smallest inventory [L, ML] in post-tonic position. This inventory is the perfect way to achieve a two-tone inventory, while having no H, no rises, and keeping the level tones at least 100 per cent of the pitch range apart. The high ranking of SPACE-100% is undoubtedly related to the brevity of the unstressed syllable, and therefore the difficulty of perceiving F_0 distinctions.

(32)   *Comparison of possible inventories in unstressed post-tonic position*

	2T	*RISE	*H	SPACE-100%
a. L	*!			
b. L, LM		*!		
c. L, H			*!	
d. L, HL			*!	
e. L, M				*!
☞ f. L, ML				

In sandhi positions there are four tones [H, M, L, ML], and the SPACE-100% requirement has been demoted off the right edge of the tableau, and is not shown here. Instead, the less stringent SPACE-50% plays a role in limiting the number of level tones to three, and forcing them to be equally spaced H, M, L. The four-tone inventory is achieved by adding the least marked contour tone, a fall from ML that includes no H (tableau 33).

(33)   *Comparison of possible inventories in sandhi (non-head) position*

	SPACE-50%	4T	*RISE	*H
☞ a. H, M, L, ML				*!
b. H, M, L, HM				**!
c. H, M, L, LM			*!	*
d. M, L, ML, LM			*!	
e. H, M, L		*!		*
f. H, M+, M, L	*!			*

Finally, the six-tone citation inventory [H, M, L, ML, HM, LM] still observes SPACE-50%, again limiting the number of level tones to three, so the six tones are achieved by adding three contours. To do this, *RISE and *H must unavoidably be violated, but the minimum violations are achieved with two falls, ML and HM, and one rise, LM (tableau 34).

(34)   *Comparison of possible inventories in citation (head) position*

	SPACE-50%	6T	*RISE	*H
a. H+, H, M+, M, L+, L	*!			**
b. H, M, L		*!		*
c. H, M, L, ML, MH, LM			**!	**
d. H, M, L, ML, HM, MH			*	***!
☞ e. H, M, L, ML, HM, LM			*	**

Once the inventory is defined for a given context, it constrains the particular output by requiring that the tone be part of the inventory set. It does not, however, explain why a given lexical item chooses the tone that it does, and here, as I said earlier, I tend to the view that the pairings are indeed lexical, a position I have resisted for years but at present see no alternative to. The interested reader might look at Kirchner 1996 on chain-shifts as a possible starting point for a more interesting analysis.

It might be instructive, before leaving this topic, to recall how recalcitrant this Min circular chain-shift has proved in previous frameworks. For example, in Yip

1980a the following less-than-illuminating rule was proposed as one of a total of three rules needed to account for the facts:

(35)   [α Upper] → [−α Upper] / _____
                                    /   \
                                  [βT]   [βT]

Other attempts were at least as bad, if not worse. See Yip 1980a for a summary.

7.4.2   Sandhi domains

I now turn to the environment in which these sandhi changes take place. Up until now I have talked of 'final' and 'non-final', but final in what? Chen (1987) on Xiamen in an influential paper refers to the relevant units as 'tone groups', and shows that they are defined by the syntax in a rather interesting way. They do not coincide with syntactic constituents, but the right edge of each non-adjunct XP marks the right edge of a tone group, shown here with a cross-hatch. The left edge, on the other hand, is ignored:

(36)

$_{NP}$[old lady]$_{NP}$ $_{PredP}$ [not $_{VP}$[believe $_S$[$_{NP}$[parrot]$_{NP\ PredP}$ [can $_{VP}$[talk]$_{VP}$]$_{PredP}$] $_S$]$_{VP}$]$_{PredP}$
       lao tsim-a-po #   m   siong-sin   ying-ko #   e   kong-we #

The simplicity of the alignment between XP edges and tone group edges is marred by the need for a condition excluding adjuncts from participating in this alignment. However, Lin (1994) shows that a more elegant and precise statement of the condition that Chen formulates as 'if not an adjunct' can be had in terms of lexical government: the right edge of any XP that is not lexically governed ends a tone group. This formulation has the advantage that it appears necessary for phrasing in other languages, especially Papago (see Truckenbrodt 1999). For more detailed discussion of this and other issues, see chapter five.

7.4.3   Syllable weight and tone sandhi in Fuzhou

The other main phenomenon of interest in Min dialects is the interaction between vowel quality, rhyme structure, and tone in Fuzhou; the relationship between vowel height and tone was discussed briefly in chapter two, but here I focus on the influence of syllable weight. See Wright 1983 and Chan 1985 for details. Penultimate syllables have a duration about half that of final syllables, and this is associated with several other alternations. Tones undergo a set of changes, among which are simplification of the extra-complex /LHL/ tone to H(L), and of /HL/ to

H or L, with the choice depending on the following tone. At the same time some diphthongs monophthongize, and vowels tend to tense and raise. Although the details are somewhat messy, it seems clear that one part of the story is that in Fuzhou an iambic foot is constructed over the last two syllables. In this foot, the final, head, syllable is bi-moraic, and can support extra-complex tones and diphthongs. The penultimate non-head syllable is mono-moraic, and prefers simple tones and monophthongs. The TBU, then, is the mora in Fuzhou.

7.5   Types of tonal changes found in Chinese

I now shift my focus to the details of the tonal changes we find in Chinese. Although at first glance they look tonally very different from African languages, the differences can be attributed to independent properties of the language families in question, as pointed out by Chen (1992). In Chinese, each syllable has an underlying tone, but this is not the case in many African languages, where toneless syllables abound. As a result, opportunities for tones to move onto toneless syllables, sometimes at a distance, are much more common in African languages than in Chinese languages, where they tend to stay on their original syllable or spread locally only. Where toneless syllables are found, as in Mandarin neutral tone or Shanghai compounds, then we see both tonal spreading and tonal movement or flop, just like in African languages. Lastly, spreading tends to target toneless syllables and be blocked by pre-existing tone associations, so again it can be expected to be rare in Chinese, where virtually all syllables have pre-existing tones. Even local spreading is less likely in Chinese, because of the prevalence of contour tones. Consider these two scenarios:

(37)   (a) σ   σ   (b) σ   σ
             L-⌐   ∧-⌐∧
             H   L   LH LH

Spreading in (a) creates a simple HL contour, and such rules abound in both African and Asian tone languages. Spreading in (b) would create a HLH contour on the second syllable: tones of this complexity are rare, and thus it is not surprising that sandhi rules creating them are also rare.

So what *do* we find in Chinese? Assimilation, dissimilation, and spreading are all easy enough to discover. Assimilation we saw in Cantonese, dissimilation we saw in Tianjin, and spreading we have seen in Shanghai. In chapter three, on tonal features, we saw that the entities involved in these rules could be either whole tones, register features, or tonal features. The truly distinct type of tonal rule seems to be the wholesale replacement of the Min dialects, which have no obvious counterpart outside this region. Lastly, I should mention metathesis. In some dialects we see facts like these well-known ones from Pingyao:

(38)   hai35 bing35 → 53. 35   'become ill'   MH → HM/ ___ MH
          er53 ruan53 → 35. 53   'ear soft, i.e. gullible'   HM → MH/ ___ HM

This is sometimes described as metathesis, because the terminal M and H tones of the first syllable switch places, but Chen has insightfully observed that what seems to lie behind this is a dissimilation of the complete contour tone as a unit, eliminating sequences of two rises or two falls, and that this has a functional advantage in that the resulting bisyllable has only three tonal targets instead of four, HMH and MHM respectively. Since we have already seen in Tianjin that the OCP can identify complete contours as units, and penalize sequences of such contours, Pingyao becomes simply another instance of such dissimilation, albeit with a different outcome.

Exercise 6.   How might you construct a grammar for the Pingyao changes? Take the Tianjin analysis given as an answer to Exercise 4 in section 7.2.3 as your starting point, and bear in mind that as far as possible the differences should fall out from constraint rankings or by the postulation of plausibly universal constraints. (Hint: Metathesis is usually considered to violate a constraint called LINEARITY which bans re-ordering of input elements.)

7.6   Tibeto-Burman

The Sino-Tibetan family includes both Sinitic (Chinese) and Tibeto-Burman. I will discuss four languages from the latter, Lhasa Tibetan, Burmese, Jingpho, and Bai. Tibetan will look quite similar to Chinese, but Burmese and especially Bai start to look noticeably different.

7.6.1   Lhasa Tibetan

Tibetan dialects range from atonal (Aba Tibetan) to fully tonal (Lhasa Tibetan), see Geziben 1996 for details. The devoicing of initial voiced obstruents produced a high/low tonal contrast, and the loss or debuccalization of final codas produced contours. The writing system still represents this lost consonantal contrast.

In this discussion I follow the analysis of Duanmu (1992a), who draws among others on Sprigg (1981) and Qu and Tan (1983). The OT analysis, however, is new. Lhasa Tibetan has two underlying tones, H and LH. On short vowels with or without glottal stop in isolation the H tone gets partially eaten up by a non-contrastive utterance final fall, so that it is usually reported as 53 (but see Edmondson *et al.* n.d. and Geziben 1996 for arguments that this fall is in fact contrastive). The rise, which is 14 on long syllables, does not rise as far on short syllables, so it is written 12.

(39)   H   pa53   'ape'
        H   pa:55   'to light'
        LH   pa12   'tent'
        LH   pa:14   'neck tumour'

In bisyllabic and trisyllabic compounds, the first syllable controls the output tone, with the tones of the final syllable being lost and the first tone spreading over the larger domain. The same final lowering effects on short syllables also come into play, turning a final H into a 53 drop (see (40)).

(40)

First syll.	Second syll. short	Second syll. long
H	55 53 σ σ_μ ╲╱ H	55 55 σ σ_μμ ╲╱ H
LH	11 53 σ σ_μ │ │ L H	11 14 σ σ_μμ ╲│ L H

In general, this looks remarkably similar to Shanghai (see section 7.3.3). In both languages the initial syllable is the head and keeps its tone, while the non-heads lose their tones. In both languages, an underlying contour tone is decomposed into its two component tones on a longer domain, with each tone associating with a single syllable. The one twist is the case of words that begin with an underlying /LH/ tone, and in which the second syllable is long. We find a [11 14] pattern instead of the expected [11 55], with the initial L portion being associated with both syllables, not just the first. This requires a special rule that spreads the L rightwards onto the final H of a long syllable. One might speculate that this results from an attempt to preserve the LH rise intact on a single syllable, PRES-LH, held in check by two things: (1) a general prohibition on contours, ONE-T/μ, and (2) a strong positional prohibition on non-final contours (as we have seen commonly in African languages) LICENCECONTOUR. To start the analysis, as in Shanghai HEAD-MAX-T will block tone deletion of head tones, even if they violate the prohibition on short contours. On monosyllables, then, all input tones survive, as shown in (41).

(41)

/σ_μ/ LH	HEAD-MAX-T	ONE-T/μ
☞ σ_μ $\wedge$ LH		*
σ_μ | L	*!	

In bisyllables, HEAD-MAX-T is satisfied by all candidates in which both input head tones are preserved. Non-head tones will delete, as in Shanghai. In what follows, I show only those candidates in which this is the case. If the final syllable is short, ONET/μ and LICENCECONTOUR ranked above PRES-H block the rise from staying together, even if the first syllable is long (see (42)).

(42)

$\sigma_{\mu\mu}$ σ_μ $\diagdown$ | LH T	ONE-T/μ	LICENCE-CONTOUR	PRES-LH
☞ $\sigma_{\mu\mu}$ σ_μ | | L H			*
$\sigma_{\mu\mu}$ σ_μ $\diagdown\diagdown$ L H		*!	
$\sigma_{\mu\mu}$ σ_μ $\diagdown\diagup$ L H	*!		

If the final syllable is long, the contour survives, because the contour can be kept together on the final long syllable without violating either ONE-T/μ or LICENCE-CONTOUR (see (43)).

(43)

σμμ σμμ ＼ ｜ LH T	ONE-T/μ	LICENCE-CONTOUR	PRES-LH
☞ σμμ σμμ ＼／＼ L H			
σμμ σμμ ｜ ｜ L H			*!
σμμ σμμ ＼／ L H		*!	

One final point: the rising tone, with its lower onset F_0, may have a somewhat breathy quality, and in the second syllable of compounds this too disappears along with the tone, suggesting that all laryngeal features of the non-head syllable are lost.

7.6.2   Jingpho

In the languages discussed so far, the different tones have been distinguished wholly or partly by their pitch. Shanghai and other Wu dialects have breathy variants of each tone after voiced onsets which lower the pitch, but in many Asian languages voice quality is fully contrastive and may co-exist with pitch distinctions. We can see this when we move on to other Tibeto-Burman languages. Jingpho (Maddieson and Hess 1986) cross-cuts contrastive tonal and voice quality distinctions. The language has three tones, 55, 33, 31, and each can occur with either 'tense' or 'lax' voice quality. 'Lax' voice quality is more breathy and produces a lower pitch at the start of the vowel. In these examples the tense member of each pair is underlined:

(44)   *Tense*   *Lax*
        p<u>a</u>t55   'stop up'   pat55   'with a whip'
        ka<u>n</u>33   'tense'   kaŋ33   'pull'
        k<u>a</u>31   'dance'   ka31   'speech'

Historically, the lax words began with voiced consonants, so it is reasonable to suppose a stage at which the voiced consonants were accompanied by breathy voice. Such a stage would have looked a lot like Shanghai, where each tone would have had a lowered counterpart after voiced onsets. Now the onset voicing has gone, but the voice quality distinction along with its pitch-depressing effect persists.

7.6.3   *Burmese*

In Burmese, tonal and phonation distinctions do not cross-cut each other, but seem to be mutually exclusive. Syllables either have a H vs. L tone distinction or a phonation distinction, but not both. The picture is somewhat murky, but consider the following Burmese data from Wheatley (1987), Green (1994), Okell (1969) and Bradley (1982). (The tilde under the vowel shows a creaky vowel. [c.g.] stands for [constricted glottis], a feature of the coda.)

(45)   L   khà   'shake'   khàn   'undergo'
       H   khá   'be bitter' khán   'dry up'
       [creaky]   kha̰   'fee'   kha̰n   'appoint'
       [c.g.]   kha?   'draw off'

Importantly, H and L tone do not contrast on creaky or [c.g.] syllables. The descriptions of these tones are somewhat variable in different sources, but Wheatley says that L tone has normal phonation, H tone is normal or slightly breathy, creaky has tense or creaky phonation and quite H pitch, often slightly falling. The [c.g.] syllables (which were originally stop-final) seem to be extremely variable in pitch depending on context. If anything, Justin Watkins (personal communication) suggests that the phonation 'register' differences are more robust than the very variable pitch patterns, and indeed Bradley (1982) analyses Burmese as a purely 'registral' language, not phonologically tonal at all. He notes that the creaky 'tone' is associated with higher, more fronted vowels, and the plain H (but somewhat breathy) tone is associated with lower more fronted vowels. He goes on to suggest that Burmese has a three-way ATR distinction, with 'creaky' being [+ATR], the plain L 'tone' being [0 ATR], and the breathy H 'tone' being [−ATR].

Other researchers have taken a tonal view. Green proposes an analysis in which H and L tone, creaky, and [c.g.] are all laryngeal features, and each full syllable may bear one and only one of these. [c.g.] migrates to coda position by an unspecified mechanism, but the others remain as syllable-level specifications. Since the coda may contain only one segment, if an *input* has both [c.g.] and coda [n] (something which is bound to arise in OT given its inability to restrict inputs, a hypothesis known as Richness of the Base), only one can survive, and a high-ranked Max(Lar) constraint ensures that [c.g.] wins out. One oddity about this analysis is the feature [creaky]: this is usually thought to involve glottalization, in which case the feature should be [c.g.], but Green has reserved [c.g.] for the glottal coda syllables and thus posits a separate creaky feature.

In polysyllabic words, whether monomorphemic or compounded, final syllables always have full vowels, but non-final syllables may have either full or reduced vowels. Reduced vowel syllables lose all laryngeal contrasts, including tone:

(46)

Reduced non-final vowels		*Non-reduced non-final vowels*	
θəyò	'mock'	cạuncạ	'be anxious'
khəlouʔ	'knob'	mòundáin	'storm'
cəbò:	'bug', from /càn-pò:/	yàunwɛ:	'trade', from /yàun-wɛ:/
	'floor-insect'		'buy-sell'

Green (1995) proposes that Burmese has monosyllabic, bimoraic feet, and words are always foot-final. Reduced syllables are monomoraic and unfooted. Laryngeal features, he suggests, are licensed by feet.

Exercise 7. Develop a formal OT version of Green's proposal for polysyllables. Make sure it explains why words like these are always bad. (The accents mark tone, and stress, which is always final, is shown by underlining.)

    *bə   *bòwə (from /bòwá/)   *pɔ́tò

7.6.4   Bai

One of the most elaborate sets of cross-cutting tonal and voice quality categories is found in Bai, a Tibeto-Burman language spoken in Yunnan province in China. Edmondson and Li (1994) conducted an instrumental study of these contrasts, illustrated below:

(47)

	[–nasal]		[+nasal]	
	[–tense]	[+tense]	[–tense]	[+tense]
high level	tɕi	tɕi	tɕi	tɕi
	'much'	'to mail'	'gold'	'to perceive'
high rising	tɕi	–	–	–
	'restless'			
mid level	tɕi	tɕi	tɕi	tɕi
	'to pull'	'leech'	'apricot'	'naughty'
mid falling, creaky	tɕi	–	tɕi	–
	'flag'		'bracelet'	
mid falling, breathy	tɕi	tɕi	tɕi	tɕi
	'earth'	'to chase'	'alkali'	'bow and arrow'

Not surprisingly, nasality has no significant interaction with tone, except for the gap in high rising tone on [–tense, +nasal]. It also has no phonetic effect on F_0. Tenseness, however, significantly raises pitch. The other thing to note is that creakiness and tenseness appear to be incompatible. There is some indication that tenseness involves syllable-final glottal closure, and certainly tense syllables are much shorter than non-tense ones, as one would expect if this is the case. One might then surmise that creak is also glottalization and that, if fixed on the coda, one gets the 'tense' set of tones, but if spread through the vowel one gets 'creak'. Apparently glottalization cannot be in two places at once. Lastly, note that tense syllables cannot have rising tones. This seems likely to be due to their shortness, so that they have only a single tone-bearing mora, and can only bear one, level, tone.

7.7   Austro-Tai

So far we have looked only at languages of the Sino-Tibetan family, but now we turn to Austro-Tai, which includes Tai-Kadai, Miao-Yao, and Austronesian. Tai-Kadai and Miao-Yao are certainly tonal, and I begin with two languages of the Tai branch of the Tai-Kadai family, Standard Thai, and Wuming Zhuang. Although there are strong similarities to Chinese, the differences are quite interesting. I then move on to Austronesian, which is mostly non-tonal, but includes some tonal languages, primarily in Melanesia, like those of New Caledonia.

7.7.1   Standard Thai

Although Thai is a syllable-toned language, it differs in significant ways from Chinese. First, the language has many bisyllabic morphemes (originally borrowed from Indic), and there are some limits on the tonal combinations found on their syllables. Second, whereas in Chinese any neutralization is most commonly on non-initial syllables (that is, the languages are mainly left-headed or left-dominant), in Thai any neutralization is found on non-final syllables. Thirdly, there are some interactions between syllable structure, segment type, and tone.

In Standard Thai (also known as Tai, or Siamese), there are five tones: H, M, L, HL fall and LH rise. Sonorant-final syllables may bear any of these. Stop-final syllables with long vowels may have only low, L, or falling, HL. Stop-final syllables with short vowels may have only H or L. Data from Gandour 1975.

(48)		CV(V)([+son])		CVV[–son]		CV[–son]	
	M	khaa	'be stuck'				
	L	khaa	'a kind of spice'	yaak	'to want'	phit	'be wrong'
	HL	khaa	'to kill'	yaak	'be difficult'		
	H	khaa	'to engage in trade'			phit	'poison'
	LH	khaa	'leg'				

This is of course reminiscent of Cantonese, which limits all stop-final syllables to level tones only, and for which I proposed that the TBU was the mora, and that stop-final syllables had only one mora. For Thai this proposal is even more convincing, since it is specifically the short-vowelled stop-final syllables that are subject to the restriction. The remaining puzzle is why long-vowelled stop-final syllables cannot have M, H, or LH rise. The simple *number* of tones and TBUs is not going to help here, since L and HL *are* permitted. The lack of a rise on such syllables is also found in the Chin language Zahao (Osborne 1979), which has H, L, and LH tones, but only H and L on stop-final syllables, irrespective of vowel length. I propose that rising tones are incompatible with final glottal closure in these languages, and this can be stated as an interaction on the laryngeal tier *LH[+constricted glottis] (Yip 1982). (The odd thing about this is that post-vocalic glottal stops historically raised the ending pitch of the word, and thus induced rising tones!) The absence of plain M and H on CVVC syllables in Thai remains a puzzle.

7.7.2 Tones in combination

Given the five tones of Thai, bisyllables should be able to have 25 tonal patterns. Although some researchers have cast doubt on this claim, stating that tones are lost on the first syllable, instrumental work by Gandour (1974, Gandour *et al.* 1999) has shown the retention hypothesis to be correct. Thai is right-headed. In a bisyllabic compound the first syllable is less stressed, and substantially shorter, but the full set of tonal contrasts is preserved on underlyingly long vowels even in fast, casual speech, albeit much reduced.

(49)   H + L   máay 'wood' + khìit   'draw a line' → máy khìit 'matches'
          HL + M   mɛ̂ɛ 'mother' + yaay   'grand M' → mê yaay   'mother-in-law'

The one genuine neutralization occurs if the non-final syllable has a short vowel followed by a glottal stop, when the contrast between H and L is eliminated, and these syllables show up as M, with a reduced vowel and no glottal stop: /tháʔhǎan/ H.LH → [thəhǎan] M.LH 'soldier'. See Peyasantiwong 1980 for many examples and discussion.

This combination of non-head reductions – shortening of long vowels, loss of final glottal stop, reduction of short vowels, and loss of tonal contrasts – can all be seen as instances of the Emergence of the Unmarked (TETU), in which marked structures, such as long vowels and glottal-final syllables, and marked features, such as vowel features and tone, are lost except in head position. However, because some contrasts survive (such as coda segments with oral articulations), and particularly because the features and tones of underlyingly long vowels survive, a full account is non-trivial. In a rule-based derivational framework, one could propose a rule-ordering analysis in which final glottal stop, vowel features and tone features were all deleted from short vowels, and *after* this long vowels were shortened. In non-derivational OT such an approach is not available. The most promising line of attack is to assume that there is no phonological loss of information at all, and to view the changes as phonetic. If the input has a long vowel, even after phonetic shortening in fast casual speech there will be enough time remaining to allow the articulation of pitch and vowel differences. However, if the input has a short vowel followed by a glottal stop – a syllable that is very short even in citation form – by the time it is further shortened in fast casual speech there will be insufficient time to move the articulators and achieve vowel differences, pitch differences, or glottal closure.

Although in general Thai is right-headed, so that the first syllable is shorter and has some reduction in tonal contrasts, there is one area of the lexicon where the second syllable shows fewer contrasts than the first. In Indic bisyllabic morphemes (a large part of the lexicon), if the first syllable has a short, stop-final low-toned syllable, then the tone of sonorant-initial second syllables is predictable: if that syllable is stop-final, it too is low. If it is sonorant-final, it ends in a rise:

(50)   sà?mùt L.L 'ocean'   sà?wǎːn   L.LH   'heaven'

Although there are some counter-examples that blur this generalization somewhat (see Yip 1982, Peyasantiwong 1980), it is worth discussing. This interaction between segments and tone has a historical origin. These words were originally monosyllables beginning with [s+[son]] clusters, broken up by epenthesis (Gedney 1947). The tone of the epenthetic vowel was derived by spreading from the following nucleus: /swaːn LH/ > [sa.waːn L.LH]. Spreading was blocked by stops but not sonorants, perhaps because only stops have laryngeal specifications for voicing, aspiration and glottalization, and this laryngeal material blocks spreading of the laryngeal features of tone.

7.7.3 *Wuming Zhuang*

I now turn to Wuming Zhuang, a Tai language from the N. Zhuang group spoken in Shuangqiao village in Guangxi province in China (Snyder and Lu 1997). On open syllables it has six tones:

(51)   55   ha   'five'
        33   tau   'chopsticks'
        35   suɪ   'to wash'
        24   pai   'to go'
        42   ɣam   'water'
        21   muŋ   'you'

In the right syntactic and prosodic environment, the first syllable of a sequence surfaces as follows; note that 55 and 42 do not change, and all the other tones merge with one or other of these two:

(52)   55, 35, 24   →   55
        42, 33, 21   →   42

These changes take place if and only if one of the following circumstances holds:

(53)   1. Both syllables are L register: ku33 ŋam21 > ku42 ŋam21 do-game 'play'
        2. Both syllables have identical tones (OCP) :
           ɣai35 kai35 > ɣai55 kai35 egg-chicken 'chicken egg'
        3. First syllable is 33, which nearly always changes:
           pu33 tin55 > pu42 tin55 clothes-short 'short jacket'
        4. Second syllable is stop-final, which the authors report to be much shorter
           and deem 'light', i.e. monomoraic:
           ɣin24 mak33 > ɣin55 mak33   stone-ink 'ink-stick'

These changes are unusual in that the neutralization on the first syllable is to high and high falling tones, not to the usual less marked low or mid tones. Two observations help us understand these changes. First, the output has a first syllable that is either more prominent than or as prominent as the second syllable, on the assumption that high pitch and prominence have a cross-linguistic tendency to co-occur. Second, the exact form of the output tone is produced by the addition of a H tone to the start of the syllable, so that it starts high but ends on about its original pitch, so that the tones that end underlyingly on /5/ or /4/ become /55/, and those that end underlyingly on /3/, /2/, or /1/ end on /2/. This is the mirror-image of the Cantonese changed-tone suffix we saw in section 7.1.5. These two observations suggest the following analysis. Zhuang is left-headed, and heads require H tone (as in Zoll 1997a, or de Lacy 1999b), triggering the insertion of a H tone at the left edge.

Exercise 8.   Present a formal analysis of these data, either along the lines sketched above, or offering an alternative of your own. Make sure you explain why Zhuang augments the head instead of reducing the non-head, as has been more common in other systems we have seen.

For space reasons, I cannot discuss any other Tai-Kadai languages here. Some are tonally quite inert, some have quite complex tones which have been argued by Edmondson and Yang 1989 to behave as unitary contours.

Turning briefly to the other sub-families of Austro-Tai, Miao-Yao languages are mainly known for their very rich tonal inventories, with reports of up to five level tones (Hei-Miao; Chang 1953), and up to three rises or three falls. Such systems test the limits of our feature systems for tone, and have been discussed in chapters two and three on tonal contrasts and tonal features. Finally, some Austronesian languages in Melanesia have interesting tonal systems, although rather few are well described. Rivierre (1980) describes Cemuhi as having three tones, H, M, and L. Ninety per cent of words have the same tone throughout the word: ápún 'dessin', àpùn 'cheveux', īpī 'cueillir en cassant'. Some grammatical morphemes are toneless, and 10 per cent of words have two tones per word, but more than that is extremely rare. Jabem (Poser 1981) has an interesting interaction between consonant voicing and tone: see chapter two for details. Typologically, these languages look more similar to the African languages than to those of East Asia, but so few languages have been studied, and most only sketchily, that it is hard to draw any clear conclusions. One of the most detailed is James' (1981) work on Siane, to which the reader is referred for details.

7.8   Mon-Khmer

Mon-Khmer languages, which include Cambodian and Vietnamese, are members of the Austro-Asiatic family. They are distinguished by a very different syllable structure from Sino-Tibetan in that many if not most morphemes are 'sesquisyllabic', consisting of a normal syllable preceded by a sort of vestigial half syllable called a 'minor' syllable, as in these examples from Chong (Thongkum 1991, cited in Silverman 1996,1997a):

(54)   rəko?1   'tips (of climbers and creepers)'
        kəsut2   'to come off'
        kəlaaŋ3   'ear'

Such languages often have a voice quality distinction, but less often a truly tonal one. The quality distinction, usually called register, is sometimes clearly laryngeal, as in Sedang and Chong (Silverman 1996, 1997a, Smith 1968), but sometimes pharyngeal, involving the tongue root, as in Cambodian (Gregerson 1976). In the Chong words above, the digits 1–3 stand for three of the four registers. Register 1 has clear voice and high pitch. Register 2 has 'clear-then-creaky voice, high falling pitch'. Register 3 has breathy voice and lower pitch.

In Cambodian, another Mon-Khmer language, each full syllable of a word may have either of the two registers, but if the first word is a particular type of minor syllable (roughly, one without a full vocalic nucleus), it must have the same register as the following full syllable. Register, then, has a domain larger than the syllable, perhaps the iambic foot. In Kammu, there is no voice quality distinction, and some dialects distinguish two simple tones, H and L. In other dialects, however, the distinction is still one of onset voicing, with the pitch distinction secondary. See chapter two for more on Kammu.

7.8.1   Vietnamese

Vietnamese is that rare thing, a truly tonal Austro-Asiatic language, and thus merits inclusion in this book. Its tonal system is thought to have developed quite late, and although in many ways the language looks more like southern Chinese dialects than it does other Mon-Khmer languages (particularly in its monosyllabic character), it is usually agreed to be Mon-Khmer. Northern dialects have six tones, two of which are accompanied by creaky voice. Nhàn (1984) describes them as high level [4], high rising [35], low level [2], low falling [21], and two creaky concave tones [214] and [415]. He uses a feature system with contour features, but translated into a level tone system his system looks like the one shown in (55). Each column is headed by the traditional name of the tone (minus its diacritics), below this are the numerical values of each tone, and below this are the features.

(55)

ngang	sac	hoi	huyen	nang	nga
4	35	214	2	21	415
+Upper			−Upper		
h	lh	hlh	h	hl	hlh

Stop-final syllables may take only the [35] and [21] tones, which have exactly two component tones in sequence, and can therefore be identified as a natural class. In Chinese and Thai, stop-final syllables were treated as having only one TBU, and this was assumed to explain why they took only level tones, but of course no such explanation is available here, and it would seem that a straightforward stipulation is required. In support of the mora as TBU, in certain environments (apparently less stressed) tones are neutralized to the level tone within their register. This can perhaps be understood as a context in which syllables become shortened to one mora, supporting only a single (level) tone.

Nhàn observes that [−Upper] tones are all creaky in some dialects, such as Hue. In the standard dialect, the falling and rising tones are creaky and the level tone is not, but he assumes this to be a minor phonetic fact that does not change his view of their features, which is based on how these tones group into natural classes, as

I shall now discuss. The decision to consider [214] [+Upper] and [415] [−Upper] is justified primarily by their behaviour in reduplication, to be described in the next paragraph, and their phonetic pitch is dealt with by a late rule which switches their registers prior to phonetic implementation.

The most interesting tonal alternations are observed in reduplication, where there is frequent tonal neutralization in one of the two syllables. The language is rich in reduplication, and the choice of one of the many reduplication patterns seems to be lexically determined. Be that as it may, consider one of the most common patterns, in which the six-way tonal contrast is reduced to a two-way one: if the input syllable is 4, 35 or 214, that is [+Upper] in Nhàn's system, then the prefixal reduplicant surfaces as 4, as in (a). If the input syllable is 2, 21 or 415, i. e. [−Upper], then the prefixal reduplicant surfaces as 2, as in (b):

(56)   a. RED-xanh4   → xanh4-xanh-4   'blueish'
           RED-trăng35   → trăng4-trăng35   'whitish'
           RED- do214   → do4-do214   'reddish'

        b. RED-vang2   → vang2-vang2   'yellowish'
           RED-măn21   → măn2-măn21   'rather salty'
           RED-khe415   → khe2-khe415   'rather quiet'

This then is preservation of tonal *register*, but neutralization of tonal *melody* to [h]. If we take [h] to be unmarked in Vietnamese, this can be viewed as the emergence of the unmarked tonal melody [+high]. In OT terms, FAITHBR [+/−UP-PER] >> *[+/−UPPER], but *[−HIGH] >> FAITHBR[+/−HIGH]. FAITH-IO dominates all markedness, so in the base all contrasts survive. In the reduplicant, however, markedness wins out over base-reduplicant faithfulness. Now consider what happens if the input is stop-final. Recall that stop-final syllables can only bear the bi-tonal 35 and 21 tones. This is incompatible with the tonal changes required in reduplication, so something has to give. What happens is that the tonal changes win out, and the coda then changes to the equivalent sonorant:

(57)   RED-mat35 → man4-mat35   'a little breezy'

Exercise 9.   Construct an OT grammar for this scenario.

7.9   A coda

The focus so far in this chapter has been on East and South-East Asia, but for completeness I should add that tone languages are found elsewhere in Asia too. In South Asia, the Indo-Aryan language Punjabi is tonal, having developed low pitch in the environment of historically voiced aspirates. After a syllable-initial voiced aspirate, we find a rising tone, and after a syllable-final one, a falling tone: *bhukh > pukkh24, *baddha > bʌd42da. See section 2.8 for more details. In Melanesia, Papua-New Guinea boasts tone languages, such as Siane (James 1981, Kenstowicz 1994). These languages are typologically in many ways more like Bantu languages than they are Chinese. Siane has polysyllabic morphemes, a simple tonal inventory H, L, LH that associates one-to-one left to right with the word, and tone-spreading from roots to suffixes. Conversely, lest the reader think that all East Asian languages are tonal, let me point to one sub-family that is almost entirely non-tonal: Malayo-Polynesian, which includes Malay and Indonesian.

This completes the survey of Asian tone languages.

Answers to exercises

Answer to exercise 1

Addition of 5 would give a 535 complex tone. However, *535 will force loss of the medial 3 tone: *535, *FLOAT, FAITHHEADTONE >> MAX-T.

Answer to exercise 2

Presumably, Taishan ranks *535 very low, since it allows all sorts of very complex tones.

Answer to exercise 3

The deleting morphemes all have the tones (3)5. Assuming that the morphological deletion targets only segments, *FLOAT will then produce the same results as above. The extra 3 tone resulting from deletion of tsɔ35 or hai35 will delete by the same mechanism.

Answer to exercise 4

LH.LH is still a whole-tone OCP violation. Two tones are always more marked than one, incurring more violations of *T, the general markedness constraint governing tonal specifications, so HL.LH loses to H.LH on general markedness grounds; in any case the sequence HL.LH contains a low-level OCP violation, as does the sequence L.LH. General faithfulness normally overrides the OCP at the constituent tone level, so that /L.LH/ survives unchanged, but when faithfulness cannot be satisfied by any viable output because of the higher-ranking OCP on the tones as units, the low-level OCP kicks in.

210 *Asian and Pacific languages*

/LH.LH/	OCP(WholeTone)	Faith	OCP(ConstTone)	*T
☞ H.LH		*		***
L.LH		*	*!	***
HL.LH		*	*!	****
LH.LH	*!			****
/L.LH/				
☞L.LH			*	***
H.LH		*!		***

Answer to exercise 5

Nuclear tones are not changed if at all possible, so a more marked contour tone LH is preferred to H. In Exercise 4, the nuclear tone *is* changed, but only because holding it constant as L.LH would violate the higher ranked OCP(ConstTone)

OCP(ConstTone) >> Faith-NuclearTone >> *T

/L.L/	OCP(Whole)	Faith	OCP(Const)	FaithNucTone	*T
☞LH.L		*			***
H.L		*		*!	**
HL.L		*	*!	*	***
L.L	*!		*		**

Answer to exercise 6

Assume faithfulness as used in the Tianjin analysis is actually a cover term for several constraints, and can be decomposed into its component parts including Max-T, which blocks deletion of input tones, and Linearity, which blocks their re-ordering. If Max-T >> Linearity, and OCP(ConstTone), we get Pingyao: deletion is worse than metathesis. If Linearity and OCP(ConstTone) >> Max-T, we get tone deletion as in Tianjin.

Answer to exercise 7

To ensure that words are head-final, and all and only heads keep vowel features and tones: FtBin-μ, Align-R(Word, Foot), Head-Max-Feature >>

MARKEDNESS >> MAX-FEATURE, PARSE-σ. Note that this grammar allows non-final feet as well as final ones, thereby correctly admitting words with two feet, each of which has all its vowel and tonal features.

Answer to exercise 8

ALIGN-L(HEAD, WD), ALIGN (HEAD, H), ONET/M >> DEP T, MAX T.

Answer to exercise 9

FAITH-IO >> *[+/–HIGH], TT[–SON] >> IDENT-SON, where TT[–SON] is some constraint that limits stop-final syllables to the 35 and 21 tones.

8

The Americas

Of the three regions that have merited their own chapters in this book, the Americas have the least studied tonal phonology, especially from a theoretical perspective. Since much of the apparatus of tonal theory was developed for African or Asian languages, it seemed advisable to begin with those, and then, with tools in hand, turn to this less-analysed region. I divide this chapter into three main sections. The first, and much the most detailed, looks at Central America, which is rich in tone languages, many of which are very well documented. The second deals with the rather scarce and sadly all too often dead or moribund tone languages of North America. The last deals with South America, about whose tonal systems relatively little is known.

8.1   Central America

8.1.1   Overview of families

Many of the languages of Central America are tonal, particularly the Otomanguean family, which includes Mixtec, Mazatec, Zapotec, Chinantec, Trique, and Chatino. Outside Otomanguean, we find occasional tone languages, including some Mayan languages such as Yucatec and Uspantec Mayan, and San Bartolo Tzotzil, some Tarascan languages such as Tlapanec and Cuitlatec, the San Mateo dialect of the language isolate Huave, and the Uto-Aztecan language N. Tepehuan. The tonal systems of neighbouring dialects can vary dramatically, so one does not talk of the tones of Mixtec, but of the tones of the specific dialect, such as Peñoles Mixtec, or San Miguel el Grande Mixtec. Table 8.1 shows the affiliations of representative tone languages in this area, including those discussed in this chapter. The classification is that of Suarez (1983). Many of these languages have been very well described, starting with the pioneering work of Kenneth Pike and his associates (e.g. Pike 1948, and many other publications), but there is relatively little recent theoretical work on their

Table 8.1.   *Central American tone languages*

Otomanguean	Mixtec	San Miguel El Grande, Molinos, Peñoles, Ayutla, Huajuapan (= Cacaloxtepec)
	Mazatec	Chiquihuitlan, Jalapa, Choapan
	Zapotec	Sierra Juárez, Isthmus
	Chinantec	Comaltepec
	Trique	San Juan Copala, San Andrés Chicahuaxtla
	Chatino	Yaitepec
Uto-Aztecan		N. Tepehuan
Huave		San Mateo
Tarascan		Tlapanec, Cuitlatec
Mayan		Yucatec, Uspantec, San Bartolo Tzotzil

tonal systems. Nevertheless, I will try to present a representative set of phenomena from this region.

The languages of central America occupy in some ways a middle ground between the Bantu languages of Africa, with their often highly mobile tone systems, and the Chinese languages of Asia, with their much more sedentary tones. We find languages like Chinantec in which tone is used for verbal inflection, and spreads over the verb root, and languages like San Miguel el Grande Mixtec, in which floating tones abound. On the other hand we find some Mazatec languages in which there is virtually no tone sandhi at all. Tonal inventories in these languages look at first more reminiscent of Asian systems in that there are frequently multiple levels (up to five in some descriptions), and many contour tones as well. But as in Bantu languages, these contours can often be shown to derive from concatenations of level tones, one of the level tones is often apparently unmarked, and we find upstep and downstep in some languages. On the morphological front, roots in these languages are usually either monosyllabic (Chinantec) or bisyllabic (Mixtecan), and in some languages the morphology provides fairly rich affixal possibilities. One of the most interesting phenomena in this region is the interaction of stress and tone, in both directions. We will look at cases where only stressed syllables may bear tonal contrasts (Zapotec, Trique, Huave), something familiar from Chinese, but also at systems where the placement of stress depends on the specific tones of a syllable (several dialects of Mixtec).

8.1.2   Tonal inventories

8.1.2.1   Number of levels

In central America it is common to find languages with four level tones, and some seem to use five. Many also have multiple contours, composed of sequences of levels. The tradition in this region is to use a five-digit notation, with 1 standing for the highest tone and 5 for the lowest. This is of course the reverse of the Asian tradition, but I have retained the usual practice in order to allow for cross-reference to the original sources.

One cannot conclude that just because a description of the dialect makes use of all five digits, the language contrasts five levels. Let us begin with two dialects of Trique (Hollenbach 1977), which are often cited as languages with five level and three rising tones, and therefore a problem for any feature system which only defines four levels and two rises, like the one proposed in chapter three. I start with San Juan Copala Trique (SJC), because Hollenbach gives a perfect set of minimal pairs to illustrate the tonal contrasts. SJC has the following tones on final syllables with long vowels:

(1)   *Level*   *Fall*   *Rise*
        3   yã   'he is sitting'   34   yã   'salt'   21   yã   'to be sitting'
        4   yã   'unmarried'   35   yã   'scar'   32   yã   'corncob'
        5   yã   'one'   53   yã   'Spanish moss'

On final short vowels we get /3, 4, 5, 34, 32, 53/, and on non-final syllables we get only /3, 4, 21/. There are also some restrictions on the tones in final syllables checked by [ʔ, h]. Many non-final syllables have no tone, in which case they are roughly [3] or [4] depending on the following tone. San Andrés Chicahuaxtla Trique (SAC), a closely related dialect, has a much larger array of tones on final syllables, including six falls and seven rises. On penults and antepenults we get a smaller set of level tones. If we eliminate four contours that occur in only one morpheme each, we are left with the following system.

(2)   antepenult: level   3, 4, 5
        penult   level   2, 3, 4, 5
        final: level   2, 3, 4, 5
                    fall   12, 23, 34, 35, 45
                    rise   21, 43, 53, 54
                    complex   343 354

The four level tones can be handled by our feature system, but the rises and falls are trickier. In Asian systems I proposed that underlying contours had a constant register, and thus the only possible rises were [H, lh] and [L, lh], where upper case [H, L] stand for tonal register, and lower-case [h, l] for the pitch features. If we propose that this is a typological variable, and that other languages may have underlying contours that are true tonal clusters, then we can use our four levels to represent up to six rises and six falls, sufficient for this system. Consider the rises. Here is a reasonable feature representation, followed by a pictorial depiction of the featural representation:

(3) 21 [H, lh]
     43 [L, h][H, l]
     54 [L, lh]
     53 [L, l] [H, l]

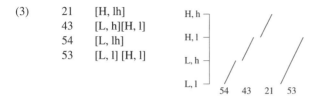

Now consider the falls. Here is a reasonable feature representation, followed again by a picture

(4) 12 [H, hl]
     23 [H, h][L, h]
     34 [H, l][L, h]
     35 [H, l] [L, l]
     45 [L, hl]

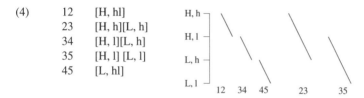

The first problem is that if we add back in to the system the extremely rare extra rises (32, 52, 51) and falls (13), the feature system cannot cope: there are then seven rises, and six is the maximum that can be composed out of four levels. The second problem is that the representations in (3)–(4) are not a very good match to the particular falls and rises chosen by this language. To see this, consider the diagram (5) in which the five-digit system is taken seriously, and the tones drawn exactly as recorded by Hollenbach. The ones in solid lines are the basic system, the ones in dotted lines are the rare ones.

(5)

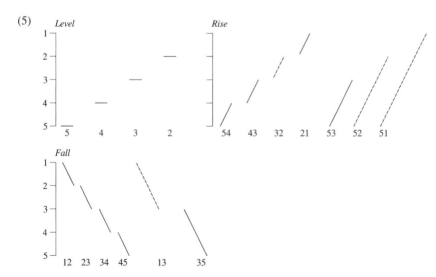

Phonetically, this system is superbly designed to maximize the use of the tone space. The contours have absolutely minimal overlap with other contours of a similar range, except for the most dramatic (but rare) rises. It is exactly the kind of system that we would expect in an approach like Flemming's (see chapter seven, §7.4 on Chaoyang), in which the perception of contrasts determines the choice of tones. However, a feature system that directly represents four non-overlapping identical contours by reference to their end-points will need to refer to at least five levels, something most of the systems proposed in this book cannot do.

These Trique dialects are a good introduction to the complex inventories of these languages, although some of course are a great deal simpler than this. In the next section I look more closely at the origins of contour tones.

Exercise 1. Discuss how one might analyse SAC by extending the tools laid out in chapter seven. Assume that SAC requires a thirteen-tone contrast, and will not space level tones more than 33 per cent of the pitch-range apart. Make sure to comment on why the following tones are rare or not found: 32, 31, 13. This is not a problem with one right answer, and a full formal account is not needed. Instead, discuss how the inventory can be seen as a perceptually tractable way to convey information effectively.

8.1.2.2 Contours as sequences

As in African and Asian languages, many of the contours in the Americas are demonstrably composed of levels. For example, Jamieson (1977) describes the Chiquihuitlan dialect of Mazatec. There are four level tones:

(6)   ǐha1   'I talk'   ki4šũ2   'landslide'
       ǐha2   'difficult'   ki4šũ4   'charcoal'
       ǐha3   'his hand'   ci1thä1   'I cough'
       ǐha4   'he talks'   ci3thä1   'I will spin it'

There are also contours, referred to by Jamieson as 'clusters', and the two-tone clusters are [14 24 34] and [21 31 41]. These have two sources, as best one can tell from Jamieson. Some result from morphological concatenation and others are the result of spreading rules. Consider the following verbal data:

(7)   ʔyu̜1   'you (pl.) drink'   ʔyu̜3   'you (pl.) know'   ʔyu̜2   'you (pl.) grind'
       ʔyu̜l4   'we (excl.) drink' ʔyu̜34   'we (excl.) know'   ʔyu̜24   'we (excl.) grind'

It would appear that a /4/ tonal suffix is associated with the first person plural exclusive morpheme, and forms a contour with the underlying tone of the verb.

Jamieson also discusses a set of tone sandhi rules which spread any preceding tone on to a /4/ tone, creating a contour:

(8)   σ   σ
         └─╲╱─┐
         T   4

The following data illustrate this process:

(9)   ho1 + khua4   →   ho1 khua14   'two + word'
         kui?42 + me4   →   kui?42 me 24   'will drink + they'
         koh3 + me4   →   koh3 me34   'with + they'

Notice that contours behave like clusters in triggering the process too: /2/ spreads off /42/ just as it does off a level 2.

The situation we have just seen is fairly common in this region. There are either no underlying contour tones, or a fairly small number, but many additional ones can be created by morphological concatenation and spreading. The constraints against many-to-one linkage are clearly much weaker than they are in Bantu languages.

8.1.2.3   Upstep and downstep

Downstep in some languages of this area looks very much like the downstep we have seen in Africa, with the cause being an unassociated low tone. A low tone is set loose to float, but its influence can be seen by the fact that it causes a following H to lower, and any subsequent H tones are realized at this new low level. We find this in Isthmus Zapotec (Mock 1981, 1988). For example, the underlying rising tone on the first syllable of *găpá* (not glossed) can lose the low part of the rise, but in that case the remaining H is downstepped, as in this sentence:

(10)   qué !gápá xpícuá' cŏlà   'my dog does not have a tail'
         | | | | | ∧ |
         H L H H H H L H L

More complex data can be found by looking at the Mixtec dialects, which have some of the most complex and interesting tonal systems of central America. Typically root morphemes are bisyllabic, and there is quite rich morphology. The tonal inventories are usually relatively simple, with two or three level tones and some contours as a result of concatenation. Peñoles Mixtec (Daly 1993) is of this type, but it also shows both downstep and upstep, and these are the subject of this section.

Consider these Peñoles data, showing three different tonal patterns on the head noun; note that low tones may drift lower in a downward glide.

(11)   H H   úní čáká   'three fish'   H L   úní tíkā   'three grasshoppers'
              [⁻ ⁻ ⁻⁻]   [⁻ ⁻ ⁻ˎ]

        L L   úní kɨtɨ   'three animals'
              [⁻ ⁻ ˎ ˎ]

What seems to be missing is the expected /LH/, but this is an illusion: its phonetic form is masked by the phenomenon of downstep. Recall that a downstepped H is found when a surface L tone causes a H to be phonetically lower than the preceding H, and also that this downstepped H may in fact be on the same level as the preceding low. It can be distinguished from a true L only by the fact that a following L is lower still. The clearest support for the existence of downstep in Peñoles comes from the realization of H-toned words embedded in phrases after L-toned words, as shown below. I separate out the tones to make the data clearer:

(12)   kwita   liʔi - de   lose rooster-his
        H L   H L   H   'His rooster will be lost'
        [⁻ -   -ˍ   ˍ]

The L tone of /(kwi)ta/ causes the following H to be realized at a lower pitch than a preceding H, and each new L further lowers any following Hs. Returning to the apparent absence of /LH/ nouns, it should now be clear that such a noun would have a downstepped H on the second syllable, which would thus be at the same pitch as the preceding L, just like the /H/ or the suffix /-de/ in the above example, which is at the same pitch as the preceding L syllable. Such nouns indeed exist:

(13)   /HH LH/   úní īná 'three dogs'   [H H L!H], phonetically identical to [H H L L]
                  [⁻ ⁻ --]

Although the /H/ of the second syllable of 'dog' is at the same level as L tones could be, it differs from a true L in that it cannot drift lower in a glide. Compare with 'animal' above. What we now see, then, is a tonal system very much like many Bantu ones, with L and H tones, and downstep.

There is another tone in Peñoles that has an unusual effect. It causes any subsequent /H/ tones to be upstepped, and its effects continue indefinitely to the right, so that each new /H/ is upstepped again. Daly represents this as /Lʰ/, but we might write /L⒣/, where ⒣ denotes a floating H. Its effects are summarized by Daly as follows:

(14)   (a) A /L⒣/tone is at a low pitch.
        (b) One or more following L tones begin a step higher and end at the level of a following H tone, or drift lower if not followed by a H tone.
        (c) The first H tone following a /L⒣/ tone is a step higher and subsequent H tones are a step higher yet.

There is a class of morphemes, including loanwords, that begin underlyingly with this /L(H)/ sequence preceding any of the four possible tone patterns that we have already seen. In addition, lexical subclasses of words with HH and LL tones may add a /L(H)/ tone to the following morpheme. One such morpheme is the enclitic /-ndo/, which has an underlying /L/ tone, assimilated to the preceding H in these examples by a regular rule. In addition /-ndo/ has a floating /(H)/, and this H plus the L set free by the earlier H spreading attach rightward to the following noun.

(15)   kini-ndo   ñaña   ' you (pl.) will see coyote'
       L H   L(H)   H H

       [- - -   ⌐ ¯]

       kini-ndo   ina   'you (pl.) will see dog'
       L H   L(H)   L H

       [- - -   _ -]

On the first syllable of 'coyote' the tonal sequence combines to produce a sharp rise from L to the upstepped high, which goes even higher on the next H. On the first syllable of 'dog' the effects of the /L(H)/ are also twofold: it is first realized as a very low tone, then the following H, instead of being downstepped as is usual for a H after a normal L (and as this would be in isolation, as shown above), is realized at the same level as the preceding Hs. In other words, the upstep cancels out the normal downstep.

   The odd thing about this upstep is its continuing effect: rows of Hs are all upstepped after a single occurrence of the /L(H)/ tone. One possible interpretation of this is that there is some kind of domino effect, with the floating H pushing a following H off its host and creating a new floating H and so on, but such an account would have to be iterative and derivational, and cannot easily be stated in OT. Note by the way that downdrift and downstep do not behave this way; after a L, the immediately following H is downstepped, but any subsequent Hs are at the same level as this H, and are not downstepped further.

8.1.2.4 Marked vs. unmarked tones

   In many languages with simple tonal inventories, H / L or H / M / L, one of the tones is taken to be unspecified, absent from the underlying representation, and inserted by later default rules. This has in fact become the standard analysis of Bantu languages, in which H is taken to be marked, and present, and L unmarked, and absent. In Chinese languages such an approach is rarely tenable, and indeed in chapter seven it was argued that positive evidence for both H and L could be found from the activity of the OCP. Not enough work has been done on this issue in Central American languages for a full picture to emerge, but in two languages researchers have argued for an unspecified tone, although interestingly it is not the expected L tone that appears to be unspecified, but rather H in one case and M in another.

Let me begin with San Mateo Huave, as analysed by Noyer (1992). Huave is a language isolate, with two surface tones, H and L. These interact in an interesting way with stress, and I will return to this topic in section 8.1.4.1. For now, what we need to know is that stress is predictable, and stressed syllables may be H or HL; this tone difference is lexically contrastive. Pre- and post-tonic syllables are L (unless they undergo H tone spreading). In the following examples the stressed syllable is marked with an acute accent; in (a–b) it is H, and in (c–d) it is HL. Syllable boundaries, inferred from Noyer's paper, are marked by dots. The syllable is the TBU, and H falls on the syllabic head. There is a late rule of vowel lengthening: see below for details.

(16)   a. o.lám   'sugar cane'   c. i.çwéak   'monkey'
            L H   L HL

        b. ʃíʌl   'wood'   d. a.ʃóood   'he rests'
            H   L HL

Noyer suggests that the simplest account of these data is to assume an underlying L vs. ø contrast, and a process that inserts a H on the stressed syllable. If that syllable is toneless, it will surface as plain H. If it already has a lexical L, it will surface as HL. If a syllable is unstressed, lexical L surfaces unchanged. If a syllable remains toneless, it will ultimately receive a default L tone. This analysis gives a simple and elegant account of the data and leads to the rather surprising conclusion that L is both the only tone marked in the lexicon, and also the default tone. This latter statement brings Huave into line with what we know about many other tone languages: that L is usually the default tone. What is new is that it breaks the link between the property of being the default tone and the property of not being lexically marked. That link, however, is not inevitable: in Chinese languages we have seen cases where all tones are lexically marked, including L, but toneless syllables nevertheless receive a default L. What is really new about Huave is that there is no *other* tone that is lexically marked. In languages with no other source of tones, this would mean that all syllables would surface as L, either lexically or by default, and the language would not appear to be tonal at all. The reason this does not happen in Huave is because Huave also has a stress system, and this stress system supplies a H to each word, which interacts with the L vs. ø distinction to create the observed surface pitches.

In closing, let me note that one might dispute this analysis and suggest that both H and L are marked. When the H supplied by the stress system is added to H, we get HH, and when it is added to L we get HL. The main reason that this analysis is not tenable is because Noyer shows that each tone in Huave needs its own vocalic mora, and that when H is added to a L syllable it therefore induces lengthening. Even already long vowels lengthen, as in the surface form [a.ʃóood] 'he rests' because they are in fact underlying /Vh/ sequences with only one vocalic mora. If the surface H syllables were in fact HH, they should also undergo lengthening, but they do not: contrast (16a–b) with (16c–d) above.

Exercise 2. Propose an OT analysis of these data. For present purposes, assume a constraint Stress = H which requires stressed syllables to have H tones. Do not try to predict stress placement.

Supplementary (harder). In OT, inputs cannot be restricted (the Richness of the Base Hypothesis). It is therefore necessary to consider inputs with specified H tones. Discuss how these could be handled.

The second case of underspecification I shall discuss is San Miguel el Grande Mixtec (SMG) as analysed by Tranel (1995, 1996). SMG has three surface tones, H, M, and L. On bimoraic words (the normal shape for Mixtec roots) almost all combinations occur, except for LL. There are no contour tones at all. Mixtec has many floating H tones (see below), and these anchor onto a following morpheme. The most general pattern is for the H to simply replace the first tone of the stem. If this is H no change is detectable, of course, but if it is M or L we get data like these. (Note: acute accent marks H tone, grave accent marks L, M are unmarked.)

(17) *Changes found after a floating H tone:*

      LM → HM   kìku → kíku   'to sew'
      LH → HH   kʷàán → kʷáán   'yellow'
      MM → HM   beʔe → béʔe   'house'

The interesting pattern comes with ML and MH inputs, when the floating H skips the M vowel and anchors to the end of the word. This means no change for MH inputs, but ML becomes MH:

(18)   ML → MH   žukù→ žukú   'branch'

        MH → MH   kučí → kučí   'pig'

Tranel's suggestion is that M vowels are toneless in this language, and that the language first and foremost respects the distinction between vowels that have tones and vowels that do not. When the floating H is looking for an anchor, it therefore avoids toneless vowels because to associate with them would change what Tranel calls the Tonal Prominence Profile of the vowel. Far from seeking out a toneless vowel, as one might expect, these floating Hs disdain them. The only occasion when they associate to a toneless vowel is when there are no toned vowels around, that is, if the input is MM, and then the H attaches to the first vowel to give HM. In OT terms, then, *FLOAT >> TONALPROMINENCEFAITH. Goldsmith (1990) takes a different view of these same data, and assumes that all three tones are specified. He is then forced to posit an *ad hoc* metathesis rule that moves a H tone around a M tone, if a H or a L follows. Tranel's account is clearly to be preferred, because it aims for a deeper explanation of the reason behind this behaviour.

We have seen the kinds of arguments that have been proposed in favour of the view that tones may be unspecified. I now turn to a topic on which these languages shed much light: the relationship between tonal features and glottal features. The first case I shall discuss comes from the same language we have just been discussing, San Miguel el Grande Mixtec.

8.1.2.5   Interaction with glottals

In general in phonology, like things interact. We do not expect to find labials causing vowel fronting, or laterals blocking rounding harmony, for example. What makes sounds 'alike' are their articulatory and acoustic properties phonologized as feature specifications. Tones are produced by modifications of the configuration of the larynx, so it would not be surprising to find interactions between laryngeal features, or laryngeal segments, and tone, and of course we do. One good example is the behaviour of depressor consonants discussed in chapters two, three and six. The Central American languages provide some interesting examples.

In the last section we discussed the fact that a floating H tone in San Miguel el Grande Mixtec will move rightward over a toneless vowel until it finds a toned vowel. So a ML input (i.e. /∅L/) after a floating H becomes [MH]. This high spreading is, however, blocked if a glottal stop intervenes, and the H then settles for the first vowel instead:

(19)   MʔL → HʔL   taʔù→ táʔù   'to beat'

Given that the floating H originates with the morpheme to the left, it is a prefix by nature. On the assumption that all laryngeals occupy a single tier in the representation, there are only two ways to associate it to the final vowel over an intervening glottal stop. One is to use a rule of metathesis (or in OT terms to violate LINEARITY), and the other is to allow association lines to cross, in violation of NOCROSSING. Mixtec apparently ranks both these highly, and in particular above TONALPROMINENCEFAITH (see (20)). (Note: Here I depart from some details of Tranel's analysis, but the essential insights are still his.)

(20)

ta?ù ‖ H + ?L	NOCROSSING	LINEARITY	TONEPROMFAITH
☞ ta?u / ‖ H + ?L			*
ta?u ‖ ?H L		*!	
ta?u ⤬ H +? L	*!		

Lastly, let me note that glottal stop can be skipped in just one circumstance; when it is the only way to associate the floating H tone. This is the case when a word begins with a glottal stop, and indeed this initial glottal allows the H to pass over: ?isò → ?isó 'rabbit'. We must conclude, then, that *FLOAT >> LINEARITY.

A second type of interaction between laryngeal articulations and tone has recently been discussed by Silverman (1997a). Languages may have different phonation types on vowels, such as breathy or creaky vowels. We have seen languages in South-East Asia in which these co-exist with tone, and the same is true here. What Silverman draws attention to is an interesting tension between these special phonation types and tone: purely tonal, pitch-based contrasts are better perceived on plain (or 'modal') vowels than they are on breathy or creaky vowels. In several Otomanguean languages, he shows that the phonation contrasts and the tonal contrasts are sequenced in time so as not to interfere with each other. First, consider Jalapa Mazatec, which has three level tones and several contours. It also has breathy and creaky vowels. Silverman observes that the breathy or creaky phonation is realized primarily in the last half of the onset and the first half of each vowel. This leaves a modal portion of the vowel vacant for tonal use. Breathiness is shown by two dots beneath the vowel, and creakiness by a tilde beneath the vowel. Tones are shown by 1 for high and 5 for low.

(21)   nn̬aa31 'nine'   nn̬ææ3 'he says'

Comaltepec Chinantec takes a different tack. As in many Chinantec languages, syllables are described as having either 'controlled' or 'ballistic' stress. According to Silverman, ballistically stressed syllables have post-vocalic aspiration, and are articulated more forcefully than controlled stressed syllables. They often rise slightly in pitch at the end, whereas controlled stressed syllables show a gradual decrease. The last part of a ballistically stressed syllable shows aperiodic noise, characteristic of aspiration. In this language, then, it is the first part of the vowel that is available for tonal contrasts.

Lastly, Silverman looks at Copala Trique, which possesses what are termed laryngeally 'interrupted' vowels, transcribed as [VʔV] or [VhV].

(22)   ga3tuʔu32   'incense-burner'
         ɾi3uhu53   'hollow reed'
         na3ʔaha32   'conversation'

These interrupted vowels are clearly single syllables: they count as one syllable for the bisyllabic word template, they have the same tonal sequences as single vowels, they do not undergo final lengthening as one would expect if they were a sequence of two short syllables, and so on. Silverman believes that a contour tone on one of these syllables is realized as two levels on each half of the intervening laryngeal: /..ʔaha32/ > [ʔa3ha2], and that again the separation of non-modal phonation from the tonal portion maximizes the likelihood of accurate perception of the tonal data. In closing, Silverman points out that languages that do not segregate non-modal phonation and tone, like Mpi, tend to use less laryngeal constriction, and thus interfere less with pitch perception.

8.1.3   Tone alternations

Although tones are not as mobile as they frequently are in Bantu, Central American languages have rich and complex tonal phonologies, showing many by-now-familiar types of interaction.

8.1.3.1   Stability

One of the traditional arguments for assigning tones to an independent autosegmental tier is the so-called stability effect. This is the name for the ability of tones to survive even after their host segments have been deleted, and then to surface on a neighbouring segment. Not surprisingly, examples of this behaviour in Central America are not particularly hard to find. I will content myself with a single example, from Comaltepec Chinantec (Pace 1990: 57). In this language, questions are formed by prefacing the sentence with a question marker /sɨMH/. However, this marker may be deleted, in which case its tones show up on the first word of the sentence, replacing the basic tones of that word:

(23)   sɨMH sʌHL hmɨːL   →   sʌMH hmɨːL   'Is there any water?'

In some cases of stability the stranded tones share their new syllable with its underlying tones, but here they displace them. It is reasonable to assume that this is because two tones are set free by deletion, and this is the maximum number that can fit on a syllable at once. As for why they triumph over the underlying tones, we know that when this is the only way for the last trace of a morpheme to achieve any kind of realization in the output, survival is common. In the segmental area, for example, Beijing Mandarin has a suffixal /-r/, and this replaces the coda of the root when added to a word like /pan/: /pan + r/ > [par]. Mandarin does not allow complex codas, and in the fight for supremacy the deciding factor is the need for every morpheme to have something to show of itself in the output. More formally, in OT terms constraints such as REALIZEMORPH have been proposed to encode this tendency (Lin 1993, 2001).

8.1.3.2 Spreading

A second reason to treat tone as independent has been its ability to spread out over more than one syllable. Sometimes this spreading is local, taking in just one extra syllable, and sometimes it is unbounded, covering any number of available target syllables. Both these are found in Central America, and to exemplify local spreading I will use the same dialect of Chinantec. The data and analysis this time are from a very interesting paper by Silverman (1997b). I start with the essentials. There is a spreading process in which H spreads off a LH tone onto a neighbouring syllable to its right. If this syllable is L or M it creates a HL or HM contour:

(24)   kwaLH toːL   →   kwaLH toːHL   'give a banana'
           kwaLH kuːM   →   kwaLH kuːHM   'give money'

This can be simply shown autosegmentally:

(25)   kwa toː
           $\bigwedge$
           L H L

The fundamental question posed by Silverman, however, is '*Why* does this happen?' In particular, he notes that this is a language in which tones bear a very large functional load, carrying as they do most verbal inflectional information (see below), and that tone sandhi is therefore dangerous because it runs the risk of neutralizing semantically central contrasts. His answer is that the sandhi is very finely tuned so as to minimize the amount of neutralization, while still making articulation easier. Consider the fact that it is only the H of a LH rise that spreads, and not a level H. We know that rising tones take longer to produce, especially if the rise involved is large, as it is here. Thus some perseveration into the next syllable is not surprising, and has been phonologized into this sandhi rule. It turns out that HL is not a lexically possible sequence, so no neutralization results. Now consider a new fact: if the target is LH, we would expect a HLH output, but instead we get MH. Silverman suggests that HLH is too complex to allow reliable recoverability of all the tones, and that instead the HL portion 'blends' into M, giving MH. Again, however, there is no neutralization, because MH is not an underlying sequence, nor does it result from any other rule. The system is quite complex, and the reader should consult Silverman for further details.

My next example is of unbounded spread, something we have seen frequently in Bantu, and also in the Wu dialects of Chinese. Here I use Huave as my example, drawing again on Noyer (1992). Recall that Huave inserts a H tone on the main stressed syllable, and that there are no underlying Hs. Since each word has one main stress, each word thus has exactly one H. However, in phrases H spreads rightward off a stressed syllable, obliterating tonal contrasts to its right. The domain of this spreading will be addressed shortly, but first here are some representative data. As before, stressed syllables are marked by an acute accent and surface tones are shown below: (a) shows isolation forms, and (b) shows the spreading of H rightwards off the first main stress.

(26)   a. ta.ha.wáw 'they saw'   na.kánc   'red'   o.lám 'sugar cane'
            L L H   L H   L H

        b. ta.ha.wáw na.kánc o.lám   'they saw red sugarcane'
            L L   H   H H   H H

Autosegmentally, this can be viewed as spreading of the first H rightward, forcing detachment of any other tones:

(27)   ta.ha.wáw na.kánc o.lám
            | | |
            L L H   L H   L H

The domain of this rule seems to be co-extensive with the syntactic phrase, and H insertion can now be seen to be limited to the phrasal head, off which it then spreads rightward. For example, NPs are right-headed, and thus all syllables to the left of the head noun's stressed syllable are L, and since the head is final right-spread is irrelevant. (Spread does not seem to happen within the final word, as shown by (28b), for reasons that are unclear.)

(28)   a. na.dám   'large'   pɛát   'mountain'   na.dám pɛát
           L H   HL   L L   HL

         b. nan.goʃ nʌt tɛat ní.ne   'big day father child' 'Christmas'
           L L   L LL H L

VPs, on the other hand, are left-headed, and here the rightward spread becomes visible, as shown by the example in (26b) above, and by this VP:

(29)   i.wʌ́n o.ʃiŋ ʃa.ma.çat   'You-sharpen nose(tip) my-machete'
         L H   H H H H   H

Noyer does not give enough information about the syntax for us to be quite sure that VP is the relevant constituent here. It could also be S, because all his examples have no overt subject, so VP and S are co-extensive.

The two examples of spreading in this section show that this region's languages include processes that are much like the local tone sandhi common in Asia and, under the name of flop, also common in Africa. Similarly the long-distance spreading of Huave, while apparently relatively rare in this part of the world, is well attested in Bantu, and it is not unlike the Wu dialects of China, where it also spreads off a stressed syllable within a syntactically defined domain. We start to see that our knowledge of tone gained by the study of unrelated language families helps us in understanding its behaviour in a new area.

8.1.3.3 Floating tones

One of the notable phenomena among African languages is the large number of floating tones, particularly L tones. Floating L tones often manifest themselves as downstep; they do not themselves surface, but they cause a following H to be downstepped. In Central America floating tones are also common. We saw earlier that Peñoles Mixtec has a floating H as part of a /L H/ complex, and that this H caused upstep. We also saw a case in San Miguel el Grande Mixtec where a floating H sought out a toned vowel to its right to attach to. Floating tones also lurk in less obvious places, as we will now see.

Throughout Mixtec we find that roots must be assigned to classes, according to whether they cause a change in the tone of the word to their right. Molinos Mixtec (Hunter and Pike 1969) is one such dialect. I present the data as in the original source, because readers will be asked shortly to perform their own analyses! Molinos Mixtec has three levels, [1, 2, 3], and these can combine. Words with /11, 22, 33, 32/ tones are either Class A, in which case they do not affect the words to their right, or Class B, in which case they do. There are Class A words and Class B words with each of these four tones, and class membership is a lexical matter. For example, in the (a) examples in (30) the second word has its tones unchanged, because the first word is Class A. In the (b) examples the tones change, because the first word is Class B.

(30)   a. Class A + Class 22A: /33A + 22A/ → [33 + 22]
              ʔu3ši3 ri2ŋki2   →   ʔu3ši3 ri2ŋki2   'ten mice'
        b. Class B + Class 22A: /11B + 22A/ → [11 + 12]
              si1vi1 ri2ŋki2   →   si1vi1 ri1ŋki2   name-mouse 'mouse's name'

Below I summarize a subset of the effects of Class B words on the following word, slightly simplified:

(31)   *Tonal changes in words that follow a Class B word*
        Underlying tone of second word

        a. 11, 12, 13   No change
            31, 22B and 32B   Change to 11
            22A, 32A   Change to 12
            23, 33 (on CV(ʔ)V roots)   Change to 13
        b. 23, 33 (on CVCV roots)   Change to 31

Exercise 3.   Propose an analysis of the data in (31a). The crucial step will be to propose what aspect of the underlying representation is different in the Class B words. After this, you will need to posit a principle that governs how the surface representations are derived. Leave the cases which change to [31] until last; if you cannot fully explain them, discuss why the tools provided so far in this chapter do not seem to work here.

Comaltepec Chinantec (Pace 1990: 26) has a system that looks quite similar, with a set of morphemes called 'perturbing' morphemes that cause tone change in the following syllable. The changes are complex, but they include changing a L into a HL fall, and a M into a H or a MH, so they also suggest that perturbing morphemes are followed by a floating H tone. This brief section on floating tones leads naturally into the next section, in which I discuss cases where morphemes consist *solely* of tones.

8.1.3.4 Inflectional morphemes

African languages make a rich use of tone for verbal tense and aspect, but this use of tone is essentially unknown in Asia, except as a result of segmental deletion with subsequent tonal reassociation. In African languages the tonal morphemes are routinely overlaid on verbs whose morphology is already complex, with a rich set of segmental affixes. The Central American languages most known for this use of tone are Chinantec, Chatino, and Mazateco, and they differ in that there are very few segmental affixes and tone carries a huge functional load. I begin with Chinantec, using data from Pace 1990. In this language verb roots are monosyllabic, and there is a set of tense-aspect prefixes. There are also reduced pronominal suffixes, which typically involve reduplication of the last root vowel. Alongside this segmental material, aspect, person and number are also conveyed by tone changes, vowel changes, and changes in whether the syllable has ballistic or controlled stress (see section 8.1.2.5; basically, ballistic stress involves post-vocalic aspiration). The fact that these three qualities form a complex that can be overlaid on the basic verb root underlines their close relationship in these languages, as discussed earlier.

A typical paradigm is given below; I have continued Pace's practice of marking the reduplicative suffix as R. This is realized as a syllabic nasal if the verb ends in a nasal, [ka^{L}kyan?^{M}-n̩^{L}] 'I slept', and otherwise as a repetition of the final vowel [dzi?^{LH}-i^L] 'I will terminate'. The acute accent marks ballistic stress.

(32)   *Verb root: /ko/ 'play'*

	1sg.	*1pl.*	*2sg.*	*3*
Progressive	kó:^{L}-R	ko:^{M}-R?	ko:^{L}-?	kó:^{L}-r
Intentive	ni^L-kó:^{LH}-R	ni^L-kó^H-R?	ni^L-kó:^{H}-?	ni^L-kó^M-r
Completive	ka^L-kó^M-R	ka^L-kó^H-R?	ka^L-ko:^{M}-?	ka^L-kó:^{L}-r

Eliminating the segmental material allows us to see the tone, length, and stress changes more easily:

(33)

	1sg.	*1pl.*	*2sg.*	*3*
Progressive	ó:^{L}	o:^{M}	o:^{L}	ó:^{L}
Intentive	ó:^{LH}	ó^H	ó:^{H}	ó^M
Completive	ó^M	ó^H	o:^{M}	ó:^{L}

There are a total of eleven major paradigms of this type, and verb membership in one or other paradigm seems to be a lexical matter. There is no clear pattern within each paradigm such that one can assign a particular tone to a particular aspect or person-number morpheme, so for the moment we must assume these are simply memorized paradigms, unsatisfactory though that is from an analytical perspective.

The Yaitepec dialect of Chatino (Pride 1963) has a similar system, but the functional load of tone is higher, because the personal pronouns are frequently absent in the singulars (that is, there is no full form present and no segmental affix, clitic, or reduced form). The tone is thus the only clue as to person. Again verbs fall into several lexical classes, and aspect and person are conveyed by a conjunction of prefix and tone. For example, in the Class E verb /li?ya/ 'carry', the first person singular is [43]. The second and third persons singular when unaccompanied by a full pronoun are [1] in the completive and continuative aspects, and [32] in the intentive. Pride does not report a ballistic/controlled distinction in this language, nor a vowel-length contrast, but nasalization may also be used for inflectional purposes. Here are some more examples of verbs from three different verb classes:

(34)

Verb class	Verb stem	Gloss	Tones		
			1sg.	*2/3sg. completive*	*2/3sg. intentive*
A	ngino̜	'hear'	32	1	32
C	ndi?o	'drink'	1	43	43
E	li?ya	'carry'	43	1	32

My last example comes from Sierra Juárez Zapotec (Bickmore and Broadwell 1998). In this language, person marking is done by a combination of segmental suffix and tonal change. The language has three tones, H [á], M [a], and L [à]. The first person singular transitive subject suffix /?à?/ is accompanied by the addition of a H tone near the start of the word; in (35a) it appears on the first syllable of the root, /xu?/, and in (35b) it appears on the habilitative prefix /ru/.

(35) a. gú-xu?nì-lu?   'you will write'
          gú-xú?nì-?à?   'I will write'

      b. ru-lábà?-lu?   'you count'
          rú-lábà?-à?   'I count'

Bickmore and Broadwell show that this tone docks to the leftmost toneless vowel, and that M must be considered the default tone supplied to syllables that remain toneless at the end of the phonology. The high tone itself is a floating tone supplied by the person suffix. Further evidence for some surface Ms being toneless comes from a rule that spreads a L off the first person intransitive suffix leftwards to any number of toneless syllables. (This suffix does not contribute a floating H.)

(36) í-yechchu   'she will bend over'
      í-yèchchù-?à?   'I will bend over'

They also show that the precise target to which the floating H docks is more accurately stated as the first *stressed* toneless syllable, which is normally the first syllable of the root, and that it can then spread back one syllable off this syllable. A step-by-step demonstration of both these processes, as well as L tone spread, is given in (37).

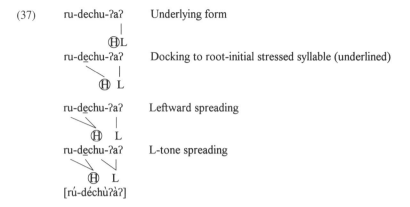

(37)   ru-dechu-ʔaʔ   Underlying form

ru-dechu-ʔaʔ   Docking to root-initial stressed syllable (underlined)

ru-dechu-ʔaʔ   Leftward spreading

ru-dechu-ʔaʔ   L-tone spreading

[rú-déchùʔàʔ]

Exercise 4. Bickmore and Broadwell argue that since the floating H associates from the suffix across tone-bearing root vowels to find a toneless vowel, the tones of the root and suffix must be on separate tiers. Draw a diagram to illustrate the problem, using [gú-xúʔnì-ʔàʔ] 'I will write' as your example. Now see if you can devise an OT analysis using ALIGNMENT that avoids this problem. You should recall that H tones are often attracted to edges and to stressed syllables (see chapter four for details).

8.1.3.5 Chainshift

In the chapter on Asian tone languages we discussed the rather striking Min dialect tone sandhi systems in which tones chainshift, each one changing into another one in the system. Amazingly, we find something similar in Central America, in Choapan Mazatec (Lyman and Lyman 1977). This language has three tones, /H, M, L/, plus the sequences MH and ML. In certain contexts we get the following chainshifts:

(38)   'Clockwise Tone Sandhi'   H > M > L > H
        'Counter-clockwise Tone Sandhi'   L > M > H

These changes happen when words from certain classes are juxtaposed, and either the first or the second word may undergo the sandhi depending on which two classes the words belong to. For example, words of class A cause following words of class B to undergo clockwise sandhi. In example (39), /luǰiH/ is Class A, and it changes /becoʔM/ to [L], and /beoL/ to [H]. (Note that when both tones are identical, they both change. This is what we would expect if a sequence of identical tones is one phonological toneme associated with both syllables.)

(39)   luǰi becoʔ   →   luǰi becoʔ   'the dog's tongue'
        H   M   H   L

        luǰi beo   →   luǰi beo   'the earthmole's tongue'
        H   L   H   H

The phenomenon, just like the Taiwanese Min Tone Circle (see chapter seven, §7.4), does not seem likely to succumb to a general phonological analysis, and it seems probable that the words that change have two allomorphs. How each allomorph is selected is mysterious, and there are not sufficient data available to tell.

This concludes a quick survey of sandhi types in Central American languages.

8.1.4   Tone and stress

8.1.4.1   Tone dependent on stress

We have seen various cases in African and Asian languages of the attraction between tone, especially H tone, and stressed syllables. In Digo, H tone moves off its source onto the stressed syllable. In Shanghai, only the stressed syllable's tone survives. In Min dialects, as stress decreases the number of tonal contrasts decreases accordingly. Both these last two phenomena are attested in Central America as well. As a preliminary, let me discuss a system, N. Tepehuan (M.-J. Kim 1997), in which the tone is not just realized on the stressed syllable, but inserted on it. As a result, there is no reason to posit lexical tone of any kind in this language. It thus provides a useful counterpoint to the truly tonal languages that follow.

Kim (1997) shows that the placement of H tone is predictable in N. Tepehuan. On words of three or more syllables, it is pen-initial: maa.kó.va 'four'. On shorter words, it is initial: bá.nai 'coyote'. All other syllables are L, with one exception to be noted shortly. Kim derives these facts by final extrametricality, and an even-iambic left-to-right parse: $(\sigma\ \acute{\sigma})<\sigma>$ and $(\acute{\sigma})<\sigma>$. A H tone is then assigned to the head. In syllables with long vowels or diphthongs, the H tone shows up usually on the second mora: taí 'fire'; so Kim suggests that syllables are right-headed, and that the mora is the TBU. The predictable placement of the H tone is further evidenced by its shift under morphological affixation: kɨɨ.li 'man' but kɨɨ.lí.-ši 'little boy'. The one case where words have more than one H tone are cases of adjacent onsetless syllables, when a H spreads back onto the preceding mora. Consider the reduplicated form of o.nó.ma 'rib', which is ó -ó.no.ma 'ribs', with the first two vowels in separate syllables. Stress and H tone are assigned to the second syllable as usual, but what is new is that the H tone then spreads left onto the adjacent vowel. This spreading rule makes it clear that the tonal tier plays an active role in N. Tepehuan, even though these tones are clearly not lexical in origin and we would not wish to call this a 'tone language'. With this as background, I now move on to languages where lexical tone and stress interact intimately.

Let us begin with another example of the attraction of H tone to stressed syllables, but now in a language that also has lexical L tone. In earlier sections I have discussed San Mateo Huave, and the reader may recall that underlyingly Noyer argues that this language marks only L tone, but that stressed syllables are assigned a H tone. On a toneless syllable, this surfaces as H, but on a L tone syllable it forms a HL contour. It now remains to show that the placement of the H tone is indeed controlled by constraints typical of stress systems. Primary word stress occurs on a final closed syllable, (40a), but final open syllables (found in function words and borrowings) never bear stress, and instead stress is penultimate, (40b); the accents in (40) show stress, not tone.

(40)   (a)   o.lám   'sugar cane'   ni.pi.lán   'people'
               na.kánc   'red'   a.koo.če.rán   'it is cut'
               ta.ta.wáw   'they saw'

        (b)   ší.ke   'I'   gá.ye   'rooster'
               be.hú.go   'vine'

This is a simple stress system with extrametrical final segments, which render final light syllables invisible to stress but leave closed ultimas still stressable. Stress is then final within the stressable domain:

(41)   ni.pi.lá\<n\>   be.hú.g\<o\>

Secondary stress, shown by a grave accent, occurs on stem syllables that would have been main stressed before the addition of suffixes, (42a), and that are not adjacent to a suffixal final stress, (42b).

(42)   (a)   a.kíiəb 'he accompanies'   a.kìiə.b-a.ran-áac 'we are accompanied'

        (b)   t-a.háw 'he saw'   t-a.ha.w-áw 'they saw'

Since a 'history' of the stress of the component morphemes is maintained in the morphologically complex form, the stress system is clearly cyclical (although in OT this morphological sensitivity is usually handled differently; see Kager 1999 for suggestions). Stress is assigned on each cycle (i.e. after each round of affixation), with the final stress being the main stress and any others surfacing as secondaries, as in (43a), unless they are deleted post-cyclically under stress clash, as in (43b).

(43)   *Cycle 1*   *Cycle 2*   *Post-cyclic*
        a. a.kíiəb   →   a.kíiə.b-a.ra.n-áac   → a.kìiə.b-a.ra.n-áac
        b. t-a.háw   →   t-a.há.w-áw   → t-a.ha.w-áw

It is only stress assignment that is cyclic, not tone assignment, with H tone being assigned only to the phrasal head, not to any other word stresses, as shown by the absence of a H tone on the word stress in [nahmbókLL] in the phrase below:

(44)   nahmbók a çíç   'bad sour-thing'
　　　　 L   L L H

The assignment of H is therefore a late post-lexical matter.

The second type of dependency of tone on stress that we observe in this region is the shrinking of tonal inventories in less stressed positions. I illustrate this from San Juan Copala Trique (Hollenbach 1977). SJC has the tones shown in (45) on final syllables with a long vowel. I repeat the data from section 8.1.2.1 for ease of reference.

(45)

Level			*Fall*			*Rise*		
3	yã	'he is sitting'	34	yã	'salt'	21	yã	'to be sitting'
4	yã	'unmarried'	35	yã	'scar'	32	yã	'corncob'
5	yã	'one'				53	yã	'Spanish moss'

On final short vowels we get /3, 4, 5, 34, 32, 53/. Most non-final syllables, on the other hand, have no tone, in which case they are roughly [3] or [4] depending on the following tone. Some non-final syllables, mainly fused compounds or Spanish loanwords, do have tone, but only one of /3, 4, 21/. There are also some restrictions on the tones in final syllables checked by [?, h].

In San Juan Copala Trique, there is an enormous amount of non-tonal evidence that final syllables are special. Non-final syllables have greatly reduced sets of contrasts in all areas, consonantal, vocalic, and tonal (see Table 8.2).

Table 8.2

Contrasts found in final syllables	Reduced contrasts in non-final syllables
Always has tone.	Often has no tone.
May end in ?, h.	Open syllables only.
Lenis stops realized as fricatives.	Lenis stops remain stops.
May begin with affricates, fortis stops or sibilants.	No affricates, fortis stops or sibilants.
Long or short vowels in open syllables.	Long vowels only.
All long vowels occur.	In native words, /iː, uː, aː/ only; /eː, oː/ rare, usually before another /e, o/.
Vowels usually invariant.	Free variation in many vowels; vowel often reduced or devoiced.
Nasalized vowels; nasalization then spreads leftwards across /y, w, ?/ to preceding vowels.	Only nasalized under influence of following final vowel.
Location of phrasal stress, which occurs on final syllable of first or second word of phrase. Marked by intensity, and by emphasis on vowel length contrast (long vowels longer, and short vowels shorter with longer fortis onsets).	No phrasal stress.

The only plausible explanation for this constellation of properties is to say that final syllables in this language are stressed, and that unstressed syllables cannot license the full set of tonal (or segmental) contrasts. In OT, this is often dealt with in terms of positional faithfulness constraints, and I will now outline such an account. For a functionally based OT explanation of this phenomenon, look at chapter seven, section 7.4 on Min dialects.

I start with the native words with no tone on non-final syllables. Assuming final syllables are indeed stressed, or heads, we formulate a faithfulness constraint specific to heads (Beckman 1997, Alderete 1995) which will allow any underlying tone to surface:

(46)   HEAD-FAITH: No deletion, insertion, or changes to head material.

The presence of any tone incurs a violation of the maximally general markedness constraint, *TONE. Since tones may occur on heads, it must be the case that HEAD-FAITH >> *TONE. In non-head position, however, tones are not present, so *TONE >> FAITH. This is the standard ranking for a system in which more contrasts occur in head position than elsewhere.

What about syllables where tones *do* occur on non-heads? The strategy is to break *TONE down into its components. Consider level tones first. Only two occur, and Hollenbach says they are [3], described as mid, and a tone that lies between [4] and [5], for which she uses [4], and which is thus quite L. Contours are also rare, so we might assume from these two observations that *H and *CONTOUR outrank general faithfulness, which in turn outranks *M and *L, allowing these to surface even in non-heads. The complication comes from the existence of the high rising tone [21] on some non-heads. and here I will speculate that these are cases from Spanish loans in which the penultimate syllable was stressed, and thus the high pitch is a memory, so to speak, of that Spanish stress. Under this view these are words that are not yet fully nativized, and these syllables would have some marking that identifies them as heads, and that they have the highest tone in the system, [21], as a reflex of the Spanish stress. Unfortunately, there are not enough data to check whether this is correct: only one example is given, and this does not look like a Spanish loan: ya21nuh53 'drum'!

Isthmus Zapotec, as described in work by Mock (1981, 1988), has two tones. Each word has a two-tone melody, which shows up on the stressed syllable, and then spreads right. Syllables before the stressed syllable are L. Some fairly complex rules then simplify and adjust these tones so that their surface manifestation is not always transparent. Taking one simple example, a trisyllabic word with a HL melody and penultimate stress shows up as [L.HL.L], as in [nà.xâ.dà] 'short', where the stressed syllable is underlined. Since only one syllable in the word may surface with a lexical tone, but its position may vary, Mock takes this to be a pitch-accent system, but it is fairly unusual in that it has four different pitch accents, LL, HH, LH, and HL. The tones of the accent are lexically determined, although position seems to contrast only in bisyllables: [gù.riâ] 'margin' vs. [guiû.bà] 'fast'. Mock says that in non-compound words the stressed syllable is the first syllable of the root, and thus always one of the last two syllables of the word, although the data suggest the possibility of a quantity sensitive system, with stress on the second syllable of the word unless the first is heavy, in which case it gets the stress. I leave this question open for lack of data, but it seems reasonable to assume that one way or another the location of stress is predictable. In that case this is simply a lexical tone language, and the tones are attracted to the stressed syllable. There is no reason to suppose that the tones are a property of that syllable underlyingly, but rather they seem to be morphemic. Note also that the attraction between tone and stress is true for all tones, not just H tones, which is somewhat surprising in view of the facts in the next section.

8.1.4.2 Stress dependent on tone

In several dialects of Mixtec there is an interesting interaction between stress and tone. The placement of stress is dependent on the particular tones of the word, not just on the presence or absence of tone. The analysis I shall present here is from de Lacy 1999, who discusses three dialects. In each of these dialects stress is placed on the leftmost (or rightmost) syllable which is followed by a lower toned syllable, that is, either a H before a M or a L, or a M before a L. If no such sequence exists, stress defaults to one or other end of the word. The details of which tonal sequences are singled out varies, as does the direction of default. Phonetically, stress is realized as duration and higher pitch. In the Ayutla dialect, there is segmental evidence for the stress/non-stress distinction too. In unstressed syllables without onsets, vowels devoice before voiceless consonants, and unstressed vowels may delete if the result is syllabifiable: /sánárà/ > [sn̩rà].

De Lacy proposes that there is a preference for stressed syllables to be H and for unstressed syllables to be L. In other words, H is intrinsically more prominent than L. He posits two constraint hierarchies to capture this, restated slightly here

(47)   *Hᴅ/L >> *Hᴅ/M >> *Hᴅ/H
       *NᴏɴHᴅ/H >> *NᴏɴHᴅ/M >> *NᴏɴHᴅ/L

With this background, let us now look at de Lacy's analysis of Huajuapan Mixtec (Cacaloxtepec) (Pike and Cowan 1967). The facts are shown in (48).

(48) a. Stress the leftmost syllable which is followed by a syllable with a lower tone:

H<u>H</u>L	sádínà	'he/she/they/(known) are closing it'
H<u>M</u>L	kǫ́nāà	'a wide thing'
<u>M</u>LH	ñą̄nǐnį́	'your (sg. adult) brother'

b. Otherwise, stress the leftmost syllable:

<u>H</u>HH	sádíní̧	'you (sg. adult) are not closing it'
<u>L</u>LH	ɗù̧kùnį́	'your (sg. adult) niece'

Think of the stressed syllable and the following syllable as a binary trochaic foot. The head of the syllable always has a higher (i.e. more prominent) tone than the non-head. In the two constraint hierarchies given above, the two highest ranking constraints are *HD/L and *NONHD/H. What de Lacy points out is that the three well-formed feet, HM, ML, and HL, are exactly the three feet that satisfy these two conditions. In fact there is one other, too, MM, but de Lacy suggests that this can be ruled out by the OCP applying within the foot. Chart (49) shows all possible tonal feet, and which constraints they violate.

(49)

Constraint	Violated by
*HD/L	<u>L</u>L, <u>L</u>M, <u>L</u>H
*NONHD/H	L<u>H</u>, M<u>H</u>, H<u>H</u>
OCP(FOOT)	<u>L</u>L, <u>M</u>M, <u>H</u>H

These constraints (together with FTBIN and FTFORMTROCHEE) define acceptable feet, but the location of the foot – leftmost – requires a further constraint, ALIGN-L(HEAD-σ, PRWD). Let us now see how these constraints produce the desired forms. First consider a case with one falling sequence, not at the left edge of the word (50). Stress still falls on the start of that sequence, because the constraints on tonal sequences inside feet outrank ALIGN-L.

(50)

/HHL/	*HD/L	*NONHD/H	OCP(FOOT)	ALIGN-L(ó-PRWD)
(<u>H</u>H)L		*!	*	
☞ H (<u>H</u>L)				*

Now take a word with two falling sequences (51): here ALIGN-L will pick out the leftmost.

(51)

/MLHL/	*HD/L	*NONHD/H	OCP(FOOT)	ALIGN-L(ó-PRWD)
ML(H̲L)				**!
☞ (M̲L) HL				

Finally, consider a case with no falling sequences (52). Here any footing will violate one of the tonal constraints, so all footings will tie and ALIGN-L will again decide things.

(52)

/MMH	*HD/L	*NONHD/H	OCP(FOOT)	ALIGN-L(ó-PRWD)
M(M̲H)		*		*!
☞ (M̲M) H			*	

Exercise 5.   There are some words without falling sequences for which this grammar will not place the stress on the leftmost syllable, contra the data generalizations given above. Which inputs are these? Show where the stress is predicted (wrongly) to fall.

In these sections I have tried to give an overview of the sorts of tonal phenomena found in Central America and sketch out their analyses. I now turn to North and South America.

8.2   North America

Although accentual languages exist in North America, fully tonal languages are quite rare, and widespread only in the Kiowa-Tanoan and Athapaskan families. Outside these, we find tone in Iroquoian (Cherokee, Mohawk), Muskogean (Choctaw), Uto-Aztecan (Hopi), and some Salishan and Wakashan languages, such as Heiltsuk. For many of these languages the tonal phonology is not well understood, and some of them are probably more accentual than tonal. A widespread historical source of tonal contrasts in North America, as Mithun (1999) notes, is lowering before a laryngeal glottal stop or /h/, with subsequent loss of the laryngeal segment. Table 8.3 shows the family affiliations of the tonal languages discussed here, and is based on Mithun 1999.

Table 8.3   *Some North American tonal languages*

Athapaskan	Northern Athapaskan	Carrier, Slave (= Hare), Sekani, Tanacross, Chipewyan
	Apachean	Navajo
Iroquoian	Northern Iroquoian	Onondaga, Mohawk
	Southern Iroquoian	Oklahoma Cherokee
Uto-Aztecan		Hopi, Yaqui, N. Tepehuan
Muskogean		Alabama, Choctaw
Kiowa-Tanoan	Tewa	Rio Grande Tewa
Wakashan		Heiltsuk

8.2.1   Athapaskan

One of the best described tonal Athapaskan languages is Navajo, a member of the Apachean or Southern branch, and in what follows I depend largely on McDonough's excellent 1999 treatment.

The Athapaskan languages typically have two tones, H and L, but they differ in which one is specified underlyingly, and which is the default tone. Some look more accentual, such as Carrier, and some look truly tonal. The distinction between accentual and tonal is, as we have repeatedly seen, a dubious one, but generally speaking truly tonal languages have more tones and a phonological output that has all or most syllables tonally specified going into the phonetics. By this last criterion, Navajo appears to be tonal, as we shall now see.

Navajo is often assumed to have H specified and L as default (Kari 1976). The tones are sufficiently sparsely distributed in the word that one might ask whether Navajo should be called accentual, not tonal, in which case we would expect that the phonetic facts would be something like Japanese, with certain syllables bearing accentual tones and others unmarked on entering the phonetics. However, deJong and McDonough's (1993) and McDonough's (1999) phonetic investigations have cast doubt on whether either tone is truly unspecified by the time phonetic implementation takes place. They show that both H and L behave like firm targets, with no more contextual variation in the pitch of L syllables than of H ones. Every syllable has a tonal target. This is very different from accentual languages like Japanese, where unspecified syllables have their pitch determined by the pitch of surrounding syllables, and suggests that Navajo ultimately has a tone specified on each syllable. Nevertheless, it is entirely possible that the lexical tonal specifications are for H only, and the Ls are inserted by default before the phonetics. We shall see shortly that this is apparently the case for inflectional morphemes.

Although Navajo may be tonal, it only has lexical contrasts on a subset of morphemes. In verbs, the stems and clitics have tonal specifications but the inflectional prefixes generally do not. Let us take a closer look at the verbal morphology. The verbal complex consists of a final monosyllabic verb stem, preceded by an inflectional 'conjunct' component. These two domains are optionally preceded by a pro-clitic 'disjunct' domain, mainly adverbial in function. The boundary between this disjunct domain and the rest is well established. Some examples of lexical tone on verb roots are given below in (53a), followed by examples of the grammatical use of tone to show aspect in (53b), and an example of a morphologically complex verb in (53c), where D = disjunct, I = inflectional conjunct and V = verb. # and // show domain boundaries.

(53)   (a) /bąąs/   'globular object'   vs.   /chííd/   'act with fingers or arms'

        (b) yicha   'he's crying, imperf.'   vs.   yícha   'he cried, perf.'

        (c) ch'iníshkaad
            chí   # nish   // kaad
            'up or out' # nperf./1sg. // 'flat, spreading': perf.
            D   #   I   //   V
            'I tossed out (something spreading)'

Summarizing, a verb will typically have a H or a L verb stem, usually no specification on the preceding inflectional conjunct portion, and optionally H or L pro-clitics. H tone on inflectional morphemes is found, but it is the exception to the usual L pattern, and so a picture emerges in which tone looks lexical on verb stems (and clitics), but more accentual in the inflectional domain. McDonough argues that this is indeed an accurate view of Navajo tone. She further shows that verb stems show a cluster of properties usually associated with prominence: a full set of phonemic contrasts, longer duration, wider pitch range, and a larger syllable inventory. This she sees as the beginnings of a stress system, and thus a language in which tonal contrasts are limited to stressed syllables, and elsewhere the language is accentual in character.

The tones of the verb stem and any tones on the inflectional conjunct do not interact, but there is interaction across the disjunct/conjunct boundary, where there is a local H spreading rule which spreads Hs such as the H of the iterative clitic /ná-/ onto the first syllable of the following stem: [ha#nishchaa] vs. [haná#níshcha'] 'iterative'. This rule is blocked if the potential target has a long vowel: /ni#ná#hiil-niih/ > [nináhiilniih]. One might suppose that this is because purely local spreading here would create a syllable with two vowel moras with different tones, like the third syllable of the hypothetical but non-existent *[ni.ná.híil.niih]. In OT this can be captured by saying that *CONTOUR outranks the constraint responsible for spreading, here just called SPREAD. However, since contour tones on long vowels *can* be created by leftward spreading from a final H enclitic, this explanation is somewhat dubious (and would require an elaboration of the OT grammar so that LEFTSPREAD >> *CONTOUR >> RIGHTSPREAD (Hyman personal communication)). In any case I should note that the interaction between spreading, vowel length, and other prosodic and morphological phenomena is quite complex, and McDonough questions whether this rule is truly phonological or perhaps just co-articulation.

The picture that emerges, then, is of underlying representations that are L or H in verb stems and clitics (which, being mostly adverbial, may perhaps also be thought of as stems), but unspecified or H in inflectional morphemes. Rightward spreading takes place from H clitics onto the unspecified inflectional morphemes. At the end of the phonology, any unspecified syllables receive a default L before the phonetics.

8.2.1.1 Slave and Sekani

Under some but not all accounts, the Athapaskan languages Slave and Sekani are also tonal. Taking a tonal view, Rice (1999a, 1999b) addresses the puzzle of why these closely related Athapaskan languages have developed opposing tonal systems for historically related words, with H in one and L in another. The data in (54) illustrate the situation with noun stems.

(54)

Slave (Hare)	Sekani	Gloss
yáʔ	yàʔ	'louse'
sǫ́ʔ	tsǫ̀ʔ	'excrement'
téʔ	tèl	'cane'

Historically, these roots had final glottalization, so the first puzzle is why it should have given rise to H in one language and L in another. The second puzzle is synchronic: each of these languages has a rule of glottal-stop insertion, but in Slave it applies after word-final H vowels, and in Sekani it applies after word-final L vowels:

(55)   *Slave*   *Sekani*

  sá?   'beaver'   tsà?   'beaver'
  sádǫ   'beaver food storage place' tsàè   'beaver-possessed'
  sásho   'large beaver'

Rice gives several arguments that these glottal stops are indeed epenthetic.

The connection between tonal and laryngeal features is well attested (see section 8.1.2.5), but, confusingly, historically glottalization sometimes lowered and sometimes raised the tone. Kingston (1985) takes the norm to be raising, and attributes the lowering to tone reversal after the loss of the glottal stops. Rice's explanation is a little different. She suggests that markedness under the laryngeal node is linked, in the sense that glottal markedness induces tonal markedness, and vice versa. Historically, Athapaskan languages inserted a Tonal node in the presence of a Glottal Aperture specification, and this Tonal node was then interpreted differently in the two languages. Synchronically, both still simply have a Tonal node, with no subordinate H or L, and interpret this node differently. They retain a common process in which this marked Tonal node now induces (re)insertion of a marked Glottal Aperture node word-finally. The diagrams in (56) may make things clearer.

(56)   *Historically*

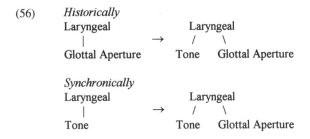

The remaining puzzle is why each language should interpret [Tone] differently, but Rice points out that cross-linguistically we know that either H or L may be unmarked, and so all she is doing is suggesting that the crucial marking in the phonology is one step removed from the phonetics, being simply [Tone] or its absence, and the decision as to how to interpret this lies elsewhere. The advantage is that it allows for a unified account of the Slave/Sekani puzzle, but the disadvantage is that it raises a new problem: what determines how [Tone] is interpreted in a given language.

8.2.2   Oklahoma Cherokee and other Iroquoian languages

By and large, Iroquoian languages do not seem to be tonal, but Cherokee as analysed by Wright (1996) may be an exception. Michelson

(1988) in a comprehensive study of Lake Iroquoian accent shows that tone depends on stress placement, and that stress placement is predictable (except on a few particles and loanwords). Historically, these languages had penult stress, or antepenultimate stress if the penult was epenthetic. Tone is then assigned to stressed vowels. In Mohawk, for example, stressed vowels have level tone except before glottal stop or [h] + resonant sequences, when they have falling tone. Prince (1983) analyses this as the association of a LĤL melody with the accented vowel. The H then spreads rightward within the syllable. Laryngeals have an inherent L and the vowel then lengthens into the laryngeal slot, giving a falling tone. In Onondaga, the highest pitch occurs *before* the stressed syllable, usually on the pre-tonic syllable, although in words of four or more syllables, final stress, and a short penult, it may occur on the antepenult. In any case, as in Mohawk the placement of high pitch is determined by a stress-based system, and neither of these languages can be considered truly tonal.

Contrast this with Wright's (1996) interesting tonal analysis of the Southern Iroquoian language Oklahoma Cherokee. He shows that Cherokee has six surface tones derived from an underlying H vs. zero contrast, association at the level of the mora, and interactions with laryngeal features and with prominence. Toneless syllables receive a L by default before the phonetics, and Wright gives phonetic evidence for the stability of L targets. Let us now look at this in more detail.

Apart from final syllables, which are always high in pitch, Cherokee contrasts six surface tones on long vowels. I give their values here in the Meso-American numbering system, with 1 high and 5 low, extrapolating from Wright's descriptions; unfortunately he does not give syllable boundaries, nor does he comment on the symbol [v] in words like [nvvya] (see (57)).

(57)

		Tone of first syllable	*Wright's terminology*	*U R*
aama	'salt'	2	high	μμ ∨ H
ama	'water'	4	low	μμ
taali	'three'	24	falling	μμ | H
sgooya	'bug'	42	rising	μμ | H
nvvya	'rock'	45	low falling	
nooya	'sand'	21	high rising	

The first four tones are found rather freely, and are represented as shown in the right-hand column of (57), with Ls filled in later by default. The last two tones will be discussed below. There is local H spreading one mora to the right in Cherokee, and this is the source of many level Hs on long vowels when tone spreads within the syllable, and also of falling tones when tone spreads from a preceding syllable. The examples in (58) show how each underlying H surfaces on two adjacent moras.

(58)   H   H   H
                      | | |
                ka - l -iisk -oo'i   aa - ktoost - iisk- oo'i
                3sA - take out - imp - hab 3sA - look at - imp - hab
        Surface form: kaaliískóo'i   aaktoóstíískóo'i

Like other truly tonal languages, Cherokee shows evidence of a floating H tone. The distributive prefix /dee-/ contributes a H tone to the first syllable of the verb stem in (59).

(59)   kanóóyee'a   deekánóóyee'a
         'he is fanning her'   'he is fanning them'

I now turn to the last two tones in (57). Wright argues that the low fall is the result of a L tone on a syllable whose second mora bears the feature [constricted glottis], which pulls the pitch of its mora even lower. For example, the low tone of the first syllable of the verb stem /-teetóska/ may undergo a regular pronominal inflection process which inserts glottalization into the stem. As a result the tone of the first syllable becomes low falling instead of low level. This tone is described as still having glottalization at its lowest point.

The high rise is rather interesting. It is only found on verbs in subordinate clauses, deverbal nouns, locatives, and adjectives, which must bear this tone somewhere in the word. The placement is determined by principles typical of stress systems: the rightmost long vowel, or failing that the first vowel of the word. It replaces any lexical tone on that vowel. Wright sees this as a remnant of the quantity-sensitive stress system still found in some Iroquoian languages such as Cayuga, but in Cherokee it co-exists with a tonal system.

8.2.3   Tone and stress: Choctaw and Hopi

In Mexican languages we saw quite complex interactions between tone and stress, but north of the border the situation is usually much simpler. The most common situation is that tone is not lexical, but inserted on prominent syllables as it is in Mohawk. It may, however, sometimes be misinterpreted as lexical. Two systems that share characteristics with the Mexican language N. Tepehuan (see section 8.1.4.1) are Yaqui and Hopi, also Uto-Aztecan. In Yaqui, there is a H on one of the first two moras, which may spread to the right. In Hopi (Jeanne 1982), it is one of the first two syllables that bears the H. The choice of syllable is determined in a way typical of quantity-based stress systems: choose the first syllable if heavy, otherwise the second syllable, so long as it is not word-final. As in N. Tepehuan, there is a superficial contrast between CV.V́ taávo 'cottontail' and CV́.V náapi 'leaf', but Jeanne points out that the CV́.V cases are actually derived from CV?. sequences like /na?pi/, and can be understood as stressing the vowel of this closed syllable in the usual way, and then vocalizing the glottal by a regular rule of Hopi. There is thus no need to posit underlying Hs on different vowels.

In some N. American languages there is evidence for underlying accent, which can be understood as the presence of lexical H tone on some syllables. For example, the Muskogean languages Alabama and Choctaw are reported to have lexical accents. The following discussion is taken from Lombardi and McCarthy 1991, and references therein. Choctaw has a completive verb form known as the y-grade which involves reduplication of some portion of the word, sometimes with insertion of /y/, to give an output with a heavy syllable with H accent:

(60)   binili   bínniili   'to sit'
       pisa   píyyiisa   'to see'
       toksali   toksáyyaali   'to work'

Although the details are quite complex, for our purposes what matters is that the heavy accented syllable may be analysed as the result of insertion of an infix of the form:

(61)   μ
       |
       H

The mora causes gemination, and the H tone is the accent. We thus have a morphological use of tone as affix in this language. Again, though, to call this language tonal is an overstatement. It has some lexical tones, but only at most one per morpheme, and always H, so only the placement is contrastive.

This completes a survey of North American tonal systems. The dearth of detailed tonal studies has meant that I have not ventured on a full theoretical analysis of any of them, but I hope that the transitional nature of many of these systems somewhere on the continuum between tone and stress has emerged from these brief sketches.

8.3   South America

Relatively few of the many languages of South America have been well studied, and of these very few are reliably reported to be tonal. Three of the best-studied language families, Carib, Guarani, and Quechua, are clearly non-tonal. A number of others are reported to be tonal, but this is disputed by other authorities. Among the more reliable reports are Pirahã (Brazil; D. Everett 1986, K. M. Everett 1998), Barasana (Colombia; Gomez-Imbert and Kenstowicz 2000), Maimande (Eberhard 1995), Iñapai (Peru; Parker 1999), Bora (Weber and Thiesen 2000), and Yagua (Payne and Payne 1986). The affiliations of these languages are as follows, based mainly on Derbyshire and Pullum (1986):

(62)   Mura   Pirahã
        Tukanoan   Barasana, Tatuyo
        Witotoan   Bora
        Namiquara   Maimande
        Maipuran (Arawakan)   Iñapai
        Peba-Yaguan   Yagua

With such a small number of well-analysed tone languages, it is hard to make generalizations about the languages of this region. They appear to resemble African languages more than those of Asia or Central America. It is often hard to decide whether a language should be truly characterized as tonal or accentual. Those putatively tonal languages for which I have sufficient data have the following characteristics. There are limited tonal contrasts, typically H vs. L on the surface, although underlyingly Yagua is argued to have a three-way H/L/zero system. Contour tones are rare, and usually limited to long vowels (Barasana, Maimande). Tones are often attracted to stressed syllables (Pirahã, Iñapai), causing spreading or tonal flop. They may also be deleted on less-prominent syllables (Barasana). Downstep is not often reported, but see Gomez-Imbert 2001 on Tatuyo. Let us look at some sample cases.

8.3.1   *Bora*

Bora is a Witotoan language that shows a tonal system in some ways reminiscent of the Bantu languages of Africa, with the major difference that it seems to have L as the marked tone and H as unmarked. The data and insights come from

Weber and Thiesen (2000). Most morphemes have an underlying tone, but these tones are generally not associated underlyingly, and tend to associate to the preceding morpheme. The complex suffixing morphology means that words may be long and polymorphemic. The TBU is the syllable. The following data are typical:

(63)   All low: wàjpì   'man'
        All high: ájtyúmɨtúrónáa   'not-see'

Sequences of low tones are only found at the end of a tonal phrase, suggesting that the OCP is in operation. Sequences of high tones are found anywhere, so the authors suggest that L is the marked tone and H is the default.

In polymorphemic words with underlyingly linked tones, tones may simply stay on their hosts, as in (64a), but many morphemes have floating tones, and these attach to the left to the last free syllable of the preceding morpheme, like the floating L of /-vu/ in (64b); (note that this example also has a final phrasal L%; see Weber and Thiesen 2000 for details).

(64)   a. /nohco - wu/   'little stork'   [nòhcó-wù]
              | |
              L   L

        b. /umehe-vu/   'to the tree'   [úméhè-vù]
                    \ \
                   Ⓛ L%

The most interesting aspect of Bora tone is the effect of the restriction on sequences of L tones, which are banned (except phrase-finally). This prohibition disrupts the usual tone association, forcing the skipping of TBUs so as to avoid two adjacent Ls. (65) shows a simple example in which the floating L of the suffix is unable to associate without violating the OCP.

(65)   /umɨhe -vu/   'to the field'   [úmɨhévù]
             | \
             L   Ⓛ L%

In the more complex example (66) the stem /ɨhvete/ 'finish' has a linked L on the second syllable. Each of the next three morphemes has a floating L of its own, and the word ends in a phrasal boundary L%, which must occupy the final TBU. Association proceeds from the initial root rightwards, but the L tone of /tso/ cannot link to the free TBU /te/ at the end of the root because to do so would be to violate the OCP. Instead, it associates to the next TBU /tso/. For the same reason, the L of /te/ skips /te/ and associates to /ro/. The underlying L of /ro/ does not associate at all, sandwiched as it is between two other Ls, and unable to associate without violating the OCP. As a result the final output shows only four low-toned syllables, even though the input contains five Ls.

(66)   ɨhvete - tso- te- ro -Vbe   → ɨhvèté - tsò- té- rò -obè   'In vain did he go
       | /   ⁄   \   to make it stop'
       L Ⓛ Ⓛ Ⓛ   L%
       'Finish-cause-go to do- CE-Sg.masc.'

The effect of the OCP is extremely pervasive in Bora. It can also force underlying delinking of L tones. As a result many Bora words show surface alternating high-low patterns across the word.

8.3.2   Barasana

I now move on to Barasana, basing my account on two thoughtful papers by Gomez-Imbert and Kenstowicz (1999, 2000), based on fieldwork by the first author. Morphemes are H or HL, with an optional extra-tonal mora at the beginning which surfaces L, shown here with <>. Morphemic nasalization is shown by a preceding tilde. Roots are (C)V(C)V, with a few tri-moraic stems. Since some of these surface as HLL, and none as HHL, tonal association appears to be left-to-right, a situation of course familiar from African languages (see (67)).

(67)   H   gáwá   'white people'   <V>H   bujá   'cotton'
       HL   ~wádi   'fish sp.'   <V>HL   boká-~bi   'he met'

Many mono-moraic suffixes are toneless, and take their tone from the root, like the 3sg. masc. suffix /-~bi/: [wáré-~bí] 'he was awake' vs. [bíbi-~bi] 'he sucked'. Bi-moraic suffixes may be HL (or H). Their tone only surfaces after a H root; after a HL root, the suffixal HL is lost: /~kubuH – aka HL/ → ~kúbú-áka 'shaman, dim.', but /~bidiHL-akaHL/ → ~bídi-aka. Note also that tonal association seems to be cyclic, since tones align with the leftmost TBU of the morpheme to which they belong lexically, as can be seen by the word for 'little shaman' earlier in this paragraph.

Since toneless suffixes acquire their tone by spreading from the root, we may assume that SPECIFY and DEP-T dominate NoLONGTONE. Extratonality can be handled with a NONINITIALITY constraint, akin to the more common NONFINAL-ITY, well known in stress systems. This will of course dominate SPECIFY. Lastly, we must explain the absence of contour tones on single moras. For this the constraint *CONTOUR has been used in earlier chapters. If there are more tones than moras, as in extratonal HL roots, the language either drops the L tone or lengthens the vowel. This optionality can be handled in OT by free ranking of constraints, here the constraints MAX-T and DEP-MORA (which blocks lengthening) as shown in tableau (68). Violations of Max-T and Dep-Mora will be given equal weight, so the first two candidates will tie as winners.

(68)

<we>koHL	*Contour	*Float	Max-T	Dep-Mora
☞a. wekoo || HL				*
☞b. weko | H			*	
c. weko | H L		*!		
d. weko /\ H L	*!			

In the case of a HL root plus HL suffix, the authors observe that in many languages HL is the melody associated with an accent, and that one property of accents is that a domain typically only allows one accent to survive. They propose that Barasana inverts this state of affairs, by accenting all HLs, and then assigning particular prominence to the first accent. Less prominent accents are then deleted. For further details, see Gomez-Imbert and Kenstowicz 2000.

This proposal raises some interesting issues for de Lacy's theory of tone–prominence interaction discussed in section 8.1.4, on Mixtec. De Lacy proposed that L tone is avoided on heads, and formulated the hierarchy *Hd/L >> *Hd/M>> *Hd/H. In Barasana, however, it appears that HL is singled out as a head, in preference to H, in direct contravention of this hierarchy. If we look at Barasana alongside Mixtecan, the commonality is that falling contour seem to be prominent. De Lacy cleverly reduced this in Mixtec to constraints on the component tones, but this strategy is not obviously extendable to the Barasana case.

8.3.3   Pirahã

The Everetts (D. Everett 1986, K. M. Everett 1998) give the basic facts of tone in Pirahã, a Mura language spoken in Brazil. There are two tones, H and L, although these give rise to four phonetic levels, with H being realized as H or M, and L as L or extra-low depending on the phonological environment. Tone is a feature of the word or morpheme, and in general it seems rather stable without a lot of alternations. However, it can be attracted off its own morpheme onto an accented syllable. Accent is assigned to one of the last three syllables in the word by an unusual quantity-sensitive system that pays attention to vowel length and onset voicing, but not to tone (see Everett and Everett 1984 for details). So, for example, the high tone of /soí/ 'skin' is on its own final accented syllable in isolation, but moves onto the stressed penult of the following verb in the morphologically complex word [so.'báa.gí] 'sell skin'. If the accent stays on the original syllable for independent reasons, as in the following example, the tone does not move: /si. 'toí + xo.ga.ba. 'gaí/ 'egg + want' > [si.'tòó.ga.ba.'gaí] 'want eggs'. After elision of the velar fricative /x/, and deletion of the vowel /í/, the underlying high tone of the deleted vowel /í/ of 'egg' shifts onto the following vowel, and surfaces on the merged syllable [tòó] of which it is a part. Clearly a theory that includes constraints encouraging H tone on stressed syllables can readily deal with this kind of attraction, which is strongly reminiscent of the rightward movement of H tones to prominent final or penultimate syllables in Bantu languages. The feature of particular interest is that the prominent syllable in Pirahã is determined by a quantity-sensitive system, as in Huave, and not simply by position in the word, as is common in Bantu.

The last fact of interest is a piece of evidence suggesting that L may be the less-marked tone. Epenthesis inserts a vowel, [a] or [i], that is always low-toned: /sogsai/ > [sogisai] 'want-NOM'. However, the reason for the low tone here may have nothing to do with the possibility that L is unmarked. Notice that epenthetic vowels create light syllables and are thus rarely stressed; since H tone usually moves to stressed syllables, unless the data include a stressed epenthetic syllable it is hard to read too much into these facts.

8.3.4   *Iñapai*

Iñapai is a Maipuran Arawakan language spoken in Peru. Data and the basic analysis are taken from Parker 1999. Iñapai seems to be basically accentual (see chapter one for a discussion of accentual languages), and does not properly belong in this book at all. However, I have included it to show some of the range of tonal behaviours in this little-studied part of the world.

Words have a LHL melody, and H falls on one or more of the last four syllables. In words of three or more syllables, the first mora is always low. The position of the H is not, however, completely predictable, and must be lexically specified:

(69)   mára   'people'   mará   'outside'
        anáwa   'they'   arawá   'canoe'
        ahetíri   'stairway'   ahétíri   'orphan, masc.'
        aparépá:nári   'equal'   amáteniri   'wild'

When there is more than one H, the Hs are always adjacent and apparently the result of spreading. There is an attraction to penult position; notice for example that
the multiple highs in the data in (69) always end on the penult. This attraction can
give rise to alternations, sometimes by spreading, as in (70a), and sometimes by
shifting, as in (70b). These alternations are lexicalized, and not very productive.

(70)   a. uteíro   'machete'   uteíróhi 'knife, dim.'

        b. yunári   'ocelot'   yunarísi 'cat, dim.'

So far, this looks like a fairly classic accentual system that can be characterized by
underlying Hs associated to one particular mora. There is, however, also some evidence of a metrical stress system. In addition to the tendency for penults to be H,
on long enough words secondary Hs radiate out in both directions from the lexical primary H in a binary alternating pattern: pàriʔàreróti 'niece', itápéxïpïrï 'post,
pole'. It is not clear if these are phonetically at the same or a lower pitch than the
'primary' H. Such extra Hs can also be added to break up a span of three or more
L syllables when two words are juxtaposed in a phrase. All this is typical of stress
systems, which frequently avoid lapses. Stress here, however, is realized as high
pitch, and is partially lexical. After that, the metrical system takes over, avoiding
H on initial syllables (NONINITIALITY) and final syllables (NONFINALITY), and
avoiding long low stretches, *LAPSE. In parallel, however, the tonal nature of the
accent persists, so that H may spread rather than simply shift.

Exercise 6. Consider *only* these two words of Iñapai, repeated from above,
where the accents show the H tones associated with main stress (acute accent) and
secondary stress (grave accent):

        a. aparépá:nári
        b. pàriʔàreróti

Bear in mind the generalizations about tone and stress outlined above. Taking
each word separately, propose underlying representations for each of the above
forms, and show precisely how their surface forms are selected by an OT grammar. Assume that stress, but not tone, is lexically marked on exactly one syllable per word. Make sure that you explain why the following outputs are not
found:

        a. aparépa:nàri, aparépá:nárí, aparépa:nari
        b. pàriʔàrerótí, pàriʔàrèróti, pariʔareróti, paríʔáréróti

We have seen tantalizing glimpses of tonal phenomena in South America, but no strong overall typological picture emerges. It is to be hoped that further research on these languages will improve our understanding of their tonal phonology.

Answers to exercises

Answer to exercise 1

To explain the spacing of the contour tones, one could propose an extension of the SPACE-X% constraints so that they penalize overlapping contours. The profusion of contours arises because SPACE-33% limits one to four level tones. The greater number of falls than rises is because *RISE >> *FALL, and the greater number of lower rather than higher tones is because *H >> *L. One might perhaps expect that of the rises the highest of all would be missing, instead of the second highest, but of course the actual system spreads the various rises out better in the tone space.

Answer to exercise 2

STRESS = H >> DEP-H
ONE-T/μ >> PRES-WT
SPECIFYT >> DEP-L

Answer to exercise 2 (supplement)

Because of the lack of lengthening, the correct output clearly has only one H. This is in fact expected because STRESS = H does not require H insertion, just the presence of a H, and so it is satisfied already by an underlying H. Insertion of an extra H would just incur an unmotivated violation of DEP-H, so even inputs with underlying Hs would only surface with one H if stressed, and no lengthening would be expected. An output-based theory can thus handle these data without underspecification of H!

Answer to exercise 3

Extremely similar to San Miguel el Grande dialect discussed in section 8.1.2.4–5, but you needed to discover this for yourselves. Class B words end in a floating H, which associates to the right. Thus almost all the outputs begin with a H tone (i.e. a [1]), which displaces the tone of the first syllable. The second syllable tone is unchanged. The extra twists: 22A becomes 12 straightforwardly, but 22B becoming 11 needs explanation. Perhaps its *own* floating H attaches to its end, squeezing out the M? The second twist is that while the H can skip to the final vowel, as in 23 becoming 31, this skipping is blocked not just by glottal stop, but also in long vowels. A Tranel-style explanation in which the glottal feature is on the tonal tier and blocks spreading (see 8.1.2.5) is therefore problematic. Finally, the skipping happens in the 33 cases too, and nothing in Tranel's analysis leads us to expect this. Instead, it seems as though the H is trying to replace a L whenever possible, so that L only survives if there were two Ls in the input. This suggests an analysis in which L is unspecified, and H does indeed seek out the toneless vowel.

Answer to exercise 4

(Only one of several possibilities.) Assume alignment constraints ALIGN(H, ǿ), and ALIGN (H, LEFT). These are ranked below the faithfulness constraints that penalize delinking, so they can not disturb underlying associations, but above LINEARITY, which penalizes re-ordering. Thus the free H can be relocated to the left of existing tones to attach to the stressed syllable, and to spread leftwards.

Answer to exercise 5

Inputs where one of the possible foot types violates two tonal foot constraints, not just one. These are (LL) feet and (HH) feet, which violate both the OCP and either *HD/L or *NONHD/H. An input with such a foot initially, such as (LL)M will be judged worse than the footing L(LM), since (LM) violates only one constraint. The sad face ☹ shows the incorrect winner.

/LLM/	*HD/L	*NONHD/H	OCP(FOOT)	ALIGN-L(ǿ-PRWD)
(LL)M	*		*!	
☹☞ L(LM)	*			*

In trisyllabic inputs this is actually the only problem case. Any input with initial /HH/ must have a lower following tone, so the final foot will be a perfect one.

Answer to exercise 6

The underlying forms will be /aparepaːnari/ and /pariʔareroti/, where the underlined syllables have lexical stress. Tone assignment results from undominated

HEAD = H >> DEP-H. Spreading comes from ALIGN-R(H, PRWD) ruling out [aparépaːnari]. Secondary stresses result from parsing syllables into feet, in satisfaction of PARSE. Tone avoids final syllables because NONFINALITY >> ALIGN-R(H, PRWD), explaining why [aparépáːnárí] is bad. If ALIGN-R>>PARSE, spreading will be preferred to binary footing to the right of a lexical stress. This explains why [aparépaːnàri] is bad. [pàriʔàrerótí] with rightward spreading violates NONFINALITY. [pàriʔàrèróti], which has spreading inside the second foot, violates the OCP because the spread H will be adjacent to the H of the next foot. [pariʔareróti] violates PARSE. [paríʔáréróti] has unmotivated spreading to the left, in violation of *ASSOCIATE.

9

Tone, stress, accent, and intonation

9.1   Introduction

By and large up until now I have emphasized the independence of tone from the rest of the phonology, with the major exception of its interaction with laryngeal features, especially voicing. However, tone bears a close relation to stress, and to intonation, and this interaction is the topic of this chapter. Tonal features can enter the phonology from a number of sources. Here there is a real difference of degree between tonal and segmental features, with segmental features being (almost) entirely associated with lexical items, rather than such things as prosodic heads, phonological phrases, or declarative intonation. Imagine what a language would sound like if the right edge of every phonological phrase ended in a voiced uvular fricative – we would have something very like the comedian Victor Borge's famous 'Phonetic Punctuation', where all commas are pronounced with a sort of gargle!

In tone languages, although the obvious source is lexical tone, it is by no means the only source. The overall picture that emerges is that the tonal phonology must accept not only input direct from the lexicon, but also from insertion during the lexical phonology, and from the utterance after lexical insertion. At this stage in addition to lexical items the representation may include certain abstract markers such as [FOCUS] and also syntactic structure, which in turn influences prosodic structure. The lexical entries that contain tones include not only the traditional lexical items such as nouns, verbs, roots, and affixes, but also functional elements and operators such as [WH], [FOCUS], [TENSE], prosodic phrases such as Phonological Phrase or Intonational Phrase, and pragmatic tunes such as Declarative. The phonology takes all this as input, perhaps in one go, or perhaps step-by-step, with word-level phonology preceding phrase-level phonology. See chapter one for more detailed discussion and references.

With this as background, I start with a discussion of stress languages, accentual languages, and tone languages, arguing that accentual languages are just a special kind of tone language. Then I spend the bulk of the chapter on intonation, beginning with the basic mechanisms, then looking at how they are used in non-tone languages, and then in tone languages. Lastly, I look at the interaction of speech rate and tone.

One sometimes hears languages categorized as 'stress languages' vs. 'tone languages', and there is a mysterious third category 'accent languages'. Let us begin by clarifying what we mean by these terms. First, let us dispose of what they do *not* mean! To call a language a 'stress language' is not to imply that pitch plays no role at all. On the surface particular syllables may have significantly different pitches from other syllables, and this difference may be an important perceptual clue to the listener, signalling pragmatic, semantic, syntactic, morphological, and even lexical information. Conversely, to call a language a 'tone language' is not to say that there are no differences in prominence among its syllables. Certain syllables may be noticeably longer or louder than others, or more prone to attract tonal contrasts. See Downing forthcoming for useful discussion.

What we mean by a 'stress language' is best captured by a quote from Hayes (1995: 8):

> stress is the linguistic manifestation of rhythmic structure. That is, in stress languages, every utterance has a rhythmic structure which serves as an *organizing framework* for that utterance's phonological and phonetic realization.

There are three possible subtypes. The most common two are (1) languages with a stress fixed at or near one end of the word, where 'near' means no more than two syllables away from the end (e.g. antepenultimate) and (2) languages with binary alternating patterns across the word. The third type is languages with fixed lexical stresses. Cross-cutting these three types is the distinction between languages in which stress falls preferentially on heavy syllables – ones with a long vowel or final consonant – versus languages that are indifferent to this distinction. Stress, then, is essentially positional in nature. Its phonetic realization is extremely variable, including duration, loudness, and pitch. Because pitch is one possible reflex of stress, it may be an important part of the final utterance, but it is not lexically specified.

In a 'tone language', on the other hand, tones are crucially part of the lexical representation, as we have seen. The interesting part comes when we consider what a language might be like that had both stress and tone. Such languages exist, and, depending on the division of labour, they are either placed into the category that seems like the best fit, or they are placed in the third class, accentual languages. First, consider a tone language in which every morpheme is potentially specified for tone, but in which the surface position of those tones is determined, at least in part, by the type of positionally driven rhythmic structure typical of stress languages. We have seen many such languages. In many African languages (Downing forthcoming), tones are attracted to the final or penultimate syllable, cross-linguistically a favoured position for main stress. In many Chinese languages, syllables are grouped into larger units that sometimes show a preference for being binary, and in these units only one tone survives. Again, the binary preference found in these tone languages is an instance of a strong cross-linguistic bias found in stress systems. In both these cases, the languages are almost always called 'tone languages', making it clear that everybody's working definition of a tone language is 'a language that has lexical tones', and that the definition does not also commit to an absence of stress!

Picking a case of the opposite type, consider Roermond Dutch (see below). This language has a Germanic-style stress system, with a main stress and secondary stresses on longer words, all assigned on positional grounds. But it also has a lexical tonal contrast, in that words may have no tones, or a single H tone, and this H then shows up on the last mora of the main stressed syllable. This sort of language does not fit neatly into either categorization. It does have lexical tone, but of a very impoverished type both in terms of numbers of tonal contrasts (one versus none) and numbers of possible tones per word (one), and in this particular language (but not all accentual languages) the position of this tone is entirely controlled by the position of main stress. It is for languages like this that the term 'accentual' has been proposed, but it is important to realize that no special mechanisms are needed to analyse such languages: the tools of metrical and tonal phonology combined can handle the facts.

I shall continue to use the term 'accentual language' as a descriptive convenience, but analytically the majority of such languages have lexical tones, and what makes them special is that these tones have a small number of contrasting tones, sparsely distributed, absent on some words, and frequently lexically associated with specific TBUs. There is no absolute division between accent languages and tone languages, just a continuum from 'accent' to 'tone' as the number and denseness of tones increases, and they become freer to move around.

9.2   Tone assignment in stress languages

Many stress languages realize stressed syllables with particular tonal melodies. The usual way to handle this is to assume that, after the metrical phonology has done its work, some particular tonal melody is assigned to each head syllable. The tonal melody may vary, but the mapping will stay constant.

For example, the word 'assimilation' said as a statement has the melody $\overset{*}{\text{M}}\text{HL}$ (Hayes 1995), where the starred tone $\overset{*}{\text{H}}$ associates to the stressed syllable *-la-*. If used as a question 'Assimilation?' the melody is $\text{ML}\overset{*}{\text{H}}$, but the starred tone $\overset{*}{\text{L}}$ still associates to the stressed syllable. Try this with other words, such as 'serendipity', 'pontoon' or 'Massachusetts', and you should find that the same observation holds. Since the pitch of each syllable can vary depending on the intonation pattern it is clear that the tones are not lexically determined. The melodies are language-specific matters, by the way: Malayalam main stress (Mohanan 1986) tends to have low pitch with a following rise in the unmarked intonation pattern, or $\text{L}\overset{*}{\text{H}}$, versus the $\text{H}\overset{*}{\text{L}}$ of RP English.

This tendency for tones supplied by the phrase-level component to be attracted to stressed syllables is one aspect of the close affinity between prominence and high tone which we have encountered over and over again. Stressed syllables are good carriers of tonal melodies: they tend to be louder and longer, so the melodies are readily produced and perceived.

9.3   Accentual languages

Accentual languages typically have a lexical contrast between tone and no tone, with each morpheme having a maximum of one tone or tonal complex whose location must be lexically specified, and even morphologically complex words often allowing only one tone to surface. They have been analysed in two main ways in the literature. One tradition identifies accented syllables with a diacritic mark, usually an asterisk, posits various rules that insert and delete asterisks, and then assigns tones at the end of the phonology to any surviving asterisks. This makes accentual languages look like stress languages, where the stresses are lexical, and the melodies are assigned to the eventual winner. The other, more recent, approach is to posit underlying tones instead of asterisks, and have the phonology operate directly on a tonal representation. Accented morphemes are those that have tones, unaccented morphemes are those that do not. This makes accentual languages look like tone languages, albeit ones of a fairly impoverished sort. It has the considerable theoretical advantage that it allows us to do away with the otherwise unmotivated abstract diacritic * markings.

Blevins (1993) analyses Lithuanian nominal accent as a tonal system. Accented morphemes have a H tone linked to the first mora (these are called the grave and acute accents), and unaccented morphemes do not. In some morphemes (called circumflex), the first mora is extra-tonal (not available for association), so the tone associates to the second mora (see Example (1)).

(1)   *Lithuanian accent types*

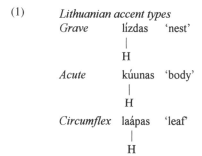

The phonetics of these accents are not well studied, but one description says that the grave and acute accents in (1a–b) have a short rise, followed by a fall, while the circumflex accent has a steady rise. This is consistent with the representations in (1); the initial short rise on the grave and acute accents is due to the normal time lag in reaching a peak.

Like many Baltic and Slavic languages, in morphologically complex words Lithuanian picks one accent to be the word accent, according to the following principle (Kiparsky and Halle 1977):

(2)   *Basic Accentuation Principle (BAP)*
If a word has more than one accented vowel, the first of these gets the word accent. If a word has no accented vowel, the first vowel gets the word accent.

Translated into tonal terms, this means that if there is more than one H tone, the second one deletes, and that a toneless word acquires a H on the first mora. For example, /víir-é/ > [víire] 'man, LOC. sg.' and /kelm-aa/ > [kélmaa] 'stump, ACC. sg.'. In OT terms, these two effects can perhaps be seen as the result of ALIGN-L (H, WORD), and of *HD/L (following de Lacy, see chapter eight for details). In any case, both are common tonal processes, entirely what one would expect to find in a tone language. Even more tellingly, there is a law known as de Saussure's Law which says that if two tones become adjacent at a morpheme boundary, the first one deletes. Nowadays we would see at work the influence of the OCP: /raát-é/ > [raaté] 'wheel, LOC. sg.'. One final piece of evidence that a tonal approach is promising comes from a different dialect of Lithuanian spoken in Zhemayt, in which neither the BAP nor the OCP is observed. Instead, multiple H tones can surface, so that /veít-á/ > [veít-á] 'place, NOM. sg.' surfaces unchanged. In sum, a tonal analysis of these data seems extremely convincing, and suggests that strictly speaking languages termed accentual are simply a subclass of tone languages.

Other languages of this type include Tonga, New Chongming Chinese (Chen 2000), Serbo-Croatian (described below in section 9.4.3), Swedish, and Japanese. Japanese has been extensively analysed both from a diacritic and a tonal point of view. The tonal perspective is most fully laid out in Poser 1984 and Pierrehumbert and Beckman 1988, although they differ on the details. Japanese has many dialects, and the following description is that of Tokyo Japanese. One class of words has a sharp fall somewhere in the word. These are called accented. In polysyllabic words the location of this fall is lexically specified. The other class has no such fall, and these are called unaccented. Superimposed on these patterns is a lowering of an initial short unaccented syllable. Pierrehumbert and Beckman generate these patterns by assuming that accented syllables have a branching HL contour tone associated with them in the lexicon. This produces the fall heard in accented words. In an utterance, words are grouped into accentual phrases with their own enveloping H%L% boundary tones. The H% links to the second sonorant mora, leaving the first one L. The L% links if possible to the first sonorant mora of the following phrase, if it is short and toneless, producing the initial lowering. Again, then, we have a truly tonal analysis of an accentual language.

I shall assume, then, that 'accentual' is a convenient descriptive term for a particular type of language in which tone is used in a rather limited way, with one (or perhaps two) tone melodies, either lexically linked to particular TBUs or perhaps attracted to a syllable selected as prominent by rhythmic principles. Such languages occupy a transitional ground between pure stress languages and pure tone languages.

We are now ready to look more closely at intonation and tone.

9.4   Intonation as phrasal-level tones: a reminder of prosodic hierarchy

A useful working definition of intonation is that of Ladd (1997): 'the use of suprasegmental phonetic features to convey "postlexical" or sentence-level pragmatic meanings in a linguistically structured way'. We might broaden this slightly by changing the words 'pragmatic meanings' to 'information', thereby encompassing syntactic and semantic information as well as pragmatics.

One might think that true tone languages would reserve tone entirely for the purposes of lexical contrast, but this is not the case. Intonation in tone languages is only slightly more limited than it is in non-tonal ones. There are four main mechanisms at the phrasal level. First, the entire pitch register may be moved up or down, so that all tones are higher or lower in pitch than usual. Second, the pitch range may be widened or narrowed, with highs and lows either moving further apart or closer together. Third, boundary tones may be inserted at domain edges, and these may then surface either on the closest head or on the edgemost syllable. Fourth, downstep may apply within some prosodic domain, such as the phonological phrase or intonational phrase, but at domain boundaries downstep may be suspended and the register reset. These mechanisms may be associated with particular syntactic, semantic, or pragmatic environments, such as questions vs. statements, focus or emphasis, certainty vs. suggestion, and so on. As pointed out by Chao (1968), there is no cross-linguistic guarantee that any particular semantics is associated with any particular intonation. For example, echo questions in American English usually have a high rising intonation, but in Mandarin they are low and breathy.

The main difference between tonal and non-tonal languages is that in a tone language these mechanisms, for obvious reasons, cannot be given as free a rein. In a non-tonal language boundary tones associating with heads and edges may completely determine the pitch contour of an utterance, and any given sentence may surface with one of several entirely different pitch contours. Individual lexical items of the same prosodic shape may be substituted without an effect on the pitch contour. In a tonal language the lexical tones must remain at least somewhat retrievable, and their complete obliteration by an intonational pattern is usually avoided. Substitution of lexical items with their own associated lexical tones is likely to change the overall pitch contour. Chao (1968) compares lexical tone and intonation in Chinese to 'small ripples riding on larger waves'. In other words, intonation affects the overall register, but the lexical tones retain their relative pitches and shapes and are mapped on to this registral 'wave'. He also notes that there are utterance-final intonational tones even in Chinese, but these are not allowed to replace the lexical tones; instead they are additive, so that, for example, the final rising intonational tone when added to a final lexical fall produces a lengthened syllable on which is realized a fall-rise sequence.

Research on intonation has offered several alternative models, but since this is not a book on intonation, but on tone, I shall assume without argument those theories of intonation that represent intonational melodies with level tones similar to those used in this book for lexical tone. See Cruttenden 1986, Hirst and de Cristo 1998, Ladd 1983, 1986, Pierrehumbert 1980, Beckman and Pierrehumbert 1986, Pierrehumbert and Beckman 1988, and references therein for discussion and argument. If both components of surface pitch use the same vocabulary, their phonological interaction is not only expected, but also easily discussed.

We start with simple examples of some of these mechanisms: downstep and phrasal tones. Then we take a closer look at the placement of intonational tones in non-tonal languages of two types: stress languages and accentual languages. With this as background, we move on to our main topic, the interaction of intonation with lexical tone.

9.4.1   Sample mechanisms

9.4.1.1   Declination, downdrift, and downstep

Although declination, downdrift, and downstep (catathesis) are most often associated with African languages, they have been shown to be common in many other language families, including English, Japanese, and Mandarin. Declination, recall, is gradual phonetic lowering across an utterance, whereas downdrift and downstep are names for lowering which is triggered by a specific phonological tone, typically either a L (as in many African languages) or a HL (as in Japanese). This tone may be realized on the surface, in which case the lowering is properly called downdrift, or automatic downstep, or the trigger may be a floating tone, in which case it is called non-automatic downstep, or just plain downstep. In common usage the term downstep is often used for all lowering caused by a L, whether overt or floating, and that is how I will use it here.

Most of the literature gives only examples in which the domain of these phenomena is the entire utterance, but a few researchers (e.g. Pierrehumbert and Beckman 1988 on Japanese, Pankratz and Pike 1975 on Ayutla Mixtec) have shown that the domain may be smaller, and that it is sensitive to intonational factors. Inkelas and Leben (1990) give the following example sentence from Hausa: Yaa aikàa wà Maanii / làabaarìn wannàn yaaròn alàrammà 'He sent Mani news of this boy of the alaramma' . The L tones, marked by grave accents, lower any following H tone below the level of the preceding H. In a statement, this lowering happens after the L of wà, but after the phrase boundary shown by the slash '/' the highs rise back again, and the downstep restarts from a new starting point and continues to the end, with successive lowerings after the Ls of ìn, àn, òn, and là. In the same utterance produced as a question, on the other hand, there is no downstep at all in the second phrase, and there is also an extra raising of the final high to an extra-high level. These facts show two things. First, the domain of downstep may be smaller than the utterance. Second, intonation can suspend downstep. Inkelas and Leben represent the intonational morpheme for Hausa questions with a Register feature, [H], which is inserted on every high tone, using the features of Hyman (1992), as discussed in chapter two, section 2.1.2. This blocks spreading of [L] Register from a preceding low tone, thus suspending downstep. Note, crucially, that lexical tone distinctions are preserved in both intonational patterns, making downstep suspension a functionally effective way of implementing intonational distinctions.

Truckenbrodt (2000a, 2000b) on Southern German provides strong evidence for treating utterance-medial re-setting of the register as a tonal morpheme. German, although not tonal, has a L$\overset{*}{H}$ pitch accent on each stressed syllable, where the asterisk denotes the tone which associates with the stress itself. Within an intonational phrase, the Hs fall steadily. At an intonational break they rebound to more or less their original level. Interestingly, however, the rebound comes not at or after the boundary, but for some speakers before the boundary, at the last stress of the first phrase. In example (3) each stress is underlined, and the stress at which the reset occurs, *Lama,* is bolded and in capitals. The pause marking the intonational phrase boundary is shown by ...

(3)   Der M<u>au</u>rer und sein L<u>eh</u>rling wollen dem W<u>e</u>rner in K<u>a</u>merun ein **Lama** malen... und der M<u>a</u>ler will im J<u>ä</u>nner in M<u>u</u>rnau wohnen.

'The bricklayer and his apprentice want to paint a llama for Werner in Cameroon ... and the painter wants to live in Murnau in January.'

We know (see below) that phrasal boundary tones may surface on the closest stress, so this placement of downstep reset strongly suggests that it is itself a phrasal boundary tone.

In passing, it is worth pointing out that in order to get an unbroken pitch-track, intonational data are often elicited (as here) by constructing utterances consisting of as many voiced sonorants as possible. This sometimes results in a rather unlikely choice of lexical items!

9.4.1.2 Tonal markers of phrasing

In many languages tonal markers of phrasing do not seem to have any particular semantics, although it may just be that the reported data is that of 'neutral' intonation, and many other intonational patterns can also be found. These neutral phrasal intonation patterns show one of intonation's most important functions: that of signalling morphological and syntactic structure indirectly by their placement at or near phonological phrase boundaries. The English sentence 'I love American history and politics' is ambiguous on the written page, but in speech, the two meanings usually have distinct intonations associated with the two structures [American [history and politics]] or [[American history] and [politics]]. Pitch, then, can convey lexical information (in a tone language), morphosyntactic information, semantic information, or pragmatic information.

Examples abound. In a famous study, Beckman and Pierrehumbert (1986) (and Pierrehumbert and Beckman 1988) look at Japanese. Japanese is an accentual language, and words may be unaccented or accented, in which case the accented syllable carries a HL melody. Utterances are grouped into accentual phrases, each of which also has a H%L% melody, with the two tones appearing at or near the two edges of the phrase. As we move to larger units, the intermediate phrase is the domain of downstep. At the level of the utterance, Japanese has an initial apparently semantically neutral // boundary tone, and in questions a semantically significant final // boundary tone. The % and // symbols are conventional for phrasal boundary tones; here I use % for the smaller unit, the accentual phrase, and // for

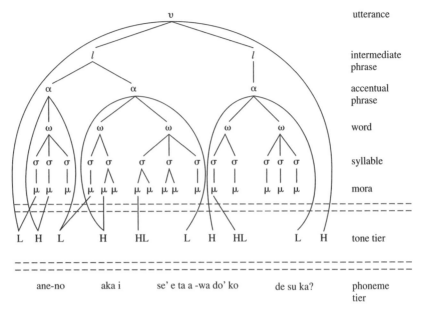

Figure 9.1   *Phrasal boundary tones in Japanese. From Pierrehumbert and Beckman 1988: 21*

the larger unit, the utterance. The example in Figure 9.1 illustrates the surface representation of the question 'Where is big sister's red sweater?'

The rules for associating tones to moras are complex, and the reader is referred to Pierrehumbert and Beckman 1988 for details.

My second example is drawn from Hale and Selkirk's 1987 work on Papago, a non-tonal American Indian language. Papago creates phonological phrases whose right edges line up with the right edges of maximal projections that are not lexically governed. For details, see also Truckenbrodt 1999. Each phonological phrase has a surface (L)HL pitch contour. The H associates with all stressed syllables, and any intervening unstressed syllables. Any preceding and following syllables are L. The final syllable gets a L boundary tone, and if the final syllable is stressed and therefore H, this creates a fall.

Phrasal tones are of two types. One type, termed a pitch accent, surfaces on a stressed or prominent syllable. It is shown with a following *: /H*/. The other type, a true boundary tone, surfaces on or near the edgemost syllable. It is shown with %: L%. Let us look at some actual words; stress is shown by the acute accents, and surface tones are shown above (Example 4).

(4)   (4) (H* L L%) (H*   H*L%) (L H* L L%) (L H*   H*L%)
              | | | ∨ | | | ∧ |
            'ó' odham hú uñ-máḍ   ha-jéweḍ-ga   e- pá al-wákon
            'person'   'ear of corn' 'their land' 'to baptize, IMPERF.'

Each stressed syllable gets H*, and so, by spreading, do any syllables trapped between stressed syllables. The final L% is a boundary tone, appearing on the final syllable even if that is already H, as we can see in the second example in (4). The initial L, on the other hand, is optional, surfacing only on any syllables that do not already have tones. It is not a true boundary tone, but more like a default tone, and can therefore be omitted from the input phrasal melody. Using the now-standard formalism, the H would be a H*, and the final L would be a L%, where the * denotes a pitch accent, and the % a boundary tone. The entire melody, then, is H*L%, with H spreading to fill in between adjacent Hs, and any remaining toneless syllables getting L by default.

Papago is not alone in showing both types of intonational tone. A second example is Bengali (Hayes and Lahiri 1991). Yes/No question intonation places a L on the questioned (and thus main-stressed) element, and then a HL fall at the end of the utterance. Its melody is thus L*(HL)%, where HL is treated as a unit. Central Alaskan Yupik (Woodbury 1989) has L*H* on the accentual phrase, where L* goes on the first stress and H* on the last stress if there is more than one. The intonational phrase then adds a L% boundary tone to the utterance.

In some languages only one type of intonational tone is in evidence. The Korean accentual phrase (Jun 1998) has boundary tones, but no pitch accents. The melody is (LH)%(LH)% or (HH)%(LH)%, depending on the laryngeal features of the initial consonant (see chapter two). The first two tones associate to the first two syllables, and the last two tones to the last two syllables. If the phrase is less than four syllables long, the picture is quite complex: see Jun for details.

9.4.2   The melodies of non-tone languages

By now it should be clear that in non-tonal languages every syllable is not of course pronounced with the same pitch. The pitch varies depending on the syllable's position in the word, the word's position in the phrase, and the choice of intonation pattern.

Languages may have very rich collections of intonational melodies, each with its own semantics and pragmatics. These have been well studied, and the interested reader might start with the classic O'Connor and Arnold 1961 for the details of English intonation patterns. Researchers vary in the numbers of melodies they can isolate. For English, for example, Halliday (1967) has five, Ladd (1978) has eight, and Cruttenden (1986) has seven.

As an example of the sort of data to be accounted for, consider the fact that according to Pierrehumbert (1980) the single word Anna can be said with at least five different surface intonations in American English (see Example 5). I have slightly simplified things here for clarity. The * denotes the tone that associates to the main-stressed syllable in the text, here the first syllable of 'Anna'. English, a stress language, places main stress on one syllable in each word, determined largely by algorithms that count in binary rhythms from one or other end of the word, although the influence of morphological and lexical factors greatly complicates the picture (see Chomsky and Halle 1968, Burzio 1994). This stressed syllable then attracts the pitch accent.

(5)   a. H*-L L%   Used as answer to a question

b. H*-L H%   Implies that answer is incomplete

c. H*-L H-L%   Calling out to Anna

d. L*-H L-H%   Incredulity, or implies that speaker is giving only one of many possible examples

e. L*-H H%   Question

British readers may feel that in their speech the facts are somewhat different, but this does not affect the point that languages have a complex array of possible intonational patterns. The schematic pictures in (6) may help 'hear' the examples:

(6)

H_2	a	b	c	d	e
350			—	—	—
300	—	—			
250			—	—	—
200			—		
150	—	—			—
100	—			—	

Continuing with English and developing Pierrehumbert's earlier work, Beckman and Pierrehumbert (1986) give six different underlying pitch accents:

(7)   *English pitch accents*
    H*   L*   H*+L   H+L*   L*+H   L+H*

Each of these has its own semantics: for example, in the phrase 'an orange ballgown' the word 'ballgown' always has a H*, but the word 'orange' may have one of several accents. It will have H* in the standard neutral intonation used when replying to the question 'What's that?' If instead 'orange' has a H*+L accent, the answer is described as having a 'real or sarcastically feigned judiciousness'. Lastly, if 'orange' has a L* accent, we get an 'expression of astonishment or an impatient reminder'. The F_0 tracings are shown in Figure 9.2. Because English has no lexical tone, the word 'orange' can have any of these pitch accents without any danger of confusion with another lexical item.

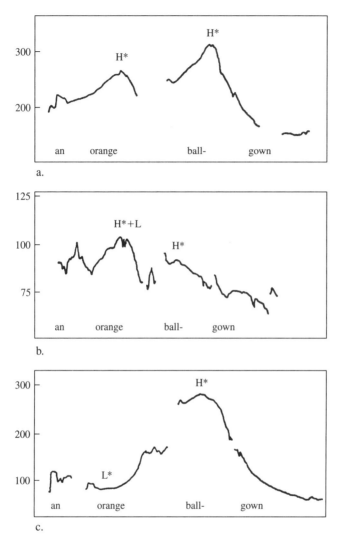

Figure 9.2   *English intonational melodies. From Beckman and Pierrehumbert 1986: 257*

Bengali, according to Lahiri and Fitzpatrick-Cole 1999, building on Hayes and Lahiri 1991, has the collection of pitch accents and boundary tones shown in (8). Note that here I use T% for a phonological or intermediate phrase boundary tone, and T// for an intonational phrase boundary tone.

(8)   *Bengali intonational tunes on the phrase containing the main stress*
        a. *Accents*
           L*   neutral question accent

H*	neutral declarative accent
L*H%	focus accent

b. *Boundary tones*

L//	declarative
L//H//	continuation
H//	offering
H//L//	yes/no

Confirming the claim that these patterns consist of tonal sequences, we can note that Bengali observes such common tonal constraints as the OCP. Consider the sentences in (9) meaning 'Amar saw Shyamoli'. I show only the tones for the object-verb portion of the utterance:

(9)   *Focussed object, declarative sentence*

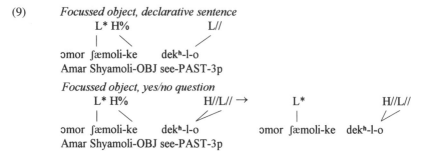

The H% of the focus melody is present in the declarative, but when a H// is added to form a question, the focus H% deletes under the influence of the OCP.

Although Bengali is not a tone language in the usual sense, it helps us demonstrate that the categorization into tonal/non-tonal languages is not as clear-cut as one might think. The set of intonation-phrase boundary tones are termed 'suffixes' by Lahiri *et al.*, and when thought of in this way they look very like the tonal equivalent of the segmental final particles so common in tone languages, and discussed in section 9.4.4.1 below. There are even cases of segmental suffixes that need lexical tones in Bengali. The emphatic clitics /=o/ 'also' and /=i/ 'even, the very, indeed' have a lexical H*, supplying the focus melody from their own lexical representation. They contrast with suffixes like /-o/ '3p', which has no tone. Consider the difference between focussing a normal phrase, and focussing one with a clitic /=o/. In the normal case, the H% always goes at the end of the phrase, which is of course always the end of a word. However, the clitic /=o/ can be attached in the middle of a complex verbal form, and in that case the H shows up on /=o/, not at the phrase edge. It seems, then, that these clitics carry their very own H, distinct from the H% of normal focus.

(10)   a.   L*   H%
                 | |
             didi-r   dæor-er
             elder   brother-
             sister-GEN   in-law-GEN

```
b.  L*   H*   L//
    |    |    /
mer-e=o-tʃʰ-e
beat-PERF=also-PRES-3p
```

In one corner of the lexicon, then, Bengali has lexical tone!

Before leaving stress languages, it is worth mentioning for completeness that one sometimes hears languages referred to as 'stress-timed' versus 'syllable-timed'. The observation is that in stress-timed languages the length of time between two stressed syllables is roughly constant, irrespective of the number of unstressed syllables intervening. Syllable-timed languages keep each syllable roughly the same length, whether it is stressed or not. It is not clear how much reality there is to this distinction; many factors can influence timing, including segmental content. To the extent the distinction is real, it interacts with intonation, because, although it is beyond the scope of this book, intonation can certainly affect length, and be affected by timing factors.

9.4.3   Intonation in accentual languages

Recall that the languages usually termed 'accentual' are ones in which there is a limited use of lexical tones. Typically, there is only one tonal melody, and words are distinguished in the lexicon by the presence or absence of that melody, and by its position. Several such languages have well-studied intonational systems, and they provide a useful first step into looking at the interaction of lexical tone and intonation.

The first thing we might expect is that languages with lexical tones rarely use pitch accents for intonational purposes, since these would risk obliterating the lexical tone contrasts. Instead, we expect to find boundary tones predominant. This is correct. In section 9.4.1.2 we saw that Japanese, with its lexical HL pitch accents, uses boundary tones at the levels of both accentual phrase and utterance. In this section I will look at two more examples, one of which shows that even a lexical tone language can use pitch accents in limited ways.

Serbo-Croatian (Inkelas and Zec 1988) has a vowel-length contrast, and a four-way contrast in lexical pitch accents, called short falling, long falling, short rising, and long rising. The authors argue that all of these can be represented by assuming that each word has one H tone linked to a particular mora. If the H is initial, the word starts H then falls, giving the two falling accents. If the mora is not initial, the H spreads one mora to the left, and produces the accents called somewhat misleadingly 'rising'. At the end of the intonational phrase, a L% boundary tone is introduced. If the final syllable is not H, this L simply attaches to the final syllable, as in (11a). If the final syllable is H, one of two things happens: if the H is doubly linked as a result of the spreading mentioned earlier, the phrasal L bumps it off the final syllable, leaving it attached only to the preceding mora, as in (11b); if the H is singly linked, as in a monosyllable, then the L is simply added to it, creating a fall, as in (11c).

(11)   *Serbo-Croatian utterance-final forms*

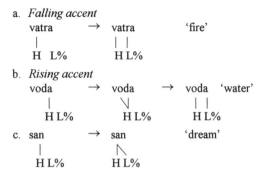

a. *Falling accent*
   vatra   →   vatra   'fire'
   | | |
   H   L%   H L%

b. *Rising accent*
   voda   →   voda   →   voda   'water'
   | ⟍ | |
   H L%   H L%   H L%

c. san   →   san   'dream'
   | ⟍
   H L%   H L%

What is interesting here is that phrase-finally the lexical distinction between the falling accent of (a) and the rising accent of (b) is neutralized by the intonational phrase boundary tone. This should hardly surprise us: segmental distinctions such as voicing, or prosodic ones such as vowel length, are frequently neutralized in word- or phrase-final position, and there is no reason why tonal distinctions should be especially privileged. Serbo-Croatian tonal and intonational phonology is extremely interesting in other ways too. The lexical tones themselves are manipulated in various ways, spreading rightwards, delinking, and so on. The interested reader should consult Inkelas and Zec 1988 for details.

For my last example, I turn to Roermond Dutch (Gussenhoven 2000). On long main-stressed syllables, Roermond has a lexical contrast between two pitch accents. One is unmarked (Accent I), and the other has a H tone on the second mora (Accent II). Short syllables are always unmarked. If a word is focussed in a declarative sentence, the main-stressed syllable attracts a H* tone to its first mora. If it is focussed in an interrogative sentence, it has a L*. Since the lexical tone contrast is on the second mora, the focus marker can co-exist with it, and the lexical distinctions can be maintained (although in Accent II in the interrogative, as I will discuss in section 9.5, the lexical H assimilates to the L* focus marker).

(12)   *Roermond Dutch accent*

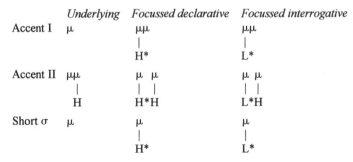

	Underlying	Focussed declarative	Focussed interrogative
Accent I	μ	μμ	μμ
		|	|
		H*	L*
Accent II	μμ	μ μ	μ μ
	|	| |	| |
	H	H*H	L*H
Short σ	μ	μ	μ
		|	|
		H*	L*

This section has shown that even lexical pitch accent languages, with their admittedly limited lexical tonal contrasts, can use intonational pitch accents in addition to boundary tones.

9.4.4 Intonation in true tone languages

We now return to the central topic: the interaction of lexical tone and intonation. This section starts with an alternative to intonation: sentence particles. With this out of the way, we turn to the use of boundary tones in tone languages, then look at a different strategy, adjustment of the overall pitch register, and end with a tone language that uses accents. Examples are drawn from a wide range of languages, although there is very little from American languages, about whose intonation too little is known to include them in this section.

9.4.4.1 Sentence particles

It is a commonplace that many lexical tone languages avoid the potential conflicts between intonation and lexical tone by using a different mechanism altogether: the sentence-final particle. Some languages also use these at sentence-internal phrase boundaries, particularly for topics or focussed elements, but this seems to be rarer. East Asian languages are extremely rich in these. For example, Vietnamese (Đo *et al.* 1998) has more than twenty. Chao (1968) gives a list of twenty-eight particles for Mandarin. Twenty-six of these are segmental. They are short, unstressed, and toneless, taking their pitch from the preceding syllable like any other toneless syllable. Two of the particles are purely tonal. One is an extra-high tone, which adds on to the end of the last tone to produce a rise. The other is a low tone, producing a fall. Particles can appear in combination, with additive meanings. In the example in (13b), the particle *ne* imparts a sense of a continuing state, and this is nested inside the particle *ba*, which shows that the remark is a supposition on the part of the speaker. In the example in (13d), the outer particle is purely tonal, and conveys reassurance. It produces a falling pitch on the segmental particle *a*.

(13)   a. ne   'continuing state'
             ba   'supposition'

          b. Ta mei   lai   'He hasn't come'
             He PERF-NEG come
             Ta mei lai ne   'He hasn't come yet'
             Ta mei lai ne ba   'He hasn't come yet, I suppose'

          c. a   'command'
             L%   'reassurance'

    d. Bie pa   'Don't be afraid!'
                                          (Straight command, as to a soldier)
    IMP-NEG fear
    Bie pa a-FALL   'Don't be afraid!'
                                          (Reassuring, as to a small child)

Cantonese (Law 1990) has thirty-five to forty particles, and in fact almost every Cantonese utterance ends with a particle. If the semantics do not demand a particular particle, speakers tend to place [a] at the end anyway, apparently as a semantically empty carrier for intonation. Every syllable of Cantonese bears one of the six lexical tones (seven by some counts, if one distinguishes between high level and high fall, which for most speakers have merged). Tones bear a heavy functional load, and a strategy that provides a toneless carrier for intonation is obviously useful. Superimposed on this [a], which has no lexical tone, is one of three 'intonational' tones. If [a] is mid, the utterance is neutral. If [a] is high, the utterance 'invites the hearer to agree to the action proposed'. If [a] is low, the utterance has an air of impatience and boredom. Law suggests that mid is the default tone, high is a tonal particle (or boundary H% in our terms) which 'weakens' the force of the utterance, and low is a tonal particle, L%, which strengthens it. The same set of tones can show up on several other particles that do not seem to have tones of their own, and also on some that do. In the latter case they add on to the end of the lexical tone, so that the high boundary tone turns a lexically low particle like [wɔ11] into the rising [wɔ13]. Semantically, [wɔ11] shows surprise on the speaker's part, and [wɔ13] disclaims responsibility, implying that the assertion is hearsay.

Other tonal particles can add directly onto the last lexical item in a sentence, with no intervening segmental particle. Echo questions, for example, are formed by the addition of a high tone to the end of the utterance. This combines with the preceding tone to form a new tone which starts on the pitch of the original tone and ends high. Essentially, then, the sentence ends either with a high level tone (if the original tone started high), or with a rising tone. Since Cantonese has six tones (seven by some counts) on sonorant-final syllables, this represents considerable neutralization, but recoverability is not a problem, since this is an echo-question, by definition repeating at least part of a previous utterance!

African languages may also use particles. Hausa (Inkelas 1988), a language with two tones, High and Low, has a discourse-marker, *fa*, which attaches to a focussed element. For example, in the sentence 'Audu fa ya tafi' 'Audu (emph.) 3sg. leave', the word 'Audu' is emphasized. Hausa (Leben 1989) also makes extensive use of intonation, as we shall see below. Gokana (Cross River, Hyman 1990) has a WH-particle, /E/, which can be shown to be a component of the intonational phrase. The evidence comes from conjoined questions, which have two intonational options. The /E/ may occur once at the end of the utterance, which Hyman argues is a single intonational phrase in that case. Or it may occur twice, once at the end, and once at the end of the first conjunct, in which case he argues that there are two intonational phrases. Crucially, it can never occur after the first conjunct only.

There is another type of phrasal marker that is neither segmental nor tonal, but simply length. In Nupe (Neil Smith personal communication) a Yes/No question is the same as the corresponding statement, except that the final vowel is lengthened.

(14)   u bé   'He came'   u béé   'Did he come?'
        u lō   'He went'   u lōō   'Did he go?'

The simplest autosegmental analysis of these facts is to assume that the question marker is a mora, or TBU, and that it acquires its segmental and tonal properties by spreading from the preceding mora.

Hyman notes that other African languages, such as Kinande, use boundary tones for intonational phrases, and he emphasizes the parallelism between segmental particles and boundary tones. It is to these tones that we now turn.

9.4.4.2   Phrase-level tones

The most commonly described intonational mechanism in tone languages is the addition of a phrase-level tone. As in Cantonese, these can be thought of as a type of particle that lacks segments, consisting solely of tone. Returning to Hausa, Inkelas and Leben (1990) give an example from Newman and Newman 1981 of a Yes/No question tonal particle. A low tone is optionally added to the end of the question, and attaches to the final lexical tone. As a result the lexical distinction between /H/ kái 'you' and /HL/ kâi 'head' is neutralized in favour of [HL] at the end of a question. Staying with African languages, examples are not especially hard to find. Kimatuumbi adds a H tone to the end of certain phrases: see chapter five for more details. Kinande (Hyman 1990) has a H% at the end of the phonological phrase, and a L// at the end of the intonational phrase. Luganda (which is variously analysed as accentual or tonal) has a H// boundary tone at the right edge of the intonational phrase in some intonations, and it associates to any toneless moras at the right edge of the phrase (Hyman 1990).

Rice (1987) gives the example of Slave, an Athapaskan language of North America. Slave contrasts high and low tone. It makes extensive use of segmental particles where English uses intonation, but it also has a phrase-level low tone that Rice argues is inserted at the end of every intonational phrase (IP). These intonational phrase boundaries can be found utterance-internally, for example after subjects and topics, as well as utterance-finally, and Rice suggests that the right edge of every daughter of S, S' or S" initiates the right edge of an IP. In contrast to Hausa, where a phrasal low forms a contour with a lexical high, in Slave the phrasal low overwrites the lexical high, merging underlying /H/ and /L/ tones as [L]. As a result there is considerable tonal neutralization at the end of Slave IPs.

Pike (1975) discusses the Otomi language Mazahua. This language solves the problem of how to accommodate lexical tones and phrasal tones by placing them on entirely different syllables. Lexical tones are limited to non-final syllables, leaving the final syllable free to bear phrasal tones. Utterance-medially, word-final syllables are normally mid. Utterance-finally, they bear a tone provided by the intonational system. In normal declarative sentences, they are low. In continuation intonation, they are mid (as in the utterance-medial environment). In confirmation questions or echo questions, they are normally high:

(15)   thùs?ə̀   'a cigar'   thùs?ə̀   'a hat'
        thùs?ə̄   '… and a cigar…'   thùs?ə̄   '.. and a hat…'
        thùs?ə́   'a cigar, you say?' thùs?ə́   'a hat, you say?'

Returning to Asian tone languages, in many Chinese languages we see the effects of intonational boundary tones, even though they are often not recognized as such. The most common is utterance-final lowering. The effects of utterance-final lowering on tonal analysis are quite insidious, because when citation forms of words are elicited in isolation, the words form their own utterances and undergo any utterance-level effects. Thus we find a remarkably high number of falling tones reported for Chinese dialects, but for many of them the fall is quite small, and almost certainly a result of the utterance-final effect.

Of course, not all falls on citation tones can be attributed to utterance-final lowering. In order to be sure, we need data from utterance-internal forms of the word, and such data are frequently missing. When they are available, the results are sometimes surprising. One language for which we have good data is Taiwanese (Peng 1997), and the data here suggest caution in being too quick to assume that the falls in citation tones are the result of utterance-final falls, since the 'level' tones are, surprisingly, falling utterance-internally as well for many speakers!

Returning to our main theme, Peng's data show two clearly intonational effects. First, we see the addition of a final high boundary tone at the end of an imperative, added to the end of the last lexical tone. Mid-level tones thus become rising, while high level tones either do not change or acquire a slight rise that suggests the boundary tone might be an extra-high tone. Second, utterance-final tones are lower in overall pitch than non-final tones, and the effect is large enough that for one speaker the utterance-final reflex of a high tone is on the same pitch as the utterance-medial reflex of a mid tone.

In Thai (Luksaneeyanawin 1998), questions appear to be formed by the addition of a high tone to the end. If the original tone was falling, the fall is neutralized, and a level tone results. In Vietnamese (Ðo *et al.* 1998) questions usually end in a particle, but all the question particles have high tone (e.g. sao, ai, nhé, không, and many more; the diacritics mark vowel quality, not tone), so that the sentence overall rises at the end. The same rising pattern is found in one type of interrogative with no final particle, suggesting that the high pitch is a question intonation superimposed on inherently toneless particles, or on the last syllable of a sentence with no particle, and is thus a type of boundary tone.

There is a subtler intonational boundary effect in many tone languages, not usually thought of as intonational at all. Instead of the phrase supplying an additional tone to the representation, existing tones may migrate to the boundary and, by doing so, signal phrasal information. In African languages this is extremely common. See the discussion of Kikamba and Kimatuumbi in chapter five.

Before leaving this section, there are two further points to make about boundary tones. One might suppose that a boundary tone would always be realized at a boundary, but this is not necessarily the case. Under certain circumstances they can migrate away from the originating boundary, as shown by Hyman (1990), for Luganda super-high tones, and Gussenhoven (2000), for Dutch phrasal tones. See below for details. One might also suppose that the boundary tone of a larger constituent is always realized outside the tones of any smaller constituents, be they lexical tones or other boundary tones, but again this is not necessarily correct, as Gussenhoven shows.

In the next section we look at a third mechanism used for intonational purposes in tone languages, pitch-range adjustment.

9.4.4.3   Pitch register adjustment

When the overall pitch register is adjusted, tones retain their relative pitches and their shapes, but become higher or lower. If both the upper and the lower limits of the pitch register are adjusted in the same direction, high and low tones raise or lower equally. If the two limits are adjusted in opposite directions, the effect is an overall widening or narrowing of the pitch space. These register adjustments most often cover an entire phrase, rather than just the final word or syllable.

One type of register adjustment is declination: a gradual fall in the pitch of high-toned syllables, and sometimes also low-toned syllables, across an utterance. As we have seen, this is extremely common, and it has been reported for African languages, European languages, and Asian languages. It serves intonational purposes in two ways. Firstly, it may be suspended altogether in certain intonation patterns, such as questions. Secondly, it may occur within some domain, and be reset and re-started in the next domain. In this latter case it may not have any particular semantics, but it does signal phrasal boundaries. These effects were exemplified and discussed in section 9.4 and will not be further explored here.

Overall lowering of the complete pitch register, including both limits, is found in Taiwanese (Peng 1997). Interestingly, it specifically affects the final syllable, not the whole utterance. There is a great deal of inter-speaker variation, but the lowering can be substantial, as much as 50 Hz in Peng's data. The shapes of the tones are unchanged: falling tones are still falling, rising tones are still rising.

Overall raising is found in Hausa questions, where, as one of a package of several intonational effects in questions, Inkelas and Leben (1990) show that the entire question is uttered at a higher pitch than the corresponding statement. They are careful to distinguish between this overall raising, which they see as carried out in the phonetics, and two other tonal characteristics of questions: the suspension of downdrift, and the raising of the pitch on the final syllable, both of which they argue to be phonological. As a second example of overall raising, we can cite Mandarin, where several studies, including Xu 1999a, have found that the first syllable of an utterance, usually the topic of the discourse, is considerably raised from normal levels.

Expansion of the pitch range is used for emphasis in Mandarin (Shih 1987). Highs become much higher, and lows become somewhat lower. After the emphasized constituent, the pitch range returns to normal, although Xu (1999a) finds that it is not just normal, but compressed.

9.4.4.4 Pitch accents in a tone language

Pitch accents are tones assigned to stressed syllables, where stress is assigned on the basis of syllable count and/or weight, and are usually found in languages with no lexical tones. In one recent analysis, however, a language has lexical tones, and assigns stress based on these tones. Then pitch accents are assigned to the stressed syllables.

Tanacross (Athapaskan; Holton forthcoming) has high, low, falling, and rising lexical tones. Holton identifies four intonational melodies, each composed of a pitch accent, a phonological phrase tone %, and an intonational phrase tone //. The notation has been changed from Holton's for consistency:

(16)   *Tanacross intonation melodies*
    Declarative   H*   L% L//
    Interrogative   H*   H% H//
    Imperative   L*   L% L//
    Content interrogative L+H* L% L//

The pitch accent associates to the most prominent syllable, where prominence is located as follows. Note that stems are word-final.

(17)   *Prominence in Tanacross*
    a. The stem syllable is prominent
       unless

    b. the stem is low and the preceding syllable is high, when the pre-stem syllable is prominent.

Although Holton's description is not easy to follow, he is quite explicit that the intonation melody takes precedence over the lexical tone melody at the end of a phrase. Nonetheless, it appears that Tanacross finds ways of rendering lexical tone distinctions recoverable. In some cases, this is direct. Consider the declarative. A high stem will always be prominent, and will thus receive an accentual H*. A low stem preceded by a H prefix will not be prominent, will not receive a H*, and instead will get the phrasal L. One might expect neutralization in the remaining case, a low stem with a low prefix, because such a stem would be prominent, and would get an accentual H*, just like a H stem, but here another mechanism kicks in. Tanacross spreads accentual tones onto the preceding syllable, but it does not spread lexical tones. Thus the accentual H* in the final case will spread, but the lexical H will not, retaining the distinction. Unfortunately, Holton gives no worked-out examples to show how this works, but it is included here as one of the very rare studies of intonation in an American tone language.

9.4.4.5   Theoretical implications

If we step back now and take a look at the theoretical implications of the ways in which lexical tone and phrasal intonation interact, the most striking finding is how similar they are. The following list is a brief summary of some similarities:

(18)   a. Both use level tone primitives.

    b. Both migrate towards prominence, and edges.

    c. Both can be subject to the OCP.

    d. Both prefer to associate one-to-one, but can associate many-to-one (contours) or one-to-many (plateaux).

    e. Both can occur with segmental morphemes (i.e. phrasal particles, in the case of intonation).

    f. Both can occur independent of segmental morphemes, as floating tones.

    g. Downdrift and downstep occur with both.

Hyman (1990) provides a nice example of a language whose lexical and intonational tones share several behaviours. Kinande (Bantu) has two lexical tones, plus toneless syllables, and the intonation system uses the same two tones, in the guise of a H% that attaches to phonological phrases, and a H// and L// that attach to intonation phrases. Some data have been simplified for expository purposes.

H tones win out over L tones, and this is true whether the H is lexical or phrasal. In the first example, a lexical H spreads left within the phonological phrase, delinking a lexical L at the end of the preceding word:

(19)   e-ki-tsungu 'potato' è-kitsùngú kí-nénè 'big potato'
        | |
        L   L H H%L//

In the next example, the H// interrogative phrasal tone bumps off the final lexical L:

(20)   e-ki-koba   'rope' è-kí-kòbá   'rope, INTERROG'
        | | | | | |
        H L L   H L L H//

A third point of convergence is the possibility of limiting tonal insertion to toneless targets, a limitation seen in both the lexical and phrasal phonology. In the phrasal case, consider the two verb forms for present and past tense 'we see/saw' when they end a relative clause, and thus a phonological phrase:

(21)   tu-ka-langır-a 'we see' tu-a-lang-ır-a 'we saw'
        | | | | |
        H   H H L L

'We see' ends with a toneless mora, and is thus available for the insertion of a H% phrasal tone. 'We saw' ends in a L mora, and no H% is inserted:

(22)   a. ...tù-ká-làngìr-á   ...(shoe that REL) we see]$_{PhPh}$ (is falling)...
              | |
              H   H%
        b. ...tw-á-lángìr-à   ...(shoe that REL) we saw]$_{PhPh}$ (is falling)......
              | | | |
              H H L L

A fourth point of similarity is that intonational tones, like lexical tones, may migrate some distance from their point of origin. Here the clearest data come from Luganda. Question intonation supplies a super-high tone, S, shown with a double acute accent, at the right edge of an utterance. However, it shows up immediately after the last H of the utterance, not at the actual edge:

(23)   tu-ba-gulilila → tú-bǎ-gùlílílà   'Are we bribing them?'
        | | | | | |||
        H L   H S L LLLL

I conclude that there are good reasons for analysing intonation and tone with similar mechanisms.

As a coda to this section, there is a residue of intonational effects that demand a subtler approach. Chief among these are the register lowering and raising effects, which cannot be attributed to the simple addition of a new tone to the tonal string. Instead, Hyman (1993), Inkelas and Leben (1990), and Truckenbrodt (2000) have argued that we must use the same mechanisms for intonation that were proposed for downstep in the non-phrasal phonology, where downstep may be the addition of a tone that associates at a higher, registral, level, and has the effect of moving the entire register up or down a notch. Crucially, this effect then persists throughout the rest of the domain.

If intonation and lexical tone are phonologically so similar, we might expect that the same type of grammar could be used to advantage to analyse either. This is of course correct. Gussenhoven (2000) offers an OT analysis of intonation in Roermond Dutch, to which I now turn.

9.5   An OT account of Roermond Dutch

The basic facts in (24) are repeated from section 9.4.3, for convenience. The lexical tonal contrast is found only on long main-stressed syllables.

(24)   *Roermond Dutch accent*

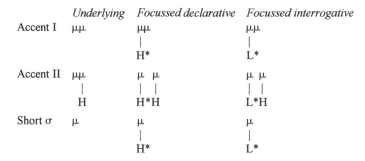

In addition to the H* Focus shown above there is also a L* Focus used in the interrogative. There is a L// Declarative boundary tone, and also a HL// Interrogative intonation. If you think back to the way in which OT handles the association of lexical tones to prominent syllables, or to edges, it is done by means of alignment constraints. Gussenhoven uses the same tools for the facts of intonation here. The basic facts are covered by four constraints.

First, lexical H must be placed correctly:

(25)   ALIGNLEXRIGHT (H, σ́): Lexical H is aligned with the right edge of the main-stressed syllable.

Second, focus tones associate to the first mora, which is the head mora. Gussenhoven does not state this constraint, but we may reasonably assume something like this:

(26)   ALIGNFOCUSLEFT (T*, μ̣): Accents are aligned with the head mora of the
stressed syllable.

The interest comes when we look at the phrasal tones. We start with the plain L//
melody. This always anchors at the right edge of the utterance, but then it spreads
leftwards. The pitch tracks are shown in Figure 9.3

If the syllable has Accent I, and is focussed, so that it has H* on the first mora
and a toneless second mora, then the L spreads to this mora and the fall from the
accent H to the phrasal L// is immediate and abrupt, taking place during the
focussed syllable, as shown in pitch track (a). In the other cases of focussed

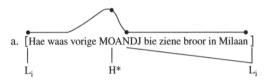

a. [Hae waas vorige MOANDJ bie ziene broor in Milaan]

L_i H* L_i

'He was last month with his brother in Milan.'

b. [Hae waas vorige WAEK bie ziene broor in Milaan]

L_i H* H   ← L_i

'He was last week with his brother in Milan.'

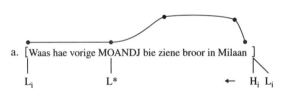

a. [Waas hae vorige MOANDJ bie ziene broor in Milaan]

L_i L*   ← H_i L_i

'Was he last month with his brother in Milan?'

b. [Waas hae vorige WAEK bie ziene broor in Milaan]

L_i L*L   ← H_i L_i

'Was he last week with his brother in Milan?'

Figure 9.3   *Roermond Dutch phrasal tones. From
Gussenhoven 2000: 139, 141*

syllables the second mora is not available, since it bears the H. In these cases there is a much more gradual fall from the focused H to the terminal L. This is shown in pitch track (b). It appears then that the phrasal tone is only realized at the left edge of its span if it is associated with a focussed syllable. We can formulate two alignment constraints, ranked as given:

(27)   ALIGNT //RIGHT(T//, IP): Align the right edge of an IP boundary tone with the right edge of IP.

(28)   ALIGN T//LEFT(T//): Align the left edge of an IP boundary tone as far left as possible.

Gussenhoven assumes that the second alignment constraint pulls the tone leftwards, but it is only realized on the focussed syllable, and at the boundary, and deleted elsewhere. In the case of Accent I, the L// will be realized at both ends, giving the early fall within the focussed syllable.

(29)   σ σ σ σ σ σ σ

In the case of Accent II (or the short syllable), it will be realized only at the boundary, since the focussed syllable is not available, and the fall will be a gradual one across the span as a result of phonetic interpolation. I follow Gussenhoven in using an arrow to show alignment without realization:

(30)   σ σ σ σ σ σ σ

Now let us look at the interrogative melody, HL//. Recall that interrogative focus is marked by L*, not H*. The pitch tracks are shown in Figure 9.3(c–d). We might expect in the case of Accent I a sharp rise from L to H within the syllable, but Roermond only allows syllable-internal rises utterance-finally. This can be stated as a constraint:

(31)   *RISE: $(\mu\,\mu)_\sigma$
                   | |
                   L H

This has two effects. First, in Accent II syllables, which would have the sequence L*H from a focus L* followed by a lexical H, the lexical tone assimilates, giving

L*L. As a result, when the H of the HL// IP melody tries to associate leftwards, there is no empty focal mora for it to surface on. The entire focussed syllable thus stays steadily low, and the rise is delayed, as can be seen in pitch track (d) in Figure 9.3

(32)

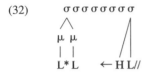

Second, the intonational H// of the HL// cannot associate to the free mora of an Accent I syllable because to do so would create an illicit rise. In OT terms, *RISE >> ALIGNT//LEFT. It does not assimilate, because its survival is licensed by the association to the boundary.

(33)   σ σ σ σ σ σ σ
             ∧
            μ μ   ╱|
            | ╱ |
            L*   ← H L//

The rise here can start during the syllable, but only as a result of phonetic interpolation. The result is the pitch track in Figure 9.3 (c). Note that there is no sharp phonological rise within the syllable equivalent to the sharp fall in the previous condition.

One final effect is particularly spectacular. Consider an utterance where the focussed syllable is a final syllable with Accent II, in the declarative. Focussed Accent II syllables have a H* followed by a lexical H, and there is also a L// IP boundary tone, so we would expect to find a high pattern, with a final fall during the last mora. Instead, we get a rise! How could this be? Gussenhoven argues that it can be construed as evidence for the ranking ALIGNLEXRIGHT >> ALIGNT//RIGHT, so that the lexical H surfaces *outside* the phrasal L//:

(34)   *Accent II, final, focussed, declarative:*
         b e i n
         | | \
         H*L//H

This is a striking example of the mobility of phrasal tones in response to the overall phonology of the language, which has the power to pull or push them away from the phrasal edge deeper into the phrase.

This concludes the discussion of Roermond Dutch. There are further interesting complexities, for which the reader is referred to Gussenhoven's work.

9.6   Phrasing, speech rate, stylistics

When tones occur in context, there are influences at work other than intonation in the strict sense. Speech rate and style – formal vs. casual – can affect
the realization of tones quite dramatically (as indeed they can segmental realization!). A declarative sentence said quickly and casually does not necessarily have
the same tonal properties as a declarative sentence said slowly and formally. And
indeed speech rate and speech style are themselves partly independent variables.
There is not a great deal of published work on this question, but an excellent
study by Ao (1993) on Nantong Chinese, analysed in OT in Yip 1999, is worth
summarizing here.

Roughly speaking, as speech gets faster the phrasing changes in the direction of fewer longer prosodic constituents. In Nantong the constituent whose
size changes most drastically is the foot, which is binary in slow speech,
but larger in faster speech. Inside the foot, only the head bears tone, and all
other tones are deleted. This in OT is handled with a positional faithfulness constraint, HEAD-MAX-T, which dominates the markedness constraint *T,
ensuring the survival of tones on head syllables. The markedness constraint
dominates simple faithfulness, MAX-T, forcing deletion of all other tones. For
arguments that the relevant constituent is indeed the foot, see Yip 1999. A
somewhat similar, though not identical, account has been arrived at independently by Matthew Chen (2000).

I first propose an analysis in which as speed increases the constraint that
places an upper bound on foot size is demoted. In very slow speech, on the other
hand, the faithfulness constraint MAX-T is promoted, resulting in less tone loss
at very slow speeds. Under this approach, the grammar itself is altered at different speech rates. This account is then contrasted with an approach in which
there is a single constant grammar, and in which the speech-rate-related differences are attributed to a change in the mapping from phonology to phonetics
(see chapter one for discussion). Strictly speaking, in this second analysis, the
speech rate changes do not affect the grammar, but only the way in which they
are realized by the phonetics. All the data, insights, and generalizations in this
section are from Ao 1993.

9.6.1   A phonological account

The examples in (35) show the foot structure of morpho-syntactically flat
cases, such as lists of numbers or polysyllabic monomorphemic words; phonologically, all feet are of the (Tooo…) type, where T shows a surviving tone, and o
shows a toneless syllable, and parentheses mark foot boundaries.

(35)   *Nantong tones at different speech rates*

Segments	Underlying tones	Slow	Normal	Fast	Gloss
ə ə ə ə	T T T T	(T) (T) (T)(T)	(T o) (T) (T)	(T o o) (T)	'2 2 2 2'
ə ə ə ə ə	T T T T T	(T) (T) (T) (T) (T)	(T o) (T o) (T)	(T o o o) (T)	'2 2 2 2 2'
puliniʃȝjɔ	T T T T T	(T) (T) (T) (T)(T)	(T o) (T o) (T)	(T o o o) (T)	Polynesia
Prosodic words		[ ] [ ]	[ ]	[ ]	

Ao gives precise foot diagnostics, including tone deletion on non-head syllables, followed by spreading or default, and Onset and Coda Lenition in weak syllables. He also gives many Prosodic Word diagnostics, including raising of LM to MH in feet that are non-final in the Prosodic Word.

Notice first that, at all speeds, all syllables are footed, and the final syllable forms a foot on its own. I will not consider candidates that violate these generalizations, which can be attributed to an undominated pair of constraints PARSE-σ and FINAL-STRESS. At normal speeds, feet are binary, left-to-right, but unary feet are allowed in two circumstances: to satisfy FINALSTRESS or to satisfy PARSE-σ. Feet of more than two syllables are never found, suggesting that FTBINMAX (Hewitt 1994) is undominated. Thus far, then, we can construct a grammar with the following ranking: PARSE-σ, FINALSTRESS, FTBINMAX >> FTBINMIN, ALLFTLEFT. For reasons of space I will not formulate these familiar constraints here: statements can be found in any OT work on stress such as Kager 1999. Within a foot, tones are deleted, in violation of MAX-T. These violations occur because of the need for feet to be binary, showing that FTBINMIN >> MAX-T. The relevant portion of the grammar is thus PARSE-σ, FINALSTRESS, FTBINMAX >> FTBINMIN, ALLFTLEFT >> MAX-T.

At fast speeds, feet enlarge, even though this means the loss of more tones, and of course violates FTBINMAX. The advantage of fewer and larger feet is that they better satisfy ALLFTLEFT, which must thus dominate FTBINMAX. The fast speech grammar is thus PARSE-σ, FINALSTRESS >> FTBINMIN, ALLFTLEFT >> MAX-T, FTBINMAX. The change from normal to fast speech thus involves demotion of FTBINMAX, as shown below by the arrow linking the normal to fast speech grammars.

At slow speeds, each syllable forms its own foot, in violation of FTBINMIN, and incurring even more violations of ALLFTLEFT. There is, however, a dramatic improvement in the eyes of MAX-T, since no tones are lost. It is clear then that MAX-T has been promoted above FTBINMIN and ALLFTLEFT. The slow speech grammar looks like this: PARSE-σ, FINALSTRESS, FTBINMAX, MAX-T >> FTBINMIN,

ALLFTLEFT. The change from normal to slow speech thus involves promotion of MAX-T, as shown by the arrow linking the normal to slow speech rate grammars.

(36)   *Summary of constraint rankings at varying speeds*
Slow: PARSE-σ, FINALSTRESS, FTBINMAX, MAX-T >> FTBINMIN, ALLFTLEFT

Normal: PARSE-σ, FINALSTRESS, FTBINMAX >> FTBINMIN, ALLFTLEFT >> MAX-T

Fast: PARSE-σ, FINALSTRESS >> FTBINMIN, ALLFTLEFT >> MAX-T, FTBINMAX

Here I take the normal speed grammar to be the real grammar, and derive the others from it by simple, principled changes. Which grammar is used at which speed must surely be predictable: no language would presumably show the opposite matching of grammars to speeds. However, it is not clear how OT, with its commitment to explaining linguistic typology as the result of constraint reranking, would ensure the right match of grammar to speech rate.

By allowing feet to vary from one syllable (slow speed) through binary (normal speed) to n-ary (fast speed), we can stick to a unified statement of tone deletion: tones delete in the non-head position of a foot. On the other hand, if only the binary units are called feet, then in fast speech we must say there are no feet, and that tones are lost in the non-head position of prosodic words. This needs two changes in the grammar instead of one: the loss of the foot level, and a change in the tone deletion conditions.

9.6.2   A tempo-based alternative

The previous analysis assumes that as speech rate increases, the grammar itself changes. This seems rather unlikely, and has the undesirable and implausible consequence that the shifts from fast to normal to slow should be discrete and categorical (Myers personal communication). A more attractive alternative would be to assume that the grammar is held constant, but the mapping onto the phonetics is affected by speech rate. Below I outline such an approach.

By hypothesis, the constant grammar will supply a single structured output to the phonetics at all speech rates. What must this structure look like? Across speech rates, we see that the tonal facts require access to syllables, to binary units, which I will call feet, ϕ, to a final unary unit, which I will also take to be a foot, ϕ, and to an n-ary unit that encompasses the whole word except the final syllable, which I will call the super-foot, ϕ', since it is larger than the foot but smaller than the prosodic word. The crucial difference here is the addition of the extra ϕ' level, and this move is rendered unavoidable by the hypothesis that a single structure is present at all speech rates, since that single structure must simultaneously encode the binary pattern of normal speed and the n-ary pattern of fast speech. Thus the binary and the n-ary units must be *different* units, rather than two instances of a single unit, and the term foot can be reserved for those that are maximally binary.

The structures required for four- and five-syllabled strings are thus as shown in (37).

(37)

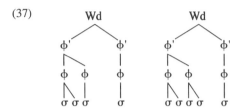

These structures will be chosen as optimal by the normal-speed OT grammar from the previous section, with the addition of an undominated constraint requiring the prosodic word to be strictly binary at the level of the super-foot.

There are two differences that concern us as speech rate increases. First, obviously, the output is faster! Secondly, more tones are deleted. I will deal with each of these in turn. To characterize the additional speed, let us assume that the timing is controlled by the mapping of prosodic units onto timing units, which I will call beats. For a somewhat similar use of the timing tier, see Dresher and van der Hulst 1995: 10. At slow speeds, smaller units are mapped onto these beats; at higher speeds, larger units are mapped onto the beats. I will assume the beats are grouped into measures, [xx]. For Nantong, the mapping is given in (38).

(38)   Slow speed: Map σ to [xx]
         Normal speed: Map φ to [xx]
         Fast speed: Map φ' to [xx]

The beat representation is located at the phonology–phonetics interface. It cannot replace the prosodic structure, nor is it a final phonetic specification, since its translation into actual duration is influenced by any number of factors, including most obviously syllable count and segment quality. I have in mind something similar to the 'sonority specification' of Beckman *et al.* (1992: 83), who develop their model 'to describe the quantitative properties of the lengthenings associated with nuclear accent... and overall tempo decrease in terms of some abstract phonetic representation that can mediate between the prosodic hierarchy and the gestural dynamics'.

Turning to the tonal facts, a rather surprising consequence follows from this analysis. If the phonological output structure is constant at all speeds, but the tonal deletion facts vary, then any phonological statement of tonal deletion will have to differ at different speech rates. In fact, the same is true for any other alternations in the weak position in a foot, such as Onset and Coda Lenition. For reasons of space, I will confine my discussion to the tonal case.

(39)   *Phonological tone deletion*
        Slow speed: No deletion
        Normal speed: Delete tones in the weak positions of feet, ɸ.
        Fast speed: Delete tones in the weak positions of super-feet, ɸ'.

As speech rates increases, then, the phonology does not stay constant after all, but varies in its choice of tone deletion rule. This then undermines the initial premise of this section: that speech rate differences are better handled in the phonetics than in the phonology.

However, suppose that tone deletion is not a phonological but a phonetic matter. In that case it can be simply and uniformly stated at all speech rates as follows:

(40)   *'Phonetic' tone deletion:*
        Delete all tones except the first in a [xx] measure.

At slow speed, each syllable is a measure, and keeps its one and only tone. At normal speed, each foot is a measure, so this is equivalent to retaining tone on the head only. At fast speed, each super-foot is a measure, and in the initial n-ary super-foot only the first tone will survive. Attractive though this rule may be, we have to stop and ask ourselves what kind of rule it is. To call it phonetic is misleading; like the mapping from prosodic structure to beats and measures, it more properly belongs on the interface between phonology and phonetics, where phonological structures are interpreted. Under this view, consider the stages in the interpretation of a five-syllabled structure at fast speed in (41).

(41)   *Prosodic structure*   *Mapping to beats:*   *Deletion of non-initial T*
                                    each ɸ' maps to [xx]   *in each [xx] measure*

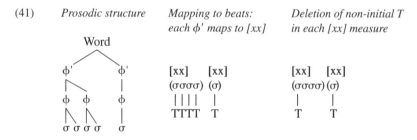

So far, then, this approach gives a straightforward account of speech rate changes by locating them entirely at the phonology–phonetics interface.

The model I have outlined in this section makes some interesting predictions that await experimental verification. If [xx] represent measures of two beats of roughly constant phonetic duration, these mappings will result in a 4σ phonological word occupying four measures at slow speed, three measures at normal speed, and two measures at fast speed. A 5σ phonological word will occupy five measures at slow speed, three measures at normal speed, and two measures at fast speed. Notice that this leads to several strong predictions: *ceteris paribus,* at normal and fast speed, phonological words of four and five syllables will be of the same approximate duration as each other: three measures at normal speed and two measures at fast speed. Ao (personal communication) tells me that this is essentially correct. A second and even more startling prediction is that at fast speed *all* phonological words will occupy exactly two measures, irrespective of length. A third prediction is that in such phonological words the final syllable, which is a φ' unto itself, will be of the same duration as the entire preceding substring. The theory can be made subtler by allowing for some variation in beat duration, so that there is a continuum of speeds under the umbrella of 'fast speed', but this does not affect the three predictions made above, which concern 'within speed' durations. Testing these predictions experimentally is tricky because we know that in 'foot-timed' languages feet are not really of equal duration, but that their duration is heavily influenced by a number of things, including most obviously syllable count and segment quality. I leave this question for future research.

I have presented an account of Nantong speech-rate changes, which has the following central characteristics: (a) The grammar builds a single prosodic structure. (b) In slow speech, limited restructuring takes place at the prosodic word level, dividing the string into two or more smaller prosodic words. (c) The phonology–phonetics interface maps prosodic units onto measures. As speech rate increases, the unit that is mapped onto a single measure enlarges from σ to φ to φ'. (d) The phonology–phonetics interface deletes all non-initial tones in a measure. This account has a clear conceptual advantage over the purely phonological account of the preceding section in that it allows us to assume that the speaker has a single grammar, rather than many. The tone deletion generalization is stated at the level of the interface with the phonetics, at the beat level. Interestingly, this interface level is the same level at which I have suggested that default tones are inserted in some languages (see chapter three, section 3.6), raising the possibility that during the transition from the phonology to the phonetics one of the allowable changes is a change in the presence or absence of specification on non-head syllables. A final advantage of this proposal is that it avoids the problem of explaining why particular grammars are chosen at particular speeds: the variation in mapping is systematic, working its way up to larger units as speed accelerates. In fact, the increasing size of the prosodic units that map onto a single measure could be seen as the definition of what it means to speak at a faster rate!

9.7   Conclusion

This chapter has looked at the interaction of tone and intonation. The primary finding has been how similar and how intertwined they are, and how rich a use of intonation we find even in languages with lexical tone. A full investigation of intonation itself is well beyond the scope of this book, but it is hoped that the reader whose interest has been piqued will pursue some of the references cited here.

10

Perception and acquisition of tone

In the introduction I talked a little about how tones are produced, but of course this is only half the picture. For tones to be used in communication, they must also be perceived by the hearer, and not just as musical pitch, but as linguistic objects. Successful perception is also the first prerequisite for tonal acquisition, and that is the reason for combining in this chapter two apparently unrelated topics, perception and acquisition. I will begin with adult perception and then move on to the child. On adult tone perception, one of the most useful references is the excellent survey in Gandour 1978, still useful as I write this text.

10.1   Adult tone perception

10.1.1   Fundamental frequency, pitch and tone

I begin by reminding the reader of the difference between fundamental frequency (F_0), pitch, and tone, already discussed in chapter one. In this order, the terms move from a purely phonetic term, F_0, to a truly linguistic one, tone. F_0 is an acoustic term referring to the signal itself: how many pulses per second does the signal contain, measured in Hertz (Hz) where one Hz is one cycle per second. The next term, pitch, is a perceptual term. What is the hearer's perception of this signal: is it heard as high or low, the same pitch as the previous portion of the signal or different? The mere existence of F_0 differences may not be enough to result in the perception of pitch differences. The F_0 changes could be too small, or be the result of segmental or other factors for which the hearer unconsciously compensates. Pitch can be a property of speech or non-speech signals such as music. Tone, on the other hand, is a linguistic term that refers to a phonological category that distinguishes two words or utterances, and is thus only relevant for languages in which pitch plays some sort of linguistic role. The perception of tone must be dependent in whole or in part on pitch perception, and thence on fundamental frequency. For distinct tones to be perceived, the signal must contain F_0 fluctuations, and these must in turn be large enough to be perceptible as pitch differences. Of course, one cannot ignore the possibility that other properties of the signal also play a role, such as duration and amplitude, a point to which we will return.

10.1.2   Pitch detection

Given the preceding discussion, let us start not with tone perception proper, but with its precursor, pitch detection. How sensitive is the human ear? Experiments addressing this issue usually use pure pitches as stimuli, rather than speech signals, and investigate the minimal detectable frequency difference. Others, more relevant for our purposes, use synthetic speech stimuli complete with harmonics (formants). The main reason this is important is that the periodicity of the fundamental frequency is reproduced in the fine structure of the harmonics as well, so information relevant for linguistic pitch discrimination can be found in any sound with harmonics (i.e. sonorants, including vowels, glides, liquids, and nasals).

One of the best-known studies is that of Klatt (1973). He found that the minimal detectable difference for sounds with a level F_0 was in the region of 0.3 Hz, a very tiny difference. For sounds with an F_0 ramp, or slope, the minimal detectable difference was larger, but still only 2 Hz. For comparison, a musical semitone is around 6 Hz. It is also clear even from Klatt's pioneering work that formants play a role in pitch perception. For example, Klatt showed that pitch is easier to discriminate on a steady-state vowel than on a non-steady vowel, such as a diphthong, where formants change during the vocalic portion of the syllable. Further, we know that pitch perception gets slightly worse if the formants are filtered out, although the relative contribution of lower vs. higher formants is not clear. See Moore 1997 for discussion. In natural speech, of course, formants are always present during vowels, and this suggests a reason for the preference for linguistic tone on vowels rather than, say, on fricatives. Fricatives have no formant structure, and thus detection of linguistically significant pitch on a fricative might be impaired. It also, as Silverman (1997a) suggests, offers an explanation for the avoidance of contrastive pitch on breathy or glottalized vowels: their impaired formant structure interferes with pitch perception. Klatt's work also suggests a reason for the lack of linguistic pitch on onsets, even sonorant onsets. Klatt showed that when F_0 changes rapidly, pitch detection is harder. Zhang (2000) speculates that, since we know that the point of transition from onset to nucleus is a period of rapid transitions in formant frequencies, this might interfere with pitch perception, and thus be a poor position to realize linguistically significant pitch.

Despite the great sensitivity of the ear to just noticeable differences (JNDs) as tiny as 0.3 Hz, it is clear that human languages do not exploit such fine distinctions. Instead, tones tend to be much further apart in the tonal space, and much fewer in number. For example, Mambila (Connell 2000) has four level tones, and they are spaced an average of 10 Hz apart. This is consistent with Rietveld and Gussenhoven's (1985) finding that pitch differences of 1.5 semitones (about 10 Hz) can reliably be interpreted as prominence differences. Pollack (1952, 1953) presented listeners with a series of equally spaced pure tones and asked them not whether a particular pair were the same or different, but instead asked them to identify each tone in a series as being tone number one, number two, and so on. Subjects were able to name up to five tones rather reliably, but their performance seriously deteriorated if the number of tones was six or more, even though the larger number of tones were no closer together in their frequencies than the smaller number.

It is also clear that the detection of contours requires extra effort. In particular, contours cannot be perceived if the syllable is less than about 40–65 ms long (Greenberg and Zee 1979). Shorter signals are perceived as level even if the frequency is actually changing. In fact, for a really robust percept of 'contouricity' the entire signal duration, including a necessary steady-state initial stretch, is about 130 ms. This is longer than the actual length of the stop-final syllables in many Chinese dialects, which are only about 120 ms long, and may explain why they are typically described as having only level tones.

In sum, the human auditory system can detect very small differences in fundamental frequency, particularly if aided by formant structure. However, there may be an upper limit on the number of such distinctions that can be handled, and contours may require extra time. For these reasons, the perceptual system may constrain the size and types of tonal inventories in natural languages. We now move on to the perception of natural language tones.

10.1.3 Is F_0 the main cue for tonal discrimination?

I have so far assumed that F_0 is the primary cue for pitch, and therefore tone, perception, but this cannot be taken for granted. In tone languages different tones frequently differ not only in F_0, but also in duration, amplitude, and voice quality. For this reason a number of researchers have tested the contributions of these various components towards the ability of native speakers to discriminate actual natural language tones. Gandour (1978) gives a useful summary of early work on this issue. It appears that in a wide range of unrelated tone languages, including Thai, Mandarin Chinese, Yoruba, and Swedish, fundamental frequency is the one absolutely indispensable cue to tonal recognition. If the signal is manipulated so that all other cues are removed, native speakers can still discriminate between the various tones with a very high degree of accuracy (Fok 1974, Abramson 1978). On the other hand, if the other cues such as duration and amplitude are left

intact, but the original frequencies of the various stimuli are suppressed and replaced with a constant F_0, tonal discrimination is substantially impaired, although
different researchers have found different degrees of impairment. For example,
Whalen and Xu (1992) found that, if they removed all F_0 information including
that inherent in the fine structure of the harmonics, a recognition rate of about
80 per cent was still achieved. Fu and Zeng (2000) found a somewhat lower
overall rate of nearer 70 per cent.

One can also wonder exactly which aspects of the remaining information are
primarily responsible for this relative success, and it appears to be largely due to
amplitude. In some languages, like Mandarin Chinese, there is a close correlation between pitch contour and amplitude contour (Garding *et al.* 1986, Sagart
1986, Whalen and Xu 1992). For example, the high falling tone begins with a
high amplitude, which falls during the syllable at much the same rate as the
pitch falls. This being so, it is not surprising that if not only pitch but also duration cues are removed, while amplitude contours are retained, a relatively high
degree of pitch recognition of about 60 per cent is still possible (Fu and Zeng
2000). The contribution of duration they found to be non-significant except in
the case of the third tone, which is known to be much longer than the other tones
in isolated syllables.

We conclude then that F_0 is indeed the primary cue for the discrimination of
tones in natural languages, but that to the extent that the F_0 contour is mirrored in
the amplitude, amplitude too is a useful cue.

10.1.4 Tone identification

If one asks English speakers to identify the vowel in the word 'beet',
based on hearing a single recorded instance of this word with no context of any
kind, you will still get a highly accurate response. The hearer does not have to
compare 'beet' to 'boot', or even to 'bit', before making a decision. It is less
obvious that one would expect the same to be true for tones. The F_0 of a male
speaker's high tone may be lower than the F_0 of a female speaker's low tone,
and the F_0 for the mid tone of a Yoruba speaker might be similar to the F_0 of either of the two mid tones of a Cantonese speaker. Without some context, tone
identification might be difficult, if not impossible. It is thus somewhat surprising to discover that native speakers of tone languages seem to be pretty good at
tonal identification even when presented with stimuli deprived of any linguistic context. Abramson (1975) showed this quite clearly for Thai, and his results
have been replicated with other languages. He also showed that it is not amplitude and duration that are responsible for this effect, since if the signal is manipulated so that these are held constant, F_0 alone is enough to allow accurate

identification. When two tones *are* confused, it is usually tones with very similar shapes, and Abramson concluded that tone *contour* is an important component of tonal identification, a finding confirmed by Lin and Repp (1989). Rising and falling tones are rarely confused (except with other rising or falling tones). Level tones are sometimes confused with each other. Of course, real 'level' tones usually show some slight pitch movement, and if this is artificially eliminated so that the tones are truly level, mis-identifications increase, especially for mid tones.

It is well known that distinctions of place of articulation or voice onset time (VOT) are perceived categorically, but vowels may be perceived continuously. One can wonder whether tones are perceived categorically or not. Chan *et al.* (1975) looked at the boundary between high level tone (Tone 1) and high rising tone (Tone 2) in Mandarin. They synthesized the syllable [i] with tones whose rise varied between 0 Hz (i.e. a level tone) and 30 Hz. They found a sharp boundary for native speakers when the rise covered about 12 Hz. Less than that, and the stimulus was perceived as level. More than that, and it was perceived as rising. For English-speaking subjects, however, no such category boundary was evident. Instead, they seemed to distinguish mainly between the phonetically level tone and all the others, suggesting that this was more like psycho-physical pitch discrimination than tone perception. Similar results were obtained by Leather (1987). Of course, this is exactly what one would expect. Categorical perception requires the formation of categories, and adult speakers of a non-tonal language are not likely to have categories for tone. It is clear, then, that for native speakers of Mandarin tonal identification taps into their linguistic knowledge of tonal categories.

Nonetheless, there do seem to be differences between tone discrimination and segmental discrimination. Cutler and Chen (1997) looked at tone processing in Cantonese. They asked native speaker subjects to decide whether a given stimulus was a word or a non-word. The non-words could differ from actual words in various ways, including onset consonant, nuclear vowel, tone, or some combination of these. When only a single difference was present, non-words were rejected least accurately if the only difference was tonal, although the error rate was never above 30 per cent. Second-worst performance came if the only difference was in the nuclear vowel. In a second experiment, subjects were asked to judge whether two syllables were the same as each other or different. Again, if the only difference was tonal, their accuracy was less, and the response times were slower, than if the differences were segmental. Finally, the experiment was repeated with native speakers of Dutch who did not know any tone language, with essentially the same results. (There were some other differences related to lexical knowledge that need not concern us here.) Cutler and Chen speculate on the reasons for the poorer

294 *Perception and acquisition of tone*

performance on tone. They make two suggestions. First, tonal information arrives late in the syllable. First comes the onset, then the vowel, and the tone, which is carried on the vowel, but which cannot be fully identified until its contour is apparent, often quite late in the vowel. Second, tones (and vowels) are more variable in context than consonants, and hearers may thus exercise caution before making their identification.

We conclude that hearers may perceive tone categorically, that they pay attention to the shape of tones, and that tone may be processed somewhat later and more cautiously than segmental information. We now turn to the effects of context on tone perception.

10.1.5 Compensation for context

We know that tones may change in context for various reasons, including declination, downdrift/downstep, and tone sandhi. Accurate tone identification requires the hearer to allow for this, and there is considerable evidence that they are able to do exactly that.

Pierrehumbert (1979) looked at declination in English. In normal intonation, successive high peaks in an English sentence are lowered. Using a natural nonsense utterance like *ma-MA-ma-ma-MA-ma*, and varying the frequencies of the peaks, she asked her subjects which of two peaks was higher in pitch. They heard them as the same in pitch when the second one was in fact substantially lower, showing that they were expecting, and compensating for, declination.

Xu (1994) looked at Mandarin. He notes first that contour tones in a 'conflicting context' may in fact have a contour very different from their canonical one. For example, a rising tone that is preceded by a high and followed by a low, as in H.LH.L may be level or even slightly falling, because coarticulation effects caused by the finite speed with which articulators can move may raise the beginning of the rise under the influence of the preceding H, and depress the end under the influence of the following L. Despite this phonetic fall, subjects identify these tones in these contexts correctly as rising with a high degree of accuracy, although not as high as in contexts that do not radically distort their shapes. Xu then played these excised stimuli to his subjects without any context, in which case they identified them as level H most of the time, and occasionally as level L. Lastly, he excised tones from these conflicting contexts and transplanted them to contexts where no such effect would normally take place. For example, the central LH 'rise' from the 'conflicting context' of the sequence LH.LH.LH in which it was phonetically level or even slightly falling was excised and placed in the 'compatible' context HL.___.HL, where an underlying rise would normally remain rising. He then asked hearers to identify this middle tone. Not surprisingly, it was heard as a HL fall, since in this context an underlying HL would itself be almost level, given that its H would be depressed by the preceding L, and its L would be raised by the following H. To sum up, one phonetic signal, a slightly falling tone that was the surface manifestation of an underlying rising tone, was heard as three different things: level in isolation, rising in its original context, and falling in the mirror-image context. The hearers are clearly basing their identification on the surrounding context and compensating for it.

The tonal changes discussed in the previous two paragraphs are clearly phonetic, but there are also of course phonological tonal changes. In Mandarin, the famous third-tone sandhi rule has been much studied in this regard, starting with Wang and Li (1967) and most recently in Peng (2000). A third tone, usually low-level non-finally and low-rising finally, changes to a high-rising second tone before another third tone. The output is usually thought to be indistinguishable from an underlying second tone. Peng looks at the output of this rule from three angles: production, perception, and categorization. From the production perspective, he shows that the output tone is phonetically of *exactly* the same shape as an underlying second tone, but very marginally lower, about 2 Hz throughout. From the perception point of view, he shows that hearers cannot reliably distinguish the output of the rule from an underlying tone 2, performing at chance, and confirming earlier work such as Wang and Li. Lastly, he conducted an experiment to assess how hearers categorized the tones they hear. Interestingly, although these output tones were produced almost identically to tone 2, and perceptually indistinguishable from tone 2, they were uniformly categorized as tone 3, showing again that hearers can retrieve the underlying forms of the tones even from radical phonological transformations.

10.2   First-language acquisition

Until now we have confined ourselves to an exploration of adult speakers' tonal phonology, but we can also ask how this knowledge was acquired, and what path the child takes en route to the adult steady state. At the present time very little is known about the acquisition of tone, and many otherwise thorough books on acquisition, such as Ingram 1989, do not mention tone at all. This portion of this chapter will summarize our current understanding and raise questions for future research. It is divided into five main sections. Section 10.2.1 discusses the earliest evidence for infants' perception of tonal distinctions. Section 10.2.2 looks at early production data. Section 10.2.3 looks at the tonal phonology proper, including tone sandhi rules and other tonal alternations. Sections 10.2.4 and 10.2.5

look briefly at child-specific phonology and at second language acquisition. Of these, early production is the best-studied area.

10.2.1   Perception of tone in infants

A necessary early step in learning a language is to perceive the contrastive sounds of that language. Without this, production is impossible, and lexical items cannot be acquired. If the contrast between [t^h] and [d] is not detected the words *Tigger* and *digger*, dear to the heart of small children, cannot be distinguished and stored. A considerable body of research has looked at the earliest age at which infants pay attention to distinctions such as voice onset time, or place of articulation, but almost nothing is known about the age at which tonal distinctions are detected. Of course, it requires considerable ingenuity to ascertain whether a tiny infant can tell any two sounds apart: we cannot simply ask! A number of techniques have been used to address this question, all relying on behavioural signs that a child has noticed a change in the signal, such as changes in sucking rate, or head turning. Different techniques are better suited to different ages and sample sizes. For example, we know that infants tend to suck faster when presented with a novel stimulus. If one sound is played repeatedly, sucking rate declines slowly as the child loses interest. If a new stimulus is then played, it increases again. It follows that an increase in sucking rate following a change in stimulus suggests that the child has detected the difference between the new stimulus and the old one. No change in sucking rate suggests the two stimuli were perceived as the same. For a useful review of procedures, see the appendix to Jusczyk 1997.

Most of the work done in this area has been segmental, and nearly all on English. In the case of voice onset time (VOT), for example, we know that English infants as young as one month can detect very small differences between stimuli differing only in VOT (Eimas *et al.* 1971). What is more, their discrimination is categorical. They do not pay equal attention to any VOT discrepancy, but only to discrepancies that occur at particular points that roughly coincide with the English adult difference between voiced and voiceless obstruents. Later research has shown the same ability to discriminate place of articulation of stop consonants at under two months of age. Since place of articulation is cued mainly by formant transitions, this implies an ability to detect changes in formant frequency. It is worth noting here that categorical perception may well not be limited to humans (chinchillas and even quails can do it too), and in humans it may not be limited to speech sounds. Nonetheless, even if this fascinating ability is not limited to human language, it has clearly been recruited for language purposes. See Jusczyk 1997 for an excellent summary of the material discussed in this paragraph.

More relevant for our purposes are studies on vowel perception by infants. Here too they seem able to discriminate pairs such as [a] vs. [i] and [i] vs. [u] at under four months. There are two interesting points about the vowel facts. First, the acoustic distinction between vowels is one of frequency: different vowels have different resonating frequencies, or formants. To tell [a] from [i] it is necessary to detect that (for a male speaker) [a] has a first formant (F1) of about 700 Hz and a second formant (F2) of about 1100 Hz, whereas [i] has an F1 of about 300 Hz and an F2 of about 2300 Hz. What is more, as high vowels [i] and [u] have very similar F1s, and are distinguished mainly by F2 alone, with [u] having an F2 typical of back vowels of around 1000 Hz. Vowel discrimination thus implies frequency discrimination, a skill that is of course crucial for tonal discrimination too. Indeed, the actual frequencies that matter overlap. For example, the difference between [ɪ] and [ɛ] for one male speaker of Australian English is mainly the difference between first formants of about 320 Hz and 420 Hz. In my speech, these are the fundamental frequencies of mid and high tones respectively. Second, vowel discrimination, unlike consonant discrimination, does not seem to be categorical for either adults or infants. We can detect differences too small to be contrastive – the sort of thing that subtly differentiates different regional accents, for example.

If vowel discrimination and place of articulation discrimination require frequency discrimination, and vowel discrimination is present very early, then one would expect tone discrimination to be in place at much the same time. So how much do we know? Physiologically, the cochleae in the ear have reached adult sizes at around six months foetal age and begin to function for low frequency sounds soon thereafter (Kjellin, e-mail OT Listserv 2001). This is the frequency range needed to detect prosody, and suggests that it could be detectable very early, perhaps even in utero. There has been some work on prosody in English, showing that young infants can distinguish between bisyllables that have either first- or second-syllable stress, a distinction at least partially encoded as pitch. Morse (1972) and Kuhl and Miller (1982) have shown that infants around two months can distinguish between stable vowels with either rising or falling pitch.

Somewhat surprisingly, there seems to be almost no work addressing this question for infants in the environment of a tonal language. One recent study on Yoruba deserves attention. Yoruba has three lexical tones, high, mid, and low. Harrison (1998, 1999, 2000) carried out perception studies for both adults and children. He used isolated syllables and showed that Yoruba adults readily discriminate high from anything else even in these isolated syllables, but mid vs. low are not readily distinguished by adults. He then looked at Yoruba and English infants aged six to eight months. In a pilot study, the infants heard synthetic instances of [ki] with different pitches. Each pair of stimuli differed by either 10, 20, or 40 Hz. The English infant was completely unable to detect any of these differences, but the Yoruba child could at least in some cases detect differences of 20 or 40 Hz, but not of 10 Hz.

In the main study, the stimuli all had a 20 Hz differential. Again, the six English children failed utterly to notice the difference. The six Yoruba children were more successful, but only around a boundary of 190–210 Hz. Above or below this pitch range they also failed to distinguish. Interestingly, this boundary comes at the same point for both infants and adults, and appears to suggest that at all ages the only distinction that is paid attention to is the 'high' versus 'other' distinction. Harrison uses this to argue for a phonological analysis in which L is absent, and the surface L/M difference is prosodically based. Be that as it may, this study seems to show clearly that, by the age of six to eight months, the language environment has affected the ability to detect tone. The English children have lost that ability (assuming from the earlier studies on English children that they once had it), but the Yoruba children have kept it and focussed in on the particular discontinuity that is relevant in their language environment. What is more, if Harrison is right, they have acquired some phonology: they are discriminating the phonological contrast between High and not High, but not the phonetic contrast between the two allotones of non-High, that is Mid and Low.

One major question does not seem to be clearly answered in Harrison's work. The actual frequency of the boundary between high tones and all others will vary widely from speaker to speaker, especially from male to female. The 200 Hz boundary discovered by Harrison is that for male speakers. For female speakers this boundary would be more likely to separate mid from low. In synthetic stimuli, the child has few other cues as to the sex of the speaker, so it remains unclear how one can conclude that the boundary they detect is the one between high and mid, rather than the one between mid and low. Indeed, if one makes the assumption that they spend more time with female care-givers than with male ones, there might be a pre-disposition towards interpreting the speech as female! I should note that one property of Harrison's stimuli leaves open the possibility that the speech was still identifiably male: the stimuli were synthesized from copies of a natural token produced by a male, and other than the frequency variation they retained the other characteristics of the original signal.

What can we conclude from this limited evidence? It seems clear that very young infants, certainly by six months, but probably as early as one month, can perceive pitch differences. They use this not only in discriminating tone, but also to distinguish vowel quality and place of articulation. By six months there is evidence that they are paying more attention to the distinctions that matter in their ambient language, such as tone in Yoruba but not in English. Beyond these essentials, we know very little. How many distinct tonal levels can an infant detect? Can they detect the difference between level tones and contour tones? Is the 20 Hz difference that seemed to be the minimum for the Yoruba infants universally true, or might a different ambient language trigger a different threshold? Are there really asymmetries as to which distinctions they can detect, of the type Harrison claims to have found for Yoruba?

What would we find in a comparison between infants raised hearing a predominantly level-tone language versus infants raised hearing a language with elaborate contour tones? Answers to these questions are hard to come by – infant research is notoriously difficult because they get tired and cranky easily, get distracted by extraneous factors, or fall asleep during sessions, and furthermore parents may be loath to give permission for them to take part.

10.2.2 Early production of tones

Once differences are perceived by the child, the next step is to produce these distinctions, mimicking as accurately as possible the adult speech. Production of pitch differences is primarily achieved by laryngeal means, and the child will presumably have to learn control over the laryngeal musculature just as he or she learns to control the tongue and lips. In the absence of such control, pitch tends to fall during the utterance. Kent and Murray (1982) observe that infants from three to nine months tend to have level or falling tonal contour over the utterance, and if there is a rise it is followed by a fall. They suggest that this tendency to fall may be attributed either to a decrease in sub-glottal pressure as the utterance progresses, or a gradual relaxation of the larynx. In either case, muscular effort is required to overcome this tendency and sustain a rise, and indeed rising contours are often delayed until late in the first year. Nonetheless, the early production stages known as babbling are often observed to have adult-like variable pitch contours, but there is little experimental data in support of (or indeed in refutation of) the anecdotal material. In what follows I rely heavily on Vihman 1996.

10.2.2.1 Babbling

'Canonical' or 'reduplicated' babbling, which typically begins around six months, consists of repeated syllables beginning with a stop consonant, and followed by an open central vowel, as in *babababa*. This is followed by (and may overlap with) 'variegated' babbling, which becomes very frequent around twelve to fourteen months. Now the consonants vary, and the sounds approximate utterances in the native language. They often have a sentence-like intonation, suggesting the beginnings of pitch control. Word production begins around this time. During these early stages the vocal apparatus is still not fully developed. The larynx is much higher than it is in adults, and does not descend until the third year.

There is disagreement about how close babbling is to the native language. Some researchers have thought that there was a discontinuity between babbling and word production, while others have hypothesized that babbling is a natural and perhaps necessary part of language acquisition that leads to, and can even overlap with, the first word stage. If this is the case, one might expect that as babbling progresses its sounds and structures would become gradually closer to those of the adult language, and there is some evidence that this is true, although the data are certainly somewhat mixed. In the segmental domain, Boysson-Bardies *et al.* (1989) found that the formant patterns of vowels in the babbling of ten-month-olds drift towards those typical of the adult language (in this study, French, Arabic, English, and Cantonese). In a 1992 paper, Boysson-Bardies *et al.* followed infants from nine months to the twenty-five-word stage and found that the proportion of consonants typical of the native-language inventory increased over time. On the other side of the debate, some studies show that adults cannot reliably identify the native language of the babbling infant (although other studies suggest that they can!).

A few projects have looked at the babbling of infants from tone language environments, but the focus of the studies was not tone itself. See, for example, Boysson-Bardies *et al.* 1984 and Boysson-Bardies *et al.* 1989. One study on intonation by Whalen *et al.* (1991) found significant differences in the babbling of American English and French infants of six to twelve months. The American children had a falling pitch contour on each utterance, but the French children had a roughly equal number of rising patterns. This single finding is consistent with the view that babbling shows the beginnings of the acquisition of language-specific phonology (or at least phonetics), and that even in the first year of life children perceive pitch as significant, and have some degree of the necessary muscular control to reproduce what they hear.

10.2.2.2 First-word stage

Our first serious data on tone production come from the first-word stage of acquisition, roughly one- to two-year-olds. This is hardly surprising. It is only at this point that one can directly compare the child's output to the adult output, and ask whether their speech is adult-like and if not how it differs from the adult forms. During babbling, one can ask whether children can raise and lower the pitch of their voice, but not whether they raise or lower it in the right places. From the word stage, if children consistently use high tone for high-toned words and low tone for low-toned words it is reasonable to assume that they have acquired the phonological tonal contrast. Of course, the inability to reproduce the adult tones consistently tells us little. They may indeed have acquired the tones, but not yet have sufficient control to produce them reliably, or have a phonology of their own that renders the tones distinct from the adult ones on the surface, much as

children may use consonant harmony to turn *dog* into [gɔg] even though [d] occurs in other words, like [dada].

Sadly, by comparison with the amount of work on segmental production, there
is very little on tonal production, and for some reason we have a larger number of
studies on Asian tone languages, primarily Cantonese, Taiwanese, and Mandarin
Chinese, than on African tone languages. Only Sesotho and Zulu have any detailed work available.

The most frequently repeated comment in the work on tonal acquisition is that
tones are acquired before segmental inventories. This remark is worth looking at
in some detail, because it oversimplifies the situation. First, notice that, if it is
true, it is not especially surprising for the following reasons. We have seen that
pitch perception is a necessary prerequisite to perceiving many segmental contrasts, particularly vowel quality (formants) and place of articulation (transitions). It may also contribute to detecting voicing, with voiced consonants being
associated with lower pitch. Once the child starts to produce speech, the added
challenge of articulation means that motor control of the appropriate musculature
must precede accurate production, and thus mastery of the system. For segments,
the crucial articulators are oral and nasal, and involve very finely tuned movements of, in particular, the tongue, which must hit and hold specific target regions
in order to produce sounds accurately. For tone, the main articulators are the
muscles that control the vocal folds and the larynx. Control of these is also an acquired skill, which is one reason that opera divas are so well paid, but in speech,
unlike in music, no precise target is required. Tone is a relative matter – High and
Low should really be called Higher and Lower – and it may be that sufficient
control to achieve this comes earlier than the necessarily precise control of the
tongue muscles.

Reasonable though the claim that tones are acquired early may be, it is not
clear how true it is, because the phrase 'acquired tone' can mean many different things. Firstly, the child may have categorized two words as tonally distinct, say H and L, but may produce the distinction quite differently, perhaps as
H vs. HL or H vs. M. Such a child will be reported as 'acquiring' H before L,
but we must recognize that the claim is only one about the accuracy of repro-
duction, and not necessarily about mental representation. Secondly, the child
may have acquired some tones, but not others, so that words with certain tones
may be produced reliably, whereas words with other tones may not be. Thirdly,
the child may have acquired lists of lexical items with the correct tones, but not
yet have acquired any tonal phonology, so that regular tonal rules may not be
applied at all, or not consistently. Most of the extant studies focus on the first
or second question and very few address the third. Of course, this is partially
related to the age of children studied. Tonal alternations and the effects of rules

cannot usually be seen until complex morphology is mastered, or multi-word utterances are used. At the one-word stage, then, tonal inventories must be the focus of our attention.

10.2.2.3 Tonal inventories

Let us start by looking at the literature on the acquisition of tonal inventories. Like all acquisition data, it must be treated with a degree of caution. Adult transcribers find it difficult to transcribe anything that does not fit into the adult phonological system. For example, if a language has four tones, [55, 35, 21, 41], the transcription tends to show these tones, rather than [44, 34, 31, 43], even if the child's speech would be more accurately transcribed with the latter set. Indeed some researchers use a notation system such as a fixed set of diacritic accents which does not admit of recording any tone outside the adult system. We would then be led wrongly to the conclusion that the child's tonal production is the same as the adults. Good research practices like using several transcribers and checking for the degree of agreement among them can reduce but not eliminate this problem. Instrumental work would be ideal, but is virtually non-existent. We need not give up all hope, however. Even if the transcription is inaccurate, it may be possible to tell whether the child has acquired the contrasts of the language, whether or not they are reproducing them precisely as the adult does. Our hypothetical child from earlier in this paragraph, for example, is keeping all four tones distinct, even though the precise pitches differ from the adult model.

A different data problem is that the studies are typically done with a very small number of children, often only one child. It is clearly very risky to make claims about normal order of acquisition based on a single child.

The earliest studies we have go back to the later 1970s. Li and Thompson 1977, still the largest study I know of, looked at seventeen Mandarin-speaking children aged 1; 6 to 3 years. Mandarin, the reader will recall, has four tones:

(1)   *Mandarin adult tones*
        High level   55
        High falling 41
        High rising   35
        Low level   21   or dipping (utterance-finally only) 214

Li and Thompson find that at the earliest one-word stage, high level tones are produced first, followed by high falling tones. Rising and dipping tones are later, and syllables with such tones are either avoided or changed to level or falling. When these last two tones are acquired, at first they are quite often confused, and this confusion continues on into the two- to three-word stage. The confusion takes place mainly in final position, where both have a rising portion. The apparently greater likelihood of confusing rising tones fits with the literature on adult perception (Klatt 1973), and suggests that the difficulty is not necessarily one of production, but lies deeper, in the difficulty of perceiving and then representing the tones correctly in the first place. Of course, rising tones are also harder to produce, needing a longer time-span for their realization (Ohala and Ewan 1973, Sundberg 1973). Clumeck (1980) studied two Mandarin-speaking children, and confirms this order of acquisition. The data below are pooled over the age-range 1;10-2;10 for one child in his study. and show only citation or utterance-final words:

(2)   *Accuracy rate of Mandarin-speaking children*
       Tone   *Accuracy (%)*
       High level   97.2
       High falling   95.8
       High rising   61.3
       Low-dipping   73.9

An older child studied between 2;3 and 3;5 still had only 83.3 per cent accuracy on the high rising tone, and the errors were overwhelmingly produced as low-dipping tones rather than any other tone.

Clumeck points out that there may be another reason for Mandarin children to confuse rising and dipping tones. In adult speech, the first in a sequence of two dipping tones becomes high rising. This means that a lexical item with a dipping tone may surface in the adult's speech as dipping (utterance finally), high rising (before another dipping tone), or low level (elsewhere). (This description should be treated with caution, since in fluent speech the 'dipping' tone is very rarely dipping. It is possible however that it is more often dipping in Motherese.) By contrast, the other three tones are essentially invariant. This explanation for the problem cannot be entirely right, because it leads one to expect the most trouble with the dipping tone, whereas the hardest of all seems to be the rising tone, even though this is invariant in Mandarin.

Both Li and Thompson and Clumeck agree that the children have more or less mastered the tones at a stage when segmentals are still quite far from adult forms. For example, one of Li and Thompson's later stage subjects said [yaba day dəyi] for [labadžaydzəli] 'the horn is here', but the tones were perfect [21 55 41 41 214].

Once we leave Mandarin, the picture on the order of tonal acquisition becomes much murkier, and we are forced to hesitate before concluding that rising tones are universally acquired later, and therefore before concluding that the Mandarin data are due to universal perceptual and production difficulties. Tse (1978) looks at a Cantonese child over a period from 1;2 to 2;8 years. See also So and Dodd 1995. Cantonese has the following tones. The three high level tones have short variants on syllables closed by stops.

(3)   *Cantonese adult tones*
      High level   55 (sometimes 53)
      Mid level   33
      Low level   22
      Extra low level 11 (sometimes given as 21)
      High rise   25
      Low rise   13

Tse found that the earliest tones to appear, at 1; 2–1; 4, were the two extreme level tones, 55 and 11. These were followed by the mid level 33 and the higher rising tone 25, at 1; 5–1; 8. Last were the low rise 13 and the remaining level tone 22, at 1;9, by which time the child had advanced to the two–three word stage. By the time the child is using longer utterances, tonal errors have almost completely disappeared, although segmental errors persist. Lee (1996) reports on a study by A. Tse (1992), who found that the last two tones acquired were not 13 and 22, but 13 and 11. We thus find disagreement as to whether 22 or 11 is the hardest to acquire.

Based on these studies, Cantonese- and Mandarin-speaking children agree on acquiring high tones first and on the rough time-scale of acquisition, but on little else. One of the rising tones in Cantonese, the high rise, is acquired before one of the level tones, the 22 low level, a finding not in line with suggestions that rising tones are universally acquired last. Apart from one anecdotal case, there seems to be little evidence in Cantonese, unlike in Mandarin, for systematic confusion of the two rising tones.

One other oft-cited study belongs in this section, Tuaycharoen 1977 on Thai. Thai has the following tones:

(4)   *Thai adult tones*
      High   Rising
      Mid   Falling
      Low

Tuaycharoen's child acquired mid and low level tones first at about one year, and then the rising tone. High and falling did not appear until four months later. This is almost the exact reverse of the Mandarin data and strongly suggests that the order of acquisition is language-specific.

A recent very interesting paper by Tsay (2001) looks at the acquisition of tone by Taiwanese-speaking children. These children, like the Cantonese and Mandarin children, make few tonal errors after the age of two; as in Mandarin, the rising tone is the most error-prone. Unlike most previous work, which focusses on the production of pitch contrasts, Tsay looks mainly at the little-studied question of duration. Taiwanese tones show systematic but non-contrastive length differences, and it is well known that very young children pay attention to quite small differences in duration and may use them to detect prosodic structure and hence infer syntactic structure. One might therefore expect that Taiwanese children would master not only the pitch but also the duration aspects of the tonal system, and this turned out to be the case. Most strikingly, for syllables closed by glottal stop in adult speech, which have specially short variants of the tones, the single child in the study dropped the final glottal stop but still used the extra-short tonal variant.

I pointed out earlier that most of the studies on early tone acquisition have been on Asian tone languages. When we look at African languages, the reason becomes apparent. The question asked by all the above researchers was 'What order are the tones acquired in?', but this question cannot be asked unless a language has a large tonal inventory. In Africa, many languages have only a H/L contrast, so the acquisition of tonal contrasts is an all-or-nothing affair! In Sesotho (Demuth 1992, 1993, 1995), the lexical contrast between H and Ø on verbal roots has been successfully mastered by age three. Before that, there is a tendency to prefer H, and treat some toneless roots as if they were H. For example, at 2;1 years the low-toned verb /kul-/ 'to be sick' and the high-toned verb /hán-/ 'refuse' both surface with H on the first syllable of the root: [tea-hána] 'I refuse' and [a-kúla] 'You are sick'. By three years, though, we get a contrast between the low-toned /kop-/ 'ask' and the high-toned verb /ngól-/ 'write', as in [o-ngólá lengolo] 'Are you writing a letter?' versus [ke-kopa motoho] 'I'm asking for porridge'. This may seem late compared to the Asian data, but the complex morpho-phonology of a language like Sesotho means that the lexical tone of a root does not necessarily surface as such on the root itself, and considerable phonological analysis is a prerequisite to successful acquisition of the tonal contrasts. Just as in Mandarin, where the existence of alternations between low and high rising may delay acquisition of these tones, so in Sesotho the abundance of H/L surface alternations may delay acquisition of the root contrasts. Support for this view comes from the fact that a different lexical contrast in Sesotho, the H/Ø contrast on subject markers, is acquired much earlier, and is evident at 2;1 years. Subject markers normally surface with their lexical tone, making it much easier for the child to identify.

We are left with more questions than answers. We see that children successfully master lexical tonal contrasts by around their third year, earlier if the language does not have too many alternations. They produce the tones quite accurately at a stage when some adult-like segmental production is still eluding them. The order in which particular tones are acquired is far from clear. There is some likelihood that high tones are acquired early, and the Sesotho data support this, but after that the variability exceeds the consistency, and must await further research.

10.2.3 Multi-word stage and phonological rules

Once a child starts constructing multi-word utterances (or polymorphemic words) the possibility of tonal alternations arises. True mastery of the tonal system includes a knowledge of these as well as of the lexical entries of the language. Unfortunately, even less is known about this than about the acquisition of lexical contrasts. Here I will report on the few studies known to me.

We begin with Asian languages. Yue-Hashimoto (1980) reports that her subject used the Mandarin third-tone sandhi rule, which changes a low tone to a high rise before another low tone, productively from 2; 3 years. Li and Thompson report that the oldest children in their study, aged 3;0, did apply the third-tone sandhi rule, but still rather erratically and hesitantly. The few examples given in their paper show a tendency to leave the low level tones as level and not use either the correct high rise on the first one or the full pre-pausal dipping form either. For example, *hai you xiao yu* 'There are more small fish' surfaces as [35 21 21 35], instead of the adult [35 35 21 35]. Unfortunately, their study did not continue past the age of 3; 0, so we have no way of knowing when this rule is finally reliably and solidly present.

Demuth's work on Sesotho is the most detailed look at the acquisition of phonological rules for tone. She studied one child longitudinally from 2; 1 to 3; 0 years, and a group of twelve children, three each from ages 3; 0, 3; 6, 4; 0, and 5; 0 years of age. She looks at several rules, and we will take each of them in turn. First, adult Sesotho has a rule that lowers the tone at the end of the VP. Sesotho children at first misapply this, lowering at the end of the utterance instead. This is noticeable by age three. However, by age five they have learnt to lower in the appropriate place, at the end of VP. Of course, we cannot tell whether their rule has changed over this period or whether the syntactic analysis has changed!

Demuth also looks at two purely phonological tonal rules, a rule of High Tone Doubling (HTD) and two delinking rules triggered by the OCP. High Tone Doubling spreads a high tone from a prefix or verb root one syllable to the right. The recipient syllable can be a tense-marker, or verb root. Demuth's data seem to show that this rule is absent at 2;6 years, but present by three years.

(5)   2; 6 é-**a**-tsamaya koloi yaka   (Demuth 1995: 124)
        SM-PRES-leave car POSS-my
        (*adult form:* é-á-tsamaya ...)

       3; 0 dí-á-tsamaya ..   (Demuth 1995: 125)
        SM-PRES-leave

The OCP-triggered delinking rules are argued by Demuth to repair HH sequences created by spreading. For example, the rule delinks H from the second vowel in this example, because it is adjacent to another H:

(6)   ba-a-bona   'They see/understand'

$$\overset{\diagdown}{H}\quad\overset{\diagup}{H}$$

(For arguments that the correct analysis requires spreading followed by delinking, rather than blocking of spreading in the first place, see Demuth 1995.) Even at the age of three years, children do not seem to have learnt this rule, since we find surface forms like [é-**á**-tjéna] 'SM-PRES-enter' where the vowel that should have been delinked is shown in boldface. Demuth gives some cases where some delinking seems to have taken place, but of the wrong vowel, so that, for example, the form in (6) would delink H from the first vowel instead of the second. She argues that this is a sign of some early awareness of the existence of the rule, but an incomplete mastery of its details.

From an OT perspective, this last finding is problematic. In OT, the raison d'être for the delinking rule is the supposedly universal OCP, which must be ranked above the constraints that cause High Tone Doubling (see chapter four, section 4.6) called here for brevity HTD. As a result the OCP blocks doubling from applying in the first place. For the adult, then, the grammar would look like tableau (7).

(7)

/e-a-tjena/ $\mid$ $\mid$ H H	OCP	HTD
☞/e-a-tjena/ $\mid$ $\mid$ H H		*
/e-a-tjena/ $\diagup$ $\mid$ H H	*!	

The child who produces a form like [é-á-tjéna] still has the OCP relatively low ranked, and has not yet learnt that it outranks and thus blocks HTD. However, the child who produces a form like [e-á-tjéna], which for Demuth has undergone the rule of HTD, followed by delinking of the H from the first vowel instead of the second, is not so easily explicable in an OT framework. One would have to assume that the child has wrongly decided that Sesotho has tonal flop, rather than spreading, and also that the OCP is still low ranked. Such a child would presumably consistently flop tones one syllable to the right, whether or not another H followed, rather than spreading them. The data are not sufficient to help us tell whether this is correct. See Demuth 1995 for further data, and for an interesting discussion of the status of the OCP.

One of the more striking results of Demuth's exemplary research is that in Sesotho lexical tone acquisition and tonal rule acquisition seem to go hand in hand. As she points out, this is in fact not surprising. The one cannot be fully acquired without the other. Consider the verb root /kul-/. This surfaces with high tone after a high-toned subject prefix as a result of HTD. In order for the child to realize that it is in fact toneless, he or she must first discover the existence of HTD. Conversely, the high-toned root /bón-/ shows up as low after the high-toned prefix /bá-/, in the form [bá-boná] 'They see X', as a result of another OCP-triggered delinking rule. Again, for the child to discover the underlying tone he or she must first decipher the rule. This symbiotic relationship means that both lexical contrasts and rules emerge at much the same time, around three years.

Demuth's point about the interdependence between tonal acquisition and the rest of the grammar is reinforced when we look at the ways in which tonal phonology is related to prosodic structure, and thence to syntactic structure. Recall that in Taiwanese, where all tones have both phrase-internal and phrase-final allotones, these are related in a chained circular relationship and thus the phrase-final variant of one tone may be the phrase-internal variant of another tone. The child can thus only identify the tone (and hence the lexical item) if they know the prosodic phrasing, and Tsay (1999) and Tsay *et al.* (1999) argue that the crucial cues here are durational, with phrase-final syllables being significantly longer. Detection of these longer syllables thus gives the child access to two things: tonal identification and syntactic structure (since the end of each phrase is the right edge of an XP). Unfortunately, Tsay does not discuss evidence for when the child is able to reliably produce the two allotones of each tone, although Tsay and Huang (1998) report that the tonally related phrase-internal process that deletes syllable-final glottal stops is in place for one subject between two and two and a half.

10.2.4   Child phonology

There are a number of well-recorded cases of children creating their own phonologies. Under this rubric one can include systematic deviations from the adult model such as consonant harmony, more extensive sets of phonological rules such as we find in twin languages, and children's word games. In the case of tone, there are very few reports of such phenomena, but there is no doubt that they do exist.

Clumeck reports on allotonic rules specific to child language in Mandarin, but unfortunately his report is somewhat misleading and hard to assess. He reports that falling and rising tones both become high level before a low-pitched syllable, but his examples are all ones in which the second syllable is not lexically low, but lexically toneless: /zhei41geØ/ > [zhei55geØ]. Such toneless syllables have a variable phonetic pitch depending on the pitch of the preceding syllable. Assuming that this levelling process only happens before toneless syllables, and not before lexical lows, it may be related to the stress pattern of such bisyllables, which is uniformly trochaic. Perhaps the strong first syllable requires a high tone, and any non-high portion is simply ignored. Whatever the reason, this is one of the few child-specific alternations reported in the literature, and deserves inclusion here for that reason alone.

Yue-Hashimoto (1980) presents an interesting case of a Mandarin-speaking child who created a word game at around the age of 2;0, and prolifically from 2;3 onwards, in which words were replaced with a fixed tone pattern. There were three tonal melodies.

(8)   Bisyllables   map to H.L t'au35 wan35 > t'au55 wan11
       Monosyllables reduplicate, and   map to H.L yən35   > yən55 yən11
                      split into bisyllable, map to L.H k'ua53   > k'ɯ11 a55

As Yue-Hashimoto points out, tone play implies tonal distinctions, and this particular word game shows an ability to manipulate tone separately from the segmentals of the language. The child has apparently arrived at what a phonologist would call an auto-segmental representation of tone!

Cross-linguistically, if we look at the behaviour of tone in word games, we find considerable variability. Hombert (1986) gives examples in which tone and segments behave as a unit, such as Thai rhyme-exchange games where *kôn jàj > kàj jôn* 'big bottom'. Here the tone and segments move together. This contrasts with games like that of Bakwiri, where syllables exchange places, but the tones are left behind: *kóndì > ndíkò* 'rice'. Hombert suggests that the inseparability of tones and segments is more common in Asian languages, but Hashimoto's Mandarin child shows that from a very early age, even in an Asian language, tones and segments are independently manipulable.

10.3   Second-language acquisition

In section 10.1.4, we looked at the perception of tone by native and non-native speakers. One can ask how the non-native speaker, with his or her limited perception of tonal contrasts, goes about acquiring a tone language. Unfortunately, we know essentially nothing about this interesting topic. Although non-native speakers do much worse at tone identification than native speakers, it appears that with simple training they can learn to improve their scores to near-native levels. Wang *et al.* (1999) found that untrained non-native speakers of Mandarin can identify tones with an accuracy of about 67 per cent, but after training this increases to 90 per cent or above, approaching the native speakers' 100 per cent. The poor performance of the untrained speakers is not surprising given the findings of Leather (1987) that English and Dutch listeners vary much more in the location of the crossover of tonal categories than do native speakers.

There are very few studies on second-language acquisition of tones, particularly on the production end. Wong 1993 looks at the perception of Cantonese tones by English-speaking learners, and Szeto 2000 looks at the production of Cantonese tones by native speakers of English. Wong finds that the easiest tone to perceive is the high level 55 tone followed by the extra-low 11 tone. The hardest to perceive is the low 22 tone. This exactly mimics the order of acquisition by first-language learners of Cantonese in Tse's 1978 study.

Szeto's production data are more confusing. The most striking fact is how well the learners do: for most tones, accuracy rates were judged by two native speakers at around 90 per cent or above. The extra-low 11 tone is the least accurately produced, at below 80 per cent accuracy. For reasons that are not clear, the accuracy was much higher if the target syllable was the first syllable of a bisyllable than if it was the second syllable, or a monosyllable. The difficulty with the extra-low tone mirrors Tse's 1992 data, which has it as one of the last tones to be mastered in first-language acquisition. In sum, the L2 data for Cantonese, like the L1 data, variously single out 22 and 11 as particularly hard to acquire, simply reinforcing the confused state of our current knowledge. We should also bear in mind the possibility that these early learners are still at the stage of mimicking the teacher's tones, rather than truly learning them.

We might also note that there is no obvious property of English that would make either 22 or 11 harder than the other tones to acquire in a second language, so the topic must be left for further research. One very surprising aspect of Szeto's small study (three speakers) is that there was an inverse correlation between length of time in the Cantonese-speaking environment (Hong Kong) and tonal accuracy. The most accurate speaker had been there three months, and the least accurate three and a half years. One suspects that this tells us more about the considerable variation in adult second-language learning abilities than it does about the effects of duration of stay!

Bibliography

Note: All references to ROA# refer to papers available on the Rutgers Optimality Archive on the web, at http://roa.rutgers.edu

Abramson, A. 1975. The tones of Central Thai: some perceptual experiments. In J.G. Harris and J. Chamberlain (eds.), *Studies in Tai Linguistics.* Bangkok: Central Institute of English Language, pp. 1–16.

    1978. Static and dynamic acoustic cues in distinctive tones. *Language and Speech* 21: 319–25.

Akanlig-Pare, George. 1997. Tonal structure of Buli phonological nouns. *Gur Papers/ Cahiers Voltaïques* 2: 63–7.

Akinlabi, A. 1985. Tonal Underspecification and Yoruba Tone. PhD Dissertation, University of Ibadan.

    (ed.) 1995. *Theoretical Approaches to African Linguistics.* (Proceedings of the 25th Annual Conference on African Linguistics). Trenton, NJ: Africa World Press.

    1996. Featural affixation. *Journal of Linguistics* 32: 239–89.

Akinlabi, A., and M. Liberman. 1995. On the phonetic interpretation of the Yoruba tonal system. *Proceedings of the International Congress of Phonetic Sciences 1995.* Stockholm, Sweden, pp. 42–5.

    2000a. The tonal phonology of Yoruba clitics. In B. Gerlach and J. Grizenhout (eds.), *Clitics in Phonology, Morphology and Syntax.* Amsterdam/Philadelphia: John Benjamins Publishing Company.

    2000b. Tonal complexes and tonal alignment. Paper given at the Tone Symposium, University of Tromsø. To appear in the *Proceedings of NELS* 31.

Alderete, J. 1995. Faithfulness to prosodic heads. ROA# 94-0000.

Anderson, S. 1974. *The Organization of Phonology.* New York: Academic Press.

    1978. Tone features. In V. Fromkin (ed.), *Tone: A Linguistic Survey.* New York: Academic Press, pp. 133–76.

Antilla, A., and A. Bodomo. 1996. Stress and tone in Dagaare. MS, Stanford University. Also ROA# 169–1296.

    (in press). Tonal polarity in Dagaare. *Proceedings of the 28th Annual Conference on African Linguistics,* Cornell University.

Ao, B. 1993. Phonetics and Phonology of Nantong Chinese. PhD Dissertation, Ohio State University.

Archangeli, D., and T. Langendoen (eds.) 1997. *Optimality Theory: An Overview.* Oxford: Blackwell.

Armstrong, R.G. 1968. Yala (Ikom), a terraced-level language with three tones. *Journal of West African Languages* 5: 41–50.

Asongwed, T., and L. Hyman. 1976. Morphotonology of the Ngamambo noun. In L. Hyman (ed.), *Studies in Bantu Tonology*. Los Angeles: University of Southern California, pp. 23–56.

Awedoba, A.K. 1993. *Kasem Studies Part 1: Phonetics and Phonology*. (Research Review, Supplement No. 7) Legon: University of Ghana, Institute of African Studies.

Baart, J.L.G. 1997. *The Sounds and Tones of Kalam Kohistani*. Arlington, TX: Summer Institute of Linguistics and National Institute of Pakistan Studies.

Bahl, K.C. 1957. Tones in Punjabi. *Indian Linguistics* 17: 139–47.

Banti, G. 1988. Two Cushitic systems: Somali and Oromo nouns. In H.van der Hulst and N. Smith (eds.), *Autosegmental Studies on Pitch Accent Systems*. Dordrecht: Foris, pp. 11–49.

Bao, Zhi Ming. 1990. On the Nature of Tone. PhD dissertation, MIT.

 1999. *The Structure of Tone*. Oxford: Oxford University Press.

Barrett-Keach, C. 1986. Word-internal evidence from Swahili for Aux/INFL. *Linguistic Inquiry* 17: 559–64.

Bearth, T., and H. Zemp. 1967. The phonology of Dan (Santa). *Journal of African Linguistics* 6: 9–29.

Beckman, J. 1997. Positional Faithfulness. Doctoral dissertation, University of Massachusetts, Amherst.

Beckman, M., J. Edwards and J. Fletcher. 1992. Prosodic structure and tempo in a sonority model of articulatory dynamics. In G. Docherty and R. Ladd (eds.), *Papers in Laboratory Phonology II: Gesture, Segment, Prosody*. Cambridge: Cambridge University Press, pp. 68–86.

Beckman, M., and J. Kingston. 1990. *Between the Grammar and Physics of Speech. Papers in Laboratory Phonology I*. Cambridge: Cambridge University Press.

Beckman, M., and J. Pierrehumbert. 1986. Intonational structure in Japanese and English. *Phonology Yearbook* 3: 255–310.

Bendor-Samuel, J. 1989. *The Niger-Congo Languages*. Lanham, MD: University Press of America and SIL.

Bernot, D. 1979. Un point de syntaxe Birmane. Paper given at the 12th International Conference on Sino-Tibetan Languages and Linguistics, Paris.

Beyer, K. 1999. La morphologie du verbe en pana. Paper presented at the 2nd Colloquium on Gur Languages, Cotonou, Benin.

Bhatia, T.K. 1993. *Punjabi: A Cognitive-Descriptive Grammar*. London and New York: Routledge.

Bickmore, L. 1996. Bantu tone spreading and displacement as alignment and minimal misalignment. ROA# 161–1196.

Bickmore, L., and G.A. Broadwell. 1998. High tone docking in Sierra Juárez Zapotec. *International Journal of American Linguistics* 64.1: 36–67.

Bird, S. 1990. Constraint-Based Phonology. PhD Dissertation, University of Edinburgh.

Blakemore, D. 1992. *Understanding Utterances: An Introduction to Pragmatics*. Oxford: Blackwell.

Blanchon, J.A. 1998. Tonology of the Kongo noun phrase. In L. Hyman and C. Kisseberth (eds.), *Theoretical Aspects of Bantu Tone*. Stanford: CSLI Publications.

Blevins, J. 1993. A tonal analysis of Lithuanian nominal accent. *Language* 69: 237–73.

Bodomo, A. 1997. *The Structure of Dagaare.* Stanford: CSLI Publications.

Bolinger, D. 1986. *Intonation and its Parts.* Stanford: Stanford University Press.

Boysson-Bardies, B. de, P. Hallé, L. Sagart and C. Durand. 1989. A cross-linguistic investigation of vowel formants in babbling. *Journal of Child Language* 16: 1–17.

Boysson-Bardies, B. de, L. Sagart and C. Durand. 1984. Discernible differences in the babbling of infants according to target language. *Journal of Child Language* 11: 1–15.

Boysson-Bardies, B. de, M. Vihman, L. Roug-Hullichius, C. Durand, I. Landberg and F. Arao. 1992. Material evidence of infant selection from target language: A cross-linguistic phonetic study. In C.A. Ferguson, L. Menn and C. Stoel-Gammon (eds.), *Phonological Development: Models, Research, Implications.* Timonium, MD: York Press.

Bradley, D. 1982. Register in Burmese. In D. Bradley (ed.), *Tonation.* (Pacifica Linguistic Series A-62) Canberra: Research Centre of Pacific Studies, Australian National University, pp. 117–32.

Bradshaw, M. 1995. Tone on verbs in Suma. In Akinlabi 1995: 255–72.

  1999. A Cross-Linguistic Study of Consonant-Tone Interaction. PhD Dissertation, Ohio State University.

Bunn, G., and R. Bunn. 1970. Golin phonology. In S.A.Wurm (ed.), *Papers in New Guinea Linguistics, No. 11.* Canberra: Australian National University.

Burzio, L. 1994. *Principles of English Stress.* Cambridge: Cambridge University Press.

Cahill, M. 1992. *A Preliminary Phonology of the Kɔnni Language.* (Collected Field Notes Series No. 20) Legon: The Institute of African Studies, University of Ghana.

  1998a. Tonal polarity in Kɔnni nouns: an Optimal Theoretical account. *OSU Working Papers in Linguistics* 51: 19–58.

  1998b. Tonal associative morphemes in optimality theory. Paper presented at Linguistic Society of America meeting, New York, NY.

  1999. Aspects of the Morphology and Phonology of Konni. PhD Dissertation, Ohio State University.

Carlson, R. 1983. Downstep in Supyire. *Studies in African Linguistics* 14: 35–45.

  1994. *A Grammar of Supyire.* New York: Mouton de Gruyter.

Casali, R.F. 1995. An overview of the Nawuri verbal system. *Journal of West African Languages* 25.1: 63–86.

Cassimjee, F. 1998. *Isixhosa Tonology: An Optimal Domains Theory Analysis.* Munich: Lincom Europa.

Cassimjee, F., and C. Kisseberth. 1998. Optimal domains theory and Bantu tonology: a case study from Isixhosa and Shingazidja. In Hyman and Kisseberth 1998: 33–132 [also ROA# 176-0297].

  2001. Zulu tonology and its relationship to other Nguni languages. In Shigeki Kaji (ed.), *Cross-linguistic Studies of Tonal Phenomena: Tonogenesis, Japanese Accentology, and Other Topics.* Tokyo: Institute for the Study of Languages and Cultures of Asia and Africa (ILCAA), Tokyo University of Foreign Studies, pp. 327–59.

Chan, M. 1985. Fuzhou Phonology: A Non-linear Analysis of Tone and Stress. PhD dissertation, University of Washington, Seattle.

  1987. Tone and melody interaction in Cantonese and Mandarin songs. *UCLA Working Papers in Phonetics* 68: 132–69.

Chan, S.W., C.K. Chuang and W.S.-Y. Wang. 1975. Crosslanguage study of categorical perception for lexical tone. *Journal of the Acoustical Society of America* 58: 119.

Chang, K. 1953. On the tone system of Miao-Yao. *Language* 29: 374–8.

Chao, Y.-R. 1930. A system of tone letters. *Le Maître Phonétique* 45: 24–7.

1933. Tone and intonation in Chinese. *Academia Sinica BIHP* 4.2, pp. 121–34.

1968. *A Grammar of Spoken Chinese.* Berkeley: University of California Press.

Chatterji, S.K. 1969. *Indo-Aryan and Hindi: 8 Lectures Originally Delivered in 1940 before the Gujarat Vernacular Society, Ahmedabad.* (Second edition).

Chen, M. 1987. The syntax of Xiamen tone sandhi. *Phonology Yearbook* 4: 109–50.

1992. Tone rule typology. In L.A. Buszard-Welcher, J. Evans, D. Peterson, L. Wee and W. Weigel (eds.), *Proceedings of the Berkeley Linguistics Society, Special Session on Tone.* Berkeley: Berkeley Linguistics Society, pp. 54–66.

2000. *Tone Sandhi.* Cambridge: Cambridge University Press.

Cheng, C.-C. 1973. A quantitative study of Chinese tones. *Journal of Chinese Linguistics* 1.1: 93–110.

Cheng, T. 1973. The phonology of Taishan. *Journal of Chinese Linguistics* 1.2: 256–322.

Chomsky, N., and M. Halle. 1968. *The Sound Pattern of English.* New York: Harper and Row.

Chumbow, B.S. 1982. Contraction and tone polarization in Ogori. *Journal of West African Languages* 12.1: 89–103.

Chumbow, B.S., and E.G. Nguendjio. 1991. Floating tones in Bangwa. *Journal of West African Languages* 21.1: 3–14.

Clark, M. 1978. A Dynamic Treatment of Tone. PhD Dissertation, University of Massachusetts, Amherst.

1990. *The Tonal System of Igbo.* Dordrecht: Foris.

Clements, G.N. 1978. Tone and syntax in Ewe. In D.J. Napoli (ed.), *Elements of Tone, Stress, and Intonation.* Washington, DC: Georgetown University Press, pp. 21–99.

1979. The description of terraced-level tone languages. *Language* 55: 536–58.

1981. The hierarchical representation of tone features. In I.R. Dihoff (ed.), *Current Approaches to African Linguistics.* Dordrecht: Foris, vol. 1, pp. 145–76.

1984. Principles of tone association in Kikuyu. In G.N. Clements and J. Goldsmith (eds.), *Autosegmental Studies in Bantu Tone.* Dordrecht: Foris, pp. 281–339.

1985. The geometry of phonological features. *Phonology* 2: 225–52.

1989. A unified set of features for consonants and vowels. MS, Cornell University. [Revision appeared as: Place of articulation in consonants and vowels: a unified theory. In *Working Papers of the Cornell Phonetics Laboratory* 5: 77–123.]

1990. The status of register in intonation theory: comments on papers by Ladd and by Inkelas and Leben. In J. Kingston and M. Beckman (eds.), *Between the Grammar and Physics of Speech.* (Papers in Laboratory Phonology I) Cambridge: Cambridge University Press, pp. 58–71.

2000. Phonology. In Heine and Nurse 2000: 123–60.

Clements, G.N., and K. Ford. 1979. Kikuyu tone shift and its synchronic consequences. *Linguistic Inquiry* 10: 179–210.

Clements, G.N., and Elizabeth Hume. 1995. The internal organization of speech sounds. In John Goldsmith (ed.), *The Handbook of Phonological Theory.* Oxford: Blackwell, pp. 245–306.

Clifton, J.M. 1975. Nonsegmental Tone in Lango. Proceedings of the Sixth Conference on African Linguistics. *OSU Working Papers in Linguistics* 20: 99–105.

Clumeck, H. 1980. The acquisition of tone. In G.H. Yeni-komshian, J.F. Kavanagh and C.A. Ferguson (eds.), *Child Phonology, Vol. I, Production.* New York: Academic Press, pp. 257–75.

Cole, J., and C.W. Kisseberth. 1994. An optimal domains theory of harmony. *Studies in the Linguistic Sciences* 24: 101–14.

1995. Paradoxical strength conditions in harmony systems. *Cognitive Science Technical Report UIUC-BI-CS-95-03 (Language Series)*. University of Illinois, Beckman Institute.

Connell, B. 1999. Four tones and downtrend: a preliminary report on pitch realization in Mambila. In P. Kotey (ed.) *New Dimensions in African Linguistics and Languages*. Trenton, NJ: Africa World Press, pp. 75–88.

2000. The perception of lexical tone in Mambila. *Language and Speech* 43: 163–82.

Connell, B.A., R.J. Hayward and J.A. Ashkaba. 2000. Observations on Kunama tone (Barka dialect). *Studies in African Linguistics* 29. 1: 1–41.

Connell, B., and D.R. Ladd. 1990. Aspects of pitch realization in Yoruba. *Phonology* 7: 1–29.

Cox, M. 1998. Description grammaticale du ncam (bassar), langue gurma du Togo et du Ghana. Thèse de diplome, Ecole Pratique des Hautes Etudes, Paris.

Creissels, D., and C. Grégoire. 1993. La notion de ton marqué dans l'analyse d'une opposition tonale binaire: le cas du mandingue. *Journal of African Languages and Linguistics* 14.2: 107–54.

Crouch, M. 1985. A note on syllable and tone in Vagla verbs. *Journal of West African Languages* 15.2: 29–40.

Cruttenden, A. 1986. *Intonation*. Cambridge: Cambridge University Press.

Cutler, A., and H.-C. Chen. 1997. Lexical tone in Cantonese: spoken-word processing. *Perception and Psychophysics* 59.2: 165–79.

Daly, J. 1993. Representation of tone in Peñoles Mixtec. MS, Summer Institute of Linguistics, Dallas.

de Lacy, P. 1999a. Morphological haplology and correspondence. MS, University of Massachusetts, Amherst. ROA# 298.

1999b. Tone and prominence. MS, University of Massachusetts, Amherst. ROA# 333.

deJong, K., and J. McDonough. 1993. Tone in Navajo. In K. deJong and J. McDonough (eds.), *UCLA Working Papers in Phonetics*. Los Angeles: UCLA, pp. 165–82.

Dell, F. 1985. A propos de: Svantesson J.-O., 'Kammu Phonology and Morphology'. *Cahiers Linguistiques de l'Asie Orientale* 14.2: 259–75.

Demuth, K. 1992. The acquisition of Sesotho. In D.I. Slobin (ed.), *The Cross-linguistic Study of Language Acquisition*. Hillsdale, NJ: Lawrence Erlbaum Associates, vol.3, pp. 557–638.

1993. Issues in the acquisition of the Sesotho tonal system. *Journal of Child Language* 20: 275–301.

1995. The acquisition of tonal systems. In J. Archibald (ed.), *Phonological Acquisition and Phonological Theory*. d Hillsdale, NJ: Lawrence Erlbaum Associates, pp. 111–34.

Derbyshire, D.C., and G.K. Pullum. 1986. *Handbook of Amazonian Languages*. (4 vols.) Berlin: Mouton de Gruyter.

Dimmendaal, G.J., and S.A. Breedveld. 1986. Tonal influence on vocalic quality. In K. Bogers, H. van der Hulst and M. Mous (eds.), *The Phonological Representation of Suprasegmentals*. Dordrecht: Foris, pp. 1–34.

Dolphyne, F.A. 1988. *The Akan (Twi-Fante) Language: Its Sound Systems and Tonal Structure*. Accra: Ghana Universities Press.

Downing, L. 2001. How ambiguity of analysis motivates stem change in Durban Zulu. *UBC Working Papers in Linguistics.*
In press. Accent in African languages. In R.E.W.N. Goedemans and H.G. van der Hulst (eds.) *Stress Patterns of the World: Data.* Amsterdam: John Benjamins.

Dresher, B.E., and H. van der Hulst. 1995. Head-dependent asymmetries in prosodic phonology. MS, University of Toronto and University of Leiden.

Duanmu, S. 1990. A Formal Study of Syllable, Tone, Stress and Domain in Chinese Languages. PhD dissertation, MIT.
1991. Stress and syntax-phonology mismatches: tonal domains in Danyang and Shanghai. *Proceedings of the West Coast Conference in Formal Linguistics* 10: 127–38.
1992a. An autosegmental analysis of tone in four Tibetan languages. *Linguistics of the Tibeto-Burman Area* 15.1: 65–91.
1992b. End-based theory, cyclic stress, and tonal domains. *Chicago Linguistics Society* 28.2: 65–76.
1993. Rime length, stress and association domains. *Journal of East Asian Linguistics* 2.1: 1–44.
1994. Against contour tone units. *Linguistic Inquiry* 25.4: 555–608.
1997. Recursive constraint evaluation in optimality theory: evidence from cyclic compounds in Shanghai. *Natural Language and Linguistic Theory* 15.3: 465–508.
1999. Metrical structure and tone: evidence from Mandarin and Shanghai. *Journal of East Asian Linguistics* 8.1: 1–38.
2000. *The Phonology of Standard Chinese.* Oxford: Oxford University Press.

Dwyer, D. 1976. The analysis of Bambara polarization. *Studies in African Linguistics,* Supplement 6: 27–38.

Đo The Dung, Tran Thin Huong and G. Boulakia. 1998. Intonation in Vietnamese, in D.Hirst and A. de Cristo (eds.), *Intonation Systems: A Survey of Twenty Languages.* Cambridge: Cambridge University Press, pp. 395–416.

Eberhard, D. 1995. *Maimande Stress: The Need for Strata.* Arlington: Summer Institute of Linguistics, University of Texas.

Edmondson, J.A. 1992. A study of tones and initials in Kam, Lakkja, and Hlai. In C.J. Compton and J.F. Hartmann (eds.), *Papers on Tai Languages, Linguistics, and Literatures: In Honor of William J. Gedney on his 77th Birthday.* (Occasional Paper No. 16. 1992. Monograph Series on Southeast Asia) DeKalb, IL: N. Illinois University Center for Southeast Asian Studies, pp. 77–100.

Edmondson, J. A., Deji-Sezhen Geziben and M. Fillippini. n.d. A cross-lectal study of Tibetan tones: analysis and representation. MS, University of Texas, Arlington.

Edmondson, J.A., and Shaoni Li. 1994. Voice-quality and voice quality change in the Bai language of Yunnan province. *Linguistics of the Tibeto-Burman Area* 17.2: 49–68.

Edmondson, J., and D. Solnit. 1988. *Comparative Kadai: Linguistic Studies beyond Tai.* (SIL/UTA Series in Linguistics No. 86) Dallas: Summer Institute of Linguistics.

Edmondson, J., and Q. Yang. 1989. Phonological geometry in Kam-Sui: contours, edges and dimorphism. MS, University of Texas, Arlington, and Central Institute of Nationalities, Beijing.

Edmondson, J.A., J. Bateman and H. Miehle. 1992. Tone contours and tone clusters in Iau. In L. Buszard-Welcher, J. Evans, D. Peterson, L.Wee and W. Weigel (eds.), *Special Session on the Typology of Tone Languages. Proceedings of the 18th Annual Meeting of the Berkeley Linguistics Society. Berkeley:* Berkeley Linguistics Society, pp. 92–103.

Eimas, P., E. Siqueland, P.W. Jusczyk and J. Vigorito. 1971. Speech perception in infants. *Science* 171: 303–18.

Essien, O.E. 1990. *A Grammar of the Ibibio Language.* Ibadan: University Press.

Everett, D. 1986. Pirahã. In D.C. Derbyshire and G.K. Pullum (eds.), *Handbook of Amazonian Languages,* Berlin: Mouton de Gruyter, Vol. 1, pp. 200–325.

Everett, D., and K. Everett. 1984. On the relevance of syllable onsets to stress placement. *Linguistic Inquiry* 15: 705–11.

Everett, K.M. 1998. The acoustic correlates of stress in Pirahã. *Journal of Amazonian Languages* 1: 104–62.

Firth, J.R. 1948. Sounds and prosodies. *Transactions of the Philological Society,* pp. 127–52. Also in F.R. Palmer (ed.), *Prosodic Analysis.* Oxford: Oxford University Press, 1970, pp. 1–26.

Flemming, E. 1995. Auditory Representations in Phonology. Doctoral dissertation, UCLA, Los Angeles.

1997. Phonetic optimisation: compromise in speech production. In V. Miglio and B. Moren (eds.), *University of Maryland Working Papers in Linguistics, Vol. 5. Proceedings of the Hopkins Optimality Theory Conference (HOT).* College Park: University of Maryland, pp. 72–91.

Fok, C.Y.-Y. 1974. *A Perceptual Study of Tones in Cantonese.* Centre of Asian Studies, University of Hong Kong.

Fountain, A.V. 1998. An Optimality Theory Approach to Navajo Prefixal Syllables. PhD dissertation, University of Arizona.

Fromkin, V. A. (ed.). 1978. *Tone: A Linguistic Survey.* New York: Academic Press.

Fu, Q.-J. and F.-G. Zeng. 2000. Identification of temporal envelope cues in Chinese tone recognition. *Asia Pacific Journal of Speech, Language and Hearing* 5: 45–57.

Gandour, J. 1974. On the representation of tone in Siamese. *UCLA Working Papers in Phonetics* 27: 118–46.

1975. On the representation of tone in Siamese. In J.G. Harris and J.R. Chamberlain (eds.), *Studies in Tai Linguistics in Honor of William J. Gedney.* Bangkok: Central Institute of English Language, Office of State University, Bangkok.

1977. On the interaction between tone and vowel length: evidence from Thai dialects. *Phonetica* 34: 54–65.

1978. The perception of tone. In Fromkin 1978: 41–76.

Gandour, J., N. Satthamnuwong and A. Tumtavitikul. 1999. Effects of speaking rate on Thai tones. *Phonetica* 56: 123–34.

Garber, A.E. 1987. A Tonal Analysis of Senufo: Sucite Dialect. PhD Dissertation, University of Illinois at Urbana-Champaign.

Garding, E., P. Kratochvil, J.O. Svantesson and J. Zhang. 1986. Tone 4 and tone 3 discrimination in modern Standard Chinese. *Language and Speech* 29: 281–93.

Gedney, W. 1947. Indic Loanwords in Spoken Thai. PhD Dissertation, Yale University.

George, I. 1970. Nupe tonology. *Studies in African Linguistics* 1: 100–22.

Geziben, Deji-Sezhen. 1996. *Trochaic Structure in Tibetan Phonology: A Metrical Analysis of Tone in Lhasa Tibetan.* MA Thesis, University of Texas, Arlington.

Goldsmith, J. 1976. Autosegmental Phonology. PhD Dissertation, MIT.

1984. Meeussen's Rule. In M. Aronoff and R. Oehrle (eds.), *Language Sound Structure.* Cambridge, MA: MIT Press, pp. 245–9.

1990. *Autosegmental and Metrical Phonology.* Cambridge: Basil Blackwell.

Gomez-Imbert, E. 2001. More on the tone versus pitch accent typology: evidence from Barasana and other Eastern Tukanoan languages. In S. Kaji (ed.), *Proceedings of the Second Symposium on Cross-linguistic Studies of Tonal Phenomena.* Tokyo: ICLAA Tokyo University of Foreign Studies.

Gomez-Imbert, E., and M. Kenstowicz. 1999. Barasana tone and accent. MS, CNRS and MIT.

2000. Barasana tone and accent. *International Journal of American Linguistics* 66.4: 419–63.

Gordon, M. 1998. The process-specific nature of weight: the case of contour tone restrictions. In K. Shahin, S. Blake and E.-S. Kim (eds.), *Proceedings of WCCFL-17.* Stanford, CA: Stanford University and CSLI.

Green, A.D. 1994. Syllable structure in Burmese: a constraint-based approach. MS, Cornell University.

1995. The prosodic structure of Burmese: a constraint-based approach. *Working Papers of the Cornell Phonetics Laboratory* 10: 67–96.

Greenberg, J. 1963. *The Languages of Africa.* Part 2, *International Journal of American Linguistics* 29.2.

1966. Some universals of grammar with particular reference to the order of meaningful elements. In Joseph Greenberg (ed.), *Universals of Language* (2nd edn). Cambridge, MA: MIT Press.

Greenberg, S., and E. Zee. 1979. On the perception of contour tones. *UCLA Working Papers in Phonetics* 45: 150–65.

Gregerson, K.J. 1976. Tongue-root and register in Mon-Khmer. In P. Jenner, L. Thompson and S. Starosta (eds.), *Austroasiatic Studies.* Honolulu: University of Hawaii Press, Part I, pp. 323–69.

Grimes, B. 2000. *Ethnologue: Languages of the World* (14th edn, CD-ROM). Dallas: International Academic Bookstore.

Gussenhoven, C. 2000. The boundary tones are coming: on the non-peripheral realization of boundary tones. In M. Broe and J. Pierrehumbert (eds.), *Acquisition and the Lexicon: Papers in Laboratory Phonology V.* Cambridge: Cambridge University Press, pp. 132–51.

Gussenhoven, C., and P. van der Vliet. 1999. Tone and intonation in Venlo. *Journal of Linguistics* 35.1: 99–136.

Guthrie, M. 1967–71. *Comparative Bantu.* 4 vols. Farnborough: Gregg International Publishers.

Hale, K., and E. Selkirk. 1987. Government and tonal phrasing in Papago. *Phonology* 4: 151–83.

Halle, M. 1983. On distinctive features and their articulatory implementation. *Natural Language and Linguistic Theory* 1: 91–105.

Halle, M., and K. Stevens. 1971. A note on laryngeal features. *Quarterly Progress Report* 101. MIT.

Halliday, M.A.K. 1967. *Intonation and Grammar in British English.* The Hague: Mouton.

Haraguchi, S. 1977. *The Tone Pattern of Japanese: An Autosegmental Theory of Tonology.* Tokyo: Kaitakusha.

Hargus, S., and K. Rice. in press. *Athapaskan Prosody.* Amsterdam: John Benjamins.

Harris, J. 1990. Segmental complexity and phonological government. *Phonology* 7.2: 255–300.

Harris, J. 1999. Release the captive coda: the foot as a domain of phonetic interpretation. *UCL Working Papers in Linguistics* 11: 165–94.

Harrison, P.A. 1998. Yoruba babies and unchained melody. *UCL Working Papers in Phonetics* 10: 33–52.

1999. The Acquisition of Phonology in the First Year of Life. PhD Dissertation, University College London.

2000. Acquiring the phonology of lexical tone in infancy. *Lingua* 110: 581–616.

Haudricourt, A.-G. 1954. De l'origine des tons en vietnamien. *Journal Asiatique* 242: 68–82.

1972. Two-way and three-way splitting of tonal systems in some Far-Eastern languages. (trans. C. Court). In J. Harris and R. Noss (eds.), *Tai Phonetics and Phonology*. Bangkok: Central Institute of English Language, Mahidol University 58–86.

Hayes, B. 1995. *Metrical Stress Theory: Principles and Case Studies*. Chicago: University of Chicago Press.

Hayes, B., and A. Lahiri. 1991. Bengali intonational phonology. *Natural Language and Linguistic Theory*. 9: 47–96.

Heine, B., and D. Nurse (eds.). 2000. *African Languages: An Introduction*. Cambridge: Cambridge University Press.

Hewitt, M. 1994. Deconstructing foot binarity. MS, University of British Columbia.

Hewitt, Mark, and Alan Prince. 1989. OCP, locality and linking: the N. Karanga verb. In E.J. Fee and K. Hunt (eds.), *Proceedings of WCCFL 8*. Stanford: SLA, pp. 176–91.

Hirose, H. 1997. Investigating the physiology of laryngeal structures. In W.J. Hardcastle and J. Laver (eds.), *The Handbook of Phonetic Sciences*. Oxford: Basil Blackwell, pp. 116–36.

Hirst, D., and A. de Cristo (eds.). 1998. *Intonation Systems: A Survey of Twenty Languages*. Cambridge: Cambridge University Press.

Hoa, M. 1983. *L'accentuation en pékinois*. (Editions langages croisés) Paris: Centre de recherches linguistiques sur l'asie orientale.

Hoffman, C. 1963. *A Grammar of the Margi Language*. Oxford: Oxford University Press.

Hogan, J., and M. Manyeh. 1996. A study of Kono tone spacing. *Phonetica* 53.4: 221–9.

Hollenbach, B.E. 1977. Phonetic vs. phonemic correspondence in two Trique dialects. In W. Merrifield (ed.), *Studies in Otomanguean Phonology*. Dallas: Summer Institute of Linguistics, pp. 35–68.

Holton, G. in press. Pitch, tone and intonation in Tanacross. In Hargus and Rice in press.

Hombert, J.-M. 1978. Consonant types, vowel quality and tone. In Fromkin 1978: 77–112.

1986. Word games: some implications for analysis of tone and other phonological constructs. In J.J. Ohala and J.J. Jaeger (eds.), *Experimental Phonology*. Orlando, FL: Academic Press, pp. 175–86.

Hombert, J.-M., J.J. Ohala and W.G. Ewan. 1979. Phonetic explanations for the development of tones. *Language* 55: 37–58.

Howie, J.M. 1972. Some experiments on the perception of Mandarin tones. In A. Rigault and R. Charbonneau (eds.), *Proceedings of the 7th International Congress of Phonetic Sciences*. The Hague: Mouton, pp. 900–4.

Hsieh, Hsin-I. 1976. On the unreality of some phonological rules. *Lingua* 38: 1–19.

Hualde, J.I. 1991. *Basque Phonology*. London: Routledge.

1999. Basque accentuation. In Harry van der Hulst (ed.), *Word Prosodic Systems in the Languages of Europe*. Berlin: Mouton de Gruyter, pp. 947–93.

Hualde, J.I., G. Elordieta, I. Gaminde and R. Smiljanić. forthcoming. From pitch-accent to stress-accent in Basque. In C. Gussenhoven and N. Warner (eds.), *Papers in Laboratory Phonology VII*. Cambridge: Cambridge University Press.

Huang, J.C.-T. 1980. The metrical structure of terraced level tones. *Cahiers Linguistiques d'Ottawa* 9: 257–70.

Hulst, H. van der, and K. Snider (eds.). 1993. *The Phonology of Tone: The Representation of Tonal Register.* Berlin: Mouton de Gruyter.

Hunter, G.G., and E.V. Pike. 1969. The phonology and tone sandhi of Molinos Mixtec. *Linguistics* 47: 24–40.

Hyman, L.M. 1972. *A Phonological Study of Fe'fe'-Bamileke.* (Studies in African Linguistics, Supplement 4). Los Angeles: University of California, Los Angeles.

Hyman, L. 1979. A reanalysis of tonal downstep. *Journal of African Languages and Linguistics* 1: 9–29.

1981. Tonal accent in Somali. *Studies in African Linguistics* 12: 169–203.

1985. Word domains and downstep in Bamileke-Dschang. *Phonology Yearbook* 2: 47–83.

1986. The representation of multiple tone heights. In K. Bogers, H. van der Hulst and M. Mous (eds.), *The Phonological Representation of Suprasegmentals*. Dordrecht: Foris, pp. 109–52.

1987. Downstep deletion in Aghem. In D. Odden (ed.), *Current Approaches to African Linguistics*. Dordrecht: Foris, Vol. 4, pp. 209–22.

1990. Boundary tonology and the prosodic hierarchy. In S. Inkelas and D. Zec (eds.), *The Phonology-Syntax Connection*. Chicago: University of Chicago Press, pp. 109–25.

1993. Register tones and tonal geometry. In H. van der Hulst and K. Snider (eds.), *The Phonology of Tone: The Representation of Tonal Register.* Berlin: Mouton de Gruyter, pp. 75–108.

2000. Privative tone in Bantu. Paper given at Symposium on Tone, ILCAA, Tokyo.

In press. Tone systems. In M. Haspelmath, E. König, W. Oesterreicher and W. Raible (eds.), *Language Typology and Language Universals: An International Handbook.* (2 vols.) Berlin and New York: Walter de Gruyter.

Hyman, L., and E.R. Byarushengo. 1984. A model of Haya tonology. In G.N. Clements and J. Goldsmith (eds.), *Autosegmental Studies in Bantu Tone.* Dordrecht: Foris, pp. 53–103.

Hyman, L., and F. Katamba. 1993. A new approach to tone in Luganda. *Language* 69.1: 34–67.

Hyman, L., and C. Kisseberth (eds.). 1998. *Theoretical Aspects of Bantu Tone.* Stanford, CA: CSLI Publications.

Hyman, Larry M., and Daniel J. Magaji. 1970. Essentials of Gwari grammar. Occasional Publication No. 27 of the Institute of African Studies, University of Ibadan Press, Nigeria.

Hyman, L., and A. Ngunga. 1994. On the non-universality of tonal association 'conventions': evidence from Ciyao. *Phonology* 11: 25–68.

Hyman, L., and R. Schuh. 1974. Universals of tone rules: evidence from West Africa. *Linguistic Inquiry* 5: 81–115.

Hyman, L., and M. Tadadjeu. 1977. Floating tones in Mbam-Nkam. In Larry M. Hyman (ed.), *Studies in Bantu Tonology.* (Southern California Occasional Papers in Linguistics) Los Angeles: University of Southern California, pp. 57–111.

Ingram, D. 1989. *First Language Acquisition: Method, Description and Explanation.* Cambridge: Cambridge University Press.

Inkelas, S. 1988. Prosodic effects on syntax: Hausa 'fa'. In H. Borer (ed.), *Proceedings of the Seventh Annual Conference of the West Coast Conference in Formal Linguistics.* Stanford, CA: Stanford Linguistics Association, pp. 375–89.

1994. The consequences of optimization for underspecification. ROA# 40-1294.

Inkelas, S., and W. Leben. 1990. Where phonology and phonetics intersect: the case of Hausa intonation. In J. Kingston and M. Beckman (eds.), *Between the Grammar and Physics of Speech: Papers in Laboratory Phonology I.* Cambridge: Cambridge University Press, pp. 17–34.

Inkelas, S., W. Leben and M. Cobler. 1987. The phonology of intonation in Hausa. In J. Blevins and J. Carter (eds.), *Proceedings of NELS 17.* Amherst, MA: Graduate Linguistics Student Association, pp. 327–42.

Inkelas, S., C.O. Orgun and C. Zoll. 1996. Exceptions and static phonological patterns: cophonologies vs. prespecification. ROA# 124-0496.

Inkelas, S., and D. Zec. 1988. Serbo-Croatian pitch accent: the interaction of tone, stress and intonation. *Language* 64.2: 227–48.

(eds.).1990. *The Phonology-Syntax Connection.* Chicago: University of Chicago Press.

Innes, D. 1969. *Mende–English Dictionary.* Cambridge: Cambridge University Press.

Issah, D. 1993. Some Tonal Processes and Tone Representation in Dagbani. MA Thesis, University of Texas at Arlington.

Itô, J., Y. Kitagawa and A. Mester. 1996. Prosodic faithfulness and correspondence: evidence from a Japanese argot. *Journal of East Asian Linguistics.* 5: 217–94.

Itô, J., and A. Mester. 1998. Markedness and word structure: OCP effects in Japanese. MS, University of California, Santa Cruz. ROA# 255.

Iwata, R., and H. Imagawa. 1982. An acoustic study of tone, tone sandhi, and neutral tone in Lian-Yun-Gang dialect of Chinese. *Annual Bulletin of the RILP* 16: 37–50.

Jagger, P. 2001. *Hausa.* (London Oriental and African Language Library) Amsterdam and Philadelphia: Benjamins.

James, D. 1981. An autosegmental analysis of Siane. MS Summer Institute of Linguistics, Oklahoma.

James, D.J. 1994. Word tone in a Papuan language: an autosegmental solution. *Language and Linguistics in Melanesia* 25: 125–48.

Jamieson, A.R. 1977. Chiquihuitlan Mazatec tone. In William Merrifield (ed.), *Studies in Otomanguean Phonology.* Dallas: Summer Institute of Linguistics, pp. 107–36.

Jeanne, L.M. 1982. Some phonological rules of Hopi. *International Journal of American Linguistics* 48.3: 245–70.

Jiang-King, Ping. 1998. An Optimality Account of Tone-Vowel Interaction in Northern Min. PhD dissertation, Chinese University of Hong Kong.

Jun, S.-A. 1998. The accentual phrase in the Korean prosodic hierarchy. *Phonology* 15.2: 189–226.

Jusczyk, P.W. 1997. *The Discovery of Spoken Language.* Cambridge, MA: MIT Press.

Kager, R. 1999. *Optimality Theory.* Cambridge: Cambridge University Press.

Kager, R., and W. Zonneveld (eds.). 1999. *Phrasal Phonology.* Nijmegen: Nijmegen University Press.

Kaji, S. 1996. Tone reversal in Tembo (Bantu J.57). *Journal of African Languages and Linguistics* 17: 1–26.

Kanerva, J.M. 1990. Focussing on phonological phrases in Chichewa. In Inkelas and Zec 1990: 145–62.

Kari, J. 1976. *Navajo Verb Prefix Phonology.* New York: Garland Publishing.

Karlgren, B. 1966. *Analytic Dictionary of Chinese and Sino-Japanese.* Taipei, Taiwan: Cheng-wen Publishing Company.

Kaye, J., and H. Koopman. 1982. Les tons du système verbal en bété (gbadi). Paper presented at the Thirteenth Annual Conference on African Linguistics, Montreal.

Kebikaza, K.K. 1994. Les tons du verb kabiyé dans les formes de l'inaccompli. In Thomas Geider and Raimund Kastenholtz (eds.), *Sprachen und Sprachzeugnisse in Afrika: Eine Sammlung philologischer Beiträge, Wilhelm J.G. Möhlig zum 60. Geburtstag zugeeignet.* Cologne: Köppe, pp. 263–79.

Kedrebéogo, G. 1997. Tone in Samoma. *Gur Papers/Cahiers Voltaïques* 2: 97–108.

Kennedy, J. 1966. *The Phonology of Dagaari.* (Collected Field Notes Series No. 6) Legon: University of Ghana, The Institute of African Studies.

Kenstowicz, M. 1972. Lithuanian phonology. *Studies in the Linguistic Sciences* 2: 1–85. 1994. *Phonology in Generative Grammar.* Oxford: Basil Blackwell.

Kenstowicz, M., and C. Kisseberth. 1990. Chizigula tonology: the word and beyond. In Inkelas and Zec 1990: 163–94.

Kenstowicz, M., E. Nikiema and M. Ourso. 1988. Tonal polarity in two Gur languages. *Studies in the Linguistic Sciences* 18.1: 77–103.

Kent, R.D., and A.D. Murray. 1982. Acoustic features of infant vocalic utterances at 3, 6, and 9 months. *Journal of the Acoustic Society of America* 72: 353–63.

Kidima, L. 1990. Tone and syntax in Kiyaka. In Inkelas and Zec 1990: 195–216.

Kim, M.J. 1997. Tonal predictability from metrical structure in Northern Tepehuan. *Proceedings of the West Coast Conference in Formal Linguistics* 15: 257–72.

Kim, No-Ju. 1997. Tone, Segments, and their Interaction in North Kyung-Sang Korean. PhD Dissertation, Ohio State University.

Kim, S.-J. 1998. Positional effect on tonal alternations in Chichewa: phonological rules vs. phonetic timing. *Proceedings of the Chicago Linguistics Society* 34.

Kinda, J. 1997. Les tons du mòoré et leur incidence sur les segments. *Gur Papers/Cahiers Voltaïques* 2: 109–16.

Kingston, J. 1985. The phonetics and phonology of Athabaskan tonogenesis. MS, University of Texas, Austin.

Kingston, J., and R.L. Diehl. 1994. Phonetic knowledge. *Language* 70: 419–54.

Kingston, J., and D. Solnit. 1989. The inadequacy of underspecification. *Proceedings of the North Eastern Linguistic Society* 19: 264–78.

Kiparsky, P., and M. Halle. 1977. Towards a reconstruction of the Indo-European accent. In L. Hyman (ed.), *Studies in Stress and Accent.* (Southern California Occasional Papers in linguistics 4). Los Angeles: University of Southern California, pp. 209–38.

Kirchner, R. 1996. Synchronic chain shifts in Optimality Theory. *Linguistic Inquiry* 27.2: 341–9.
1997. Contrastiveness and faithfulness. *Phonology* 14.1: 83–112.

Kisseberth, C. 1984. Digo tonology. In G.N. Clements and J. Goldsmith (eds.), *Autosegmental Studies in Bantu Tone.* Dordrecht: Foris Publications, pp. 105–82.

Klatt, D. 1973. Discrimination of fundamental frequency contours in synthetic speech duplications for models of pitch perception. *Journal of the Acoustical Society of America* 53: 8–16.

Kleinewillinghöfer, U. 1999. The verb in Kusuntu. Paper presented at 2nd Colloquium on Gur Languages, Cotonou, Benin, 29 March–1 April 1999.

Krifka, M. 1998. Scope inversion under the rise-fall contour in German. *Linguistic Inquiry* 29.1: 75–112.

Kröger, F. 1992. *Buli–English Dictionary*. Münster: Lit Verlag.

Kropp Dagubu, M.E. 1986. Downglide, floating tones and Non-Wh questions in Ga and Dangme. In K. Bogers, H. van der Hulst and M. Mous (eds.), *The Phonological Representation of Suprasegmentals*. Dordrecht: Foris, pp. 153–74.

Kubozono, H. 2000. *A Cross-Linguistic Study on the Phonological Study of Compounds*. (Grant report). Japanese Ministry of Education, Science and Culture, Grant No. 09610480.

Kuhl, P.K., and J.D. Miller. 1982. Discrimination of auditory target dimensions in the presence or absence of variation in a second dimension by infants. *Perception and Psychophysics* 31: 279–92.

Ladd, D.R. 1978. *The Structure of Intonational Meaning: Evidence from English*. Bloomington, IN: Indiana University Press.

1983. Phonological features of intonational peaks. *Language* 59: 721–59.

1986. Intonational phrasing: the case for recursive prosodic structure. *Phonology* 3: 311–40.

1990. Metrical representation of pitch register. In M. Beckman and J. Kingston (eds.), *Between the Grammar and Physics of Speech. Papers in Laboratory Phonology I*. Cambridge: Cambridge University Press, pp. 35–57.

1997. *Intonational Phonology*. Cambridge: Cambridge University Press.

Ladefoged, P. 1975. *A Course in Phonetics*. (4th edn 2001) Fort Worth, TX: Harcourt College Publishers.

Ladefoged, P., and I. Maddieson. 1996. *The Sounds of the World's Languages*. Oxford: Blackwell.

Lahiri, A., and J. Fitzpatrick-Cole. 1999. Emphatic clitics and focus intonation in Bengali. In R. Kager and W. Zonneveld (eds.), *Phrasal Phonology*. Nijmegen: Nijmegen University Press, pp. 119–44.

Laniran, Y. 1992. Phonetic aspects of tone realization in Igbo. *Progress Reports from Oxford Phonetics* 5: 35–51.

1993. *Intonation in Tone Languages: The Phonetic Implementation of Tones in Yorùbá*. Ithaca, NY: Department of Modern Languages and Linguistics, Cornell University.

Laughren, M. 1984. Tone in Zulu nouns. In G.N. Clements and J. Goldsmith (eds.), *Autosegmental Studies in Bantu Tone 3*. Dordrecht: Foris, pp. 183–235.

Law, S.-P. 1990. The Syntax and Phonology of Cantonese Sentence-Final Particles. PhD Dissertation, Boston University.

Leather, J. 1987. $F_\emptyset$ pattern inference in the perceptual acquisition of second language tone. In A. James and J. Leather (eds.), *Sound Patterns in Second Language Acquisition*. Dordrecht: Foris, pp. 59–81.

Leben, W. 1973. Suprasegmental Phonology. PhD Dissertation, MIT.

1978. The representation of tone. In Fromkin 1978: 177–220.

1989. Intonation in Chadic: an overview. In Z. Frajzyngier (ed.), *Current Progress in Chadic Linguistics*. Amsterdam: Benjamins, pp. 199–217.

Lee, T.H.-T. 1996. Theoretical issues in language development and Chinese child language. In C.-T.J. Huang and Y.-H.A. Li (eds.), *New Horizons in Chinese Linguistics*. Dordrecht: Kluwer, pp. 293–356.

Li, C., and S. Thompson. 1977. The acquisition of tone in Mandarin-speaking children. *Journal of Child Language* 4: 185–99.

Li, F.-K. 1949. Tones in the riming system of the Sui language. *Word* 5.3: 262–7.

1977. *A Handbook of Comparative Tai*. Honolulu: University Press of Hawaii.

Li, X.-J., and S.-X. Liu. 1985. Tone sandhi in the Tianjin dialect. *Zhongguo Yuwen* 1: 76–80.

Liberman, M. 1978. The Intonational System of English. PhD Dissertation, MIT.

Liberman, M.J., M. Schultz, S. Hong and V. Okeke. 1993. The phonetic interpretation of tone in Igbo. *Phonetics* 50.3: 147–60.

Lin, H.B., and B. Repp. 1989. Cues to the perception of Taiwanese tones. *Language and Speech* 32.1: 25–44.

Lin, J. 1994. Lexical government and tone group formation in Xiamen Chinese. *Phonology* 11: 237–76.

Lin, Y.-H. 1993. Degenerate affixes and templatic constraints: rime change in Chinese. *Language* 69.4: 649–82.

2001. An Optimality-theoretic account of dialect variation in *Er* suffixation: a case-study of Zhejiang Wu dialects. In De Bao Xu (ed.), *Chinese Phonology in Generative Grammar*. New York: Academic Press, pp. 193–222.

Lindblom, B. 1986. Phonetic universals in vowel systems. In J. Ohala and J. Jaeger (eds.), *Experimental Phonology*. Orlando: Academic Press, pp. 13–44.

1990. Phonetic content in phonology. *PERILUS* 9: 101–18.

Lombardi, L. 1990. The non-linear organization of the affricate. *Natural Language and Linguistic Theory* 8.3: 375–426.

Lombardi, L., and J. McCarthy. 1991. Prosodic circumscription in Choctaw morphology. *Phonology* 8.1: 37–72.

Longacre, R. 1952. Five phonemic pitch levels in Trique. *Acta Linguistica* 7: 62–82.

Luksaneeyanawin, S. 1998. Thai. In D. Hirst and A. Di Cristo (eds.), *Intonation Systems*. Cambridge: Cambridge University Press, pp. 376–94.

Lyman, L., and R. Lyman. 1977. Choapan Zapotec phonology. In William Merrifield (ed.), *Studies in Otomanguean Phonology*. Dallas: Summer Institute of Linguistics, pp. 137–62.

Lyovin, A. 1997. *An Introduction to the Languages of the World*. Oxford: Oxford University Press.

Maddieson, I. 1978. Universals of tone. In J.H. Greenberg (ed.), *Universals of Human Language, Volume 2: Phonology*. Stanford, CA, Stanford University Press, pp. 335–66.

1979. Tone spacing: evidence from bilingual speakers. *UCLA Working Papers in Phonetics* 45: 84–88.

1997. Phonetic universals. In W.J. Hardcastle and J. Laver (eds.), *Handbook of Phonetic Sciences*. Oxford: Basil Blackwell, pp. 619–39.

Maddieson, I., and S. Hess. 1986. 'Tense' and 'lax' revisited: more on phonation type and pitch in minority languages of China. Paper given at the 19th International Conference on Sino-Tibetan Languages and Linguistics, Columbus, Ohio.

Manfredi, V. 1993. Spreading and downstep: prosodic government in tone languages, in van der Hulst and Snider 1993: 133–84.

Maran, L.R. 1971. Burmese and Jingpho. A study of tonal linguistic processes. *Occasional Papers of the Wolfenden Society on Tibeto-Burman Linguistics*, Vol. 4.

1973. On becoming a tone language: A Tibeto-Burman model of tonogenesis. In L. Hyman (ed.), *Consonant Types and Tone*. (Southern California Occasional Papers in Linguistics 1) Los Angeles: The Linguistics Program, University of Southern California, pp. 99–114.

Matisoff, J.A. 1973. Tonogenesis in Southeast Asia. In L.Hyman (ed.), *Consonant Types and Tone*. (Southern California Occasional Papers in Linguistics 1) Los Angeles: The Linguistics Program, University of Southern California, pp. 73–95.

McCarthy, J. 1986. OCP effects: gemination and antigemination. *Linguistic Inquiry* 17: 207–63.

1988. Feature geometry and dependency: a review. *Phonetica* 43: 84–108.

1999. Sympathy and phonological opacity. *Phonology* 16: 331–99.

2000. The Fundamentals of Optimality Theory. MS, University of Massachusetts, Amherst.

2002. *A Thematic Guide to Optimality Theory*. Cambridge: Cambridge University Press.

McCarthy, J., and A. Prince. 1993. Prosodic Morphology I: Constraint Interaction and Satisfaction. To appear, MIT Press. Rutgers University Center for Cognitive Science, Report TR-3. Available at http://ruccs.rutgers.edu/publicationsreports.html.

1994. The emergence of the unmarked: Optimality in prosodic morphology. In Mercè Gonzàlez (ed.), *Proceedings of the North-East Linguistics Society 24*. Amherst, MA: Graduate Linguistics Students Association, pp. 333–79. ROA# 13.

1995. Faithfulness and reduplicative identity. In J.N. Beckman, L.W. Dickey and S. Urbanczyk (eds.), *Papers in Optimality Theory*. Amherst, MA: Graduate Linguistics Students Association, University of Massachusetts, pp. 249–384.

McDonough, J. 1999. Tone in Navajo. *Anthropological Linguistics* 41.4: 503–39.

Meeussen, A.E. 1967. *Bantu grammatical reconstructions*. (Annales du Musée Royal de l'Afrique Centrale, Série 8, Sciences Humaines, 61.81-121). Tervuren: Musée Royal de l'Afrique.

Michelson, K. 1988. *A Comparative Study of Lake-Iroquoian Accent*. Dordrecht: Kluwer.

Miller-Ockhuizen, A. 1997. Towards a unified decompositional analysis of Khoisan lexical tone. MS, Ohio State University. ROA# 203–0697.

1999. Reduplication in Juǀ'hoansi: tone determines weight. In P. Tamanjio, M. Hirotani and N. Hall (eds.), *Proceedings of NELS 29*. Amherst, MA: Graduate Linguistics Students Association, University of Massachusetts, pp. 261–75.

Mithun, M. 1999. *The Languages of Native North America*. Cambridge: Cambridge University Press.

Mock, C.C. 1981. Tone sandhi in Isthmus Zapotec: an autosegmental account. Spanish version appeared in *Proceedings of the Ithaca Symposium of PILEI*. Ithaca, NY: Latin-American Studies Center, Cornell University.

1988. Pitch accent and stress in Isthmus Zapotec. In H. van der Hulst and N. Smith (eds.), *Autosegmental Studies on Pitch Accent*. Dordrecht: Foris, pp. 197–223.

Mohanan, K.P. 1986. *The Theory of Lexical Phonology*. Dordrecht: D. Reidel.

Moore, B.C.J. 1997. Aspects of auditory processing related to speech perception. In W.J. Hardcastle and J. Laver (eds.), *The Handbook of Phonetic Sciences*. Oxford: Basil Blackwell, pp. 539–65.

Moreton, E. 1999. Non-computable functions in Optimality Theory. MS, University of Massachusetts, Amherst. ROA# 364.

Morse, P.A. 1972. The discrimination of speech and non-speech stimuli in early infancy. *Journal of Experimental Child Psychology* 13: 477–92.

Mugele, R. 1982. Tone and Ballistic Syllable in Lalantla Chinantec. PhD Dissertation, University of Texas, Austin.

Myers, S. 1987a. Tone and the Structure of Words in Shona. PhD Dissertation, University of Massachusetts, Amherst.

1987b. Vowel shortening in English. *Natural Language and Linguistic Theory* 5: 485–518.

1997. OCP Effects in Optimality Theory. *Natural Language and Linguistic Theory* 15.4: 847–92.

1999a. Surface underspecification of tone in Chichewa. *Phonology* 15.3: 367–92.

1999b. Tone association and F$_0$ timing in Chichewa. *Studies in African Linguistics* 28: 215–39.

1999c. AUX in Bantu morphology and phonology. In L. Hyman and C. Kisseberth (eds.), *Theoretical Aspects of Bantu Tone*. Stanford, CA: CSLI, pp. 231–64.

Myers, Scott, and Troi Carleton. 1996. Tonal transfer in Chichewa. *Phonology* 13.1: 39–72.

Nash, J. 1992–4. Underlying low tones in Ruwund. *Studies in African Linguistics* 23: 223–78.

Nespor, M., and I. Vogel. 1986. *Prosodic Phonology*. Dordrecht: Foris.

Newman, P. 1986. Contour tones as phonemic primes in Grebo. In K. Bogers, H. van der Hulst and M. Mous (eds.), *The Phonological Representation of Suprasegmentals*. Dordrecht: Foris, pp. 175–93.

1992. The development of falling contours from tone bending in Hausa. In L.A. Buzard-Welcher, J. Evans, D. Peterson, L. Wee and W. Weigel (eds.), *Proceedings of the Berkeley Linguistics Society, Special Session on the Typology of Tone Languages*. Berkeley: Berkeley Linguistics Society, pp. 128–33.

1995. Hausa tonology: complexities in an 'easy' tone language. In J. Goldsmith (ed.), *The Handbook of Phonological Theory*. Cambridge, MA: Basil Blackwell, pp. 762–81.

2000. *The Hausa Language: An Encyclopedic Reference Grammar*. New Haven, CT: Yale University Press.

Newman, P., and R. Newman. 1981. The *q* morpheme in Hausa. *Afrika und Übersee* 64: 35–46.

Nhàn Nhô Thanh. 1984. The Syllabeme and Patterns of Word Formation in Vietnamese. PhD Dissertation, New York University.

Noyer, R. 1992. Tone and stress in the San Mateo dialect of Huave. In *Proceedings of the Eighth Annual Meeting of the Eastern States Conference on Linguistics*. Columbus, OH: Ohio State University Department of Linguistics, pp. 227–88.

O'Connor, J.D., and G.F. Arnold. 1961. *Intonation of Colloquial English*. London: Longmans.

Odden, D. 1981. Problems in Tone Assignment in Shona. PhD Dissertation, University of Illinois, Champaign-Urbana.

1982. Tonal phenomena in KiShambaa. *Studies in African Linguistics* 13: 177–208.

1984. Stem tone assignment in Shona. In G.N. Clements and J. Goldsmith (eds.), *Autosegmental Studies in Bantu Tone*. Dordrecht: Foris, pp. 255–80.

1986. On the role of the obligatory contour principle in phonological theory. *Language* 62: 353–83.

1987. Kimatuumbi phrasal phonology. *Phonology* 4: 13–36.

1990a. Tone in the Makonde dialects: Chimaraba. *Studies in African Linguistics* 21.1: 61–105.

1990b. Syntax, lexical rules, and postlexical rules in Kimatuumbi. In Inkelas and Zec 1990: 259–78.

1991. Vowel geometry. *Phonology* 8.2: 261–90.

1995. Tone: African languages. In J. Goldsmith (ed.), *Handbook of Phonological Theory.* Oxford: Blackwell, pp. 444–75.

1998. Principles of tone assignment in Tanzanian Yao. In Hyman and Kisseberth 1998: 265–314.

Odden, D., and R.R. Roberts-Kohno. 1999. Constraints on superlow-tone in Kikamba. In Kager and Zonneveld 1999: 145–70.

Ohala, J.J. 1978. Production of tone. In Fromkin 1978: 5–40.

Ohala, J.J., and W. Ewan. 1973. Speed of pitch change. *Journal of the Acoustical Society of America* 53: 345.

Okell, J. 1969. *A Reference Grammar of Colloquial Burmese.* (2 vols.) London: Oxford University Press.

Osburne, A. 1979. Segmental, suprasegmental, autosegmental contour tones. *Linguistic Analysis* 5.2: 183–94.

Pace, W.J. 1990. Comaltepec Chinantec verb inflection. In William R. Merrifield and Calvin R. Rensch (eds.), *Syllables, Tone and Verb Paradigms.* (Studies in Chinantec Languages 4) Dallas: Summer Institute of Linguistics, and University of Texas at Arlington, pp. 21–62.

Pankratz, L., and E. Pike. 1975. Phonology and morphotonemics of Ayutla Mixtec. In R. Brend (ed.), *Studies in Tone and Intonation.* Basel: S. Karger, pp. 131–51.

Parker, S. 1999. A sketch of Iñapai phonology. *International Journal of American Linguistics* 65.1: 1–39.

Payne, D.L., and T.E. Payne. 1986. Yagua. In Derbyshire and Pullum 1986, Vol. 2: 431.

Peng, S.-H. 1997. Production and perception of Taiwanese tones in different tonal and prosodic contexts. *Journal of Phonetics* 25: 371–400.

2000. Lexical versus 'phonological' representations of Mandarin sandhi tones. In M.B. Broe and J.B. Pierrehumbert (eds.), *Acquisition and the Lexicon: Papers in Laboratory Phonology V.* Cambridge: Cambridge University Press, pp. 152–67.

Peterson, T.H. 1971. Mooré Structure: A Generative Analysis of the Tonal System and Aspects of the Syntax. PhD Dissertation, UCLA, Los Angeles.

Peyasantiwong, P. 1980. Stress in Thai. Paper presented at the 13th International Conference on Sino-Tibetan Languages and Linguistics, University of Virginia, October 1980.

Pierrehumbert, J. 1979. The perception of fundamental frequency declination. *Journal of the Acoustical Society of America* 66: 363–8.

1980. The Phonology and Phonetics of English Intonation. PhD Dissertation, MIT.

Pierrehumbert, J., and M. Beckman. 1988. *Japanese Tone Structure.* Cambridge, MA: MIT Press.

Pike, E. 1975. Tonemic-intonemic correlation in Mazahua (Otomi). In R. Brend (ed.), *Studies in Tone and Intonation.* Basel: S. Karger, pp. 100–7.

Pike, E., and J.H. Cowan. 1967. Huajuapan Mixtec phonology and morphophonemics. *Anthropological Linguistics* 9.4: 1–15.

Pike, K. 1948. *Tone Languages: A Technique for Determining the Number and Type of Pitch Contrasts in a Language, with Studies in Tonemic Substitution and Fusion.* (University of Michigan Publications in Linguistics, No. 4) Ann Arbor: University of Michigan Press.

Poletto, R. 1996. Base-identity effects in Runyankore reduplication. *OSU Working Papers in Linguistics* 48: 183–210.

1998. Constraints on tonal association in Olusamia: an optimality theoretic account. In Hyman and Kisseberth 1998: 331–64.

Pollack, I. 1952. The information of elementary auditory displays. *Journal of the Acoustical Society of America* 24.6: 745–9.

1953. The information of elementary auditory displays II. *Journal of the Acoustical Society of America* 25.4: 765–9.

Poser, W.J. 1981. On the directionality of the tone-voice correlation. *Linguistic Inquiry* 12.3: 483–8.

1984. The Phonetics and Phonology of Tone and Intonation in Japanese. PhD Dissertation, Massachusetts Institute of Technology.

Pride, L. 1963. Chatino tonal structure. *Anthropological Linguistics* 5.2: 19–28.

Prince, A. 1983. Relating to the grid. *Linguistic Inquiry* 14: 19–100.

1990. Quantitative consequences of rhythmic organization. In M. Ziolkowski, M. Noske and K. Deaton (eds.), *Parasession on the Syllable in Phonetics and Phonology*. Chicago: CLS, pp. 355–98.

Prince, A., and P. Smolensky. 1993. Optimality theory: constraint interaction in generative grammar. Rutgers University Cognitive Science Center Report TR-2. Available at http://ruccs.rutgers.edu/publicationsreports.html.

Pulleyblank, D. 1983. Extratonality and polarity. In *Proceedings of the West Coast Conference on Formal Linguistics*. Stanford, CA: Stanford Linguistics Association, Vol. 2: 204–16.

1986. *Tone in Lexical Phonology*. Dordrecht: D. Reidel.

1997. Optimality theory and features. In Archangeli and Langendoen 1997: 85–101.

Qu, Aitang, and Kerang Tan. 1983. *Ali Zangyu* (Ali Tibetan). Beijing: Chinese Academy of Social Sciences Press.

Rennison, J. 1997. *Koromfe*. (Routledge Descriptive Grammars) London: Routledge.

Reynolds, W.T. 1997. Post-high tone shift in Venda nominals. ROA# 194-0597.

Riad, T. 1996. Remarks on the Scandinavian tone accent typology. *Nordlyd: Tromsø University Working Papers on Language and Linguistics* 24: 129–56.

Rialland, A., and M. Badjimé. 1989. Réanalyse des tons du bambara. *Studies in African Linguistics* 20: 1–28.

Rice, K. 1987. On defining the intonational phrase: evidence from Slave. *Phonology* 4: 37–60.

1999a. How phonetic is phonology? Evidence from tones in Athapaskan languages. Talk given at Conference on Distinctive Feature Theory, ZAS, Berlin.

1999b. Featural markedness in phonology: variation. Part I. *GLOT International* 4.7: 3–6, Part II. *GLOT International*. 4.8: 3–7.

Rietkerk, D. 1999. The Mbelime verb system. Paper presented at 2nd Colloquium on Gur Languages, Cotonou, Benin, 29 March–1 April 1999.

Rietveld, A.C.M., and C. Gussenhoven. 1985. On the relation between pitch excursion size and prominence. *Journal of Phonetics* 13: 299–308.

Rivierre, J.-C. 1980. *La langue de Touho: Phonologie et grammaire du Cemuhi (Nouvelle-Caledonie)*. Paris: SELAF.

Roberts, R.R. 1991. A non-metrical account of Sukuma tone. In E. Hume (ed.), *Papers in Phonology*. (OSU Working Papers in Linguistics 41) Columbus, OH: Ohio State University, (pp. 135–48.

Roncador, M. Von. 1999. Remarques sur la morphologie verbale du nootré. Paper presented at 2nd Colloquium on Gur Languages, Cotonou, Benin, 29 March - 1 April 1999.

Russell, J.M. 1985. Moba Phonology. MA thesis, Macquarie University, Sydney.

Sagart, L. 1986. Tone production in modern Standard Chinese: an electromyographic investigation. *Cahiers de Linguistique, Asie Orientale:* 205–21.

Sagey, E. 1986. The Representation of Features and Relations in Nonlinear Phonology. Doctoral dissertation, MIT.

Schuh, R.G. 1978. Tone rules. In Fromkin 1978: 221–57.

Scobbie, J. 1991. Attribute Value Phonology. Doctoral dissertation, University of Edinburgh.

Selkirk, E. 1984. *Phonology and Syntax: The Relation between Sound and Structure.* Cambridge, MA: MIT Press.

1986. On derived domains in sentence phonology. *Phonology Yearbook* 3: 371–405.

Selkirk, E., and T. Shen. 1990. Prosodic domains in Shanghai Chinese. In Sharon Inkelas and Draga Zec (eds.), *The Phonology–Syntax Connection.* Chicago: CSLI, pp. 313–38.

Shen, X.-N.S. 1990. *The Prosody of Mandarin Chinese.* (University of California Publications, Linguistics Vol. 118) Berkeley: University of California Press.

Shi, F., L. Shi and R.R. Liao. 1987. An experimental analysis of the five level tones of the Gaoba Dong language. *Journal of Chinese Linguistics* 15.2: 335–61.

Shih, Chilin. 1986. The Prosodic Domain of Tone Sandhi in Chinese. PhD Dissertation, University of California, San Diego.

1987. *The Phonetics of the Chinese Tonal System.* AT&T Bell Laboratories Technical Memorandum. MH 11225.

1988. Tone and intonation in Mandarin. *Working Papers of the Cornell Phonetics Laboratory* 3: 83–109.

1997. Mandarin third tone sandhi and prosodic structure. In Jialing Wang and N. Smith (eds.), *Studies in Chinese Phonology.* New York: Mouton de Gruyter, pp. 81–124.

Sietsema, B. 1989. Metrical Dependencies in Tone Assignment. PhD Dissertation. MIT.

Silverman, D. 1996. Phonology at the interface of phonetics and morphology: root-final laryngeals in Chong, Korean and Sanskrit. *Journal of East Asian Linguistics* 5.3: 301–22.

1997a. Laryngeal complexity in Otomanguean vowels. *Phonology* 14.2: 235–62.

1997b. Tone sandhi in Comaltepec Chinantec. *Language* 73.3: 473–92.

Smith, K.D. 1968. Laryngealization and de-laryngealization in Sedang phonemics. *Linguistics* 38: 52–69.

Smith, N.V. 1967. The phonology of Nupe. *Journal of African Languages* 6: 153–69.

1968. Tone in Ewe. *Quarterly Progress Reports, Research Laboratory of Electronics, MIT* 88: 290–304. Reprinted in E. Fudge (ed.), *Phonology: Selected Readings.* Harmondsworth: Penguin Books, 1973: 354–69.

Snider, K. 1990. Tonal upstep in Krachi: evidence for a register tier. *Language* 66: 453–74.

1998. Phonetic realization of downstep in Bimoba. *Phonology* 15.1: 77–102.

1999. *The Geometry and Features of Tone.* (Publications in Linguistics 133) Dallas: SIL and University of Texas, Arlington.

Snyder, W.C., and Tianqiao Lu. 1997. Wuming Zhuang tone sandhi: a phonological, syntactic and lexical investigation. In Jerold A. Edmondson and David S. Solnit (eds.), *Comparative Kadai: The Tai Branch.* Dallas, TX: Summer Institute of Linguistics, pp. 107–40.

So, L., and B. Dodd. 1995. The acquisition of phonology by Cantonese-speaking children. *Journal of Child Language* 22: 473–95.

Somé, P.-A. 1998. L'influence des consonnes sur les tons en dagara, langue voltaïque du Burkina Faso. *Studies in African Linguistics* 27: 3–47.

Sperber, D., and D. Wilson. 1982. Mutual knowledge and relevance in theories of comprehension. In N. Smith (ed.), *Mutual Knowledge*. New York: Academic Press.

Sprigg, R.K. 1981. The Chang-Shefts tonal analysis, and the pitch variation of the Lhasa-Tibetan tones. *Linguistics of the Tibeto-Burman Area* 6.1: 49–59.

Stahlke, H. 1977. Some problems with binary features for tones. *International Journal of American Linguistics*. 35: 62–6.

Steedman, M. 2000. Information structure and the syntax-phonology interface. *Linguistic Inquiry* 31.4: 649–89.

Steele, M., and G. Weed. 1966. *The Phonology of Konkomba*. (Collected Field Notes Series No. 3) Legon: University of Ghana, The Institute of African Studies.

Steriade, D. 1991. Moras and other slots. In D. Meyer and S. Tomioka (eds.), *Proceedings of the 1ˢᵗ Meeting of the Formal Linguistics Society of the Midwest*. Madison: University of Wisconsin.

—— 1995. Underspecification and markedness. In J. Goldsmith (ed.), *Handbook of Phonological Theory*. Oxford: Basil Blackwell, pp. 114–74.

Stevens, K.N. 1997. Articulatory-acoustic-auditory relationships. In W.J. Hardcastle and J. Laver (eds.), *The Handbook of Phonetic Sciences*. Oxford: Basil Blackwell, pp. 462–506.

Stevens, K.L., and S.J. Keyser. 1989. Primary features and their enhancement in consonants. *Language* 65: 81–106.

Stevens, K., S.J. Keyser and H. Kawasaki. 1986. Toward a phonetic and phonological theory of redundant features. In J. Perkell and D. Klatt (eds.), *Invariance and Variability in Speech Processes*. Hillsdale, NJ: Lawrence Erlbaum, pp. 863–5.

Suarez, J.A. 1983. *The Meso-American Indian Languages*. Cambridge: Cambridge University Press.

Sundberg, J. 1973. Data on maximum speed of pitch changes. Royal Institute of Technology, Stockholm. Speech Transmission Laboratory. *Quarterly Progress and Status Report* 4: 39–47.

Svantesson, J.-O. 1983. *Kammu Phonology and Morphology*. (Travaux de l'Institut de linguistique de Lund 18) Malmö: CWK Gleerup.

Szeto, K. 2000. Learning the Cantonese tones by English-speaking learners. Talk given at Linguistics Society of Hong Kong Annual Research Forum, City University of Hong Kong.

Tak, H.K. 1977. Derivation by tone change in Cantonese. *Journal of Chinese Linguistics* 5.2: 186–210.

Tesar, B., and P. Smolensky. 2000. *Learnability in Optimality Theory*. Cambridge, MA: MIT Press.

Thongkum, T.L. 1991. An instrumental study of Chong registers. In J. Davidson (ed.), *Essays on Mon-Khmer Linguistics in Honor of H.L. Shorto*. London: School of Oriental and African Studies, pp. 141–60.

Thurgood, G. 1980. Consonants, phonation types and pitch height. *Computational Analyses of Asian and African Languages* 13: 207–19.

Tranel, B. 1995. On the status of universal association conventions: evidence from Mixteco. In J. Ahlers, L. Bilmes, J. Guenter, B. Kaiser and J. Namkung (eds.), *Proceedings of the Berkeley Linguistics Society* 21: 299–312.

1996. Rules vs. constraints: a case study. In J. Durand and B. Laks (eds.), *Current Trends in Phonology: Models and Methods.* Paris: CNRS, and Salford: University of Salford, pp. 711–30.

Trigo, L. 1991. On pharynx-larynx interactions. *Phonology* 8: 113–36.

Truckenbrodt, H. 1998. Register-features in intonation: a theory of their phonological distribution and their phonetic implementation. MS, Rutgers University.

1999. On the relation between syntactic phrases and phonological phrases. *Linguistic Inquiry* 30.2: 219–56.

2000a. The representation of the reset in intonational phonology: evidence from Southern German. MS, Rutgers University.

2000b. A new kind of boundary tone. Paper presented at the 31st meeting of the North East Linguistics Society, Georgetown University. To appear in the Proceedings.

Tsay, J. 1994. Phonological Pitch. PhD Dissertation, University of Arizona.

1996. Neutralization of short tones in Taiwanese. In *The First Seoul International Conference on Phonetic Sciences.* Seoul: The Phonetic Society of Korea, Seoul National University, pp. 136–41.

1999. Bootstrapping into Taiwanese tone sandhi. In Y.-M. Yin, I.-L. Yang and H.-C. Chan (eds.), *Chinese Languages and Linguistics V: Interactions in Language.* (Symposium series of the Institute of Linguistics (Preparatory Office), Academia Sinica, No. 2) Taipei, Taiwan: Academia Sinica, pp. 311–33.

2001. Phonetic parameters of tone acquisition in Taiwanese. In M. Nakayama (ed.), *Issues in East Asian Language Acquisition.* Tokyo: Kuroshio Publishers, pp. 205–26.

Tsay, J. and J. Myers. 1996. Taiwanese tone sandhi as allomorph selection. *Berkeley Linguistics Society* 22: 394–405.

Tsay, J., and T.-Y. Huang. 1998. Phonetic parameters in the acquisition of entering tones in Taiwanese. In E. Zee and M. Lin (eds.), *The Proceedings of the Conference on Phonetics of the Languages of China.* Hong Kong: City University of Hong Kong, pp. 109–12.

Tsay, J., J. Charles-Luce, and Y.-S. Guo. 1999. The syntax-phonology interface in Taiwanese: acoustic evidence. In J.J. Ohala, Y. Hasegawa, M. Ohala, D. Granville and A.C. Bailey (eds.), *Proceedings of the XIVth International Congress of Phonetic Sciences.* San Francisco: University of California, Berkeley, pp. 2407–10.

Tse, A. 1992. The Acquisition Process of Cantonese Phonology: A Case Study. MPhil thesis, University of Hong Kong.

Tse, J.K.P. 1978. Tone acquisition in Cantonese: a longitudinal case study. *Journal of Child Language* 5: 191–204.

Tuaycharoen, P. 1977. The Phonetic and Phonological Development of a Thai Baby: From Early Communicative Interaction to Speech. Doctoral dissertation, University of London.

Urua, Eno. 1995. The status of contour tones in Ibibio. In A. Akinlabi (ed.), *Theoretical Approaches to African Linguistics.* Trenton: African World, pp. 329–43.

Vance, T. 1987. *Introduction to Japanese Phonology.* Albany, NY: SUNY Press.

Vihman, M. 1996. *Phonological Development: The Origins of Language in the Child.* Oxford: Basil Blackwell.

Wang, Jialing. 1987. The representation of neutral tone in Chinese Putonghua. In Jialing Wang and N. Smith (eds.), *Studies in Chinese Phonology.* New York: Mouton de Gruyter, pp. 157–84.

Wang, W. 1967. The phonological features of tone. *International Journal of American Linguistics* 33.2: 93–105.

Wang, W., and K.P. Li. 1967. Tone 3 in Pekinese. *Journal of Speech and Hearing Research* 10: 629–36.

Wang, Y., M.M. Spence, A. Jongman and J.A. Sereno. 1999. Training American listeners to perceive Mandarin tones. *Journal of the Acoustical Society of America* 106: 3649–58.

Ward, I.C. 1944. A phonetic introduction to Mende. In K.H. Crosby (ed.), *An Introduction to the Study of Mende*. Cambridge: Heffer and Sons, pp. 1–7.

Weber, D., and W. Thiesen. 2000. A synopsis of Bora tone. MS, Summer Institute of Linguistics.

Welmers, W.E. 1963. Associative *a* and *ka* in Niger-Congo. *Language* 39: 432–47.

1973. *African Language Structures*. Berkeley: University of California Press.

1976. *A Grammar of Vai*. (University of California Publications in Linguistics 84) Berkeley: University of California.

Whalen, D.H., A.G. Levitt and Q. Wang. 1991. Intonational differences between the reduplicated babbling of French- and English-learning infants. *Journal of Child Language* 18: 501–16.

Whalen, D.H., and Y. Xu. 1992. Information for Mandarin tones in the amplitude contour and in brief segments. *Phonetica* 49: 25–47.

Wheatley, J.K. 1987. Burmese. In B. Comrie (ed.), *The World's Major Languages*. New York: Oxford University Press, pp. 834–54.

Wichser, M. 1994. Description grammaticale du Kar, langue senoufo du Burkina Faso. Thèse de diplome, Ecole Pratique des Hautes Etudes, Paris.

Williamson, K. 1986. Igbo associative and specific constructions. In K. Bogers, H. van der Hulst and M. Mous (eds.), *The Phonological Representation of Suprasegmentals*. Dordrecht: Foris, pp. 195–208.

Wong, C.S.P. 1993. The perception of Cantonese tones by English-speaking learners. MS cited in Szeto 2000.

Woo, N. 1969. Prosody and Phonology. PhD Dissertation, MIT.

Woodbury, A. 1989. Phrasing and intonational tonology in Central Alaskan Yupik Eskimo: some implications for linguistics in the field. In J. Dunn (ed.), *1989 Mid-America Linguistics Conference Papers*. Norman: University of Oklahoma, pp. 3–40.

Wright, M. 1983. A Metrical Approach to Tone Sandhi in Chinese Dialects. PhD thesis, University of Massachusetts, Amherst.

Wright, R. 1996. Tone and accent in Oklahoma Cherokee. In P. Munro (ed.), *Cherokee Papers from UCLA*. Los Angeles: Department of Linguistics, UCLA, pp. 11–22.

Xu, Y. 1994. Production and perception of coarticulated tones. *Journal of the Acoustical Society of America* 95.4: 2240–53.

1998. Consistency of tone-syllable alignment across different syllable structures and speaking rates. *Phonetica* 55: 179–203.

1999a. Effects of tone and focus on the formation and alignment of F0 contours. *Journal of Phonetics* 27: 55–105.

1999b. F_0 peak delay: when where and why it occurs. In J. Ohala (ed.), *International Congress of Phonetic Sciences 1999*. San Francisco: n.p., pp. 1881–4.

Xu, Y., and Q.E. Wang. 2001. Pitch targets and their realization: evidence from Mandarin Chinese. *Speech Communication* 33: 319–37.

Yip, M. 1980a. The Tonal Phonology of Chinese. PhD Dissertation, MIT. Published 1990, New York: Garland Publishing.

1980b. Some fragments of the tonal phonology of Mandarin. *Cahiers de Linguistique-Asie Orientale* 7: 47–57.

1982. Against a segmental analysis of Zahao and Thai: a laryngeal tier proposal. *Linguistic Analysis* 9: 79–94.

1988. The obligatory contour principle and phonological rules: a loss of identity. *Linguistic Inquiry* 19.1: 65–100.

1989. Contour tones. *Phonology* 6.1: 149–74.

1990. Tone, phonation and intonation register. *North Eastern Linguistics Society* 20: 487–501.

1993a. The spreading of tonal nodes and tonal features in Chinese dialects. In L.A. Buszard-Welcher, J. Evans, D. Peterson, L. Wee and W. Weigel (eds.), *Proceedings of the Berkeley Linguistics Society, Special Session on Tone.* Berkeley: Berkeley Linguistics Society, pp. 157–66.

1993b. Tonal register in East Asian languages. In van der Hulst and Snider 1993: 245–68.

1995. Tone in East Asian languages. In J. Goldsmith (ed.), *Handbook of Phonological Theory.* Oxford: Basil Blackwell, pp. 476–94.

1999. Feet, tonal reduction and speech rate at the word and phrase level in Chinese. In Kager and Zonneveld 1999: 171–94.

2000. The complex interaction of tones and prominence. To appear in the *Proceedings of NELS 31.*

Yip, V., and S. Matthews. 1994. *Cantonese: A Comprehensive Grammar.* New York: Routledge.

Young, S. 1991. *The Prosodic Structure of Lithuanian.* Lanham, MD: University Press of America.

Yue-Hashimoto, A.O.-K. 1972. *Studies in Yue dialects I: Phonology of Cantonese.* Cambridge: Cambridge University Press.

1980. Word play in language acquisition: a Mandarin case. *Journal of Chinese Linguistics* 8.2: 181–204.

Zec, D. 1988. Sonority Constraints on Prosodic Structure. PhD Dissertation, Stanford University.

2000. Footed tones and tonal feet. *Phonology* 16: 225–64.

Zee, E., and I. Maddieson. 1980. Tones and tone sandhi in Shanghai: phonetic evidence and phonological analysis. *Glossa* 14.1: 45–88.

Zemlin, W.R. 1981. *Speech and Hearing Science: Anatomy and Physiology.* (2nd edn) Englewood Cliffs, NJ: Prentice-Hall.

Zhang, Jie. 2000. Phonetic duration effects on contour tone distribution. In M. Hirotani, A. Coetzee, N. Hall and J.-Y. Kim (eds.), *Proceedings of NELS 30.* New Brunswick NJ: Rutgers University, Vol 2, pp. 775–85.

2001. The Effects of Duration and Sonority on Contour Tone Distribution – Typological Survey and Formal Analysis. PhD Dissertation, UCLA. ROA # 452–0701.

Zhang, Sheng Yu. 1981. Chaoyang fangyan de yuyin xitong [An outline of Chaoyang phonology]. *Fangyan* 1: 27–39.

Zhengzhang, Shangfeng. 1964. Wenzhou fangyande liandu shengdiao [Wenzhou dialect tone sandhi]. *Zhongguo Yuwen* 1964: 106–52.

Zhou, Z.-Y. 1987. Sound change as a means of indicating diminutives in the dialect of Rongxian. (In Chinese). *Fangyan* 1987.1: 58–65.

Zoll, C. 1997a. A note on multiple prominence and tone mapping. *MIT Working Papers in Linguistics* 30: 97–111.

1997b. Conflicting directionality. *Phonology* 14: 263–86.

1998a. Lexical underspecification and tone melodies. Handout for talk given at MIT Phonology Circle.

1998b. Positional markedness, positional faithfulness, and licensing. MS, MIT.

Author index

Subject index